Voices from the Carpathia

VOICES FROM THE CARPATHIA:
RESCUING RMS TITANIC

GEORGE BEHE

The History Press

For my wife Pat

By the same author

Titanic: *Psychic Forewarnings of a Tragedy* (Patrick Stephens, 1988).

Lost at Sea: Ghost Ships and Other Mysteries, with Michael Goss (Prometheus Books, 1994).

Titanic: *Safety, Speed and Sacrifice* (Transportation Trails, 1997).

'Archie': *The Life of Major Archibald Butt from Georgia to the* Titanic (Lulu.com Press, 2010).

A Death on the Titanic: *The Loss of Major Archibald Butt* (Lulu.com Press, 2011).

On Board RMS Titanic: *Memories of the Maiden Voyage* (The History Press, 2012).

First published 2015

The History Press
The Mill, Brimscombe Port
Stroud, Gloucestershire, GL5 2QG
www.thehistorypress.co.uk

© George Behe, 2015

The right of George Behe to be identified as the Author
of this work has been asserted in accordance with the
Copyrights, Designs and Patents Act 1988.

British Library Cataloguing in Publication Data.
A catalogue record for this book is available from the British Library.

ISBN 978 0 7509 6189 9

Typesetting by Thomas Bohm, User Design
Printed and bound in Great Britain by TJ International Ltd.

CONTENTS

Acknowledgements

Although the majority of the material in this book has been culled from the author's own files, a considerable number of people and institutions generously provided me with the texts of additional documents that I might otherwise never have seen.

First and foremost, I would like to thank Ed and Karen Kamuda and the *Titanic* Historical Society and *Titanic* Museum for granting me permission to reproduce a number of rare documents that were published in back issues of the society's journal, the *Commutator*. As always, Don Lynch came through for me by sharing a number of rare documents from his personal collection. Kalman Tanito generously translated several rare accounts that were originally published in Hungary. Craig Sopin kindly provided me with the texts of several rare documents from his personal collection, and Randy Bryan Bigham unhesitatingly shared transcriptions of a number of documents that he uncovered during his own research. Malcolm Cheape was incredibly kind in providing me with the texts of hundreds of documents from the family archive of Joseph Bruce Ismay, and Jim Harper went above and beyond the call of duty in transcribing the texts of numerous original documents from the Frank Blackmarr scrapbooks.

Other individuals were equally kind in making the texts of unique documents available to me, and, so as not to show apparent favouritism to one person at the expense of another, I'm forced to list these people in alphabetical order: Virginia Birt Baker, Richard M. Barbour, David Billnitzer, Patrick Bogue of Onslows, the family of Roger Bricoux, Muffet Brown, Shelley Dziedzic, Gordon Gardiner, Kristen Iversen, John Lamoreau, Anita Leslie, Olivier Mendez, Beverly Anne Mitchell, Charles and Lee Ann Otter, Tony Probst, Steve Rigby, Helen Ryder, Steve Santini, Eric Sauder, Les St Clair, Richard Stead, Craig Stringer, Geoffrey Ward, Gladys Weaver, Joan Webb, Ed Weichsler, Mrs Lawrence Grant White, Geoff Whitfield and Bill Wormstedt.

A number of institutions and archives were equally generous in sharing the texts of documents from their collections: the Franklin Delano Roosevelt Library, Library of Congress, Maritime Museum of the Atlantic, Blunt White Library, British *Titanic* Society, Fishburn Archives at Park University, Marconi Company

Limited, National Archives, National Maritime Museum, Public Archives of Nova Scotia, Naval Historical Center, Royal Mail Streamline, Smithsonian Archives of American Art, Society of Professional Journalists, Straus Historical Society and the State Historical Society of Wisconsin.

To all of these individuals and institutions I offer my sincere thanks.

Introduction

When the White Star liner *Titanic* began sending out distress calls after striking an iceberg in April 1912, one of the first vessels to reply to those distress calls was the Cunard liner *Carpathia*. As it turned out, *Carpathia* was the only vessel that reached the scene of the disaster in time to save the lives of any of *Titanic*'s passengers and crewmen, and after she arrived in New York, newspaper reporters crowded the Cunard pier and vied with each other to obtain detailed first-hand interviews with the survivors of the disaster. In their zeal to interview *Titanic* survivors, though, the reporters often brushed right past other people who could have provided their own eyewitness accounts of the *Titanic* rescue – *Carpathia*'s own passengers.

Although there were occasional exceptions to the rule, the *Carpathia*'s passengers and crewmen were usually left to their own devices as to how and when they discussed their own participation in the aftermath of the world's greatest maritime disaster. A few *Carpathia* passengers wrote letters to relatives describing the things they had witnessed during the *Titanic* rescue, and a few others wrote accounts that were specifically intended for publication. Although the number of such first-hand accounts that have come to light since 1912 has been relatively small, one advantage of this fact is that the present author has been able to collect the texts of most of these documents and reproduce them in a single volume – the volume you are holding in your hands. For the most part, these first-hand accounts have never been utilised in telling the story of the *Titanic*, and they are being offered here as a new source of information for future historians of the disaster.

In a similar vein, the number of *Carpathia* passengers who were interviewed by newspaper reporters in 1912 was so small that the present author has been able to gather together the vast majority of these interviews and present them here for the reader's perusal. Even though these newspaper interviews are second-hand accounts whose reliability cannot be regarded with the same level of confidence as first-hand letters and memoirs, the interviews nevertheless assume importance as being the only surviving record of the experiences of many of those people on the *Carpathia* who witnessed the rescue of the *Titanic*'s passengers.

In reading this collection of letters and interviews, historians will soon discover that not every word of these accounts can be accepted as gospel, since some of the documents contain information that was undoubtedly obtained second-hand on board the *Carpathia*. Even so, the documents contain enough solid facts to make them a valuable supplement to the existing body of evidence surrounding the *Titanic* disaster, and experienced researchers will easily recognise many *Titanic* passengers who remain unnamed in the documents themselves but whose described experiences in the disaster are well known.

While searching for accounts written by and about *Carpathia* passengers, the present author also ran across the texts of a number of interesting letters and accounts that were written by people on board other vessels that had a more distant connection with the *Titanic* disaster. It is hoped that these accounts will shed additional light on the tragic way the lives of many 'peripheral' people were impacted by the loss of the largest passenger liner in the world.

The author hopes that the present volume will serve as a useful sourcebook of brand new information about the *Titanic* disaster.

George Behe
Mount Clemens, Michigan

CARPATHIA PASSENGER
AND CREW LETTERS

JOHN BADENOCH

On 18 April, while the *Carpathia* was approaching New York, Mr Badenoch sent the following Marconigram to Percy Straus, the son of victims Mr and Mrs Isidor Straus:

> Every boat watched. Father and mother not on the *Carpathia*.
> Badenoch[1]

After interviewing multiple *Titanic* survivors regarding the fate of Mr and Mr Isidor Straus, Mr Badenoch dictated the following account to a reporter after arriving in New York:

> Mr. and Mrs. Straus, when the crash came, immediately appeared in the companionway and inquired about the danger. They were reassured by one of the officers as well as by several of the other passengers that there was practically no danger and were advised to go back to their stateroom at that time and took the precaution of putting on extra clothing.

Mr. Straus insisted on their maid dressing to the fullest extent, wearing the heaviest clothing that she had. They again went on deck and were again reassured by an officer that there was no danger, but that they were going to take the precaution of lowering the boats for the women and children should something unforeseen happen.

They chatted on deck for some time after that discussing the possibility of the outcome resulting seriously. At this time several of the passengers impressed upon Mr. Straus the necessity of putting on life belts.

Mrs. Straus again looked after the safety of her maid by insisting that she take her place among the women that were being placed on the nearest lifeboat. The maid seemed rather reluctant, but Mrs. Straus was insistent. After the maid had embarked, Mr. and Mrs. Straus began to realize that there was a necessity for them taking to the boats.

Mr. Straus, now convinced that this was the case, urged Mrs. Straus to get into a boat. She refused. Then he commanded her to do so, at which time several of the passengers as well as the officer of the boat then going out, which was the last to leave the doomed ship, tried to force her into the boat by main strength. She strongly resisted and absolutely refused to go. Saying to her husband:

'No, dear. I will not leave you. When you go I go, but never until then.'

By this time all of the other women near them had been removed to the other boats, and another attempt was made to persuade Mrs. Straus to go.

Finally, when Mr. Straus led his wife by the arm to the last boat, someone gave an order:

'Back, men, back'. Mr. Straus was pushed back against the walls of the cabin. Mrs. Straus left the gangway and came to him. She threw one arm around him and with the other caressed him, murmuring as she did so: 'Dear, we will stay here together.'

And so they went to their death.[2]

On 24 April Mr Badenoch wrote the following detailed letter to Percy Straus:

Dear Mr. Percy,

As per your request, I submit herewith the facts as desired. About 1:30 on the morning of April 15th I was awakened by the unusual sounds of activity on the deck over head. Just then the fog-horn blew and I got up and looked out of the port hole. It was a perfectly clear star light night and the sea was without a ripple. Of course I immediately realized that either we or some other vessel was in trouble. I then went into the companionway and saw a steward who informed me that it was the *Titanic* that was in trouble. He said they had been in communication with her since twelve o'clock and at that time, which was about 1:45, had just received her last message in which it was said she was sinking. The discipline about the *Carpathia* was perfect and she was using every ounce of steam to hurry her to the scene of the accident.

At about 3:15 we sighted the first life boat and it was alongside at 3:45, just as day was breaking. This first boat was about three quarters filled with people about one quarter of whom were women. None of those rescued in the first life boat knew whether or not your Father and Mother were on the *Titanic*. The second boat which came alongside about fifteen minutes later was fairly well filled, and almost exclusively with men. There were not more than four or five women in that boat. From one of the passengers on this second boat, I received the information that Mr. & Mrs. Straus were aboard the *Titanic*. It was not until the third boat arrived that I was able to get a *Titanic* passenger list and verify the statement that your Father and Mother were booked as passengers. I watched every boat load with intense interest and while it was almost impossible to distinguish the faces of the first arrivals, it was quite day light by the time the fourth or fifth boat arrived. After that they unloaded four boats at one time, two on the port side and two on the starboard side. As I could not watch all these boats unloading, I described your parents to a fellow passenger, so that they would not be brought aboard unobserved by me. After that, however, the boats came in singly. About from the sixth to the ninth boat, two of them came in with not over twelve people in her and the other not having more than twenty people.

At 7:30 we had taken in all the boats in sight. We then steamed at slow speed into the wreckage and again lay to, expecting to find more boats. It was then about 8:30 o'clock and the Captain of the *Carpathia* seemed to think that he had taken aboard all who were in the boats. I then spoke to an officer who appeared to be one of the White Star men, (he was the third officer) and asked him to tell me whether or not all of the *Titanic*'s boats had been accounted for. He refused at first but when I stated my reason for knowing and insisted on an answer, he told me that all the boats had been accounted for and that in his judgment there was almost no hope for those who were not already rescued. Thinking possibly that your father and mother had been taken aboard and I had missed them, I covered the entire ship from bow to stern, and searched the saloon, second and steerage. Also looked in every stateroom, irrespective of its occupants so that I could satisfy myself beyond a doubt whether or not they were aboard. By this time it was almost ten o'clock. I then wrote the message which you received Thursday morning, handed it to the Purser and explained to him the absolute necessity of getting it off at once. He replied very courteously that he would do the best he could but that the muster was just being made and that it must take precedence over private messages. This

I accepted as being reasonable. The muster was not completed until noon time when they assured everyone that the names had been sent to the offices of the line in New York. I fully expected that such being the case, all the names of the survivors would be published in the New York papers by three o'clock that afternoon. Later in the afternoon, I asked the officer if any of the private messages had been sent and he replied that he did not think any of them had been sent, but that they would surely be sent that night.

At this point Mr Badenoch wrote a rather lengthy description about the difficulty he experienced in getting a message sent. He believed his message was not sent until late Wednesday:

Realizing how anxious you would be to get the most accurate information about the last that was seen of your Father and Mother, I circulated among the survivors and although many claimed to have some knowledge of their actions, those whom you have personally interviewed are the ones I finally decided could give the most authentic account. From what I heard on board and that which I have learned since, I think that the statement given to you by Mr. Woolner is the most accurate. All the survivors agree on one fact and this is if the proper discipline had obtained, there is not the least doubt but that your Father and Mother would have been saved.

Taking the statements of eight or ten of the survivors and comparing them, I believe that the following can be considered the most accurate.

Mr. & Mrs. Straus were in bed at the time of the accident. Immediately after the boat struck they were seen in the companion-way, in bath robes. At this time an officer, as well as several of the passengers assured them that there was no trouble and the best they could do would be to return to their rooms. The maid's story after this is that your Mother seemed to realize the danger and prepared to dress, requesting your Father to do likewise. To hurry matters, she sent the maid for his valet to assist him in dressing. Shortly thereafter they both appeared on deck, fully clothed, mingled with the other passengers and discussed the danger in a perfectly calm and collected manner. They evidently did not believe that there was any great danger of the ship sinking. On the advice of the Captain, they put on life preservers over their fur coats, and assisted other passengers in doing the same. By that time the boats were being filled with women and children and your Mother was asked by an officer in charge and urged by your Father to get into one of the life boats. She refused to do so and insisted that the maid take her place in boat No. 8. They stood by while other boats were being filled, all the while your Father continuously urging your Mother to enter one of them. Finally when it became apparent that there was no hope of the *Titanic* staying afloat, your Father insisted that your

Mother enter the second from the last boat that was being launched from the side they were on. She still refused, saying she would not go without him, and when the officer in charge again urged her to enter, and, in fact, attempted force, aided by the urging of your Father, she placed her foot in the boat, thinking at the time that your Father would accompany her. Just then, some demonstration seems to have been made by the men standing around and the officer in charge ordered all the men back. Mr. Isidor, thinking that your Mother was safe in the lifeboat, stepped back with the other men. Your Mother, looking around and seeing that your Father was not with her, got out of the boat, went to where your Father was standing and put her arms around him. The officer in charge seeing that it was no use in trying to get your Mother to leave your Father ordered the boat lowered away. Your Father and Mother then walked to the opposite side of the ship and when last seen were standing, clasped in each other's arms, calmly waiting for any help that might come. Just what happened after that is not quite clear, but I believe they did not attempt to enter any other boat or make any effort to get away, caused, I believe by the unruly behavior of a number of the passengers.

It is now history all over the world that they displayed the most magnificent courage, self sacrifice and devotion known to modern times.

Yours respectfully,

John A. Badenoch[3]

MAY BIRKHEAD

While on board the *Carpathia*, Miss Birkhead wrote the following account for publication:

It was half-past four on the morning of Monday, April 15, when I was awakened by much rushing around of hasty footsteps on deck above, just over my head. I got out and on deck by five and was greeted with a most beautiful sight of icebergs on every side – some of much greater dimensions than the ship, and then some baby ones – all beautiful white in the calm sea and glittering sun, a most impressive view, but one that turned from gorgeous beauty to sickening pangs when I learned the great disaster one had caused.

The sea was dotted with tiny life-boats from the *Titanic*, and much to my amazement there was one at our side and our sailors were pulling the passengers up onto our deck with ropes. Some were so cold it was impossible for them to climb the ladders, and had to be put in bags to be hauled up. Then I heard one, then another woman calling for her husband – husbands who have never yet appeared.

One gentleman (*Titanic* passenger) told me that he was in the smoking room of the *Titanic* at quarter to twelve when he felt the shock of the big ship as if it had run against something, but he thought little of it – in fact, he thought so little of it that he went to his room to retire. He was ready for bed, but hearing increasing noises he dressed with his room mates, who had been awakened by the jar but thought nothing of it, and went out to see what it was all about, having no idea that anything serious had happened.

They went on deck and found that boats were being lowered. This was before the extent of the catastrophe was even guessed. The seamen were really having difficulty filling the lifeboats, because no one had any idea that the ship would sink. A lifeboat was being lowered only about half filled, and as there were no more women close around these men got in as it was swung off the ship and out to sea. They received orders from the captain to row out until the lowest row of lights were hidden by the waves from observers in the boat.

The seamen said eight or ten hours would cover the time for the boat to sink, if it sunk at all, but after rowing out a mile from the ship it could be seen that one row of lights and then another would disappear, and the final plunge came at twenty minutes after 2 a.m. making the time from the first jar to the final plunge, two hours and a half.

Mrs. Clark of Los Angeles told me that she had just gotten into her bed when she felt this sudden jar and heard the engine's immediate stop with a death-like stillness. Thinking the engine was panting, she listened to hear it take up again. At that moment she looked at her window, the *Titanic* having huge windows instead of portholes, and instead of seeing the blackness of the night she saw a perfectly white background. She got up very calmly and not at all frightened and went to the window, and as far as she could see she saw this huge white thing. She had no thought of an iceberg – the thing was so huge she thought it a tremendous ship with its white bow at the window. She then went to her bathroom, climbed up on her tub and put her head out the porthole and there was nothing to be seen, which shows the rapidity with which the ship must have passed the huge white thing after it was hit.

From this account it evidently hit the ship a little to the side of the front and then scraped along tearing the bottom and side entirely out. After look-ing out this porthole this woman started back to bed, thinking the damage would be easily and soon repaired, but just then the steward came and told her to put on a life preserver and warm clothes and go out on deck. She did so, not at all willingly, as she had such explicit confidence in the *Titanic* and much preferred risking her life to that ship instead of a small lifeboat. This seemed to have been the general feeling. Nobody believed the boat could sink, as it had been pronounced absolutely non-sinkable by the Board of Trade of the English government.

There was absolutely no panic in getting into the lifeboats. The women, of course, were put in first. They kissed their husbands good-bye, thinking they were going out to sea for a short time only by way of precaution and would return as soon as the ship was righted. This woman whom I speak of was so perfectly sure of returning that she scarcely had a thought of her husband coming, too, and he did not offer to come. After her boat was put out to sea she could see that they had to row rapidly to get away from the ship. She realized then and only then that the ship was sinking and the suction would be great and they would have to row fast to get away from it.

In the meantime some of the men had grown frightened, and not being allowed to get into the lifeboats until the women were saved had jumped from the ship and were swimming for the lifeboats. The women who had left husbands, on seeing this, wanted to go back for them, but others wanted to row hard to get away from being sucked in by the ship.

There were only sixteen lifeboats – not nearly enough to accommodate half the passengers, so at the very best there must have been some heart-sickening scenes among the men, when they discovered there was nothing in which they could put to sea. They simply had to go down with the ship.

There was one bunch of twenty-five men and two women who made a raft of chairs and any pieces of wood that they could find. Only eight of these souls reached the *Carpathia*.

One of the women died from the cold and exposure. The other woman reached the *Carpathia* almost frozen to death. She had only her nightgown and a coat to cover her and had been standing in that icy water up to her knees for five hours. She had been prostrated ever since she was taken up by the *Carpathia*. One by one the men died and were put into the sea until just eight reached other boats. I had this story from a 13-year-old boy who was on the rafts and saw his father go down. One of the men had his feet frozen to the knee.

There were 710 persons rescued by this ship, four or five of whom died since we turned toward New York. Besides the sixteen lifeboats there were two canvas lifeboats, one of which reached us among the first of the boats. The other cannot be accounted for. Supposedly it was either capsized, was lost or picked up by another ship later in the day.

The *Carpathia* must have been anchored very near the actual spot of the sinking of the *Titanic*, as there was much debris floating around us and we were very close to a number of icebergs.

Not one vestige of the *Titanic* could be seen when the *Carpathia* came into sight of the lifeboats at dawn – not even one mast sticking up as might have been expected. That non-sinkable boat was entirely out of view in just those two and one-half hours.

I had it from the wireless operator on board the *Carpathia* that he received the 'C.Q.D.' message at twenty minutes after eleven o'clock New York Time, and the marvelous part of it is that in five more minutes he would not have received the message at all, as he was just going to bed and was ready to turn off the instrument.

However, immediately upon receiving the message our Captain Rostron turned us to the north with all possible speed and went between ninety and a hundred miles to the scene of the disaster. I am told that our small ship – very small compared to the tremendous *Titanic* – looked to those shipwrecked souls, many of whom had given up hope of being rescued, like a huge angel from heaven, larger than any ship they had ever seen.

I am also told that there was some discussion on our bridge as to taking our passengers into the dangers that had been the death of the *Titanic* and its twenty-two hundred passengers, but being warned of the icebergs, we could take the necessary precautions of a good watch, and there was only the one thing left to do, and our captain did it.

Among the rescued ones who came on board the *Carpathia* was the president of the White Star Line. Mr. Ismay, who naturally feels the loss most keenly, and a pitiable sight he was – hatless, as they all were, but with Romeo slippers and pajamas on and an overcoat.

I am told that the lookout of the *Titanic*, who is on board the *Carpathia* now, says he signaled the bridge that icebergs were ahead, and there was no response. It was alleged that there was no officer on the bridge at the time, but this is not authentic and scarcely seems possible. I am also told that Captain Smith of the *Titanic* shot himself with a pistol as the ship was going down. On the other hand, I have heard it contradicted, and it is said he went down with the ship, as did the second officer. The second officer, Lightoller by name, had the most wonderful escape of which I have yet heard. He actually went down with the ship and was blown out by an explosion, which occurred after the ship had sunk with tremendous force. After going down the second time he was blown near a raft of men, and as he was being pulled on the raft he was struck by some funnel part of the ship which had been blown out and was knocked off the raft. Then he was pulled on again and is here to tell the tale.

From all I can gather the truth of the *Titanic* seems to be that it was not completed. It seems that the workmen were pushed very hard to start her on the day she was booked and consequently left numerous little things undone. For instance, the lifeboats were not supplied as they should have been with food and brandy and such necessities, and one can realize what horror might have been added to the already too great disaster had our ship not received the 'C.Q.D.' message, it being the only ship that did receive the message. Those people would have been left to drift the seas in hunger and to reach their death through starvation.

These poor souls say after leaving the *Titanic* in the lifeboats that the cries for help of those left to go down were the most harrowing. They will never forget them as long as they live if they live for a thousand years, and some can't sleep at night for hearing those awful cries.

After the bottom was taken out of the *Titanic* by this iceberg I was told that the water reached E deck almost immediately. The cafe or dining room, which I assume was forward, was filled with water at once, and hardly any of those attached to it were saved.

After we picked up the lifeboats with their passengers we circled around the scene to see if we had missed any. We were within two miles of the most tremendous floe of ice that has ever been known in that part of the Atlantic. By actual count we steamed fifty-two miles by the side of this ice monstrosity before we could get around it, and it loomed near enough to be reached with a stone's throw. There were at least twenty-five icebergs in plain view from where we were anchored.

After not being able to get into one of the lifeboats Mr. Williams and son jumped into the water and clung to some part of the ship, but the water dislodged them and the father was overcome and sank. The son, being stronger, eventually succeeded in gaining a lifeboat after the *Titanic* had gone down. He feared that the dreadful suction of the sinking ship would draw him under before he reached his objective point, but it seemed to have the contrary effect of driving him away.

Those saved from the *Titanic* by the *Carpathia* were:

First class	220
Second class	120
Third class	160
Crew	201
Total	710

The total crew on board the *Titanic* was 900.

I am told the band was playing as the big ship went down, and when last heard it was playing 'Nearer My God, to Thee'.

Sir Duff Gordon with his wife, Lady Duff Gordon, and her maid and two oarsmen were among the first to be taken on board the *Carpathia* from a small boat containing only those five persons. They seemed to have really the easiest time of all with life.

There are several children on board who have lost their parents – one baby of eleven months with a nurse, who, coming on board the *Carpathia* with the first boat, watched with eagerness and sorrow for each incoming boat, but to no avail. The parents had gone down.

There is a woman in the second class cabin who lost seven children out of ten, and there are many other losses quite as horrible. Such a loss of life has never before been known on the sea, and who is to be blamed can scarcely be told. All seems to have been done that could have been on board the *Titanic* after she started to sink. The implicit confidence of her passengers seems to have been their undoing. I have not yet found any one among those rescued ones who was frightened when they started out to sea in the small boats or who had a thought of its being anything but a temporary arrangement.

The work of the crew on board the *Carpathia* in rescuing was most noble and remarkable, and these three or four days that the ship has been over-crowded with its 710 extra passengers could not have been better handled. The stewards have worked with undying strength – although one was over-come with so much work and died and was put into his grave at sea.

Every cabin had been filled with women and children sleeping on the floors in the dining saloon, library and smoking rooms. The passengers of the *Carpathia* have divided their clothes with the shipwrecked ones until they have at least kept warm. 'Tis true that many women have had to appear on deck in kimonos and some in underclothes with a coat thrown over them, but their lives have been spared and they have not thought of dress. Some children were entirely without clothes in the second cabin, but the women have joined together and made warm clothes out of the blan-kets belonging to the *Carpathia* and with needles and thread they could pick up from passenger to passenger.

Among other notable passengers rescued we have Mrs. J.J. Astor, Mr. Astor having been lost with the majority. Mrs. Astor has been ill ever since she came on board, and many others have not so far been able to recover from the dreadful loss.

After we got the *Titanic*'s passengers on board our ship it was a question as to where we should take them. Some said the *Olympic* would come out and meet us and take them on to New York, but others said they would die if they had to be lowered again into small boats to be taken up by another, so we finally turned toward New York, delaying the *Carpathia*'s passengers eight days in reaching Gibraltar.

These subscriptions were taken up on board the *Carpathia* on Monday:

Mrs. William Bucknell	$250.00
Mrs. Walter Clark	$200.00
Mr. Washington Dodge	$150.00
Mr. Richard Beckwith	$100.00
Mrs. George N. Stone	$100.00
Mrs. Leo D. Greenfield and Mr. William B. Greenfield	$100.00
Mr. E.N. Kimball, Jr.	$100.00
Dr. H.W. Frauenthal	$100.00
Mr. Robert W. Daniel	$200.00

Mr. F.C. Spedden	$100.00
Mrs. J.J. Brown	$100.00
Mrs. E.E. Lines	$5.00
Mr. Frederick H. Seward	$20.00
Mrs. C. Williams	$50.00

Other subscriptions were made by Mr. Charles Whilems, Mrs. G.L. Longley Hudson, Mrs. Edward S. Robert, Miss Georgette Madill, Miss Elizabeth W. Allen and Mr. Harry Anderson.

One woman who was in the first lifeboat told me that when the order first came for her to get into it she declined, saying, 'I do not believe the *Titanic* is in danger. I will stay here with my husband.'

To that the officer replied, 'Madam, if you do not obey orders you will spread confusion among the other ladies of the ship. You owe it to yourself and to everybody on board to do as you are told in this matter.'

Then the woman obeyed, taking her place.

Five women saved their pet dogs, carrying them in their arms. Another woman saved a little pig, which she said was her mascot. Though her husband is an Englishman and she lives in England, she is an American and was on her way to visit her folk here. How she cared for the pig aboard ship I do not know, but she carried it up the side of the ship in a big bag. I did not mind the dogs so much, but it seemed to me to be too much when a pig was saved and human beings went to death.

Mrs. Isidor Straus was drowned because she would not leave her husband. A person who was standing beside the aged couple on the deck of the *Titanic* heard Mr. Straus say to his wife, 'Get into the lifeboat.' To that she replied, 'I will not leave you. I will get into the boat only if you will.'

Mr. Straus refused to make a move toward the boat. They must have died together.

The attitude of Mrs. Straus seemed to typify that of the other women who were saved. They went into the boats because they obeyed, and I heard several of these express regret that they had not been allowed to remain and drown with their husbands.

Though most of the women were overcome by the disaster when they realized its enormity, that was not invariably the case. One woman whose husband was drowned never mentioned him, but never ceased to bewail the loss of her jewels, which she repeatedly assured all who would listen to her were worth $30,000.

Some of the costumes which the women wore into the lifeboats seemed similarly inappropriate. Lady Duff Gordon had a moleskin coat over a purple silk kimono.

All night the people in the lifeboats sang, according to Lord Duff Gordon. This was in part to keep their ears and minds closed to the awful cries for help which came from the *Titanic* when it became clear that the ship was going down.

A steward who was saved told me that when he went to one of the first cabin passengers – a woman – and told her to dress and put on a life preserver, she merely laughed.

'If that little bump is all that has happened, I'll stay right here,' she said.

'Madam,' replied the steward, 'my orders are from the captain to tell you to dress and put on a life preserver.'

'My orders to myself are to get back into bed and go to sleep again,' said the woman. And she did. She paid for that with her life.

A woman from Wisconsin said that she was not called at all, and if she had not heard Mrs. Astor out in the passageway crying she would have remained in her stateroom.

One first class passenger, after all the lifeboats had been put out, heard several stokers saying that they knew where there was a collapsible boat, which they proposed to put overboard. So the passenger kept close to the stokers and, sure enough, they launched the boat. He got in it with them and was saved. These same stokers yesterday decided to put some cheer into the dreary atmosphere on board the *Carpathia*, so they took an accordion and several tin pans and gave a burlesque entertainment. That served to dispel some of the gloom.

Two French children, three and five years old, were brought aboard the *Carpathia* without their father, who was lost. They could not speak to us, and it was not known at first whether they were speechless from cold or could not speak English. Spoken to finally by a Frenchman, they answered in their native tongue, and were soon crying for their father. Women in the boat with them comforted them as best they could.

In the boat with Mrs. John Jacob Astor, who wanted to put back toward the *Titanic* to rescue men who after plunging overboard were struggling to save themselves, were other women who wanted to keep going forward. Mrs. Astor was inclined to return to the men, her own husband had been left behind, and she was urged to offer the oarsmen any amount of her wealth if they would put back; but the will of those who were opposed prevailed and the oarsmen rowed onward.

Mrs. Astor was ill aboard the *Titanic*, but she bore up well in the lifeboat. She was taken aboard the *Carpathia* in negligee costume. The captain of the *Carpathia* gave up his cabin to her and she was made perfectly comfortable. She did not leave it until New York was reached. All of the rescued women were made as comfortable as possible, passengers aboard the *Carpathia* either giving up their staterooms entirely or else sharing them.

Many of the survivors of the *Titanic*, especially women, as may be expected, were in a violent state of excitement when rescued, and one woman appeared to have lost her mind entirely. She seemed to be beyond recovery. She appeared to be in possession of her mental faculties when the rescue was being made; her husband was among the missing and she scanned every lifeboat for him. When the last lifeboat had come alongside the *Carpathia* and he was not among the passengers, then it was that her mind gave way. She became suddenly frantic, and all efforts of women and men to quiet her were in vain. The mental suffering of many others from shock was severe.

All of the men in the lifeboats, except one, conducted themselves most commendably. They worked well and rowed hard. The exception was a man who absolutely refused to work at all. There was but one other man in the boat with him. This beast (I wish I could tell you his name!) not only refused to work, but took for himself all blankets in the boat, the women having to go without and shiver and also row.

One of the women in the boat finally told this man that she would shoot him if he did not give up the blankets and work. The display of a pistol had the desired effect.

Only two of the *Carpathia*'s passengers knew at two o'clock in the morning that the *Carpathia* was rushing to the aid of those aboard the doomed *Titanic*. They were awakened by the rushing around of the crew making ready for the work that was ahead of them, and went out on deck and asked what it all meant. They were told that nothing at all was the matter, but they were convinced that something unusual and of great moment had happened. Just by accident it was learned at five o'clock what was going on.

Major Arthur Peuchen, of Canada, owes his life to the fact that he is a yachtsman. His story was one of the most interesting of those told aboard the *Carpathia*. When the boats were putting out from the *Titanic* Captain Smith noticed that one of the places for oarsmen was vacant. The sailor whose place that was was not at hand. Captain Smith, addressing the men passengers, asked, 'Can any of you men handle an oar?'

There was silence for a moment, and then Major Peuchen, stepping forward, said, 'I am a yachtsman, Captain, and am familiar with small boats, too.'

'Get aboard,' ordered Captain Smith.

Major Peuchen jumped to a rope which hung over the side and hand over hand made his way to the lifeboat below. He rowed all night, and when he came on board the *Carpathia* his hands were a mass of blisters.

Lord Duff Gordon, one of those who was saved, said that the last thing he did before entering the lifeboat was to put his pistol in his pocket, thinking that there might be trouble and he would need it.

The sea was practically calm when the rescue was made and all during the time that the rescue was being made, but shortly afterward a storm swept over the sea and, according to seamen, a lifeboat could not have gone fifty feet in it.

Lord Gordon wanted a picture of the men who had rowed him; he wanted it with the men in the life preservers, but some of the rescued women could not bear the sight of a life preserver, and out of deference none was brought out. Lord Gordon gave to each of the men a check, which he called a 'fiver', probably five pounds sterling.

As there were no other boats or life rafts of any description within sight after the last survivor had been taken aboard the *Carpathia*, we were led to believe that perhaps some were saved by other ships which might have been passing on another course.

There were no bodies to be seen afloat except that of a child, which was supported by a life preserver. It presumably had been frozen to death.

One second cabin woman lost seven children out of a family of ten.

Only the steerage passengers, we were told, were hard to handle aboard the *Titanic*. Many of these had to be driven either backward or forward as officers may have desired.

One man who persisted in his efforts to enter a lifeboat was shot dead and his body either tumbled or was thrown overboard.[4]

FRANK BLACKMARR

On 17 April, while he was on board the *Carpathia*, Dr Blackmarr bribed the vessel's wireless operator to send the following message to Chicago:

> *Carpathia* picked up 700 *Titanic*, mostly women. Over 2,000 lost. Iceberg continuous mass was twenty-five miles. Chicagoans this ship well. 8:35 a.m. Dr. F.H. Blackmarr[5]

On 18 April Dr Blackmarr cabled the following account to his hometown newspaper:

> On Monday morning at 1:15 the *Carpathia*'s wireless operator, Harold Thomas Cottam, picked up a distress signal from the steamship *Titanic*. It was the habit of this boy before retiring for the night to pick up the nearest ship and say 'Good Night'. Having received the distress signal he at once notified the officers of the ship. When we arrived at the spot the *Titanic* had sunk. The sea was covered with wreckage of all kinds, mahogany splinters, white enameled wood, silk covered couches, pillows, and

mattresses. We all saw a woman's hat floating in the debris. One fur coat floated by, suspended on a piece of wood.

From near at hand and from a distance, too, lifeboats were coming towards us, women occupying rowing seats in many of them, with a man at the tiller. Not a sound escaped their lips; no hysteria was in evidence. Their faces were pinched with cold. The task of raising them from the lifeboats to the ship's deck was difficult. The women with their blistered hands found it hard to climb any ladders. The majority of them were lifted in by a swing which consisted of a board with a rope from each side, connecting with a single large cable.

Officers, stewards, and stewardesses had been on duty for hours preparing to receive them. These same officers and crew after that had no opportunity to lie down for a rest until their journey was over.

Many of the women that came in the boats huddled together in the seats with a dead sailor lying in the bottom of the boat.

When asked why it was there were so few men saved – an estimate of one in five – a woman passenger who had lost her husband said she begged him to get into the boat with her, but that he refused out of sympathy for the poor fellows who were left.

Col. Astor, it is said, after placing his wife in a boat, as did some of the other rich men, returned to the middle of the deck of the *Titanic*, folded his arms, and went down with the ship. The conduct of these rich men goes to prove they were heroes.

The only panic at the beginning, as I understand it, was in the steerage, where there were many persons who lacked self-control. There was no shooting, as I learn, except that a steerage passenger told me he saw an officer trying to control the maddened rush by shooting two persons. The same officer shot himself a minute later.

The stairway of the *Titanic* was so crowded with steerage passengers that it was utterly impossible for some to gain the upper deck. One man told me he climbed along the ledge of the boat until he reached the deck where he loosened a collapsible boat. A moment later the lifeboat was filled on its edges with women, children, and men. It began to sink with the load, and the women and children at the edge gradually slipped off, into the ocean.

The saddest moment of all, after the boat loads had been landed on the deck, was to see the poor widows and sons and daughters whose family relations had been broken, standing at the rail, looking into the distance with hands outstretched trying in hope to see their loved ones. There were numerous sick persons on board, but the illness was not so much physical as it was mental agony.[6]

Dr Blackmarr later wrote and delivered a public address regarding the *Carpathia*'s rescue of the *Titanic*'s passengers:

The story of the most awful shipwreck of modern times may not be a pleasant subject for either the relater or the hearers, but there is an interest in the details of the loss of the *Titanic* which warrants me in telling the story. And having been on the boat which rescued the survivors, I may be able to give a more vivid description of the incidents of the rescue than have been conveyed in the manner published in the public press.

When, on the fifth day of April, I sailed from New York on the *Carpathia*, I had little thought that before the voyage ended I would act a part in the tragedy of the sea, the like of which the world had never before known. It is not for one's best interests to think of this disaster any longer than necessary. It is necessary, however, to keep this matter constantly before us. Only until you and I and the nations of the world shall see to it that proper precautions are taken in the constructions of vessels, the supplying of safety devices, the proper control and watchful care of those who hold human lives in the palm of their hands, so make a repetition of such a catastrophe an impossibility.

Speed and greed have cost thousands of human lives in the past year. Our fast train systems are the result of demand ingrained by the public, our luxurious express steamers running on scheduled time; stopping for naught, fogs or storm are the result of the public's demand. The day of restful recreation and moderate business endeavor is passing.

Increased activities in pleasures and business have associated therewith a terrific increase in the proportion of danger. At the speed of our trains and ships are increased, it is not alone coal, fuel and oil that are consumed, but the responsibilities upon those in charge of them is increased to the sapping point of their nervous energies. What I have said already gives the key to my innermost conviction concerning these matters.

The *Titanic* was, until now, the largest and most beautiful ship ever constructed. 883 feet long, 91 and one half feet broad, 104 feet high from her heel to the bridge. Figure out in your minds how many times you can place this building which you are now on top of itself to reach the length of the *Titanic*, and you could almost gain an idea what a terrific mass of steel, iron and concrete went to the bottom of the sea last April. She was built in Belfast of the world's best materials, by the world's best builders, magnificently equipped, with engines, furnaces and all the mechanisms that science could evolve to make her comfortable and seaworthy. Her passenger equipment, as you know, was all that you could find on land: magnificent suites, gymnasium, swimming tanks, squash-tennis court, a la-carte restaurant, magnificent salons for both men and women, summer gardens, etc.

I returned on the *Olympic* with the purpose of studying *Titanic*'s sister ship.

So much for comfort and luxury. On the other side of the ledger we find but sixteen 30-foot lifeboats and several hundred dead bodies to balance the account.

The *Titanic* sailed from Southampton on Wednesday, April 10 with 2,208 passengers and crew. Sunday night at 11:50 she struck a submerged spur of an enormous iceberg. Two hours and one half later, at 2:20 a.m., she plunged bow on to a depth of over 2 miles into her eternal berth. 688 of her crew and 615 passengers sank in the icy water.

Sunday night I strolled the *Carpathia*'s deck with my heavy overcoat on, gazing at the wonderful glittering stars in their black background. The ship's lights did not seem to be as bright at the deck, and were it not for those lights I doubt if I could have seen my hands before my face. Looking over the side of the ship, one could feel that they were gazing into abysmal depths. With the memory of what transpired a few hours later, I never want to see another night uncanny and cold. This night I associate in memory with a night shortly before we arrived in New York when returning with the survivors, when it seemed, with the mist, fog, rain and awful lightening, as though God and nature were displeased.

I retired shortly after 12 o'clock and had just gotten into my berth when I was aroused by a knock. The wireless operator, in going from his quarters to the bridge to deliver the *Titanic*'s CQD message, had knocked. This young man, Mr. Harold Cottam, had been very kind. His interest in high tension apparatus and therapeutics had made our acquaintance mutually interesting and resulted in my becoming familiar with his apparatus.

The wireless equipment of this ship was decidedly antiquated and consisted of two coils, one of them punctured, a tuning device, a detector, receiver, sending key and old condensers.

Immediately after reception of the messages, the ship's crew was in action and everything was quickly arranged and surely arranged, and very few of the passengers knew what was going on. Our captain, Captain Rostron, a most remarkable military man and officer of His Majesty's Naval Reserves, managed the details of the preparation for the subsequent care and nursing of the survivors without fuss or friction. Large bales of old blankets materialized.

Stimulants, hot foods, etc. seemed to come to the surface as if by magic. The ship had been put about to the rescue.

I have often wished to know what [the] sensations were that passed over and over through the mind of this brave man. [During] Captain Rostron's testimony before a court of inquiry he was asked about the dangers encountered by his own ship in this awful trip to the rescue. He said 'I took the risk of full speed in my desire to save life, and probably some people may blame me for taking such a risk'. The Senate committee assured him they would not. He also stated in his evidence that between 2:45 and 4:00 a.m. they had passed over twenty large icebergs from 100 to 200 feet high and a great many smaller ones. It was a matter of constant maneuvering to go around them and between them.

Our deck was covered with lookouts, and you can imagine with the atmospheric conditions I have briefly described how busy the Captain and crew must have been in avoiding these ghostly monsters.

When we were in the field, located as described in the *Titanic*'s message of distress, rockets were sent up to show the survivors our position. At 4 a.m. we stopped with an enormous iceberg directly in front of us, and as the dawn lifted we saw just beyond the iceberg one of the lifeboats. The crew had provided a cradle, swings and ladders for both sides of the ship to hasten the matter of rescue. The women were seated in the swings and raised with nooses under their shoulders. The men climbed the ladders. There were some who tried to climb but were so badly frozen that it made our hearts ache. The babies and small children were put in bags and raised to the deck. While these poor people were being raised to the deck I went from side to side of our vessel and looked down into their faces.

Many stories have been written and published describing these people and their behavior at the moment of their arrival; that they were hysterical and some were too dazed to realize what they were passing through. But I want to tell you that there was only evidence of one thing written on their faces – and that was gratitude, thankfulness that they were to be saved. There was absolutely no hysteria; only one woman had hysteria and that was when she was brought into the cabin of the ship and was undoubtedly due first to the joy of her being saved and the awful strain under which she had been laboring, because she was one of the women who had pulled an oar of a lifeboat.

Mr. Duff Gordon made the statement that the only hysterical individual who was in evidence that night of the disaster was a man.

The setting of this disaster, the picture that remains with me of the silvery sheen of the dawn with those magnificent great white bergs coming toward us out of the dawn. Boats filled mostly with women who wore white life preservers such as I show you. Back beyond this picture in the background later showed beautiful mountains and stretches of glittering ice. Mr. Cooper, a well-known artist, made drawings of this setting, and with my photographs which I now show you, will help you imagine the picture that I am trying to make indelible to you.

The work of raising the survivors progressed very rapidly, the boats coming up on either side of our vessel until the sea began to come up. We were worried for some time, because several of the lifeboats that were coming in from great distances were loaded down almost to the tops of the boats and the poor women who rowed them had difficulty in keeping out of the troughs of the waves.

After all but one of the boats had been emptied, I began to take notice of the wreckage. For acres and acres about our ship there seemed to be a yellow scum on the surface of the water which appeared to be like ground cork. At the right of us, we stood still, one of the lifeboats lay bottom up, steamer chairs, fine woods, clothing, what seemed to be the front of a piano, one trunk.

I counted six soft sofa pillows. In fact anything almost can be found on the surface of the water here which you can find on land. Concerning the cork or what seemed to be cork, the following letter will give you an idea about some of the recent agitation that is taking place now:

Letter Dated 20 April 1912
Dear Dr. Blackmarr,

I am enclosing a letter from the *Paris Herald* which explains itself. As I remember, you took one of the *Titanic* lifebelts to show with you, and if you still have it it would be most interesting to make a test of it. The belts I cut up on board the *Carpathia* contained a poor quality of cork, some of which I still have. Could you not make a test by floating it with, say, 160lbs of weight and see how long it will remain afloat. It would of course make some difference if the water was not salt, but that difference would be slight. I am hoping you can make this test and let me know the results.

With best regards, I am faithfully yours,

Lewis M. Ogden

In the *Paris Herald* of 11 August, Mr Ogden said:

On reading the report of the *Titanic* conditions I noticed the question of efficiency of lifebelts is not touched upon. When the *Carpathia* arrived at the scene of the disaster it was most naturally expected that numerous bodies supported by lifebelts would be found, but such was not the case. What was the reason for this? And why was such a grave question ignored by the commission? The evidence shows the following facts; first that each person on the *Titanic* was supplied with a lifebelt, second, that many testified to hearing cries for an hour after the vessel sank; third, that the *Carpathia* found practically no bodies afloat on her arrival; fourth, the bodies that were picked up a week later were found floating with belts properly adjusted. In these circumstances is it not fair to assume that the belts were constructed with improper materials which, becoming water-logged, allowed the bearers to sink only to arise later owing to natural causes?

At 4:10 a.m., an hour and fifty minutes after the *Titanic* sank, the first boat was alongside, and shortly after daybreak the *Carpathia* was in the wreckage.

The immense quantities of small squares of cork, presumably from belts, covered the sea. Also, the overturned lifeboat, a few chairs etc. etc., but to our enormous surprise there were no bodies. We are still awaiting the explanation.

The commission has answered the question 'should searchlights have been provided and used' in the negative. Nevertheless, had these three ships been equipped with searchlights, the *Carpathia* might have greatly aided in her dash through the bergs, the *Californian* might have reached the scene seven hours earlier then she actually did (which was at 8:00 a.m.), and lastly the *Titanic* might have picked up the great icefield and landed all of her people in safety.

Why not searchlights for such emergencies?

[Signed] Lewis Mansfield Ogden of London, England

I bring this question of the cork in life preservers home to you because such a matter needs critical consideration by every individual of our country who travels our lakes and rivers. It should be a criminal offense to neglect any detail of safety of a steamer, whether she be of small or large tonnage.

Back again to the deck of the *Carpathia*, we had taken the passengers all on board, raised such of the lifeboats as the Captain considered seaworthy, set adrift several that were not, and I call your attention at this point to a story that appeared in the press concerning the lifeboat found a month or so after the accident, adrift with three dead men lying on the bottom with cork in their mouths. These men were put back into this boat while alive, but died before they reached the *Carpathia*. I saw the ship's surgeon examine these bodies before the boat was set adrift. The newspaper story went on to say this boat had not been discovered and that the men had died from privation and had eaten the cork out of the structure of the boat. If there was cork in their mouths, you can readily see how it came there because the surface of the water was covered with cork where the *Titanic* went down.

The moment of mental agony that caused the passengers and crew of the *Carpathia* to make an effort to control their feelings was when the *Carpathia* started to move away from amongst the wreckage. These poor survivors, scantily clothed, with tears running down their cheeks, without an audible cry of any kind, their arms outstretched, looked into the far way to see if they could not discover just one more boat that might contain their loved ones. You and I have faced death and grief in the sick room, but imagine and words would fail to convey to you the feelings that surged through me at that time.

Captain Rostron turned his ship about for New York. It is my pleasure to show you some of the photographs of the ice which have never been published. Many pictures have appeared in the papers that were taken weeks after the disaster.

These which I show you make up the setting of the tragedy. Had it not been for the terrific extent of the ice Captain Rostron would undoubtedly have sailed for Halifax, as it was the nearest point of distance. We were late in the afternoon before we passed the mass of ice, having run nearly 75 miles to get around.

We steamed within two or three hundred yards of part of this ice floe, and at dusk we could see in the distance only a few straggling icebergs. In the testimony of the officers of different steamships, some of them have testified that they had never seen field ice, and some testified that they had never seen any icebergs at this season of the year. These photographs I show you were taken every half hour of the field ice and the bergs. According to the visibility at sea tables, one can see from the height of our deck to the horizon some six and two/tenths of a mile, and the objects on the horizon that are visible would range from 90 to 95 feet high, so [if] you will bear this in mind you can gain a fairly accurate idea of the magnitude and height of this mass of field ice and also of the bergs.

During the day, first an accounting was made of the survivors and the lost, and a memorial service was held and eight dead bodies were buried. Four of these had died on the ship from exposure and the other four had been taken out of the boats. The *Carpathia* passengers and crew busied themselves in providing clothing and comfort for the passengers. The majority of the survivors were obliged to sleep on straw mattresses that came from somewhere, no one knew where, placed on the floors of the smoking room, the ladies writing room and the dining salon. Some of the poor fellows slept out on the open deck, wrapped up in blankets. The young man that was with me joined the straw mattress throng and we gave our stateroom to four ladies who could hardly understand each other. The pathetic and ridiculous were evidenced in the selection of those whom we thought needed those beds in our room the most.

Two people we had picked out, and they had retired immediately. I went to the ladies writing room where the ladies were lying on the floor packed in like sardines, and looked about for others who needed the unfilled cots.

In the middle of the room I saw an old grey-haired woman at least sixty years old. I woke her up and asked her to come and get in one of the beds. She sat up, looked all about her, and said, 'I want to thank you oh so much, but please take someone else. There are so many that need it worse than I.'

Next to this old lady laid a very large woman. Sitting by her side, leaning up against a post was one who proved to be what she called her governess. This governess grabbed hold of my arm and demanded that I take her mistress to the bed that I was trying to give to the old lady. It took an unusually long time for this governess to unharness the large lady, and finally I was called in to try and assist her in trying to get her into the two upper ones, being the vacant ones. In the absence of steps I attempted to boost her into the berth, and just about the time when she should have ducked her head she stretched her neck, with the result that I was obliged to let her down. Three times I tried this to the accompaniment of a beautiful flow of 'French' and violent punctuations. In spite of the fact that the two ladies in the lower berths had lost everything, they began to show a slight degree of mirth and one of them asked, under her breath, 'why I didn't put her up?' Remembering my football days, I made a low tackle and this lady landed in the upper corner with a groan.

The *Carpathia* returned to New York in every kind of climatic condition imaginable; ice, sleet, rain, fog, thunder and lighting and such a chilled damp air that clothing seemed to be of no avail in keeping one warm. We had no serious illnesses on the *Carpathia* on this return trip, which means much in evidence for the efforts and unselfish attention administered by the stewardesses. To my mind, these women were entitled to most of the money and gratuities that were given out by the different organizations.

Bear in mind that we had a great many women passengers and the addition of the large number of women survivors such small quarters made their care an arduous one.

Upon my return to Chicago, I was asked if there was not a great deal of physical suffering on the *Carpathia*. I answered no, there was plenty of good food, plenty of blankets and many hands to help, but of course there was, worst of all, suspense and mental agony. So much I have given you in this brief analysis.

I will now read you [four] stories, each written for me by the survivors themselves and as yet unpublished:

[Note: at this point Dr Blackmarr read accounts by Charles Stengel, Washington Dodge, Algernon Barkworth and Eugene Daly.]

Statement by Sir Cosmo Duff-Gordon, signed by himself:
The only thing that I can say was that I was amazed at the perfect calmness of everyone concerned and the great care displayed by the officers and crew in lowering the boats.

[Signed] Sir Cosmo Duff-Gordon

A word regarding the bulletins that were posted by the Captain and the different committees on the *Carpathia*. The first one I shall read to you is posted by Captain Rostron:

NOTICE TO PASSENGERS
I hereby declare that no press messages at all have been Marconied from this ship with the exception of a short one of about twenty words to the

Associated Press, sent immediately after the passengers had been picked up, and that passenger messages have been dispatched with all possible speed. The reason for this statement is that it has come to my attention that several passengers are under the impression that the delay in dispatching their private messages is due to the instruments being used for the press.

[Signed] A.H. Rostron, Commander

When I sent the message concerning the disaster to the *Chicago Tribune* I had not read this notice and was not aware at that moment that I was offering any offense to our Captain. I was in the wireless operator's room when a reporter who was on vacation with his wife came in and requested Mr. Cottam, the operator, to send a message for him immediately, and that he did not wish anyone to send any messages to the press. After he had gone out, I succeeded in persuading him that my Chicago friends were entitled to know that the Chicago people on board the *Carpathia* were in good condition and safe. This message I learned afterwards was the second message sent off the ship:

BULLETIN
Committee to Assist Destitute Passengers Mrs. J.J. Brown, Mrs. William Bucknell, Mrs. George Stone. Important: The Committee has received assurance from Mr. Bruce Ismay, Managing Director of the White Star Line [that] passengers of the *Titanic* requiring assistance will be sent to their destinations and will be supplied with necessary clothing. In order to facilitate the collection and handling of subscriptions, it is requested that all funds be sent to J.P. Morgan and Company of New York, or to Mr. I.G. Frauenthal on this boat.

[Signed] Committee for the Survivors of the *Titanic*'

BULLETIN
To the Captain, to the Officers and Passengers of the RMS *Carpathia*. On behalf of the survivors of the *Titanic* we desire to express to each and all our heartfelt thanks for the kindness of treatment and full hearted welcome accorded us on board your ship. It will be our sincere endeavor to express our thanks at an appropriate and fitting manner at the earliest possible moment.
[Signed] Survivors of the SS *Titanic*, by the Committee. S.H. Goldenberg, F.D. Spedden, W.E. Carter, Frederic K. Seward, I.G. Frauenthal, Karl H. Behr, Margaret T. Brown, Björnström Steffanson, A.H. Barkworth.'

Resuming the return from the scene of the disaster to New York, I wish to remind you again of the climatic conditions through which we passed. Chicago is noted for fickle and absurd climatic conditions, but take the worst weather and rapid changes you have ever experienced in Chicago and add to it the limit of your powers of imagination and make it as bad as the worst, and you can't begin to equal the nightmare of that trip.

The last of the survivors was lifted to our deck at 8:30. We circled around through the wreckage, and then Captain Rostron assigned the responsibility of finding any others of the survivors to the *Californian* and the *Birma*, a Russian tramp ship. With what you have read, Captain Rostron showed excellent judgment in returning immediately to New York, and I know that you will agree that it was the best thing to be done. The field of ice was nearly 80 miles long and 12 miles wide. There is little to say now in answer to the questions 'Why did not the *Birma* come to the rescue when she was but 12 miles away?' and 'Why did not the *Californian* come to the rescue?' In answer to the first question, there was 12 miles of solid ice between the *Birma* and the *Titanic*, and it took hours for that ship to go around that massive ice to get to the point in question.

On board the *Olympic* when I returned, was a gentleman who had attended the inquiry in London. As I understood, he was a representative of the Allan Line. I asked why he thought the *Californian* did not go to the rescue and he replied, 'I do not know'. I invited him into my stateroom and showed him the pictures I am showing you tonight. I asked him 'Do you not think that the Captain of the *Californian* was afraid to move in that terrible blackness of night while he was hemmed in by such enormous masses of ice?' His reply was 'it is possible'.

I neglected to tell you a little incident concerning Dr. Washington Dodge's son. The picture that you see of the third officer holding the boy in his arms is of interest. The boy was saved, as other children were, with very little clothing on.

The ladies took the old blankets and made clothing for them. In this case, this boy's pants resembled the baggy trousers of a Holland youth, crossing the suspenders made out of a blanket front to back as you see them in the picture.

Mr. Pitman, the third officer, at first refused to have his picture taken but finally consented when I told him I wanted to give him the picture of the boy in his foreign suit of clothes. You will notice that Mr. Pitman turned his brass buttons inside so he would not be criticized.

All of the stories of our landing in New York have an edge of truth which you have by this time discerned. In brief, the lessons of this disaster are few. In England, there are several books published that take up a lot of time and space in recommending remedies to prevent catastrophes at sea. Some would cover the boat deck with lifeboats, life rafts etc.

But let me ask you a question. These wrecks seldom if ever occur when the sea is smooth. And how long do you think lifeboats filled with survivors would live in the trough of the sea?

If you have ever been in a storm, you can answer the question. If not, ask one of the *Titanic* survivors who might have been in one of the boats that was taken aboard when a light sea had risen. Also take into consideration the difficulty and hazard in lowering these boats in rough weather. The ocean's whitecaps and mountains of spray would swamp any lifeboat filled with inexperienced men and women. Too many lifeboats would make it difficult for men to work in, and there would be loss of efficiency.

Some recommended floating sections in a ship. This is a limited error of good judgment. A mountainous sea would capsize such an unwieldy mass such as they describe. To my mind, the lesson taught is along the line that I suggested at the beginning of my paper under the caps 'SPEED and GREED': the installation on every ship afloat of powerful wireless apparatus with relays of operators so that every machine can be brought into activity at any moment of danger. Increase the number of lifeboats to hold at least two thirds of the crewed capacity of the ship and that these lifeboats shall be under government inspection in every port and on every trip made by that particular vessel. The installation of searchlights to be operated over the sides of vessels to facilitate the lowering and control of boats in the water. The United States Government's suggestion of a sea patrol at certain seasons of the year is to my mind a remedy for disasters of this kind. Another feature I have omitted is the construction of the keel of a ship. You have noticed perhaps that the White Star Line has taken the *Olympic*, the sister ship of the *Titanic*, out of the water and are putting a new skin on the bottom.

So, as to why the Ruler of the Universe allows the human intelligence to so miscalculate the forces of nature to the extent that 1,500 beings are suddenly taken from time into eternity, the only answer is 'who can tell'. Was Captain Smith to blame? The answer is no. Was Mr. Ismay or the White Star Line to blame? The answer is no. If there is an answer, if only in part, what can that answer be? SPEED AND GREED.

[Signed] Dr. Frank Blackmarr, Chicago, Illinois, *Carpathia* Passenger[7]

After the *Carpathia* resumed her interrupted voyage to Gibraltar, Dr Blackmarr transcribed the address that Captain Rostron gave to his crew on the third day out from New York:

Men of the *Carpathia*, I have assembled you here to show you my sincere appreciation for what you have done for me and those that you have saved some days ago. Your loyalty and obedience to every command & order has brought to you and your ship great praise.

I am proud to have such men under my command. You my men I am proud to command.

Especially must I mention the doctors, the pursers, the stewards who have done such great work in relieving the distress of the survivors. Again I say I am proud to command such a crew.

You notice at the fore, the flag – the Stars and Stripes – which we have representing the people of the United States, another flag which I now have the honor to unfurl is the blue ensign of His Royal Majesty's Naval Reserve in which I have the honor to serve. The third flag, that of the Cunard Line which you have honored.

I want you men to remain with this ship. Do your duty. I shall always be just with you – I shall always be fair with you.

Before leaving America a gentleman came aboard and laid a package in my hands saying that he wished to make some small recompense to you for all the care and consideration that you showed the survivors, that he wished the contents of the package distributed among the men of the crew.

At an early date I shall do so.

Again I wish to thank you for what you have done for me & again I say that I am proud to have such men as you serve under my command.[8]

❖ ❖ ❖

WALLACE BRADFORD

On 15 April 1912, Mr Bradford wrote the following letter, which he later sent to the editor of the *New York Herald*:

Monday Noon, April 15 – Since half past four this morning I have experienced one of those never to be forgotten circumstances – one that weighs heavy on my soul and which shows most awfully what puny things we mortals are. Long before this reaches you the news will be flashed that the *Titanic* has gone down and that our steamer, the *Carpathia*, caught the wireless messages when seventy-five miles away, and so far we have picked up twenty boats, estimated to contain about 750 people.

None of us can tell just how many, as they have been hustled to various staterooms and to the dining saloon to be warmed up. I was awakened by unusual noises and imagined that I smelled smoke. I jumped up and looked out of my port hole, and my eyes must have bulged when I saw a huge iceberg looming up like a rock off shore. It was not white, and I was positive that it was a rock and the thought flashed through my mind, 'How in the world can we be near a rock when we are four days out from New York in a southerly direction and in mid-ocean?'

When I got out on deck the first man I encountered told me that the *Titanic* had gone down and we were rescuing the passengers. The first two boats from the doomed vessel were in sight making toward us. Neither of them was crowded. This was accounted for later by the fact that it was impossible to get many to leave the steamer, as they would not believe that she was going down. It was a glorious, clear morning and a quiet sea. Off to the starboard was a white area of ice plain, from whose even surface rose mammoth forts, castles and pyramids of solid ice almost as real as though they had been placed there by the hand of man.

Our steamer was hove to about two and a half miles from the edge of this huge iceberg. The *Titanic* struck about 11:20 p.m. and did not go down until two o'clock. Many of the passengers were in evening dress when they came aboard our ship, and most of these were in a most bedraggled condition. Near me as I write is a girl about eighteen years old in a fancy dress costume of bright colors, while in another seat nearby is a woman in a white dress trimmed with lace and covered with jaunty blue flowers.

As the boats came alongside after the first two all of them contained a very large proportion of women. In fact, one of the boats had women at the oars, one in particular containing, as near as I could estimate, about forty-five women and only about six men. In this boat two women were handling one of the oars. All of the engineers went down with the steamer. Four bodies have been brought aboard. One is that of a fireman, who is said to have been shot by one of the officers because he refused to obey orders. Soon after I got on deck I could, with the aid of my glasses, count seven boats headed our way and they continued to come up to half past eight o'clock. Some were in sight for a long time and moved very slowly, showing plainly that the oars were being handled by amateurs or by women.

No baggage of any kind was brought by the survivors. In fact, the only piece of baggage that reached the *Carpathia* from the *Titanic* is a small closed trunk about twenty-four inches square, evidently the property of an Irish female immigrant. While some seemed fully dressed, many of the men having their overcoats and the women sealskin and other coats, others came just as they had jumped from their berths, clothed in their pajamas and bathrobes.

It was a beautiful clear morning, but extremely cold, and the sufferings that those in the boats had endured for the three to four hours that they were afloat was plainly shown by their condition. Rope ladders were lowered over the sides for those that could climb aboard and canvas bags were sent down for the women and children, there being a large number of both babies and half grown children in the boats. The children were taken from the mothers and deposited in the bags and hoisted to the decks, while the anxious mothers watched eagerly for the moment when they were received by the men on deck and hurried to the dining saloon.

We cruised about until about two p.m. and are now headed for New York. Our captain has just told me that he is going to New York unless he receives wireless orders otherwise. I was standing near the second officer of the *Titanic*, who is the senior surviving officer, when he was questioned by some of the crew who had come aboard. They agreed that eighteen boats had reached the *Carpathia*. Three of the men said that one of the *Titanic*'s boats had not been cut away and the officer asserted that that left only one boat not accounted for.

I soon discovered that Washington Dodge, City and County Assessor of San Francisco, and his wife and four-year-old boy were passengers on board the *Titanic*. Several of the boats have come in, but only Mrs. Dodge and the little boy have so far arrived on our steamer. Mr. Dodge's friends in San Francisco will understand that he is the last one in the world to leave a ship while there are any women and children that have not been put into the boats.

Soon after writing this I discovered that Mr. Dodge had got aboard, having come in one of the last boats that left the ship, and it was a good deal of satisfaction to me to turn over my stateroom to them. Before we started for New York the steamer *Californian*, a freight boat, arrived and communicated for fifteen or twenty minutes with our boat with the aid of a megaphone and evidently agreeing with our captain to stay there and cruise about in the hopes of picking up more people. No more floating palaces for me. I'll take my chances on a moderate sized boat with a limited number of people.

There are two darling little French twins who left Europe with their father, their mother having died, who have finally landed on our steamer, the father having gone down with the *Titanic*. The children were brought aboard in their night clothes, but have been rigged out by some of our passengers so that they now present a neat appearance. The wireless operator caught the SOS from the *Titanic* when he was supposed to be off duty, it being his hour for sleep. We did not see anything of the steamer and the only evidence that she had gone down was a very limited amount of wreckage which floated by our steamer about two hours after we had hove to. You can imagine that the taking on of seven hundred new passengers in a steamer of the size of the *Carpathia* has demoralized to some extent the sleeping accommodations, but it is simply astonishing what fine work the culinary department of the steamer has done.

The meals are served in almost as good shape as they were before the *Titanic*'s passengers came aboard, and everybody connected with the ship, from the captain to the scullery boys, is doing his utmost to handle the passengers which overcrowded the steamer. Beds have been made up on the tables in the dining saloons, and the women who have not been able to find berths in the staterooms are occupying these beds, while the men who were occupying berths on the *Carpathia* have turned them over to the rescued passengers and are sleeping in the hallways and smoking rooms of the steamer.

A young man told me of his fearful experience. After the last boat left about fifty men who were near one of the collapsible boats on the upper deck, which up to that time they had been unable to open, finally succeeded in pulling up the moveable sides, but before they could cut her loose, the bow of the *Titanic* sank beneath the surface and they went down with her, but as the stern of the *Titanic* sunk the bow came above the surface of the water and they managed to cut loose and float off.

Of something like fifty men who left the steamer on that raft, or collapsible boat, only seventeen managed to reach the *Carpathia*. As one after another succumbed to the bitter cold, they were dropped overboard in order to lighten the weight of the raft, as those that were on the raft were standing in water up to their knees for nearly four hours.

I have talked with many of the survivors, both men and women, and all agreed that the discipline aboard the *Titanic* after she struck was first class in every respect. The officers were armed with their revolvers and in the sternest manner commanded that none but women should be put in the boats, with the exception of from four to six men who could handle oars. The women passengers were formed into line and marched to the stairway, the officers telling them that there was no immediate danger and that they were to be put into the boats as a matter of precaution and that they would all probably be taken back when the captain was satisfied that the damage to the steamer would not cause her to sink.

There are from fifteen to twenty-five women aboard, most of them being young brides, who were forced to leave their husbands and go into the boats. Among these is Mrs. John Jacob Astor, of New York. She has kept to her cabin since she has come aboard the *Carpathia*. I listened this morning to the story of the quartermaster of the *Titanic* who was at the wheel when the steamer struck. He said that the man in the crow's nest reported an iceberg ahead, but as the icebergs take on the color of their surroundings, and as the water was very dark at the time, he said that it was not likely that the lookout could have seen the iceberg much more than a quarter of a mile away, and that if the iceberg was a quarter of a mile away when he reported it the steamer would be up with the iceberg in less than two minutes, and going at the speed she was it was impossible to check her headway enough to avoid a collision in so short a time.

This seems a reasonable statement, as many of the passengers have told me that the iceberg struck the steamship up near the bow, but on the side and not full on. Some of the passengers say that the only evidence that they saw of an iceberg anywhere near the ship was several tons of crushed ice on her forward deck, while a very intelligent English woman has told me that she plainly saw the huge iceberg that the steamer struck and that it had two elevations resembling the towers of a cathedral. The case of this woman is a sad one, as she told me that her husband had sold his business in England and that he and she and their eight-year-old daughter were on their way to Payette, Idaho.[9]

HOWARD CHAPIN

While on board the *Carpathia*, Mr Chapin wrote an account of the *Titanic* disaster based upon the interviews he conducted with the survivors:

Account of the disaster told by the quartermaster at the wheel:

At 8 o'clock Sunday evening Second Officer Lightoller went on duty on board steamship *Titanic* and sent word to the lookout in the crow's nest to keep a sharp lookout for icebergs and especially for small ice. Also he ordered the ship's carpenter to look out for the fresh water pipes as the thermometer was 30 degrees and there was danger that the pipes might freeze. The *Titanic* steamed rapidly on through a sea as smooth as glass, which reflected the stars so clearly that the horizon could scarcely be discerned. The air was quite cold but no ice was seen. At 20 minutes of 12 the lookout in the crow's nest on the foremast rang three gongs, which means danger right ahead and five seconds later he telephoned to the officer on the bridge: 'Iceberg dead ahead'.

First officer, Mr. Murdoch, who was then on the bridge, turned to the quartermaster at the helm and ordered 'hard a-starboard'. The quartermaster jammed the wheel over as he repeated, 'Hard to starboard', and the sixth officer, Mr. Moody, who was at the compass to oversee the ship's course, answered, 'Helm hard a-starboard', thus reporting that the order had been carried out.

A light crash followed in two or three seconds, and immediately First Officer Murdoch shouted: 'Hard a-port'. The quartermaster twirled the wheel as he repeated 'hard a-port', and the sixth officer answered 'Helm hard a-port', showing that the order had been carried out. Immediately a terrible crash ensued, and Mr. Murdoch, the first officer, stopped the engines with a signal, rang the warning bell and pulled the lever which instantly closed all the watertight bulkhead doors. Thus he kept the ship from sinking immediately.

At this moment Captain Smith rushed to the bridge and looked at the commutator. It showed a five degree list to starboard, where the ship had been carrying a five degree list to port. This showed that the ship had struck on the starboard bow and was rapidly filling with water. Captain Smith took this in with one glance and said, 'O My God!' He realized exactly the condition of affairs. He instantly sent one quartermaster to the Marconi operator, Mr. Phillips, with orders to signal the ship's name, position and sinking condition, and to continue such signal indefinitely; he ordered the ship's carpenter to sound the forward peak and the other quartermaster to send off distress rockets. Simultaneously he ordered the boats to be lowered and the ladies to be saved. The other officers came running to the bridge, took their orders and manned the lifeboats. The captain then told the men to go to the boats, save the women and children first, and then themselves.

In one hour and three minutes the ship went down bow foremost, with the electric lights shining brightly, the orchestra playing 'Nearer, My God to Thee' and the captain on the bridge.

The *Titanic* was said to be sailing N.N.W. when she struck, and going at a speed of 25 miles per hour. The reason that the iceberg was not seen sooner was because the sea was so calm that no waves broke on the edge of the berg and that the stars reflected in the berg just as they did in the water.

The first officer tried to clear the ship's bow by putting the helm to starboard and then clear her stern by putting the helm to port, but the iceberg extended far out under the water, and there was no chance of not hitting it. The ship struck first lightly on her port bow and crashed heavily with her starboard bow, staving in the forward plates and ripping practically the entire bottom of the boat.

The ship's carpenter went to the hold to measure the leak, but never returned. Many persons scarcely felt the shock, while others near the bow felt it, but hardly realized the great peril. The officers [stood] at the boats with loaded revolvers and kept the men from going until the women had been saved. There was no panic. All were calm, few realizing the danger, and many even after they got into the lifeboats said they would feel safer back on the steamer.

The tales of individual experiences were terrible, and the suffering very great.

Colonel Gracie's Experience:
As soon as he felt the shock he went out on deck. The forward part of the deck was covered with broken chunks of ice, and the big berg loomed high above the ship. The ship was 100 feet high from the water, and the berg was still higher. Col. Gracie went up from deck to deck as the water arose and constantly helped women to their boats. He finally was driven by the water to the bridge, where he stood with the captain until that, too, sunk beneath the waves. Col. Gracie was tossed by the water over to the funnel

and hung for a few seconds to the iron railing of the smokestack. Then he, with the ship, went down under the waves. He swam under water, was pulled downward by the suction but eventually reached the surface and sat for a while on a bit of floating wreckage. Later he, with another man, got on the bottom of an upturned lifeboat and were at last picked up by another lifeboat.

Col. John Jacob Astor accompanied his wife to the lifeboat and put her into it. He asked the officer in charge if he should go also, but the officer said, 'No, only ladies now', so Astor said goodbye to his wife, lit a cigarette and walked away down the deck to his death.

Many of the officers had revolvers, and it is reported that they shot some men who tried to get into the lifeboats before the women.

Many women refused to go without their husbands, and instead stayed with them and were drowned with them.

One girl, 20 years old, stuck to her husband while six lifeboats left the ship, and finally both she and her husband left together in the last lifeboat to leave that deck, all the women having gone.

Lady Duff Gordon's Husband's Story:
Lady Duff Gordon, perhaps better known to American women as 'Lucile' and sister of Eleanor Glynn, of 'Three Weeks' fame, was on the *Titanic* with her husband, Mr. Gordon.

They felt the shock but felt no fear till the officers ordered that 'all ladies put on lifebelts'. Even then they say people seemed to think it a joke and laughed and jested about it. Many men continued to play cards, and one man lost $75 at bridge after the ship struck.

Mr. Gordon and his wife, Lady Duff Gordon, went to their rooms, got some clothes and lifebelts and went up on the upper deck after almost all the lifeboats had gone. They saw a sailor and four stokers in the captain's gig and Mr. Gordon said, 'May we go?' The sailor said, 'Pleased to 'ave you, sir' and helped them in with as much care as if they were landing from a yacht. Then they lowered the gig with great care and another man jumped in lightly. They left the ship, having seen no confusion, and rowed rapidly away. They said they really had no experience.

Mr. Williams' Story:
Mr. Williams, a young man from Philadelphia, had a far different experience. He got into a life raft with a large number of men and women. The raft collapsed and filled with water, so that they all stood up to their waists in ice water. Twice they were tossed out of the raft and had to swim into it. Men and women standing on the raft with him succumbed to the cold and exposure, died and floated away. They lay all night, or rather stood on the craft, for the weight of the people kept the raft below the surface, and were

surrounded by corpses and struggling men. Finally a lifeboat took them in tow and dragged them to the *Carpathia*.

Mr. Andrews, the designer of the *Titanic*, was on board and went down with her.

The electric lights kept burning until the ship sank, and they say it was a beautiful sight to see the ship sink head first, the lights being extinguished as they went under the water.

As the ship sank the crowds on the deck that had been unable to get away ... [several words illegible] ... cries and moans ... [illegible] ... all those struggling in the water were drowned or frozen.

Few of the lifeboats ... [went back to pick up survivors] ... although the officers in charge ordered the men to row back.

Mrs. Walter Clark, who was in one of the boats, wanted to go back, but the other women objected, and it is said they offered their jewels to the sailors if they would not row back, but Mrs. Clark turned to Mrs. Astor and begged her to help, and together they persuaded the men to go back, and so succeeded in saving eight persons.

Mr. Bruce Ismay, the managing director of the White Star Line, was on board and did excellent work in helping the ladies into the boats. He was saved but suffered a severe nervous collapse. He very kindly promised to give all needy *Titanic* passengers clothing and car fare to their homes.

Many men shot themselves rather than be drowned or frozen.

The bandsmen ... [who had been serving on board the] ... *Carpathia*, but went over to England to take the *Titanic*, did nobly to the end. They went beneath the waves playing 'Nearer, My God to Thee'.

Bleriot [Marechal] the aviator was on the *Titanic* but was saved.

Five dogs, mostly Pomeranians, were saved.

One man saw a boat pass his window and threw his dog through the porthole into the lifeboat. He was saved by another lifeboat and so got his dog again on the *Carpathia*.

At about midnight Captain Rostron of the *Carpathia* got a wireless from the *Titanic*; he immediately turned the ship's head northward and ran at full speed till he picked up the green light that one boat carried. At about sunrise he picked up the first lifeboat, and the last survivor was taken on board about noon, although everyone worked hard.

While steaming north the captain had all the lifeboats on the *Carpathia* manned and made ready to launch. The deck was covered with life preservers and breeches buoy and the sides of the steamer were lined with rope ladders.

All the crew stood by to lend a hand. One by one the passengers came on deck and were told the facts. Everything was quiet, orderly, shipshape, and all was done quickly. The captain took the *Carpathia* almost to the spot where the *Titanic* sunk and then, sighting the green light, began to pick up the survivors. Many were dead when picked up, and several more died during the trip to New York.

Everyone on the *Carpathia* was considerate and self-sacrificing, while those rescued were grateful and appreciative.

The stewards and crew of the *Carpathia* are to be especially commended for their fine conduct.

Large quantities of private Marconigrams were sent off, but owing to complaints from passengers the following notice was posted:

Notice to Passengers
I hereby declare no press messages at all have been Marconied from this ship (with the exception of a short one of about 20 words to the Associated Press, sent immediately after the passengers had been picked up) and that passengers' messages have been dispatched with all possible speed.

The reason for this statement is that it has come to my knowledge that several passengers are under the impression that the delay in dispatching private messages is due to the instruments being used for press news.

[Signed] A.H. Rostron, Commander

Later a dispatch was received from Siasconset which read as follows:

Carpathia – Wire news dispatches immediately to Siasconset or any boats. If this is impossible ask captain the reason why no news is allowed to be transmitted.

[Signed] Guglielmo Marconi

April 18th
When the captain reached the place where the *Titanic* sank, there were icebergs in all directions, and on one side there was a field of ice 10 miles long and five miles wide, out of which rose mountains of ice, while lesser bergs floated in all directions.

At noon Monday the *Californian* reached the place (Leyland line), but all had been saved then.

She stayed there the rest of the day.

Later the *Birma* of the Russian-American line came.

Howard M. Chapin[10]

Mr Chapin also wrote a more speculative account in 1913 about the *Titanic* disaster:

Every detail and circumstance of the scene pointed to the tragic consequence, the wrecking of the 'unsinkable' ship. It is interesting, in a kind of melancholy sense, is speculate upon those details.

The tragedy occurred on a calm night. The moon was not shining, though many stars were out. The sea was calm. Everything pointed to a safe and speedy voyage. In fact, undoubtedly the *Titanic*'s officers were out to make a record. They were already making it, although J. Bruce Ismay, head of the White Star Line and one of the survivors, testified that no orders to that effect had been given. Nevertheless, in a practical sense, an attempt at a record was being made. And I believe if a poll of the passengers had been taken, whether Captain Smith would try to make a record, or proceed slower for safety, would have voted for speed.

Now IF the sea had been somewhat rough, the lookout would have seen waves breaking on the iceberg, and would probably have heard them as well. Again, when the sea is rough a certain area, in the lee of a berg is comparatively smooth. Neither of these evidences presented themselves.

Again, IF the night had been foggy, the ship would have been proceeding more slowly, at any rate. Again, IF the moon had been shining, the berg would have been sooner visible to the eye of the lookout in the crow's nest. However, it was a black night, with a black sea, and black ice. Starlight did not reveal the contour of the berg, as the moon would have done.

Still another IF. IF it had been a high iceberg which menaced the *Titanic*, its contour would have blotted out some of the stars from the lookout's gaze. However, it was a low berg, not as high as the lookout's position in the crow's nest, another act that added to the tragic consequences.

Now to reconstruct the scene. The *Titanic* is steaming at nearly 30 miles an hour. That is a mile in two minutes – half a mile in one minute – and a quarter of a mile in half a minute.

Now with the visibility that was present on that night, it is probable that the lookout could not have seen the berg until it was within a quarter of a mile. That would leave only thirty seconds to give warning.

Here is what happened:

The lookout saw the mass of ice – say, a quarter of a mile away; only thirty seconds to act. It takes a second or more for him to realize the danger. He strikes the warning – three bells, meaning 'danger straight ahead'. That takes more seconds. Then he telephones to the bridge, 'Danger, iceberg dead ahead!' At best this dread warning takes a few seconds more.

The officer at the bridge tells the quartermaster at the helm. The helmsman moves the wheel, the mechanical steering device at the stern of the vessel moves the tiller – the tiller moves the rudder. The ship responds.

But all too many seconds have elapsed. Long ere this series of events can take place the thirty seconds have gone. The ship has struck. Remember too, that by far the greater part of the bulk of a mass of ice is below the surface. The bulk of the low-lying berg was spread out far away, like a gigantic knife. It ripped into the vitals of the *Titanic* like a blade, or like an enormous can-opener.

Although the helmsman instantly pulled the lever which closed every water-tight compartment, it was of no use. Those compartments had been sliced open – enough of them ruined to seal the doom of the ship, though some of them kept her afloat for a while.[11]

A year after the disaster, Mr Chapin wrote the following account for his college alumni journal:

We sailed from New York at noon on Thursday, April 11, 1912, on the RMS *Carpathia*, and Sunday evening found us steaming a little north of west in the warm waters of the Gulf Stream. It was warm too! The sun had been shining all day from a clear sky, and we had been forced to lay aside our steamer rugs and heavy coats, and late in the afternoon even to seek the shady parts of the deck in order to be comfortable. We retired at the usual time but, shortly after midnight, I was awakened from a sound sleep by hearing a man kneel down on the deck directly over my head. As I was in the upper berth, I could hear this plainly, being only a few inches beneath the deck. It happened that I had previously noticed that the painter of a life-boat was tied to a cleat just above the deck over my berth, so that when I heard the man stop there and kneel down, I felt sure he was unfastening the life-boat and that something must be wrong.

I immediately jumped from my berth, awakened my wife, put on my overcoat and hurried up on deck to question the sailor whom I had heard. He told me that we had received a wireless message from the *Titanic* saying that she had struck an iceberg and was sinking, and that we were rushing to her assistance. It was pitch dark on deck although the stars were shining overhead. The sea was quite calm with practically no swell. The temperature, however, had fallen rapidly since early evening, and it was now very chilly on deck. I returned to the cabin to get my wife, and we both put on our warmest clothes and came up on deck. It was still colder now. When we first came up, no other passengers were on deck. The deck was covered with lifebelts, breeches buoys and blankets, and the sides of the *Carpathia* were lined with rope ladders. Two lifeboats were made ready for lowering and the crew took their places by the boats. All was dark so far as we could see but the cold kept increasing. We were now sailing a little west of north, for when the *Titanic* struck the berg the *Carpathia* was 58 miles away to the southeastward of her. We were in the warm Gulf Stream when we got the message, but soon passed out of it and entered the Labrador Current in which the *Titanic* sank. Of course we hoped and fully expected to reach the *Titanic* before she sank, which indeed seemed most probable as no one believed that she could sink.

It was after three when we sighted a faint green light off our port bow which we took for the starboard light of the *Titanic*. It seemed a long time before the light became larger, and as we neared it we could see it was too low to be on a big ship. We realized at last that it was a lifeboat. Then just as it seemed we would reach it, we turned aside – a huge blackish mass became visible scarcely a hundred feet away – a cold, towering iceberg.

Circling around this berg, we went close up to the little boat and finally lay to a few hundred feet away from the lifeboat. It took only a few moments for it to reach our side, and as its occupants were rapidly and quietly taken on board, and were handed over to the doctors for examination, we learned the awful fact that the *Titanic* had gone down over an hour before. Another lifeboat reached us before the first one had been unloaded, and still another before the day dawned.

Then as the darkness became twilight, we could see all about us the dark masses of huge icebergs, which became lighter and lighter as the day increased, until finally when the sun's rays struck them, they became pure white and glittered like crystal. From fifteen to twenty icebergs were within our sight all the morning, the nearest being about five hundred feet away. This berg was long, low and flat, and according to the description given by the *Titanic*'s surviving officers was without doubt the berg on which the ship struck. Here and there among the bergs we could make out the little lifeboats as they came slowly towards us. One or two had sails but most of them used simply oars. Before one of them could be entirely unloaded, another would reach our side, so that we lay still for seven or eight hours while this mournful and bedraggled procession came over our side. Some of the survivors climbed easily up the rope ladders, while others seated on sailors' chairs climbed partly and were partly hoisted on board. Still others had to have ropes tied to them so that they could be hoisted up like bales of cotton.

Nearly all had on heavy outer garments, although very few were entirely dressed. Many men had on evening clothes, as the accident occurred before they had started to retire. Practically everyone was quiet and subdued, apparently stunned by the shock and the cold. In fact, the actual enormity of the catastrophe was apparently not fully realized by any of the *Titanic* survivors or *Carpathia* passengers until we reached New York. Only four bodies were found in the boats, and these were taken on board, our flags then being lowered to half-mast – a very sorrowful sight away out there. There were no bodies floating, although we saw a steamer chair, a few pieces of wood, some miscellaneous wreckage and a mass of reddish scum which looked like a mixture of iron rust and oil, and which spread over the surface of the water for approximately a couple of hundred square feet.

About half-past eleven in the morning, the *Californian* came alongside and signaled us. As we had picked up all the lifeboats and taken on board all the survivors and whatever lifeboats were in good condition, we got under way and steamed southward, leaving the *Californian* to cruise about the spot the rest of the day in the hope of finding other boats.

Before we got under way a funeral service was held by the Rev. Father Anderson (a brother of the Order of the Holy Cross in communion with the Episcopal Church of America). As we were over the spot where the *Titanic* lay, the service was for all those who were lost in the wreck. It also embraced a Thanksgiving service for the survivors.

As we steamed away we passed within a few hundred yards of an immense ice field, which was said to be 25 miles in width and over 60 miles in length. It was a beautiful sight, a smooth sheet of snowy whiteness, from whose midst here and there rose lofty cones of ice, whose clear-cut outlines showed up against a cold, blue sky. In front the deeper blue of the water contrasted even more strongly with the pure white of the ice. Truly it was a beautiful sight or would have been under other circumstances. Few gave even passing heed to it, for our minds were full of sadness at the terrible disaster which had occurred, and we were all anxious to do what we could to alleviate the sufferings of those whom we saved.[12]

STANTON COIT

Before he re-sailed for Europe on the *Carpathia*, Dr Coit wrote the following statement describing his vessel's rescue of the *Titanic*'s survivors:

At 5:30 Monday morning last our bedroom steward reported that the ship had stopped to rescue the passengers from the *Titanic*, which had sunk the night before. I hurried on deck, saw great icebergs about, and looking over the railing, saw some fifteen rowboats approaching us, full chiefly of women. These were drawn up on board and passed us by, most of them so stiff with cold and wet that they could not walk without being supported. Soon the tragic news spread among us that some fifteen hundred people had been drowned, and for the most part only women had been saved. My first and lasting impression was the inward calm and self poise – not self-control, for there was no effort or self-consciousness – on the part of those who had been saved. I said to one woman, whose dress, but not her face, betrayed that she was one of those who had undergone tragic experiences, 'You were on the *Titanic*?'

She answered, 'Yes, and I saw my husband go down.'

The only hysteria displayed was after the physicians had administered brandy to the half-frozen sufferers. The people struck me not as being stunned and crushed, but as lifted into an atmosphere of vision where self-centered suffering merges into some mystic meaning. Everyone reported a magnificent self-possession of the husbands when parted from their wives. Many related the cases of women who had to be forced from their husbands. Touching beyond words was the gratitude toward those of us who gave clothes and our staterooms.

More magnificent than the calm of the clear dawn was the unconsciousness of any personal horror, or need to pity, on the part of those who related how they had met their fate. One youth of seventeen told, as if it had been an incident of every-day life, that he was hurled from the deck and that as he found himself sinking he took a deep breath. When he came up and found that he was again to be drawn under, he thought it would be well again to breathe deep. Upon rising the second time, he said, he saw the upturned bottom of a canvas boat. To this he clung until he was rescued.

One woman in one boat insisted that they should row back and rescue eight men clinging to wreckage, although the oarsmen feared the suction of the great steamer might endanger their lives, and the eight were thus rescued. My feeling is that in the midst of all this horror human nature never manifested itself as greater or tenderer. We were all one, not only with one another, but with the cosmic being that for all time had seemed so cruel.

On board the *Carpathia* there was much discussion as to the possible culpability of the captain of the *Titanic*, but there was no judgment offered, and the feeling, I believe, grew upon us that only wrongs were the insufficient number of lifeboats and the full speed of the *Titanic*, and that even this great sacrifice of innocent life and happiness would have been counted by each sufferer worth making if it would help to put an end in the future to the sacrifice to commercial interests of the infinitely precious life of those we love.

But I return again to what I say was my first and abiding impression – the self-poise that is so because the human soul is not self-centered.

One young woman with whom I talked was so calm and full of stories of the heroism and the suffering of others that I said, 'How fortunate that you lost no friend!'

Then for the first time her face change, and, with tears streaming down her cheeks, she said, 'My brother, who was my only living relative, went down before my eyes. He scorned to disobey the discipline, so now I am alone.'

My faith in the deeper meaning of things has been greatly strengthened by this wonderful experience.[13]

WILLIAM COLLOPY

In later years crewman Collopy wrote the following description of his experiences on the *Carpathia*:

I was a member of the crew of the *Carpathia*, bound from Liverpool to New York and then sailing to Trieste, Fiume, calling at Naples. We were a few days out of New York when we heard of the sinking of the *Titanic*. It was springtime and the weather was then very calm.

At midnight, April 12th [14th], to my great surprise the emergency bell rang and all hands were roused to report for duty immediately. We were informed that the SS *Titanic* was sinking and needed help, but not one of us believed it was possible.

Every preparation was nevertheless made to receive passengers. Cases of brandy from storerooms, hot foods made ready, and plenty of strong coffee to serve quickly. We were all at the 'alert'. The engine room staff had on an extra watch to get the maximum speed out of the ship, which made her shake, as she was only a 14–15 knot ship now doing 17–18 knots! Every lifeboat was swung out, ready for lowering.

As we came nearer to the area given by Marconi wireless, every door in the ship's side was opened, and Jacob's ladders of rope and wooden slats were put over the side in readiness. An anxious time was spent by the captain and the crew waiting for the *Titanic*'s lifeboats to be sighted and brought alongside.

The survivors were carried or assisted into the saloon, given hot drinks, mainly coffee laced with brandy, and food. Then about four hundred people were accommodated as best as possible, some put to bed and given immediate medical attention.

As soon as all immediate help was given, the *Titanic*'s lifeboats were hoisted on deck and we made for New York with all speed.

On arrival the piers were crowded with people seeking relatives, and there were many pathetic scenes and reuniting. We were greatly affected by the sadness of it all. The American public showed great gratitude to the captain and crew of our ship, and we were literally given the freedom of New York.

Once all was cleared and details of every rescued person given, we proceeded on our voyage. We were presented with a medal from the people of the USA, and I think everyone had an extra month's pay from the White Star Line. This disaster was accounted to be one of the worst in the merchant service annals.[14]

MRS COLIN CAMPBELL COOPER

After the disaster (possibly on 18 April) Mrs Cooper wrote a letter to her sister, Mrs William Carson. The letter started out by saying that the first news of the *Titanic*'s plight was received about 12 o'clock and that at about 4 o'clock two boatloads of survivors were picked up. Later there were sixteen in all:

> I think more than half were filled with steerage passengers, and nearly all were filled with women and children. The first boats to leave the *Titanic* carried husbands with wives, but later no men were allowed to enter the boats and numbers of wives stayed with their husbands until the last boat and were urged to get in by their husbands, all of whom were calm and brave to the last. The last boat had gotten but a short distance away when the great steamer plunged her bow into the water, heaved, twisted and sank down into the depths without any of the suction that they feared would draw the small boats in the vicinity down with her.
>
> The heroism of the splendid men who remained on the *Titanic* is the talk of all on board and passengers feel that instead of filling the lifeboats with all women, the husbands should have been sent with the wives when boats were not filled, so that they might have taken the oars. In most cases there were but two or three sailors in a boat, and the women helped at the oars as they could.
>
> I have heard of one man, a sailor, who was at the helm of a lifeboat and behaved like a brute. He refused to leave the helm to a man with one arm broken, who could have helped row toward our steamer, and so been of assistance. His remarks, his conduct were simply brutal. All the others were brave and splendid through it all.
>
> But it seems wrong to have saved so many widows who are to reach New York without a cent or the addresses of relatives in some cases, while so many strong men went down to the strains of the orchestra. The music was heard until the last.

Mrs Cooper said that lack of caution was thought to be the cause of the disaster. She said that there was a great field of ice all around the ship. The view at sunrise when the ice became visible in all its colours was of much beauty and weirdness.

There are many stories of the splendid heroism of men and women and of the calmness and dignity of the entire proceeding. With very few exceptions the behaviour of all was fine. They tell of a baron who got into a boat in spite of threats and said he would kill anyone who stopped him, and refused to row, of his making himself a thick bed of blankets and that he had several jerked from under him by a furious woman.[15]

After the *Carpathia* reached New York, Marconi Operator Cottam dictated the following account of his experiences during the *Titanic* rescue:

I got the *Titanic*'s 'CQD' call at 11:20 o'clock, New York time, on last Sunday night. It was this: 'Come at once. We've struck a berg. It's a CQD call, old man.'

Then the *Titanic*'s operator followed with his position, which was latitude 41.46 north and longitude 50.14 west.

'Shall I go to the Captain and tell him to turn back at once?' I asked.

'Yes. Yes' came the instant reply.

I went to the bridge and notified First Officer Dean of the call for help. He roused Capt. Rostron, who was taking his turn below, and he issued orders to turn the ship about immediately.

I hurried back to my cabin, and just as I got there I heard the *Titanic* working the *Frankfurt*. The *Titanic* was having trouble in getting the *Frankfurt*'s signals because escaping steam and air from the expansion joint were making the signals almost indistinguishable.

I tried to get the *Frankfurt*, for he apparently only got the *Titanic*'s position, but I couldn't raise him.

I think I received the CQD seven to ten minutes after the *Titanic* struck.

It was only a streak of luck that I got the message at all, for on the previous night I had been up until 2:30 o'clock in the morning, and the night before that until 3 o'clock, and I had planned to get to bed early that night.

I thought I'd take some general news, as I didn't know how the coal strike in England was going, and I was interested in it. When I had been taking this some time there was a batch of messages coming through for the *Titanic* from the long-distance Marconi wireless station at Cape Cod, which transmits the day's news at 10:30 New York time every evening.

When Cape Cod had been going some time he started sending a batch of messages for the *Titanic*, and, having heard the *Titanic* man being pushed with work during the afternoon, I thought I'd give him a hand by taking them and retransmitting them the following morning, as I had nothing much to work on.

As I was the nearest station to the *Titanic*, it was more or less my duty to retransmit them to him. When Cape Cod finished I made up my daily list of communications and reported them to the officer on watch. On returning to the cabin I put telephones on to verify a time rush which I had exchanged with the *Parisian* early that afternoon. A 'time rush' is the slang wireless word for the exchange of ship's time, which is always made when you encounter another ship to see if your clocks agree.

I put the telephones on and called the *Titanic* and asked if he was aware that a batch of messages were being transmitted for him via Cape Cod. And his answer was: 'Come at once. We have struck a berg'.

Previous to reporting the communication to the bridge I had been in constant watch, so that I was certain that she must have struck while I was on the bridge, and that was seven to ten minutes before.

After hearing the *Frankfurt* then, I heard the *Olympic* calling the *Titanic* with a service message, and as the *Titanic* didn't reply, apparently he couldn't hear the *Olympic*. I said to the *Titanic*: 'Don't you hear the *Olympic* calling you? Go ahead and call.'

My wireless wasn't of as late type as that aboard the *Titanic*, so that my calls would have had no effect.

The only other ship I heard at this time was the *Baltic*. She was calling Cape Race. The *Titanic* exchanged sundry signals with the *Carpathia*, but apparently the *Olympic* and the *Carpathia* were the only ships that heard them.

We steamed with every ounce of steam in us in the direction given by the *Titanic*, and we reached the spot just before dawn. One of the engineers told me that the *Carpathia* had been making between 17 and 18 knots. Her usual speed is about 13 to 14 knots.

There was a double watch of men in the engine department, and everything that could be done to hasten our arrival at the location of the *Titanic* was being done.

All this time we were hearing the *Titanic*, sending her wireless out over the sea in a last call for help. 'We are sinking fast' was one which I picked up being sent to the *Olympic*.

The *Frankfurt* kept calling and asking us what was the matter, but though she must have been nearer to the *Titanic* than we were, she never arrived there until after we had picked up the survivors and left for New York.

Just before we reached the *Titanic* I got this message, and it was the last one I received: 'Come quick. Our engine room is flooded up to the boilers.'

I answered them that our boats were ready, and for them to get theirs ready also, and that we were doing our utmost to get there in time. There was no reply. It was 11:55 New York time, when I got this last signal from the *Titanic*.

I kept calling to warn them to look out for our rockets, which were being constantly sent up, but I shall never know whether he heard me or not.

From 11:55 until we reached the spot where the *Titanic* foundered I was listening for a spark from his emergency set, and when I didn't hear it I was sure that he had gone down.

The first sign we got, shortly before dawn, was a green light off the port bow of the *Carpathia*. It was a beacon on one of the small boats, and we knew then that the *Titanic* had gone, but that there were survivors for us to pick up.

I was kept busy in the wireless room for the next few minutes, and the first of the rescue that I saw was a boat alongside and the passengers being hauled aboard.

Most of them were women and children. Some were crying, and they seemed overcome by the calamity. As they were raised to the deck several of them collapsed.

I saw wood and debris from the sunken *Titanic* when dawn came, but I did not see a body in the water.

Daylight showed that we were right on the scene of the disaster, for there were ten or a dozen boats around us when it became light enough to see, and as rapidly as possible their occupants were taken aboard.

We remained near the spot, looking for additional survivors, for about three hours, and then, convinced that there was no human being alive in the sea of ice in which we floated, we started for New York.[16]

In 1914 Mr Cottam wrote the following letter in reply to a May 1912 letter from an admirer:

Kushima Maru
So. Pacific
Xmas Day 14

Dr Miss J.B. Scherer,

You will, I have no doubt, be very surprised to hear from me.

I consider it high time I wrote you a short epistle acknowledging your existence out of merest decency. A thousand profuse apologies dear young lady for not recognizing receipt of yours of May 2nd 1912, but at the time of the disaster I barely glanced at the sundry letters & cards from well-wishers in various parts of the world & only the other day while looking my bachelor junk over did I drop across your request.

If you have not been able to raise my face from a newspaper relative to the *Titanic* affair I will send you a picture on my return to London.

Hoping this finds you at 4332 Michigan Ave.

Yours Sincerely,
Harold Thos. Cottam
Ex S/S *Carpathia*
Posted Tokyo, Japan[17]

MRS CHARLES F. CRAIN

After the disaster Anna Crain wrote the following letter to a friend in Chicago:

I was the only passenger on the *Carpathia* to know about the accident until the first small boat arrived alongside. About 1:30 o'clock in the morning the ship surgeon, Dr. McGhee, came in to see my husband who was ill. He told me of the message announcing that the *Titanic* was sinking, which had just been received by wireless.

The lifeboats were made ready to lower, the rope gangways slung over the side and the baskets put in shape to haul up the children. On all sides of our ship were icebergs. The captain said we picked our way through like a snake.

Rockets were sent up, and on such a beautiful starlit night and with the sea like oil, it seemed as if we must see and be seen for miles. Finally we saw a blue light, which seemed to flicker and go out. A voice cried, 'Shut off your engines'. Then a boat came alongside. Many of the women were in evening dress.

After an hour or so we had all the survivors on board – a pitiful 700. We could hear the agonized cries for help as the stern rose high in the air and then crashed down with the waves.[18]

Mrs Crain also wrote the following story for a New York newspaper:

About half-past one o'clock Monday morning the ship's surgeon, Dr. McGhee, came in to see my husband, who was ill. As he left he said a message had been received from the *Titanic* and that the ship had turned back and was making toward her with all possible speed. The report was that her engine room was full and she was sinking fast.

I dressed and went out upon the deck. This must have been a little before two o'clock. I was greatly impressed by the work of the ship's crew, officers and men and the little group of stewardesses. Preparations for the rescue were pushed rapidly forward. One would have thought it merely an ordinary drill. The baskets were slung alongside to be used in bringing up the children, the boats were made ready to lower and the pleasant smell of coffee and piling up of soft masses of blankets told how much the comfort of the rescued was in the minds of all.

Suddenly a ghostly shape appeared off the port bow. It was an iceberg. Another and another appeared; high above the water they towered, while later on lower ones were to be seen dotting the waters like groups of tiny islands. The preparations were completed, the gangways of rope were fastened to the side and all eyes were strained to watch with fascinated gaze the nearing icebergs as we wound our way in and out among them seeking some sign of light or life from the missing ship.

Slowly the dawn crept up, a gray light spread over the sea, and showed us the huge monsters of ice that were surrounding us. Suddenly out of the darkness was seen a flickering light. It came nearer, and soon the outlines of a small boat were visible.

A voice called 'Stop your engines', and in the still waters the little craft drew alongside the swinging gangway. Who that saw it can ever forget that pitiful scene! The little handful waiting below, packed closely, each wearing a lifebelt, their strained, white faces uplifted to the decks!

A sort of rope harness was slipped over each in turn to keep them from falling should they slip, and so, quietly – and dazed with the cold and horror of the night – they were drawn on board and received by the sympathetic band of stewards and stewardesses. Occasionally the silence was broken by a wailing baby, unused to the bag which was bringing it to warmth and safety.

All were taken immediately to the dining saloon, and later the greatly afflicted were carried to the library, while the reunited ones found a place on deck and joined the watch for the missing boats.

The day soon broke, and over the water in all directions small white boats, scarcely distinguishable from the smaller icebergs, could be seen, in many cases rowed by the women, who had kept to their task all night.

Some of the boats were well filled, but in others were a mere handful, eloquent evidence of the condition that existed on the sinking vessel, where apparently no well directed efforts were made to save even those who might have found a place in the lifeboats had they been warned or called from their rooms in time.

One boat came alongside and a man was seen to shake the women seated near him gently by the shoulders and rouse them from their stupor of grief. I cannot describe the scene as boat after boat was unloaded and the agonized search began for the missing ones.

The Carpathia's passengers went among the stricken ones assisting them to places where they could see the occupants of the ever arriving boats, until the eighteen had been accounted for, and their grief and despair knew no bounds. Sounds of weeping and sobbing filled the ship and several poor souls became delirious in their grief. Some faint hope was offered, that perhaps other ships had picked up a boat, but few found comfort in what they could only believe was held out to them to temper the first anguish of their loss.

The capacity of the Carpathia was strained to the utmost. Many of her passengers gave up their rooms and generously donated clothing to the needy. Clothing was cut from the steamer rugs and made a warm covering for the shivering little ones, snatched from their beds in the night and rolled in blankets.

Many of the grief stricken ones roused themselves to help in the work, and what the doctor's soothing drugs had accomplished in the first day or two merciful labor did in the third and fourth.[19]

'EMPSIE'

After the *Carpathia* returned to New York on 18 April, Empsie wrote a letter to Mabel Dalby describing her honeymoon trip on that vessel. The letter thanked 'Mab' for writing a letter and postcard to her and 'Hutch', and for including the parting gift of a handkerchief. She mentioned that she had had to minimise the amount of luggage she took with her so that it would all fit into their state-room, and she left her pendant and engagement ring in Hutch's safe deposit box because she was afraid they might come to harm if she took them with her. She gave a list of wedding presents they had received and described how they dined at the Waldorf Astoria before the *Carpathia* sailed on 11 April.

She then told of the 'horror' of the *Carpathia*'s rescue of the *Titanic*'s survivors and mentioned the suffering and grief she witnessed. Empsie said that some of her travel plans had to be changed because of the *Carpathia*'s return to New York, but that they were nevertheless glad to have been able to help the survivors. She jokingly complained that her honeymoon trip didn't involve any 'spooning' and that she saw very little of her husband during the return voyage due to the fact that they gave up their four-berth stateroom so that four survivors could make use of the cabin.

She described how she and her husband moved into the cabin of their table companions, a married couple from St Louis, and said that it seemed very odd to sleep in a tiny cabin with strangers. She wrote that the women turned in first and slept in the lower berths, while the men came in and retired after the ladies drew their curtains. The men arose and dressed first in the morning and then left the cabin so that the ladies could dress, and there was a great deal of joking about these arrangements.

Empsie and her husband hid the fact that they were newlyweds and claimed that they had been married for two years, and Empsie wrote that their long courtship had caused the usual 'froth and goo-goo' of newly-married couples to be absent, which assisted them in carrying out their bluff. She mentioned that the ruse was so successful that a judge from Adams, Massachusetts had spoken about his own 7-year-old son and then asked them if they had any children. Empsie replied with a 'weak' no and knocked on wood, and she concluded her letter by saying that the *Titanic* disaster had ruined her good spirits and taken all the beauty out of the sea for her.[20]

MARY FABIAN

On 17 April, while the *Carpathia* was still at sea, Miss Fabian wrote the following letter to her family:

Steamship *Carpathia*
April 17th

Of course, by now, you must have heard about the terrible disaster of the *Titanic*, and our newspapers are so remarkable that you may know more about it than we do. It certainly has been a thrilling experience even for us, and at times seems like a kind of nightmare.

Our Marconi man was just going to bed on Sunday night, when he thought he might as well pick up the instrument, and see if there was any message, and got a call for help from the *Titanic*, almost 100 miles away. The boat was immediately stopped and turned right around, or rather northwest, and they say it never went so fast before, 18 knots. The *Titanic* struck the iceberg at 11:45 p.m., and sank two hours later.

The people were told at first that there was no danger, and some even went back to bed. Even the officers say that they did not think the boat was really going down, until just at the last. The first two life boats that were put off, were only about a third full, because people really refused to get into them thinking they were safer on the big boat. Then, at the last, they just crowded women and children into the boats, making the men stand back and in two of the boats, the women had to do most of the rowing.

The ship went down so suddenly that they did not have time to get off all the lifeboats. They say all the people could have been saved, if they had only realized the danger, but so far as we know only twenty boats got off.

The *Titanic*'s fifth officer says he firmly believes that no one else was saved, except those picked up by the *Carpathia*, because after the *Titanic* went down he went back with a row boat and six men, among the wreckage, and rescued four men, but that everyone else was beyond rescue. His description of it is too horrible to repeat.

Of course, all the people on board, especially those who have lost husbands, or other members of their families, are hoping that others have been saved, but it is only a hope.

I woke up some time in the middle of the night, feeling that the boat had stopped, but then heard the engines going again at full speed, so went to sleep. About five o'clock I woke again, and heard a great commotion, people running about and moaning, dishes rattling, etc., and I heard a steward say, just outside my door, 'Look, there come five more boats'. I immediately got up, inquired what was the matter, and hurriedly dressed and went on deck.

It was a wonderful and terrible sight, too. We were surrounded by icebergs, and the *Titanic* lifeboats were coming in various directions. They had all been rowing most of the night and the last ones did not reach us until about half past eight. A great many of the people were completely exhausted and hysterical, and had to be carried in.

Everything on this boat was wonderfully organized. Our steward told me they had orders to take on 2,000 passengers and in an hour and a half they were ready for them. Several hundred came on board (no one seems to know exactly how many) and were given brandy and coffee and crackers, and as quickly as possible places were found for them to lie down.

Most of the people, however, were too excited to rest until much later. When all the lifeboats in sight had been taken on, we cruised around for some time, going much nearer the icebergs, to see if there were more boats. I have been told that we went by the exact place where the *Titanic* sank, but was not on deck at the time. We saw some of the wreckage. While we were cruising around, the *Californian*, Atlantic Transport came up and she went in the other direction, and was to stay around for a few hours, and people think she may have picked up more of the *Titanic* people.

They say the berg the *Titanic* struck was about sixty feet high. The night was bright and perfectly still. The sailors on the *Carpathia* say they could see the icebergs, ten miles away. If it had been one lone iceberg, it would not have seemed so strange, but as we went nearer, (we must have gone within a couple of miles of the ice or nearer – in fact the water where we were was full of ice) we could see an immense field of ice, standing as far as one could see, with numberless separate icebergs besides. They say the *Titanic* was way north of its course.

Well, we shall be back in New York tomorrow! The captain thought at first of putting in to Halifax, but decided New York was safer, on account of the ice, and of course it would have been worse to take those people to Gibraltar; that would have taken a week, and everyone is glad that this excitement is going to last only one day more.

Most of the *Carpathia* passengers spent the whole day Monday trying to look after our 'guests'.

My room was full all day of people who wanted to dress or lie down, or arrange their hair. Many of the people had come off with only their night gowns, and perhaps a skirt or coat, so that we had to try to get clothes for them to wear. The *Carpathia*'s passengers were very generous. One girl even gave away her one suit and a steamer coat, thinking she would have a chance to get others in New York.

The boat is terribly crowded. The first night, I gave up my room to three exhausted ladies, and managed to get an upper berth in a room for four, though I had expected to sleep on deck. The dining room, library and smoking rooms are full of people each night, sleeping on mattresses on the floors and tables. The meals have been more or less confused until today, but even this morning, I saw two or three people having breakfast, standing up in the hall.

We are wondering what is to become of us, but probably shall not know until we reach New York. Some think we shall be in New York only a few hours, and some say a day. Some people are talking of giving up the trip entirely, but most are going on again.[21]

On 19 April Miss Fabian wrote the following letter to her family in Illinois:

The landing of the *Carpathia* last night was the most thrilling thing you can imagine. Newspaper boats met us away out at the *Ambrose Channel* Lightship, and one reporter even tried to get on the *Carpathia* from the pilot's row boat, but none were allowed on board until just before we reached the dock.

They say there has not been such excitement in New York for years, and it is estimated that there were 30,000 people on, or as near the dock, as they could get. Fourteenth Street was so full of people that the cars could hardly pass. Everyone was very quiet, though, and there was no disturbance.

A reporter from the *New York World* was among those rescued from the *Titanic*, and he certainly had a scoop. He did not have a chance to get his reports in, though, until about an hour before the boat docked. Then the *World* boat managed to come right alongside, and he threw his papers on board. He had two large packages tied together with a long strap, and they caught on the rope of one of the *Titanic* lifeboats, which was being lowered in order to get them out of the way. The reporter was almost frantic, but a sailor finally fished the papers off, and the *World* boat steamed away in great triumph.

The *Titanic* people were, of course, landed first, and the rest of us did not know what was going to become of us, until a few minutes after we reached the dock. Then a notice was posted that the *Carpathia* would sail at four Friday afternoon.

We were so wrought up all the time that we hardly had time to think, and the landing in New York seemed almost as bad as the actual rescue.[22]

CECIL R. FRANCIS

After the *Carpathia* arrived in New York, Mr Francis wrote the following letter to his hometown newspaper:

Dr. Blackmarr and I were the first passengers on the *Carpathia* who knew the *Titanic* was in trouble. Operator Cottam came to our cabin and told us immediately after he notified the captain. We dressed and kept a lookout until dawn, when we sighted some of the lifeboats, which looked like specks in the distance.

When the survivors were brought aboard the majority of the passengers on the *Carpathia* relinquished their staterooms and provided the unfortunates with clothing. Among the rescued were three motherless babies and a number of small children. One little fellow, a son of Dr. Washington Dodge of San Francisco, was fitted out with a pair of knickerbockers which the women made out of a steamer rug.

The sea in the vicinity of the wreck was covered with debris and floating ice. There was an icefield apparently twenty-five or thirty miles long, with a number of large bergs visible. The temperature was low and my heaviest clothing with a sweater and a big ulster was none too comfortable.

During the trip back to New York everybody, including crew and passengers, seemed to forget themselves in devoting their time and attention to trying to make the survivors of the wreck as comfortable as possible. We slept anywhere we could, a part of the time on mattresses in the cabin, and some of us slept in the dining saloon on the tables.[23]

❖ ❖ ❖

TIM H. HARDGROVE

After the rescue, Dr Hardgrove sent the following Marconigram to George Hardgrove of Fond du Lac, Wisconsin:

Our ship picked up surviving passengers of *Titanic* and we are now returning to New York. Will start again at 4 o'clock.
Dr. T.A. Hardgrove[24]

❖ ❖ ❖

On 20 April, after the *Carpathia* arrived in New York, Dr Hardgrove sent the following telegram to his hometown newspaper:

New York
April 20

The *Titanic* sent a wireless at 12:05 midnight that she was on an iceberg. A few minutes afterward we got the 'CQD' call, meaning 'Come at once'.
  'Goodbye. Our boilers are flooded.' This was the message we received at 2 a.m.

Our ship steamed straight for the icefield at 17 knots an hour. We reached the spot at 5 a.m. and began taking survivors on board at 7:56.

The *Titanic* was broken about the center and when the water rushed in, the boat went down with hundreds of souls aboard. A most awful sight to behold and to listen to the hissing sound of the dying demon and the screams of the heroes.

Fond du Lac suffers the loss of Dr. W.E. Minahan, whose wife and sister were among those taken aboard the *Carpathia* clad in nothing but a few garments. All the survivors were in about the same condition.

Almost every man on board the *Titanic* was a hero, standing back to allow women and children to go first. About 300 widows and many children, whose parents had perished, were taken aboard the *Carpathia*.

The *Titanic* was going too fast. It was too large and there were not enough life boats. Carelessness is the cause of the disaster.[25]

❖   ❖   ❖

MRS TIM H. HARDGROVE

On 17 April Mrs Hardgrove wrote the following letter to her daughter, Miss Mamie Hardgrove:

April 17, 1912

Dear Mamie, Aunt Mary and All,

Well, instead of going on our journey now, we are bound for New York again with about 875 passengers, most of them heartbroken with the loss of some loved one or ones from the *Titanic*, which lost about 1,500 people Sunday evening. We knew nothing about it until Monday morning when we woke up and heard all the excitement.

It was a terrible, terrible sight, all the people, most of them clad in scant clothing, and in such terrible misery about their lost ones.

Our boat was informed of the danger by the Marconi message between 12 and 1 o'clock. We were 60 miles away and our boat went to them, endangering ourselves with the icebergs, and putting on extra speed, but we did not know the danger surrounding us. The poor people were let out on life boats, about thirty for that whole boat full of people. Some of the women and children were thrown into the boats. They drifted (or were rowed around) until dawn. I cannot tell you all of the awful experiences they told about. There are 200 widows on this boat now. Of one family of eleven the mother and one child only are left.

Yesterday we found Mrs. Minahan on board and the doctor is missing. Of course some of the lost may be found. Some floated around all night on rafts and wreckage. There are several sick now and no wonder from the awful exposure.

We took one little English woman with two little girls into our room. One of her children is a baby, and her husband is among the missing. They are not even comfortable with clothes. We did what we could. One little girl has Maurice's blouse on for a dress, one lady my shoes, etc., but it is heart breaking to think what they will find at New York, no news of the lost. So many of them had all of their belongings with them, and all are gone. I never in my life passed through anything like it.

One little baby is saved with the nurse, the rest of the family gone. It must have been from a wealthy family. Two sweet little boys with curly hair were left alone. They were sick last night with a high fever. One lady with a seven weeks old baby and little girl is among the saved. They put the child on the steam pipes in the kitchen to bring it to life. And the lady didn't eat anything from yesterday morning until this noon. Couldn't eat in the steerage, and wasn't allowed to stay up. These are only a few incidences. It is just heart breaking.

The *Titanic* was like a palace and sank in one and a half hours. The saved watched it sink and did not know people were in it until the terrible cries were heard.

It is a lucky thing that our boat was so near or all of those people might have perished. There is not much difference in station now. They are all putting up with great inconvenience and I believe many are suffering with the cold. In the *Titanic*, the musicians played within ten minutes before the boat sank, and then were all lost. As the boat went down the people sang, 'Nearer My God to Thee'.

We have all been frightened since. Had a storm last night. I don't know what we'll do when we reach New York. We have all lost courage just now. I believe we may not start again on the voyage, but will write. This letter is not written well, but it is raining, and I am writing it out on deck.

With love,
Minnie[26]

Mrs Hardgrove wrote another letter which included the following statements:

We were 60 miles away and our boat went to them endangering ourselves with the icebergs and putting on extra speed. But we did not know the danger surrounding us. The poor people were let out on lifeboats, about 30 for that boat-full of people ... I cannot tell you the awful experiences they told about.[27]

On 24 April, after the *Carpathia* resumed her interrupted voyage to Europe, Mr Hoyt wrote the following letter:

Royal Mail Steamship *Carpathia*
Mid Ocean
April 24, 1912

Dear Bird,

In the Providence of God it has come to Emma and myself to be of assistance to our fellow men and women in the greatest 'Tragedy of the Seas' and Bird it was a tragedy. The horror of it all was appalling. Monday morning April 15 about four o'clock Emma woke me and said the boat had stopped and that there was considerable moving about. I put my head out the cabin door and was told by a steward that 'the White Star Steamer *Titanic* is in distress'. Dressing and going down on deck we learned that, about midnight our ship received a wireless and immediately changed her course, steaming 58 miles to the position of the *Titanic* arriving about four o'clock, and it was the stopping of the ship that awoke Emma. Nothing was to be seen however, and it was supposed the *Titanic* had gone down with all on board, but soon appeared out of the 'Dark of the Dawn' first one boat and the other, 18 in all, loaded with men, women & children & babies, most of them scantily clothed, some of the ladies in evening dress, and the night bitterly cold, the boats were attracted by the rockets we were sending up, and were received without any 'fuss or frather' or confusion, owing to the marvelous discipline always prevailing on a Cunarder, in fact there was so little noise that I had to awaken Mr. Weidman and his cabin mate and their room was not fifteen feet from where the rescued were coming aboard. Upon arrival of seventh or eighth boat I surrendered our cabin and we bunked with Mr. and Mrs. Reynolds during the voyage to New York, and it was soon filled with four men who were in very bad shape. By about nine o'clock all boats in sight having been cared for, and, the Leyland Liner *Californian* steaming up, we left her cruising in the vicinity and started for New York with our load of sorrow and woe and misery. We were over 1100 miles out and they were long, long days, we passed our time being mostly occupied with the poor unfortunates. There is an incident of what we were up against. I remarked to Mr. Weidman, 'that Englishman in my room is in bad shape. I'm going to get a doctor for him'; immediately a young woman lying on a lounge raised her head and said, 'I wonder if it is my husband', 'no madam he is a single man' was my reply. Just think, Bird, of the hope and despair of that one moment, and there were about 150 made widows on board and the fatherless & motherless and mothers without sons to the end of the chapter. All talk about the shrieks of women ringing through our ship which you have probably read in the papers is the worst rot, if you had seen the fortitude with which they bore their sufferings and woe you would be prouder than ever of your sex. Most of the statements in the New York papers are of like untruth, caused by our captain refusing to let the reporters aboard at the lightship. In [the] fifth boat was a sailor from the *Titanic*, who I saw shake hands with one of our sailors and pointing to an iceberg said 'that is the one that did it'. It was immense, estimated by a Civil Engineer as 180ft in height. You have no doubt seen pictures in the magazines of rescue parties in the polar seas. Well, that is the best description of the scene I can give you. In the background was an immense ice floe with berg after berg which had not broken loose, and other bergs floating around, our ship standing off the floe and the boats approaching from the direction of the floe. I think this a perfect picture of the scene. The ice floe was immense. We steamed 52 miles to get away and around it, and it extended in the other direction beyond the horizon, in fact in the New York papers some Captain reported it as 100 miles in length. We gave away many things until I was down to the underclothing I have on. The sea was calm all the way to New York. All that died of the rescued were buried at sea, four in number. As you know from the papers, we left New York again April 19th and thus far have had clear weather. We should be at Gibraltar April 29. We have no definite plans beyond that, as we have not decided how long we will remain in Spain. Emma has been remarkably well except the effect of the strain we have been under. It took almost everyone two or three days to get over that. The crew was called together Monday and thanked by the Captain for their good work. They certainly were entitled to it and appreciated his thanks as one of them said to me afterward 'he is proud of us ain't he'. He surely had reason to be. Later a picture of the officers was taken on the forward deck. We have music by the orchestra every evening at nine and at dinner and lunch. One night instead of music, Señor Jose Mardones, First Baritone Boston Opera Co., gave us several numbers. I don't know of anything more to interest you. Address c/o American Express Company, 546 Haymarket London England. Emma joins with me in love to you all.

Yours,
Luke Hoyt[28]

CARLOS HURD

While the *Carpathia* returned to New York, Mr Hurd wrote the following account for a New York newspaper:

Fifteen hundred lives – the figures will hardly vary in either direction by more than a few dozen – were lost in the sinking of the *Titanic*, which struck an iceberg at 11:45 p.m. Sunday and was at the ocean's bottom two hours and thirty-five minutes after.

The printed rolls of first and second cabins, compared with the list of the survivors on the *Carpathia*, show that of 390 first cabin passengers 212 were saved, 154 of them women and children and that of 270 second cabin passengers 116 were saved 102 of them women and children. Of the third class passengers, 800 in number, 170 survive, of whom 83 are women and children.

Of 985 officers and crew, 207, including 22 women, reached the *Carpathia*. A few in each class doubtless escaped enumeration on the *Carpathia*.

Accepting the estimate of the *Carpathia*'s officers, that 705 survivors reached the ship, comparison with the total, 2,181, shows that 1,476 are unaccounted for. There is but the faintest hope that any of these reached any other ship. Reports that the *Californian*, a cattle ship, may have rescued a few persons have given merciful respite from utter despair to some of the women. Cause, responsibility and similar questions regarding the stupendous disaster will be taken up in time by the British marine authorities. No disposition has been shown by any survivor to question the courage of the crews, hundreds of whom saved others and gave their own lives with a heroism which equated but could not exceed that of John Jacob Astor, Henry B. Harris, Jacques Futrelle and others in the long list of the first cabin missing. Facts which I have established by inquiries on the *Carpathia*, as positively as they could be established in view of the silence of the few surviving officers are:

That the *Titanic*'s officers knew several hours before the crash, of the possible nearness of icebergs. That the *Titanic*'s speed, nearly twenty-three knots an hour, was not slackened.

That the number of lifeboats on the *Titanic* was insufficient to accommodate much more than one-third of the passengers, to say nothing of the crew. Most members of the crew say there were sixteen lifeboats and the collapsible which got away to the limit of their capacity.

That 'the-women-first' rule, in some cases, was applied to the extent of turning back men who were with their families, even though not enough women to fill the boats were at hand on that particular part of the deck. Some few boats were thus lowered without being completely filled, but most of these were soon filled with sailors and stewards, picked up out of the water, who helped man them.

That the bulkhead system, though probably working in the manner intended, availed only to delay the ship's sinking. The position and length of the ship's wound (on the starboard quarter) admitted icy water, which caused the boilers to explode, and these explosions practically broke the ship in two.

Had the ship struck the iceberg head-on, at whatever speed, and with whatever resultant shock, the bulkhead system of water-tight compartments would probably have saved the vessel. As one man expressed it, it was the 'impossible' that happened when, with a shock unbelievably mild, the ship's side was torn for a length, which made the bulkhead system ineffective.

The *Titanic* was 1,799 miles from Queenstown and 1,191 miles from New York, speeding for a maiden voyage record. The night was starlight, the sea glassy. Lights were out in most of the staterooms, and only two or three congenial groups remained in the public rooms.

In the crow's nest, or lookout, and on the bridge, officers and members of the crew were at their places, awaiting relief at midnight from their two-hours watch.

At 11:45 came the sudden sound of two gongs, a warning of immediate danger.

The crash against the iceberg, which had been sighted at only a quarter of a mile, came almost simultaneously with the click of the levers operated by those on the bridge, which stopped the engine and closed the water-tight doors.

Capt. Smith was on the bridge a moment later, giving orders for the summoning of all on board and for the putting on of life preservers and the lowering of the lifeboats.

The first boats lowered contained more men passengers than the later ones, as the men were on deck first, and not enough women were there to board them.

When, a moment later, the rush of frightened women and crying children to the deck began, enforcement of the women-first rule became rigid. Officers loading some of the boats drew revolvers, but in most cases the men, both passengers and crew, behaved in a way that called for no such restraint. Revolver shots, heard by many persons shortly before the end of the *Titanic*, caused many rumors. One was that Capt. Smith shot himself, another was that First Officer Murdoch ended his life. Smith, Murdoch and Sixth Officer Moody are known to have been lost. The surviving officers, Lightoller, Pitman, Boxhall and Lowe, have made no statement.

Members of the crew discredit all reports of suicide, and say Capt. Smith remained on the bridge until just before the ship sank, leaping only after those on the decks had been washed away. It is also related that when a cook later sought to pull him aboard a lifeboat, he exclaimed, 'Let me go!' and, pulling away, went down.

What became of the men with life preservers is a question asked since the disaster by many persons. The preservers did their work of supporting their wearers in the water until the ship went down. Many of those drawn into the vortex, despite the preservers did not come up again. Dead bodies floated on the surface as the last boats moved away.

To relate that the ship's string band gathered in the saloon, near the end, and played 'Nearer My God to Thee' sounds like an attempt to give an added solemn color to a scene which was itself the climax of solemnity. But various passengers and survivors of the crew agree in the declaration that they heard this music.

To some of the hearers, with husbands among the dying men in the water and at the ship's rail, the strain brought in thoughts the words:

'So, by my woes I'll be
Nearer, My God, to Thee,
Nearer to Thee'

'Women and children first' was the order in the filling of the *Titanic*'s lifeboats. How well that order was fulfilled, the list of missing first and second cabin passengers bears eloquent witness. 'Mr.' is before almost every name, and the contrast is but made stronger by the presence of a few names of women – Mrs. Isidor Straus, who chose death rather than leave her husband's side; Mrs. Allison, who remained below with her husband and daughter, and others who, in various ways, were also entering the line of those to be saved.

To most of the passengers, the midnight crash against the mountain did not seem of terrific force. Many were so little disturbed by it that they hesitated to dress and put on life preservers, even when summoned by thundering knocks and shouts of the stewards. Bridge players in the smoking room kept on with their game.

Once on deck, many hesitated to enter the swinging life boats. The glassy sea, the starlight sky, the absence, in the first few moments of intense excitement, gave them the feeling that there was only some slight mishap – that those who got into the boats would have a chilly half-hour below, and might later be laughed at.

It was such a feeling as this, from all accounts, which caused John Jacob Astor and his wife to refuse the places offered them in the first boat, and to retire to the gymnasium. In the same way H.J. Allison, Montreal banker, laughed at the warning, and his wife, reassured by him took her time about dressing. They and their daughter did not reach the *Carpathia*. Their son, less than two years old was carried into a lifeboat by his nurse and was taken in charge by Maj. Arthur Peuchen.

The admiration felt by passengers and crew for the matchlessly appointed vessel was translated, in those first few moments, into a confidence which for some proved deadly.

In the loading of the first lifeboat, restrictions of sex were not made, and it seemed to the men who piled in beside the women that there would be boats enough for all. But the ship's officers knew better than this, and as the spreading fear caused an earnest advance toward the suspended craft, the order 'Women first' was heard, and the men were pushed aside.

To the scenes of the next two hours on those decks and in the waters below, such adjectives as 'dramatic' and 'tragic' do but poor justice. With the knowledge of deadly peril gaining greater power each moment over these men and women, the nobility of the greater part, both among cabin passengers, officers, crew and steerage asserted itself.

Isidor Straus, supporting his wife on her way to a lifeboat, was held back by an inexorable guard. Another officer strove to help her to a seat of safety, but she brushed away his arm and clung to her husband, crying: 'I will not go without you'.

Another woman took her place, and her form, clinging to her husband's became part of the picture now drawn indelibly in many minds. Neither wife nor husband reached a place of safety.

Col. Astor, holding his young wife's arm, stood decorously aside as the officers spoke to him, and Mrs. Astor and her maid were ushered to a seat. Mrs. Henry B. Harris parted in like manner from her husband, saw him last at the rail, beside Col. Astor. Walter M. Clark of Los Angeles, nephew of the Montana senator joined the line of men as his young wife, sobbing, was placed in one of the craft.

'Let him come! There is room!' cried Mrs. Emil Taussig, as men of the White Star Line motioned to her husband to leave her. It was difficult that he released her hold to permit her to be led to her place.

George B. Widener, who had been in Capt. Smith's company a few minutes after the crash, was another whose wife was parted from him and lowered a moment later to the surface of the calm sea.

Of Maj. Archie Butt, a favorite with his fellow tourists; of Charles M. Hays, president of the Grand Trunk; of Benj. Guggenheim and of William T. Stead, no one seems to know whether they tarried too long in their staterooms or whether they forbore to approach the fast-filling boats, none of them was in the throng which, weary hours afterward, reached the *Carpathia*.

Simultaneously on the upper decks of the ship the ropes creaked with the lowering of boats as they reached the water. Those in the boats saw what those on the decks could not see – that the *Titanic* was listing rapidly to starboard and that her stern was rising at a portentous angle. A rush of steerage men toward the boats was checked by officers with revolvers in hand.

Some of the boats, crowded too full to give rowers a chance, drifted for a time. None had provisions or water; there was lack of covering from the icy air, and the only lights were from still undimmed arcs and incandescents of the settling ship, save for one of the first boats. There a steward that explained to one of the passengers that he had been shipwrecked twice before, appeared carrying three oranges and a green light.

That green light, many of the survivors say, was to the shipwrecked hundreds as the pillar of fire by night. Long after the ship had disappeared, and while confusing false lights danced about the boats, the green light kept them together on the course which led them to the *Carpathia*.

As the end of the *Titanic* became manifestly but a matter of moments, the oarsmen pulled their boats away, and the chilling waters began to echo splash after splash as passengers and sailors in life preservers leaped over and started swimming away to escape the expected suction.

Only the hardiest of constitutions could endure for many minutes such a numbing bath. The first vigorous strokes gave way to heartbreaking cries of 'Help, Help' and stiffened forms were seen floating, the faces relaxed in death.

Revolver shots were heard in the ship's last moments. The first report spread among the boats was that Capt. Smith had ended his life with a bullet. Then it was said that a mate had shot a steward who tried to push his way upon a boat against orders. None of these tales has been verified, and many of the crew say the captain, without a preserver, leaped in at the last and went down, refusing a cook's offered aid.

The last of the boats, a collapsible, was launched too late to get away and was overturned by the ship's sinking. Some of those in it – all, say some witnesses – found safety on a raft or were picked up by lifeboats.

In the Marconi tower, almost to the last, the loud clicking of the sending instrument was heard over the waters. Who was receiving the message those in the boats did not know, and they would least of all have supposed that a Mediterranean-bound ship in the distant South Atlantic track would be their rescuer.

As the screams in the water multiplied, another sound was heard, strong and clear at first, then fainter in the distance. It was the melody of the hymn 'Nearer, My God, to Thee' played by the string orchestra in the dining saloon. Some of those on the water started to sing the words, but grew silent as they realized that for the men who played, the music was a sacrament soon to be consummated by death. The serene strains of the hymn and the frantic cries of the dying blended in a symphony of sorrow.

Led by the green light, under the light of the stars, the boats drew away, and the bow, then the quarter, the stacks, and at last the stern of the marvel-ship of a few days before, passed beneath the waters. The great force of the ship's sinking was unaided by any violence of the elements, and the suction, not so great as had been feared, rocked but mildly the group of boats now a quarter of a mile distant from it.

Sixteen boats were in the forlorn procession which entered on the terrible hours of rowing, drifting and suspense. Women wept for lost husbands and sons. Sailors sobbed for the ship which had been their pride. Men choked back tears and sought to comfort the widowed. Perhaps, they said, other boats might have put off in another direction toward the last. They strove, though none too sure themselves, to convince the women of the certainty that a rescue ship would appear.

Early dawn brought no ship, but not long after 5 a.m. the *Carpathia*, far out of her path and making 18 knots instead of her wonted 15, showed her single red and black smoke-stack upon the horizon. In the joy of that moment the heaviest griefs were forgotten.

Soon afterward Capt. Rostron and Chief Steward Hughes were welcoming the chilled and bedraggled arrivals over the *Carpathia*'s side.

Terrible as were the San Francisco, *Slocum* and Iroquois disasters, they shrink to local events in comparison with this world-catastrophe.

True, there were others of greater qualifications and longer experience than I nearer the tragedy – but they, by every token of likelihood, have become a part of the tragedy. The honored Stead, the adroit Jacques Futrelle, what might they not tell, were their hands to hold a pencil?

The silence of the *Carpathia*'s engines, the piercing cold, the clamor of many voices in the companionways, caused me to dress hurriedly and awaken my wife at 5:40 a.m. Monday. Our stewardess, meeting me outside, pointed to a wailing host in the rear dining room and said, 'From the *Titanic* – she's at the bottom of the ocean'.

At the ship's side a moment later, I saw the last of the line of boats discharge their loads, and saw women, some with cheap shawls about their heads, some with the costliest of fur cloaks, ascending the ship's side. And such hope as the first sight of our ship may have given them had disappeared from their faces, and there were tears and signs of faltering as the women were helped up the ladders or hoisted aboard in swings. For lack of room to put them, several of the *Titanic*'s boats after unloading were set adrift.

At our north was a broad icefield, the length of hundreds of *Carpathias*. Around us on all sides were sharp and glistening peaks. One black berg, seen about 10 a.m. was said to be that which sunk the *Titanic*.

In his tiny house over the second cabin smoking room was Harold Cottam, the Marconi operator, a ruddy English youth whose work at his post, on what seemed ordinary duty until almost midnight, had probably saved the lives of the huddling hundreds below.

Already he was knitting his brows over the problem of handling the messages which were coming in batches from the purser's office. The haste with which these Marconigrams were prepared by their senders was needless in view of the wait of two days and two nights for a land connection. 'Safe' was the word with which most of the messages began. Then in many of them the words, 'missing'.

Dishevelled women who the night before could have drawn thousands from their husbands' letters of credit or from the *Titanic*'s safe, stood penniless before the *Carpathia*'s purser, asking that messages be forwarded – collect. Their messages were taken with the rest.

The *Californian*, a cattle ship, came near us and though it gave no sign of having any of the refugees on board, its presence in the vicinity gave hope to many women who were encouraged in the belief that the *Californian* might have picked up their loved ones.

Capt. Rostron's decision to abandon the Mediterranean course begun the Thursday before and to return to an American port was soon known to the passengers. At first it was reported that Halifax or Boston would be the destination but at noon the notice of the intended arrival in New York three days later was posted. At that time the *Carpathia*, at an increase over her usual moderate speed, was westward bound and her passengers were deferring their hopes of Gibraltar, Naples and Trieste, and were sharing their rooms with the newcomers. Few men of the *Carpathia*'s passenger list slept in a bed in any of the nights that followed. They and the men of the *Titanic* lay in chairs on deck, on dining tables or smoking room couches, or on the floors of the rooms which held their hand baggage and their curtained-off guests. The Captain was the first to vacate his room, which was used as a hospital.

In the first cabin library women of wealth and refinement mingled their grief and asked eagerly for news of the possible arrival of a belated boat or a message from some other steamer telling of the safety of their husbands. Mrs. Henry B. Harris, wife of a New York theatrical manager, checked her tears long enough to beg that some message of hope be sent to her father-in-law. Mrs. Ella Thor, Miss Marie Young, Mrs. Emil Taussig and her daughter Ruth, Mrs. Martin Rothschild, Mrs. Wm. Augustus Spencer, Mrs. J. Stuart White and Mrs. Walter M. Clark were a few of those who lay back exhausted on the leather cushions and told in shuddering sentences of their experiences.

Mrs. John Jacob Astor and the Countess of Rothes had been taken to staterooms soon after their arrival on shipboard. Those who talked with Mrs. Astor said she spoke often of her husband's ability as an oarsman and said he could have saved himself if he had a chance. That he could have had such a chance, she seemed hardly to hope.

To another stateroom a tall, dark man had been conducted, his head bowed, anguish in his face. He was J. Bruce Ismay, head of the International Mercantile Marine and chief owner of the *Titanic* and her sister ship, the *Olympic*. He has made the maiden voyage on each of his company's great ships. He remained in his room in a physician's care during the voyage back to New York. Capt. Rostron, his only caller, was not admitted to see him till Tuesday evening.

Before noon, at the Captain's request, the first-cabin passengers of the *Titanic* appeared in the saloon and the passengers of other classes in corresponding places on the rescue ship. Then the collecting of names was begun by the purser and the stewards. A second table was prepared in the first cabin for the new guests and the *Carpathia's* second cabin, being better filled than its first, the second-class arrivals had to be sent to the steerage.

In the middle of the morning the *Carpathia* passed near the spot, seamen said, where the *Titanic* went down. Only a few floating chairs marked the place. The ice peaks had changed their position. Which of these in sight, if any, caused the wreck was a matter of conjecture.

Those of the refugees who had not lost their lives found subject for distress in the reflection that their money and jewels were at the bottom of the sea. Miss Edith L. Rosenbaum, writer for a fashion trade journal, mourned the loss of trunks containing robes from Paris and Tunis. Several of the late works of Phillip Mock, a miniature painter, were in his lost baggage, but the artist was not inclined to dwell on this mishap.

The child of the Montreal Allisons, bereft of both parents and carried by a nurse was an object of pitying sighs in the saloon. In the second cabin, two French children engaged pitying attention. The two boys, four and two years old, who lost their mother a year before and their father the night before, were children of beauty and intelligence, but too abashed to answer any questions even those put in their native tongue. Their surname is believed to be Hoffman. They are now in the care of Miss Margaret Hays of No. 304 West Eighty-third street.

Reminiscences of two bridge whist games of Sunday night in the smoking room were exchanged by passengers who believed that the protracted games, a violation of the strict Sabbath rules of English vessels saved their lives. Alfred Drachstedt [Nourney] was leader in the smoking room game, Miss Dorothy Gibson the other.

Mrs. Jacques Futrelle, wife of the novelist, herself a writer of note, sat dry-eyed in the saloon, telling her friends that she had given up hope for her husband. She joined with the inquiries as to the chances of rescue by another ship, and one told her what soon came to be – the fixed position of the men – that all those saved were on the *Carpathia*.

'I feel better,' Mrs. Futrelle said hours afterward, 'for I can cry now'.

Among the men conversation centered on the accident and the responsibility for it. Many expressed the belief that the *Titanic*, in common with other vessels, had warning of the ice packs, but that in the effort to establish a record on the maiden run sufficient heed had not been paid to the warning. The failure of the safety compartments, said to have been closed from the bridge directly after the accident, was the occasion of amazement and one theory offered was that the doors had, for some reason, not worked in the usual manner. Others contend that these devices are, at best, but time-savers, and said that without them the *Titanic* would have gone under before three boats could have been lowered.

The requirement that the officers on the bridge should take temperatures of the water every 15 minutes to indicate the approach of the ice was discussed.

As to the behavior of officers and crew not a word of complaint was heard from the men. They were praised as worthy Britons and true seamen. In the same breath the survivors exalted the heroism of the missing men of the first cabin who had stood calmly waiting for their turn – the turn which because of scarcity of boats and shortness of time – never came for most of them.

'God knows I'm not proud to be here,' said a rich New York man. 'I got on a boat when they were about to lower it, and when, from delays below, there was no woman to take the vacant place. I don't think any man who was saved is deserving of censure, but I realize that in contrast with those who went down, we may be viewed unfavorably.' He showed a picture of his baby boy as he spoke.

As the day passed the forepart of the ship assumed some degree of order and comfort, but the crowded second cabin and rear decks gave forth the incessant sound of lamentation. A bride of two months sat on the floor and moaned her widowhood. An Italian mother shrieked the name of her lost son.

A girl of seven wept over the loss of her teddy bear and two dolls, while her mother, with streaming eyes, dared not tell the child that her father was lost and that the money for which their home in England had been sold had gone with him. Other children clung to the necks of the fathers, who, because of carrying them, had been permitted to take the boats.

At 4 p.m. Monday service for the dead was read by Father Roger Anderson of the Episcopal Order of the Holy Cross over the bodies of three seamen and one man, said to have been a cabin passenger, who were dead from exposure when received on this ship. Some of the *Titanic*'s passengers turned away from the rail as the first of the weighted forms fell into the water.

In the hospital and the public rooms lay, in blankets, several others who had been benumbed by the water. Mrs. Rosa Abbott, who was in the water for hours, was restored during the day. G. Weikman, the *Titanic*'s barber, who declared he was blown off the ship by the second of two explosions after the crash, was treated for bruises. A passenger, who was thoroughly 'ducked' before being picked up, caused much amusement on the *Carpathia*, soon after the doctors were through with him, by demanding a bath.

Storekeeper Prentice, the last man of the *Titanic* to reach this ship, was also soon over the effects of his long swim in the icy waters into which he leaped from the poop deck.

The physicians of the *Carpathia* were praised, as was Chief Steward Hughes, for work done in making the arrivals comfortable and avoiding serious illness.

Monday night on the *Carpathia* was one of rest. Wailing and sobbing of the day were hushed as widows and orphans slept. Tuesday, save for the crowded conditions of the ship, matters took somewhat their natural appearance.

Tuesday afternoon, in the saloon a meeting of survivors was held and plans for a testimonial to the officers and crew of the *Carpathia* and survivors of the *Titanic*'s crew were discussed. It was decided that relief of the destitute should be first considered and the chairman of the meeting, Samuel Goldenberg, appointed a committee, consisting of I.G. Frauenthal, Mrs. J.M. Brown, [Mrs.] William Bucknell and [Mrs.] George Stone, to raise a fund. The first subscriptions were for $100 each and amounts were paid largely in traveler's checks or personal checks, cash being somewhat scarce among the refugees, who had kept currency in the purser's safe.

Resolutions were adopted praising the *Titanic*'s surviving officers and crew, and the officers, crew and passengers of the *Carpathia* and declaring that a memorial is needed for 'those who in heroic self sacrifice' made possible the rescue of so many others. One speaker suggested that a memorial fund be raised by popular subscription, mentioning the *World* as a suitable medium. This and other suggestions were left to the committee to develop.

Rain and fog marked the *Carpathia*'s homeward cruise, and those who were not seasick when New York was reached were none the less sick of the sea.

Capt. Rostron's rule that personal messages should take precedence of press messages was not relayed even when Thursday a message from Mr. Marconi himself asked the reason why press dispatches were not sent. The Captain posted Marconi's message on the bulletin board and beside it a bulletin stating that no press message, except a bulletin to the Associated Press, had been sent. The implication was that none would be sent, and the most urgent and respectful appeals failed to change his determination, which, he seemed convinced, was in the best interest of the survivors and their friends.

My wife was my only active helper in a task which ten newspaper men could not have performed completely. S.V. Silverthorne of St. Louis aided greatly by lending me his first cabin passenger list, one of the few in existence.

Robert Hichens, one of the surviving quartermasters of the *Titanic*, the man who was on duty at the wheel when the ship struck the iceberg, told me the story of the wreck on the *Carpathia*, Thursday. Save for the surviving fourth officer, Boxhall, whose lips are sealed, Hichens saw Sunday night's tragedy at closer range than any man now living. In the hastily compiled list of surviving members of the crew, the names of Hichens, and other quartermasters appear among able-bodied seamen, but the star and anchor on the left sleeve of each distinguishes their rank from the A.B.s.

Hichens has followed the sea 15 years and has a wife and two children in Southampton. His story of the wreck, as he told it to me and as he expects to tell it to a marine court of inquiry, is here given:

I went on watch at 8 o'clock Sunday night and stood by the man at the wheel until 10. At 10, I took the wheel for two hours. On the bridge from 10 o'clock on were First Officer Murdoch, Fourth Officer Boxhall and Sixth Officer Moody. In the crow's nest (lookout tower) were Fleet and another man whose name I don't know. Second Officer Lightoller, who was on watch while I stood by, carrying messages and the like from 8 to 10, sent me soon after 8 to tell the carpenter to look out for the fresh water supply, as it might be in danger of freezing.

The temperature was then 31 degrees. He gave the crow's nest a strict order to look out for small icebergs. Second Officer Lightoller was relieved by First Officer Murdoch at 10 and I took the wheel then. At 11:45 three gongs sounded from the crow's nest, the signal for 'something right ahead'. At the same time one of the men in the nest telephoned to the bridge that there was a large iceberg right ahead. As Officer Murdoch's hand was on the lever to stop the engines the crash came. He stopped the engines, then immediately, by another lever, closed the watertight doors. The skipper (Capt. Smith) came from the chartroom onto the bridge.

His first words were, 'Close the emergency doors.'

'They're already closed, sir,' Mr. Murdoch replied.

'Send to the carpenter and tell him to sound the ship,' was the skipper's next order. The message was sent to the carpenter. The carpenter never came up to report. He was probably the first man on that ship to lose his life. The skipper looked at the commutator, which shows in what direction the ship is listing. He saw that she carried five degrees to starboard.

The ship was then rapidly settling forward. All the steam sirens were blowing. By the skipper's orders, given in the next few minutes, the engines were to work at pumping out the ship, distress signals were sent by Marconi and rockets were sent up from the bridge by Quartermaster Rowe. All hands were ordered on deck and life belts were served to the crew and to every passenger. The stewards and other hands helped the sailors in getting the boats out.

The order 'Women and children first' was given and enforced. There was no panic. I was at the wheel until 12:25.

It was my duty to stay there until relieved. I was not relieved by anyone else, but was simply sent away by Second Officer Lightoller, who told me to take charge of a certain boat and load it with ladies. I did so, and there were 32 ladies, a sailor and myself in the boat when it was lowered, sometime after 1 o'clock – I can't be sure of the time.

The *Titanic* had 16 lifeboats and two collapsible boats. All of them got away loaded, except that one of the collapsibles did not open properly and was used as a raft. Forty sailors and stewards who were floating in the water got on this raft and later had to abandon the raft and were picked up by the different boats. Some others were floating about on chairs when picked up.

Every boat, as far as I saw, was full when it was lowered, and every boat that set out reached the *Carpathia*. The green light on one of the boats helped to keep us together, but there were other lights. One was an electric flashlight that a gentleman carried in his pocket.

Our boat was 400 yards away when the ship went down. The suction nearby must have been great, but we were only rocked somewhat.

I have told only what I know and what I shall tell any marine court that may examine me.

G. Whiteman [Weikman] of Palmyra, N.Y., the *Titanic*'s barber, was lowering boats on deck A after the collision and declared the officers on the bridge, one of them First Officer Murdoch, promptly worked the electrical apparatus for closing the water-tight compartments. He believes the machinery was in some way so damaged by the crash that the front compartment failed to close tightly, though the bridge indicator said that it was secured.

Whiteman's manner of escape was unique. He was blown off the deck by the second of the two explosions of the boilers, and was in the water more than two hours, he declares, before he was picked up by a raft.

'The explosions', Whiteman said, 'were caused by the rushing in of the icy water to the boilers. A bundle of deck chairs, roped together, was blown off the deck with me, and struck my back injuring my spine, but it served as a temporary raft.

'The crew and passengers had faith in the bulkhead system to save the ship and were lowering Berthon collapsible boat, all confident the ship would get through, when she took a terrific dip forward and the water rushed up and swept over the deck and into the engine rooms. The boat went clean down and I caught the pile of chairs as I was washed up against the rail. Then came the explosions and blew me fifteen feet.

'After the water had filled the forward compartments, the ones at the stern could not save her. They did delay the ship's going down. If it wasn't for the compartments, hardly anyone could have got away.

'The water was too cold for me to swim and I was hardly more than 100 feet away when the ship went down. The suction was not what one would expect, and only rocked the water around me. I was picked up after two hours. I have done with the sea.'

Whiteman was one of those who heard the ship's string band playing 'Nearer, My God, to Thee' a few minutes before she went down.

R.N. Williams, a Philadelphia youth, on his way home from England to take the Harvard entrance examinations, was one of the few saloon passengers at the rail excluded from the 'women first' order from the boat who was saved. His father, Duane Williams, was lost.

'There is much and yet there is little to tell of my experience,' said young Williams. 'My father and I had about given up our hope for life and were standing together, resolved to jump together and keep together if we could, so long as either of us lived. I had on my fur coat. The forward end, where we stood, was sinking rapidly; and before we could jump together the water washed my father over. Then, with explosions, the ship seemed to break in two, and the forward end bounded up again for an instant. I leaped, but, with dozens in the water between us, my father was lost to me. I swam and drifted nearly two hours before I was pulled aboard the raft or collapsible boat which served for a time as a raft. Later, with the abandonment of the raft, I was taken aboard a boat.'

Frederick K. Seward who sat next to W.T. Stead at the *Titanic*'s saloon table, told of the veteran English journalist's plans for his American visit. His immediate purpose was to aid in the New York campaign of the Men and Religion Forward movement.

'Mr. Stead talked much of spiritualism, thought transference and the occult,' said Seward. 'He told a story of a mummy case in the British Museum which, he said, had had amazing adventures, but which punished with great calamities any person who wrote its story. He told of one person after another who, he said, had come to grief after writing the story and added that, although he knew it, he would never write it. He did not say whether ill-luck attached to the mere telling of it.'

Stead also told, Seward said, of a strange adventure of a young woman with an admirer in an English railroad coach, which was known to him as it happened, and which he afterward repeated to the young woman, amazing her by repeating everything correctly save for one small detail.

Had Harold Cottam, Marconi operator on the *Carpathia*, gone to bed Sunday night at his usual time, the *Carpathia* would have known nothing of the *Titanic*'s plight, and the lifeboats, without food or water, might have been the scenes of even greater tragedy than the great death ship itself.

The *Carpathia*, an easy going Mediterranean ship, has only one Marconi man, and when Cottam had not the receiver on his head the ship was out of communication with the world.

Cottam, an Englishman of twenty-one years, told me the morning after the wreck how he came to receive the *Titanic*'s CQD:

'I was relaying a message to the *Titanic* Sunday night, shortly after 11 o'clock by my time,' he said, 'and told Phillips, the *Titanic*'s Marconi man, that I had been doing quite a bit of work for him, and that if he had nothing else for me, I would quit and turn in for the night. Just as I was about to take the receiver off my head came CQD. This was followed with "We've hit something. Come at once".

'I called a sailor and sent word to an officer, and a few minutes later the Captain had turned the *Carpathia*, at eighteen knots, in the direction of the *Titanic*, which was sixty miles of more from us. Before I could tell the *Titanic* we were coming, came their SOS, and the operator added, "I'm afraid we are gone".

'I told him we were coming, and he went on sending out signals in every direction.'

An assistant Marconi man from the *Titanic*, not on duty at the time of the wreck, was among the survivors and assisted Cottam in his work after Wednesday, having been laid up the two previous days by the shock of the chill he suffered in the water and by injuries to his legs. He said Phillips, the *Titanic*'s chief operator, was lost.[29]

While on board the *Carpathia*, Mr Hurd wrote a second account for another newspaper:

Sixteen hundred and one lives were lost on the *Titanic*, which struck an iceberg at 11:45 p.m. on Sunday and were at the ocean's bottom two hours and thirty-five minutes after. Of the *Titanic*'s 330 first cabin passengers, 210 were saved, 154 of them being women and children, and of the 330 second cabin passengers, 125 were saved, 100 of them being women and children. Of the third class, 760 in number, 200 were saved, 83 of whom were women and children. Of the 940 officers and crew, 210, including 22 women, were rescued.

No survivor can question the courage of the crew, hundreds of whom gave their lives with a heroism which equaled, but could not exceed that of John Jacob Astor, Henry B. Harris, Jacques Futrelle and other passengers in the long list of first cabin passengers.

The bulkhead system, though probably working, prevailed only to delay the ship's sinking. The position of the ship's wound on the starboard quarter admitted icy water which caused the boilers to explode, and those explosions broke the ship in two.

The crash against the iceberg, which had been sighted at only a quarter of a mile, came almost simultaneously with the click of levers operated from the bridge which stopped the engines and closed the airtight doors.

Capt. Smith was on the bridge a moment later. He summoned all on board to put on life preservers and ordered the lifeboats lowered. The first boat had more male passengers, as they were the first to reach the deck.

When the rush of frightened men and women and crying children to the decks began, the 'women first' rule was rigidly enforced. Officers drew revolvers, but in most cases there was no use for them.

Revolver shots heard shortly before the *Titanic* went down caused many rumors, one that Capt. Smith had shot himself, another that First Officer Murdoch had ended his life, but members of the crew discredit these rumors.

Capt. Smith was last seen on the bridge just before the ship sank, leaping only after the decks had been washed away. What became of the men with life preservers was the question asked by many since the disaster. Many of those with life preservers were seen to go down despite the preservers and dead bodies floated on the surface as the last boats moved away.

It is stated positively that the ship's string band gathered in the saloon near the end and played 'Nearer, My God, to Thee'.

Mrs. Isidor Straus refused to leave her husband's side and both perished together.

Harold Cottam, the marine operator of *Carpathia*, did not go to bed at his usual time Sunday night and as a result caught the first message of the *Titanic*'s plight. He had been relaying messages to the *Titanic* Sunday night and shortly after 11 o'clock bade the *Titanic* operator good night. Just as he was about to take the receiver off his head the CQD call sounded. This was followed by the words, 'We've hit something; come at once'.

Cottam at once communicated with the *Carpathia*'s officers and its course was at once changed in the direction of the *Titanic* full speed at eighteen knots for the full distance of sixty miles intervening between the two ships.

Before Cottam could make a reply to the CQD, the *Titanic*'s 'I'm afraid we are gone', Cottam sent word of the coming of the *Carpathia*. No further communication was had with the doomed ship.

The *Titanic*'s speed of twenty-three knots an hour was never slackened and it was going at that speed when it struck.

Facts which I have established by inquiries on the *Carpathia* as positively as they could be established in view of the silence of the few survivors are:

That the *Titanic*'s officers knew, several hours before the crash, of the possible nearness of the icebergs.

That the *Titanic*'s speed, nearly twenty-three knots an hour, was not slackened.

That the number of lifeboats on the *Titanic* was insufficient to accommodate more than one-third of the passengers to say nothing of the crew. Most members of the crew say there was sixteen lifeboats and two collapsibles: none say there were more than twenty boats in all. The 700 who escaped filled most of the sixteen lifeboats and the one collapsible which got away to the limit of their capacity.

Had the ship struck the iceberg head on at whatever speed, and with whatever resulting shock, the bulkhead system of water tight compartments would probably have saved the vessel. As one man expressed it, it was the impossible that happened when, with a shock unbelievably light, the ship's side was torn for a length, which made the bulkhead system ineffective.

The *Titanic* was 1,700 miles from Queenstown and 1,191 miles from New York, speeding for a maiden voyage record. The night was starlight, the sea glossy. Lights were out in most of the staterooms and only two or three congenial groups remained in the public rooms.

In the crow's nest, or lookout, and on the bridge, officers and members of the crew were at their places, awaiting relief at midnight from their two hours' watch.

At 11:05 came the sudden sound of two guns, a warning of immediate danger.

In the loading of the first boat restrictions of sex were not made and it seemed to the men who filled in beside the women that there would be boats enough for all. But the ship's officers knew better than this and as the spreading fear caused an advance towards the suspended craft, the order, 'Women first' was heard and the men were pushed aside.

To the scene of the next two hours on those decks and in the waters below such adjectives as 'drastic' and 'tragic' do but poor justice. With the knowledge of deadly peril gaining greater power each moment over those men and women, the courage of the greater part of the men, both among cabin passengers, officers, crew and steerage, asserted itself.

Isidor Straus, supporting his wife on her way to the life boat, was held back by an inexorable guard. Another officer strode to help her to a seat of safety, but she brushed away his arm and clung to her husband, crying, 'I will not go without you'.

Another woman took her place and Mrs. Straus, clinging to her husband, became part of a picture now drawn indelibly in many minds.

Col. Astor, holding his young wife's arm, stood decorously aside as the officers spoke to him and Mrs. Astor and her maid were ushered to seats.

Mrs. Henry B. Harris parted in like manner from her husband; saw him last at the rail, beside Col. Astor.

Walter M. Clark of Los Angeles, nephew of the Montana senator, joined the line of men as his young wife, sobbing, was placed in one of the craft. 'Let him come. There is room,' cried Mrs. Emil Taussig as the men of the White Star motioned to her husband to leave her. It was with difficulty that he released her hand to permit her to be led to her place.

George D. Widener, who had been in Capt. Smith's company a few moments after the crash, was another whose wife was parted from him and lowered, a moment later, to the surface of the calm sea.

Of Maj. Archie Butt, a favorite with his fellow tourists; of Charles M. Hays, president of the Grand Trunk; of Benjamin Guggenheim and William T. Stead, no one seems to know whether they tarried too long in their staterooms or whether they forbore to approach the fast filling boats; none of them was in the throng which, weary hours afterward, reached the *Carpathia*.

Only the hardiest constitution could endure for more than a few minutes such a numbing bath. The first vigorous strokes gave way to heart breaking cries of 'Help, Help' and stiffened forms were seen floating, relaxing in death.

Revolver shots were heard in the ship's last moments. The report spread among the boats was that Capt. Smith had ended his life with a bullet. Then it was said that a mate had shot a steward who had tried to push his way into a boat against orders. None of these tales had been verified, and many of the crew say the captain, without a preserver, leaped in at the last and went down, refusing the cook's offered aid.

The last of the boats, a collapsible, was launched too late to get away and was overturned by the ship sinking. Some of those in it, all say some witnesses, found safety on a raft or were picked up by a lifeboat. In the Marconi tower almost to the last the click of the sending instrument was heard over the waters.

As the screams in the water multiplied another sound was heard, strong and clear at first and then fainter in the distance. It was the melody of the hymn, 'Nearer, My God, to Thee', played by the string orchestra in the dining saloon. Some of those on the water started to sing the words, but grew silent as they realized that for the men who played the music was a sacrament soon to be consummated by death. The strains of the hymn and the frantic cries of the dying blended in a symphony of sorrow.[30]

In later years Mr Hurd described how he had come to write his 1912 account of the *Titanic* disaster:

At noon Thursday, April 11, 1912, the RMS *Carpathia* sailed from New York for Naples. My wife, since deceased, and I were passengers in the second cabin, having planned a brief traversing of the time-honored grand tour, from Naples to Liverpool. We had meant to go aboard the *Berlin*, a new and fast German ship in the Mediterranean service, but the *Berlin* had been chartered for the mid-April trip and we had taken the small and slow Cunarder.

It was a late spring, after an extremely hard winter. In St. Louis, lawns had been covered with snow until a few days before our departure on Easter Sunday. The first three days at sea were clear and chilly. By Sunday, we were beginning to diverge from the North Atlantic track toward the Pillars of Hercules.

No one but a Polar explorer could have been much farther from the world than the *Carpathia*'s passengers were that Sunday. The time was an eventful one. The Mississippi River was in flood and raging through the South. The Secretary of State was touring Central America; the Pennsylvania coal miners were striking; the Irish home-rule bill was pending; and the forces which were soon to split the Republican party were lining up. But, until we reached Gibraltar, none of the world's worries would reach us. Our wireless was a small affair, which could communicate with land only by relaying its messages through larger ships. Its limited facilities were in the care of one operator, who had no substitute. When he slept, or for any reason took off his headpiece, the *Carpathia* was out of any possible touch with the world. In three days we had seen but one ship.

The latest newspapers on board were the New York papers of Thursday morning. These carried extended news accounts of the sailing from Southampton, Wednesday, the tenth, of the new White Star liner *Titanic*, sister ship of the *Olympic*. The passenger list was one of unusual distinction.

Sunday night, April 14, was clear and cold. Monday morning I awoke to find the sun shining in my face, a thing which, owing to the ship's direction, had not happened before. I realized the startling fact that the ship was standing still.

Outside, toward the sun, lay a low jagged line of shimmering white. I half dressed and started out of my stateroom. Then came the sound of wailing, deep and prolonged, from the other side of the ship, the port side. In the hallway I met a stewardess, leading two weeping and bedraggled women. She hardly paused for my questions. 'The *Titanic* has gone down. We are taking on her passengers,' she said. I returned to the room to finish dressing and to tell my wife what had happened.

Thursday morning's *World* lay on the shelf. I tore out the story of the *Titanic*'s sailing, with the list of prominent passengers and thrust it into my pocket as I went out again. On the port side, the last of the lifeboats from the sunken ship was being cleared of its shivering occupants. The unloading process had begun while the *Carpathia*'s passengers slept.

The ordinary restrictions of the second cabin were forgotten as I hurried to the front of the ship. Women and children were being taken into the saloon-library; men who had heavy coats were still on deck. Near the bow I approached a pair of men who seemed more composed than the rest. I told them that I was connected with the *St. Louis Post-Dispatch*.

'How's my friend Billy Steigers?' said one of the men. He proved to be a buyer from a St. Louis department store, a friend of the business manager of the paper, about whom he had inquired. He and the other man, survivors of the *Titanic*, told me what they had seen of the disaster.

These two had been up late Sunday night, one on deck, the other in the smoking room, when the ship, making 23 knots, had struck the iceberg. They had seen, from different places, the rush of passengers to the decks, the lowering of lifeboats upon the glassy and starlit sea.

They had heard some refuse to get into lifeboats, saying that the ship was unsinkable, that it was silly to be panicky. They had seen others get into boats in the spirit of half jest. They had entered boats about to be lowered, where there was room for them. They had seen indifference grow to alarm and terror as the lighted ship began listing heavily, then unmistakably to sink. They had seen men, wearing lifebelts, jump into the icy water. They had seen some, the most robust, swim to the boats and clamber in where there was possible room for another person.

From a distance created by vigorous rowing, they saw the breaking and sinking of the ship. After it had disappeared, the lifeboats had drawn together and moved in the direction from which, after daybreak, the rescuing *Carpathia* appeared.

'All I saved,' said the St. Louis man, 'was what I had in my pocket. That included this list of the *Titanic*'s passengers. Take it. I want it back, but you may mark it up as much as you wish.'

In the saloon, unperturbed English stewards were bringing hot coffee to the chilled refugees. Most of these were women of refinement. Even then, the poorer women had found their way to the rear of the ship and the steerage spaces.

It was a scene of utter despair and misery. Some women were sobbing, others sat bowed in silence, still others were asking frantically for or about their husbands, whom they had left on the sinking ship.

A young woman, herself one of the rescued, talked in a comforting tone to some of the others and calmed them. She was a private teacher, who a few years before had been instructor to President Roosevelt's younger children in the White House. When there was opportunity to speak with her, I asked her about Capt. Archie Butt, noted Washington social figure, and President Taft's emissary to the Vatican, who was listed among the *Titanic*'s passengers.

She had no news of him, but she, and other women in the room, who seemed to find relief in the recital, told of the Strauses, the aged couple who had remained at the ship's rail together, refusing to be parted after their long union; of the farewell of John Jacob Astor to his young wife; and of the conflicting reports as to Captain Smith, who, however, had not been saved.

One woman with whom I talked in the library that morning was the newly made widow of a popular novelist. Near her was the widow of a Broadway show producer. Two others, who had no personal bereavement to mourn, were the original poster girl of one of the most popular artists of the time, and her mother.

It was no time to urge unwilling persons to talk, nor was there any temptation, that morning, to do so. There were enough who were willing to talk and who found a certain relief in speech. After that first morning, this ceased to be true in regard to many of the wealthier survivors. As they regained their composure, they regained also their reserve, which some of them did not again break.

I soon learned how fragmentary, and often contradictory, were the individual accounts of the happenings of the night before. Naturally, none of the rescued knew, in more than a general way, the part that the wireless had taken in their rescue. It began to appear that the wireless operator of our own ship, a ruddy English youth whom I had seen in the second cabin dining room, had a most important story to tell. I was so fortunate as to get his story early, before he and the wireless room had been made inaccessible by the captain's order.

He had been sitting in the wireless cabin, wearing his headpiece, long after the usual time, when he had heard the first signals of distress. He had reported to Captain Rostron, who had instructed him to get details of the *Titanic*'s position. Then the *Carpathia* at once made a left turn toward the North Atlantic track and the *Titanic*, fifty to sixty miles away.

Leaving the wireless room, I met Captain Rostron. I told him of my newspaper connection and added that it was my duty and intention to send a story at the first opportunity to the *New York World*, for its own use, and for transmission to the *Post-Dispatch*.

There was no hesitation about the British captain's answer. He meant to see to it that the rescued persons in his care were not annoyed by press men. Probably I would be able to pick up some incidents but positively I might not use the wireless. A list of the rescued would be made up and I might see the purser later about copying it.

The captain's no-wireless ruling was a jolt in the jaw, to put it very mildly. At that moment it made no difference, for I had just learned from young Cottam, the operator, that we were not in touch with the shore or with any other ship and were not likely to be for more than twenty-four hours. But when we should get within range of communication, I knew that every paper in New York would besiege the operator with queries and offers and I could hardly imagine that some of them would not get a reply from him.

At the first opportunity I saw Cottam at table and promised him liberal pay from my funds on hand and later from the *World* if he would get even a short message through for me. His reply showed that the captain's thorough discipline extended to the Marconi service and that no message not expressly authorized by the captain had a chance to go. Attempts to get Captain Rostron to reverse his ruling were vain, but I was to learn, on getting to New York, that all other efforts to break the wireless embargo had failed likewise. Except for a partial transmission of survivors' names, no news had gone out from the *Carpathia*. Messages filed for me by the *Post-Dispatch* and *World* were delivered to me only after arrival in New York, not having been accepted for wireless transmission.

From the time of our first stopping within sight of the ice field, word had gone through the ship that our journey to the Mediterranean was not to be continued, that we would return to the nearest port. That might have been Halifax, but before our start, late in the morning bulletins announced a return to New York.

On the deck now and then during the day, between talks with the rescued, I got distant glimpses of the icebergs. There was a burial at sea, that of an elderly man who had been one of the rescued. He had been in the water a considerable time and died of shock and exposure. That left the number of survivors at 705 and indicated that more than 1,500 persons had been lost – the number officially established later was 1,517. The exact number lost could not be computed on board the *Carpathia* for the reason that, while printed lists of the *Titanic*'s first and second cabin passengers were available, there was no complete third class list except the one kept in Southampton. Estimates of the third class passengers made by members of the crew proved somewhat too high. They pointed to a figure of about 1,600 lost.

While we did not get very near the icebergs, most attempts at photographing them being unsuccessful, we saw debris which showed that we were not far from the scene of the disaster. Deck chairs and other objects were to be seen on the surface, which still kept the calm of the night before. We saw at one point the Leyland liner *Californian*, which as shown in official inquiries later, was much nearer to the scene of the disaster than the *Carpathia* but did not respond in time to take part in the rescue.

The clear skies of the first day gave way on the return voyage to rain and fog which kept the foghorn blowing at such frequent intervals as to make conversation difficult. This affected the spirits of the rescued and bereaved.

By common consent the *Carpathia*'s passengers opened their rooms to the newcomers. In my stateroom a little boy, just sick enough to keep very quiet, was placed. He was one of the two French children who had been put into lifeboats by other passengers while their father, who did not succeed in getting into the boat, was drowned.

The other boy, who was well but not boisterous, was with his brother a part of the time but slept in another stateroom. Both received much attention from the women of our passenger list, though even those who spoke French could get no information from them. My wife and I had left two children of the same age at home, so that little sick boy could not have found a place where he would have been more welcome. The two waifs of mystery, it was found later, had been taken by their father from their mother, a Mme. Navratil of Nice, who came to New York and took them home.

I had made an early requisition on the ship's little store for tablet paper and pencils and was accumulating a mass of notes. It seemed to me that, besides and ahead of individual experiences of the survivors, the story of the disaster itself should be told. The endeavor to fit such a story together showed how fragmentary was the knowledge of individuals. One would mention an incident which could be confirmed or completed only by another. In the search for the other, new suggestions and new complications would arise. The job would have taxed the energy and resources of a dozen reporters.

An instance of this difficulty was the incident, still remembered, of the playing of hymn music by the English musicians in the sinking ship's orchestra. Several persons told of having heard this music from their boats, but, because of distracting noises, they could not be sure what the melody was. Two women who professed familiarity with sacred music said it was 'Nearer My God, to Thee'. This statement appeared in my report and gained general currency. The *New York Times* later obtained a book of music said to be a duplicate of the one which the *Titanic*'s orchestra had. It did not contain the tune 'Bethany', to which the tune already named is sung, but it did contain the hymn tune 'Autumn' which, though in different meter, is much like 'Bethany'. The *Times* concluded that 'Autumn' was the number played.

With guests in my stateroom and with all public parts of the ship crowded, I found night the most feasible time for writing. All had to be done on long-hand. My wife checked the list of survivors with the first and second cabin passenger lists of the *Titanic*, to prepare a list of the unreported – this being, as we then supposed and was soon shown, synonymous with 'lost'. Quest of the photographs made by a few of our passengers took much time, and those obtained proved to be useless because of light conditions.

Sailors who had taken charge of the lifeboats were disposed to seek pay for their stories. I paid one, who by common account had more to tell than the others of occurrences at the front of the ship before and immediately after the crash. Such stories were the nearest that could be had to an official account, for the *Titanic*'s surviving officers brusquely refused to talk. The head of the White Star Line, Bruce Ismay, was inaccessible. So much mystery was preserved about Ismay's movements that stories were circulated that the lost Captain Smith was also secreted in a forward cabin. The *Titanic*'s wireless operator, Bride, a hero of the rescue, was kept from questioners by a guard of sailors.

We knew that New York would be reached Thursday afternoon or evening. The *Carpathia*, making thirteen knots, was taking us in with the story for which the world was waiting. Continued attempts to get use of the wireless, all of which were futile, took much time and nerve force. Most of Wednesday night was spent in longhand writing and revision of copy.

As we neared Sandy Hook late Thursday afternoon, fellow passengers helped me to make a bundle of my copy, to be given to the expected emissary of the *World*, who, I hoped, would be admitted to the ship there. Knowing that the matter might have to be tossed over the ship's side, others advised me to attach some sort of buoy or ballast, as the bundle might fall into the water. A cigar box, the only thing at hand, was fastened to the bundle by a cord.

The expected tugs were at Sandy Hook. They were from all the papers. I was in the ship's hold as the lower doors were opened, but no one from the approaching tugs was permitted to come on board, or to come within a distance at which the *World* representatives could have taken my bundle. Our stop was only for a few minutes. In the maneuvering as the ship started, I caught sight of the *World*'s tug, in charge of Charles E. Chapin, city editor of the *Evening World*.

As I got back to the upper deck, my name was being called through megaphones. Not only the *World*, but the others, called for me in tones suggesting the summons of judgment day. I called back from the ship's rail and waved my bundle at the tug bearing the *World* banner as the *Carpathia* moved away in the growing dusk. Before the liner could get up its not excessive speed, the *World* tug had come alongside. Chapin's arms were extended. I threw my bundle over. The unlucky ballast cord passed over the supporting rope of one of the *Titanic*'s lifeboats, projecting from the *Carpathia*'s next deck level, and the bundle hung balanced, far out of my reach.

A sailor on the lower deck reached out, took the bundle and hesitated. 'Throw it!' cried a dozen persons. The sailor tossed the bundle to Chapin. With an acknowledging toot of the tug's whistle, the little craft churned off for the Battery as the *Carpathia* continued toward the Cunard pier on Fourteenth Street. For once, we were to land without customs inspection. The *Carpathia*'s passengers had been nowhere, the *Titanic*'s survivors had nothing.

The projecting lifeboats of the *Titanic* delayed the *Carpathia* in getting to its pier, and it was 9 o'clock before our shipload of tourists and refugees moved down the gangplanks, through the Cunard pier and to the densely thronged, but startlingly silent, spaces of Fourteenth Street. It was a night and a scene long remembered in New York.

As we reached the nearest 'L' station, newsboys were selling the *Evening World Extra*, with a hasty but effective condensation of my story. The story appeared in Friday morning's *World* and in Associated Press papers throughout the country. The *Post-Dispatch*, with an hour's advantage in time, issued a night extra and carried the full story Friday.

At the *World* office that Thursday night I was informed of the award of a $1,000 bonus and was told to add three weeks to my vacation. Eight days of this time were consumed by the return to New York, from which we sailed again Friday afternoon.

Through May and June the Continental papers told of the official inquiries into the *Titanic* disaster. Returning to Boston in mid-July, we found the *Titanic* still front-page news. The official inquiries cleared various points and affected some reputations. The complete story of the *Titanic* disaster, however, was and is as impossible to tell as the complete story of Waterloo or of Gettysburg. Three years later the sinking of the *Lusitania*, with somewhat less loss of life, became a crowning horror of the war and replaced the *Titanic* in the public mind. To this day the two lost ships are confused by many.[31]

MRS CARLOS HURD

After the *Carpathia* resumed her interrupted voyage to Europe, Katherine Hurd wrote the following letter to her sister Emily:

Cunard RMS *Carpathia*
Monday April 29

Dear Emily,
I have been wanting to write for some time but as you know there is not a great deal happening on ship board in mid ocean. Our trip back to New York was a sorrowful one – for though the rescued women were wonderfully brave it was awful to see their haggard faces and to know that nearly every one of them had lost some dear one – husband, father or son.

New York harbor was a brilliant spectacle. The city welcomed the *Carpathia* as a ship was never welcomed before. Yet all was quiet and a spirit of mourning prevailed. For until our ship came in hundreds of those in the waiting crowd did not know whether their loved ones would appear or not. We were of the first to disembark and as we passed the anxious crowd names were called out and placards held high with names upon them so that the survivors could more readily find their friends. Only those expecting friends were allowed on the pier – at first we wondered that there was not a greater mob but when we got outside the streets were packed and we learned that the lines had been tightly drawn.

The *World* received Carlos with enthusiasm. For days they had been trying to communicate with him by wireless but no messages had been delivered. So he got all the facts into note form and had them ready for the *New York World* tug boat that met us in the harbor. Several papers were represented, and not until the questions 'How many saved?' 'Is Widener there?' 'Where is Archie Butt?' came thro' the megaphones did we realize how little the world really knew of that terrible disaster. We were sent to the Belmont Hotel and felt like tramps among so much grandeur. We had no enthusiasm for another start until we received the encouraging reply to our telegram.

We have had a quiet pleasant restful voyage this time and are glad we did not give up our trip. We have a good deal of fun playing shuffleboard and ring toss in the daytime and in the evening we have a little music – and some play cards or chess. Last Wednesday evening we had a musical, the next night a dance and the next night the ship's concert. We have attended Church of England services in the 1st cabin every Sunday – the Captain and the Purser read the services and they pray for the King of England (and the President of the United States). We hope to get to Gibraltar this afternoon and I have only a few minutes in which to finish this, as I want it mailed from there. We saw three or four ships yesterday and everybody is anxiously looking for land. We hope you and Alice Baby and Alice 'my sister' will make us a nice long visit on your way back to Korea. If you decide to go back and if you don't you can make us that much longer a visit. When I come down for Clement and Emily I plan to bring family and children back with me. This is Mother's wedding anniversary, may she have many, many more.

With lots and lots of love to each one from Carlos and myself.

Affectionately your sister,
Katherine[32]

CHARLES HUTCHISON

On 18 April Mr Hutchison wrote the following letter to his parents:

At Sea
Royal Mail Steamship *Carpathia*
April 18, 1912

Dear Mother and Dad,

I started a letter to you soon after we left New York, but now I will have to write another, as everything has been upset. When we were four days out from New York our boat received a wireless from a ship in distress. It proved to be the new giant White Star liner *Titanic*, which had struck an iceberg. You have, no doubt, seen by the papers, how our ship rescued 710 of the passengers of the magnificent boat which went to the bottom. It was a wonderful sight and one which we shall never forget, the way our ship rescued the people.

It is estimated that there were very close to 2,000 went down with the *Titanic*. It has been one of the worst disasters of our time. Just think – this great ship, making her first trip, with so many notable people on board going to the bottom of the ocean. It makes me feel as though the risk of an ocean trip wasn't worth what we will gain in knowledge. However, we feel now as though we shall go on. You know we are now on our way back to New York with the 710 people we rescued from the ill-fated ship. We have made the acquaintance of a Mr. and Mrs. Iddiols from St. Louis. We have doubled up with them and have given up our cabin to a Mrs. Smith, of West Virginia. She is the daughter of Senator Hughes of West Virginia, and has lost her husband. She told me she knew of 16 women who have lost their husbands. It seems as though the women were taken off first and, when they were all off, there were no lifeboats for the men, so most of the lost were men.

Among the men were John Jacob Astor, Mr. Case of the Standard Oil Co., and Maj. Butt, aide to the President. Mrs. Astor, who was Madeline Force, is rescued and is on our ship. We expect to be in New York by tonight, and this will be mailed to you at once. We are safe and enjoyed the trip immensely until we rescued these poor ship wrecked people. Ever since the ship is more like a cemetery than a boat. I have written an account of the disaster, of some 10 pages, which I expect to send to *The Pittsburg Press*. So you may see the account in that paper. Goodbye.

Best wishes to all.
Charles M. Hutchison[33]

Mr Hutchison wrote this account for the *Pittsburg Press* on 18 April:

On board the *Carpathia*, of the Cunard Line, April 18 – The night of Sunday, April 14, 1912 was clear and the stars shining brightly. We were steaming along, some 1,200 miles east of New York on our path to Gibraltar, with not a thought of danger, when just a few minutes before midnight our wireless operator picked up the distress signal, SOS, coming from the new giant White Star liner *Titanic* on her maiden voyage from Southampton to New York.

She, in order to make a fast trip, was somewhat off her course and struck an enormous iceberg while running at full speed. I will tell what happened from facts that I have gathered since Monday from people who took part in the scenes that followed.

When the ship struck there was only the slightest imaginable shock; so slight indeed that only a few people noticed it. The promenade contained many happy people in high spirits at the approaching end of the trip. In the smoking room card games were in full blast.

When the collision occurred, the iceberg seemed simply to brush alongside the ship, and the only result was that some ice and a quantity of snow fell onto the deck. The passengers stared in delighted surprise at their first iceberg, which reared its uneven shape fully 70 feet above the water, and then finding the snow lying about the deck, started to pelt each other with snow balls.

The card players continued their games without pause. It was carelessly reported among the passengers that the ship had run into an iceberg, but the officers assured all that there was no danger, as even at the worst the airtight compartments would keep the ship afloat for a day at least. Most of the passengers had retired, and those who were awakened were told by the officers to go to bed again, as there was no danger.

It later developed that the watch in the crow's nest signaled the bridge that there were icebergs ahead, but found no one there. He signaled again, and finally left to try to get the news to the wheel house himself. By the time he reached there the ship struck the iceberg, astern of amidships.

After some time, although the passengers had been assured there was no danger, Capt. Smith issued orders to send the women off in the lifeboats. There was no difficulty in carrying out this order, as few on board thought there was any danger, and most objected to leaving the vessel.

Sixteen lifeboats and two life rafts were finally sent away from the ship, this being all the lifeboats there were on board. The collapsible rafts failed to work, and sank as soon as launched. These 16 boats and two rafts were picked up by our boat, the *Carpathia*.

The women were taken off the *Titanic* first, but when the boats were all launched there were still a great many on board. The loading of the first boats was very slow; none of the women wanted to go. They declared that the officers said there was no danger, and insisted that accordingly they did not want to get into the small boats. Comparatively few got in the first boats, and most of them declared they would be back for breakfast.

It was not a great time, however, before the *Titanic* began to settle and then the passengers were eager to get in the lifeboats, as they realized the deadly quality of their danger. The result was that the few remaining lifeboats were filled to overflowing, while passengers who failed to get a place, jumped overboard, hoping to be picked up by the life boats.

So great was the damage done by the collision that by 1 o'clock in the morning the *Titanic* was settling rapidly. When the end came she sank stern first, half broadside, and broke in half. Many of the rescued passengers claim there were 2,500 passengers on board, 710 of whom were rescued by our boat.

There were many thrilling rescues of persons who had jumped overboard in hope of being picked up by the boats. One passenger who had been thrown into the water was drawn under by the suction and raised to the surface, and finally was rescued by one of the boats. Another gentleman on board here told me he owes his life to the fact that someone pushed him overboard as he was assisting a woman into a boat. When the lifeboats became fewer and the passengers realized their danger, panic reigned and the captain shot himself. Many of those rescued were still in evening dress, not having yet retired.

As the lifeboats were in the distance, their occupants watching the ship settle in the water, the cry of help from those on board the ill fated ship could be heard. Those in the boats had to sit and watch others dear to them going down with the ship.

The lifeboats were not the ones intended for the *Titanic*, but were only temporary until the regular ones could be completed. They contained neither food nor water and not one was supplied with a lantern, while all were poorly manned. Some boats were launched with but two or three men to do the rowing, and in many instances there were women at the oars. In one boat the plug was lost out of the bottom and a woman stopped the hole with her hand.

That the boats might follow each other and keep together, bits of paper, letters and handkerchiefs torn into strips were burned. There seems to have been less than a third enough lifeboats on the *Titanic* to take care of the passengers in case of accident.

Our ship, when she received the wireless, at once turned north, to the location given by the wireless, and we covered some 60 miles before we met the first lifeboats of the *Titanic*. The giant boat, the most wonderful afloat, was nowhere to be seen on the surface of the wide sea. By this time we were entirely surrounded by an enormous field of ice and icebergs, and at one time I counted 25 of them. It was wonderful how our captain, A.H. Rostron, steered the ship in and out amongst them. The ice field has been estimated by many on board the *Carpathia*, at being 25 miles in extent, with icebergs standing up in them as high as 100 feet. Then there were countless floating icebergs which practically surrounded the ship. I have some eight or ten pictures I took of those icebergs.

After the wireless had been received as to the danger of the *Titanic*, everything on board the *Carpathia* was made ready to receive the boats with the passengers of the lost ship. The first lifeboat of the *Titanic* was sighted, and its passengers were taken on board at 4 o'clock Monday morning, April 15. The last boatload was taken on board by 7 a.m.

The last two boats each contained one dead sailor, dead from cold and exposure. Two others died later in the day. All were buried at sea, after services held at 3:30 o'clock by Father Anderson, of Baltimore, an Episcopal monk. The iron doors at the side of our boat were opened and a platform let down. The bodies, after being sewed up in sail cloth and weighted at the feet to make them strike the water feet first, were laid on slabs or boards, and covered with a British flag. After a prayer the flag was lifted and the bodies pushed off the slabs feet first, and making as little splash as possible. One, however, struck flat, and I shall never forget the sound of the splash.

Our crew worked heroically, taking the rescued onto our boat, and there wasn't the least sign of confusion. The iron doors at the side of our ship were opened and rope ladders let down. The women were drawn up on a swing, the men who were able climbed the rope ladder, and the children and babies were hauled up after being placed in a canvas sack.

About 12 of the lifeboats of the *Titanic* were raised to the deck of our ship. The balance, with the life rafts, were set adrift. Our ship, after cruising around in the hope of picking up more lifeboats, returned to the location where the *Titanic* had gone down, and at the request of our captain, Father Anderson read the prayer of interment, the benediction of interment, the prayer of consolation and the prayer of thanksgiving for those who were saved.

Our captain then decided to return to New York. All the rescued were made as comfortable as possible, and everything done for them in the way of clothing. We gave up our cabin to Mrs. Smith, daughter of Congressman Hughes, of West Virginia, who lost her husband, he being one of the men left on board the *Titanic*. We doubled up in the cabin of Mr. and Mrs. Iddiols, of St. Louis, Mo.

At noon Monday, our ship turned and put back for New York, which we hope to reach some time Thursday night or Friday morning. The fog has been heavy and we are delayed. After we had picked up all the lifeboats from the *Titanic* we sighted the *Californian*, a freight steamer. She was signaled to remain, in case there might possibly be more lifeboats adrift. Later we sighted the *Birma*, another freight steamer.

The iceberg which the *Titanic* struck was enormous in size, and reached to the upper deck of the ship, which was 70 feet above the water line.[34]

MRS CHARLES M. HUTCHISON

Mrs Hutchison wrote the following account while she was on board the *Carpathia*:

All through the early morning hours I heard steps overhead and fussing and calling and tramping, and between three and four my husband called to me, 'What's all this about? I am going to get up and see, as I have heard it long enough'.

I made no remark in particular, and he climbed down, put on his dressing gown in haste and without more words stepped into the hall. Soon he returned and reported this: 'I've been talking to a chap and he says he's been in a wreck and escaped with not an article of his belongings but the clothes on his back.'

We both thought it too bad for the fellow, and at Charles's suggestion I hurried into my clothes to go up on deck to learn how the rescuing was conducted. Neither of us had any idea of the terrible extent of the disaster, nor were we in any way apprehensive of the suffering we were to see.

Upon hurrying out of our room and crossing the main hall we saw the doors in the side of the ship half way down to the water's edge open, and immediately became interested. At the same moment I heard a seaman on duty say to a disheveled woman at my side, 'All rescued people this way, please', and I had my second hint at the rescued being a number of people, because accommodations were so extensive. They were taking them by the wholesale into the dining saloon at the end of the hall. I grabbed Charles and we hurried in wild haste to the deck, where we could get an idea what was going on.

Upon looking over the edge of the boat into the sea we saw that a lifeboat marked 'S.S. *Titanic*' was just being emptied and that many others were tied to the side of our boat, all emptied. Two others were still at large, approaching. We watched the two approaching and also were interested in noting the mode of handling passengers.

The women were placed in a seat like an ordinary tree swing consisting of a plain board and ropes up to eight feet, where they were knotted together and attached to the main rope. This swing was then hauled up by hand and the passenger taken into the doorway halfway down the vessel's side.

The women seemed to be calm enough when being raised into the boat, and although many had their hair loose to the wind, giving a wild feature to the scene, they were all orderly. The greater number of the boats we saw unloaded were of steerage passengers.

The men were able to walk up a rope ladder and the babies were put into a canvas sack and then hauled up. The women and babies appeared to be roughly knocked against the side of the vessel, but none was hurt.

When we arrived on deck all boats had been in except two. We saw two being unloaded, already made fast to our steamer, but saw two more coming in. These two I shall speak of at length.

The men rowing the boats were so exhausted they were unable to make any time, and the *Carpathia* was compelled to put on power and go up to them. They had masts up, but no sails. There were but five or six men in one boat, and perhaps twenty in the other.

Everyone had the chest life preservers strapped on his or her body. These were present in each stateroom and were put on by each passenger himself. Very few kept them on until taken onto our boat, as they removed them just before being drawn up into the *Carpathia*.

In one of these boats there was a great deal of water in the bottom and a man (a sailor) was lying in the bottom of the boat with his legs and body dipped in the water, while his head and shoulders were raised onto something higher. He was white and lifeless appearing, but I did not think he was dead, which was the case.

In the second boat a man was sitting on a seat which extends completely around the boats, but his head hung down on his chest and I guessed him frozen to death. At last blankets were thrown over him and he was huddled onto the seat and left there until all the living passengers had been raised onto our boat.

After all passengers had been taken off, these two dead men (both sailors who died from exposure) were more carefully covered with blankets, a rope tied around the waist over the blanket, and the bodies lifted to the *Carpathia*. All lifeboats but two were lifted to the *Carpathia* as protection to the extra souls now on our boat. There was apparently no room for the other two, and they were cut loose and allowed to drift. Fourteen boats were placed on the *Carpathia*, so that is the number of boats which came in.

We were informed that the *Titanic*, the largest craft afloat, on her first trip from Southampton, had, about 11:30, struck an iceberg and gone down within two hours. We made up with a sailor on deck, and he said as a rule none but women and children were saved, the men being told to wait until the women had been sent off. He said he was saved because two sailors, at least, were placed in every lifeboat to row and manage the boat. Thus it is sometimes fortunate to be a sailor.

It is not known why the iceberg was not seen, as the night was clear and beautiful and the sea was exceptionally calm. One old seaman told us it was more calm than he had seen it in thirty-six years.

The ocean had the appearance of a quiet lake. There were rises and falls, but no pure waves at all. The rescued say all the stars were reflected in the water when they started on their night's trip in the small boats, and the quiet beauty of the rising sun was an impression never to be forgotten, for daylight meant hope.

I couldn't believe, even after I was assured of it, that the giant ship *Titanic*, with all of the improvements known to modern ship construction, could have done so seemingly avoidable a thing as strike an iceberg! And added to that – to sink in two hours!

After everyone had been landed, the *Carpathia* put on power and started her cruise around the icebergs. These large icebergs could be seen all morning at a distance, and my surprise was that there were so many of them and that they were so large at such a distance. From all sides of the ship they could be seen. One egg-shaped one appeared to be the nearest of all. And there was a queer, snow-white line all around about one third of the horizon to be seen from one side of the ship.

All wondered at it, and I asked if it couldn't be a gigantic flat piece of ice, but, of course, everyone thought it impossible to be so large – miles upon miles in extent. Upon nearing the white object, with the aid of a glass we could see that it was a huge icefield of flat ice and snow, the entire frozen shore of some place having broken off as one piece and floated down.

Out of this frozen shore rose some twenty-five to thirty-five huge mountains of ice, properly called glaciers, although they were not the pure separated glacier of sea life, as they were not disengaged from the ice bed.

Our good ship *Carpathia* steamed around and circled the entire field, looking for any stray lifeboats or for any persons clinging to wreckage, although everyone declares that no one could have lived till morning in the icy waters. The morning was bitter cold on our deck because of the proximity of ice in such immense proportions.

One iceberg of any size was the sole one disengaged from the field, and it was egg-shaped in so far as could be seen above the water. All others were pointed, or ragged-topped, or split, or generally irregular. One on the icefield, an immense one, had the shape of a giant piece of cake, cut to the center of the cake and laid on its side, wedge shaped. My husband took several snapshots of these icebergs and a good one of the egg-shaped one floating out by itself separate from the ice fields.

No boats were discovered, and the *Carpathia*'s errand was futile. Swishing and grating against our boat were millions of pieces of ice in size averaging ten to five cubic feet, broken off from the icefield. None of them was a clear piece of ice, as all had opaque, snowy surfaces on them like the icebergs themselves.

The icebergs themselves were snow white and through the glass looked like snow-covered mountains rather than colossal cakes of ice. We naturally were very nervous over the icebergs being so near our boat. It seemed unsafe. But we were at a sufficient distance, and we were told no risk was taken, although it seemed so to us at the time.

We were shown the particular iceberg the *Titanic* struck, but no one seemed to be absolutely certain. One woman told us the iceberg was as high as her ship the *Titanic*, while another said it was very small above the waterline. We are informed that as a rule seven-eighths of the volume of the iceberg is below the waterline and but one-eighth alone to be seen.

This fact, and the fact also that ledges often extend out for hundreds of feet underwater, make a vessel hit the iceberg long before it appears to be really up to it.

Our boat, since it took a southern course, was not in the path of the iceberg, but upon call from the *Titanic* by wireless around 11:30 it traveled in haste sixty miles out of its course to help the ill-fated boat. It was, of course, considerable risk to our boat to approach the boat so near for the reason that they were dodging icebergs at night themselves to do so. But we knew nothing of that danger. We all noticed how bitter cold it was upon rising in the morning.

The distress on board I shall never be able to picture. One poorly clad lower class woman hurried about on the first class deck, sobbing and crazed as she peered over the sides for her family. No one could understand her in her trouble, as she spoke no English. My husband and I helped a Mr. and Mrs. Pritchard and a Mr. and Mrs. Phelps of North Adams, Mass., move all of their belongings into one room and give the vacant stateroom to a richly garbed mother and three daughters, all grown, who had lost father and son. They bore up bravely until they learned all boats were in, when they could restrain their grief no longer.

My husband and I had become well acquainted with a Mr. and Mrs. Chas. Iddiols, who sat at our table, and they made up two extra berths in their stateroom, and we went into that and gave up our room to the shipwrecked, one of them being Mrs. Smith, a young bride of a year who had been in the Holy Lands, and who is a daughter of Rep. Hughes of West Virginia. She is so beautiful and is but eighteen years old.

Mrs. Smith says her husband leisurely ate an apple while she dressed and took her onto deck and put her in a lifeboat, standing by himself to allow all women to be saved first.

Mrs. Smith blames the captain in not having been on duty on the bridge. She says that three times the watch in the crow's nest telephoned to the bridge that icebergs were in sight, but the captain was not there. She says Captain Smith was a social man and a dear old fellow and was anxious to make fine times etc., but she said he wasn't ever on duty like our captain of the *Carpathia*.

Mrs. Smith says the *Titanic* was grand beyond description. Her stateroom had a private bath, a couch, and red electric lights to imitate log fires. The deck had a walk as wide as an entire smoking room, five times the width of ours, and her husband called it a race course. Mrs. Smith said no one who had not been aboard had any idea how grand the boat really was, and also, of the size.

We also made up with a nurse girl who was saved with a baby eleven months old. Her mistress and master, she said, did not think the accident would amount to much and did not hurry to dress. The maid, however, was alarmed and dressed the baby and hurried on deck. The maid never saw them again. There was also another child, two and one-half years old.

The baby is as beautiful a child as I have ever seen, a boy. The father's name was Hudson Allison, of Toronto. The faithfulness of the nurse is pathetic, and she never left the baby for a moment.

Mrs. Gilbert, who ate at our table, went into her stateroom and asked if she could do anything for three women she had placed there, and was met with this – 'No, thank you, there is nothing you can do; we have all lost our husbands.' The shock to her was terrible.

There are three brides saved who were on their honeymoon. Two had their new husbands saved with them, the other lost hers.

Two pet dogs came aboard safely, both small long-haired curs. I have an insane desire to kick them. A woman, richly dressed, ate one day at our table and said all her party was saved, 'as it consisted of but three women'. First class women were nearly all saved. There were no boats left for the men.

Any steerage passengers who were saved forced themselves onto deck, as they were trying to keep them back until first class were saved.

Many men came on board in full dress, also women, they having not yet retired. One man, a Mr. Haven, of New York, said he was playing cards with Mr. Case, of the Standard Oil, when they heard a thud, and while they noticed it, did not think much of it.

He played on for nearly an hour, when a man told him he would better go up on deck, and he did so. Mr. Case, however, said he didn't think it would amount to anything, and that is the last he saw of Mr. Case, who has never appeared.

Mr. Haven waited, as he was ordered, until the women had been place in boats, but when he saw twenty stokers make a rush for a boat, he jumped on the back of one big sailor and was thus able to enter the boat.

While the other boats were being loaded, no man was allowed to enter, and anyone who did was ordered out or he'd be shot.

We were about 1,200 miles from New York when the accident occurred, and immediately after circling the icefield, about noon, set sail back to New York with the saved aboard.

Mr. J. Bruce Ismay, president and manager of the White Star Line, was one of the passengers aboard, and he was saved. He has not yet appeared on deck, and Mrs. Smith and other rescued of the *Titanic* say he knows better than to risk his presence among his people. It is reported that he was asked on the other ship whether he was going to leave his ship, and he replied that he intended to save himself.

Captain Smith of the *Titanic* had been promoted to his office as a mark of appreciation and was taking his last trip before retiring, he having reached the age limit, sixty years. Many say he shot himself when he found there was no hope for his boat.

The ship was seen by several of the rescued to break in half before sinking. The electric lights were burning until the lights themselves reached the water's edge, and the clicking of the wireless could be heard until the deck was to the water's edge, although the apparatus was not able to connect with our vessel after its first message.[35]

❖ ❖ ❖

CHARLES IDDIOLS

After the *Carpathia* arrived in New York, Mr Iddiols sent the following telegram to his hometown newspaper:

> Have returned with 745 of rescued *Titanic* passengers. Experienced wonderful thrilling rescue amidst floating icebergs and field of ice twenty-four miles square on which were forty icebergs. Went ninety miles out of our course after receiving wireless to reach scene of disaster, where we held memorial service before we left. Our steamer was in no danger at any time. We sail again for Naples to-morrow.[36]

❖ ❖ ❖

ARPAD LENGYEL

In May of 1912, Dr Lengyel wrote the following account of the *Carpathia*'s rescue of the *Titanic*'s survivors:

> Already a month has passed since the terrible news that shook the world that the pride of the White Star Line, the 45,000 ton *Titanic* – which was thought to be unsinkable – sank and hundreds of people died. And although time has passed, people still cannot forget the catastrophic loss of life.
>
> An odd feeling took hold of me Sunday and Monday, when I realized I was the first of my countrymen to learn about the tragedy. Only those who have been at sea can imagine the thoughts such news brings when out on the ocean and at the mercy of the sea.
>
> I will never forget the moment when my steward ran abruptly into my cabin to wake me up, and although he didn't know the reason, his behavior showed urgency and with the mobilization of *Carpathia*'s crew at

1 a.m., obviously something terrible had happened. At first I thought it concerned a patient, as often is the case, but as I was getting dressed, the British doctor came in and informed me he had important news, that the new *Titanic* was sinking. I didn't want to believe it, it seemed like a nightmare, but unfortunately it was true.

To begin, I should mention that during our stay in New York the weather was quite cold, and on 9 April, two days before *Carpathia*'s departure, it snowed. We left New York on the 11th at exactly 12 noon, and apart from the cold we had a pleasant voyage for three days.

On the 14th our passengers went to bed early, and when I retired about 11:30 p.m. with my Italian colleague, everybody was already asleep.

The sky was clear, full of stars, and the sea was calm and smooth. When I had dressed I hurried to the place designated for the officers, and there I learnt that a Marconigram received at 0:35 a.m. requested assistance for *Titanic* that was sinking; her position latitude 41.46, longitude 50.14.

Carpathia's crew of over 300 were alerted to wait for the captain's orders. Our ship was 1,095 nautical miles from New York at latitude 41.11, longitude 49.01, that is, to the southeast and some forty-five to forty-eight miles from *Titanic*.

Arthur H. Rostron, commander, informed us that we were in the vicinity of ice and that *Titanic* had hit an iceberg, and although he didn't believe there was any serious danger, *Carpathia* would steam northwest, possibly to be of help to thousands of passengers.

Along with the British and the Italian doctor, we were asked to prepare for all eventualities, for if the news were true there could be many injured and in need of medical attention.

I should mention that until 12 midnight British officer Bisset and Hungarian officer Gusztav Rath were on duty and had seen icebergs off in the distance but had assumed their proximity was not untypical from the soundings taken earlier that measured the temperature of the water.

Carpathia's average 13 knot speed was increased to the maximum of 18 on her new course. Out 1,100 passengers were sleeping peacefully and had no idea of what was happening.

A few who were awakened by the movements of the crew thought that a drill was taking place, for on Cunard ships the crew gathers at the lifeboat stations once a week. The stations of the doctors were divided so that the British doctor went to the first class dining room, the Italian doctor to second class, and I was assigned to the surgery in steerage. It is the lowest entrance on the ship, and later we lifted survivors through those doors.

It was my responsibility to classify and assign where they would stay on board. At all three medical stations we prepared alleviatives and excitants which were in abundance in our dispensary, as well as dressings and instruments. We also set up several stretchers, prepared splints for fractures, gathered cognac and whiskey – and from the kitchen prepared pots of tea and coffee as well as large quantities of food.

Our fever-ward was empty, our patients were taken there; we obtained two wards with thirty-two completely equipped beds ready to admit patients. Large quantities of blankets were brought up from storage and heated; since it was very late at night, we knew the passengers would have inadequate clothing, or that we would have to remove wet clothes from some and they would need warm blankets. Later, of course, it was proven that this foresight had not been in vain.

Central heating was turned on in every room, too, and two giant sterilizing machines on the upper deck of the ship were set right away. The stewards concerned with nursing were allocated to the surgery and to the ward to assist the doctors.

When we were finished with the medical preparation I hurried on deck and saw that by then our ship had been clearly lit by reflectors. The seamen were busy with turning the lifeboats out so that they could be used without delay; they opened the shell doors, lowered rope ladders and fastened pulleys to the gangways. About two o'clock when we thought that we were within eyesight of the disaster scene, rockets were continuously launched from the bridge so that the survivors would see that help was on its way. As my eyes became accustomed to the darkness I could begin to make out icebergs all around us, bluishly gleaming under the light of the stars, between which *Carpathia* maintained her speed which was not without danger in spite of her double watch and by the captain and the officers.

Our commander made preparations considering every possibility despite the fact at that time no one was aware of the magnitude of the catastrophe; our officers were of the opinion that there wouldn't be much amiss, but it was our duty to be ready for all possibilities.

After two o'clock a flashing blue light was sighted to starboard; this, I later learned, was the only boat in which the shipwrecked had a magnesium light. Shortly a number of small lights were glimmering all over the smooth surface of the ocean and we all realized what we'd heard about *Titanic* had been real. We agonized on the number of lives lost, estimating the ship was more than three times the size of *Carpathia*. We knew that it is normally impossible to launch all lifeboats in such a short time.

It was after three o'clock that the first boat, occupied by some twenty-five people arrived and we anxiously waited for news of the others. They were thrown ropes and they pulled themselves up to our gangway. The crying coming from the lifeboat pierced one to the marrow.

Hankinson, our chief officer, encouraged them to climb up the rope ladder hanging over the side, while one of our crew climbed down to show how it's done. However, despite repeated attempts, the people sitting in the boat couldn't manage the climb; their limbs were numb from the bitter cold and they had to be lifted one at a time by pulleys to reach the safety of *Carpathia*'s deck.

Those in the boats were mainly women and children wearing life belts. As I learnt later, only as many men were admitted in the boats as was necessary to handle them.

The children were pulled up first, one at a time, in canvas bags which kept them from falling. They were followed by the women, who were lifted onboard in a swing-like bench lowered on ropes, and lastly the men came. As soon as they were on deck, we cut their life belts off.

They all came to the surgery which was next to the gangway, and after they had been served a warm drink and given a blanket, and if they had no injuries, they were guided to their appropriate class.

Those with injuries or wounded were taken to the ward on stretchers, where they received the necessary medical attention.

The crying from some of the survivors brought immediate sympathy; upon their arrival when the realization of their loss hit, they broke out again with more crying. Some were looking for their children, others for their parents, still others for their spouses. It was terrible to watch. When I tried to say some comforting words to some of the women, they fell about my neck; often I could hardly free myself from their tight grip. But it was more horrible to listen to the awful crying from the men, to which the stoic British had two words of comfort: 'Be Englishmen' with a compassionate slap.

Members of families who had been separated in different boats were eventually reunited.

A young woman in a blue hat was crying and looking for her baby; she knew her husband was dead, the baby was her only child. I sent several children to her until she recognized the fourth one as hers and she held it closely to her breast.

One lifeboat had been commanded by only women; many were dressed elegantly, some wore men's trousers, thinking they were more practical than the narrow skirts in fashion. Many women were in evening dresses and some gentlemen wore tuxedos. Many had only bathrobes, some didn't even have time to put on their shoes.

Mr. Ismay, the managing director of the White Star Line, was one of those who were saved. A young banker called Daniels in a torn, red nightshirt kept insisting he was a doctor. I didn't want a colleague to be left without clothes so I gave him mine.

The following day, when I talked to him again, he couldn't recall. He must have been delirious!

Many people were injured jumping from the ship and over two wards were filled with patients suffering from bruises and fractures.

In some boats the occupants were sitting knee-deep in water. Five people were holding onto an ice floe, then swam and were lifted to boats not far from our ship. There were some who were in the water for some time including the second Marconi operator and two first-class passengers. One seaman who was taken on board a lifeboat was assumed dead, and it was only later that I noticed that he was alive; his condition improved during the afternoon, so much so that he complained only of being tired.

The last to board were four young officers; they were in charge of various boats and had waited for all survivors to disembark. Before coming aboard, they lifted four dead from the boats to our ship. Although I felt badly for them, I could only take a cursory look for I knew that within a few hours they would be committed to the eternal deep again. One was face down in the water in the bottom of the boat and had drowned. There were no outer marks of injury on any, which means that their cause of death had been freezing or being crushed to death, but it is also possible that the unfortunate had died of heart failure or seizure. It must have been around ten o'clock that all survivors had come aboard.

Our passengers who watched the rescue work were filled with all kinds of emotion. As I heard later, there were some among our first-class passengers who were indignant that steerage passengers were let aboard among them, and only when they learnt that the survivors were more affluent than they themselves did they try to console them. The passengers in steerage, some 800, half were Hungarian and half were Italian, had awoken earlier and accepted the restrictions without complaint in order to accommodate survivors including their first meal served late in the afternoon!

Naturally, I calmed and informed them of the work we were doing, and they were standing at the bars of their door crying and praying.

The officers, starting with the captain and the greater part of the male passengers, gave their cabins over to the survivors, and the members of our crew gave their bunks. My cabin was occupied by four women, and they gave me half an hour every day to have a wash in the cabin.

We picked up survivors from sixteen boats and, as there wasn't more space, we took thirteen with us to New York.

When daylight came I saw where the giant ship sank; a few hundred feet away there was a large patch where the clear blue water had tinged to an ugly brown; floating chairs and wooden parts marked the scene of disaster. *Titanic*'s doctors were lost, although it was said that the younger one was offered a chance to survive; he didn't accept.

It is strange that although the passengers were equipped with life belts, we didn't see anyone swimming or any corpses.

I saw a huge two-peaked iceberg emerging high above the water and as the survivors say, it stood high above the deck of *Titanic*; it can be assumed that it must have been at least ten stories high.

In one of the boats a sail had been rigged, and we also saw two empty boats that we left; there was no trace of the sunken ship, quite understandable; according to the chart the sea was 3,600 meters deep.

As soon as the rescue work was finished, we commenced separating the more seriously injured who needed medical attention immediately. There were forty-two wounded; many had broken ankles and fractures in their limbs. From a medical point of view it is interesting to note that although many were exposed to cold in inappropriate clothing, there were no cold-related illnesses.

There were two wards totaling thirty-two beds with two sick. There were many more affected emotionally. Women fainted, some had convulsions, others cried or laughed from delirium. There were many whose symptoms evaded my attention because of the linguistic barrier. I am convinced there will be many survivors whose whole life will be affected such as cases of mass hysteria reoccurring or irregular menstruation.

We did everything possible to make the women comfortable; our ladies sewed clothes from blankets and similar available material on board; everybody gave them their extra garments and the survivors expressed their deep gratitude.

It was late when we were finally finished assisting the survivors. The four dead taken from the lifeboats were committed to the deep after being sewn in canvas equipped with iron weights, having previously been identified by one of *Titanic*'s officers. According to regulations, the ship's crew stopped for a moment, the bells of the bridge and the crow's nest struck alternately. People on deck watched the sad spectacle as a priest, who was a passenger, said a prayer as the dead were dropped in the sea. There were five priests altogether on this voyage; they arranged a divine service, heard confessions and consoled the passengers.

A list of survivors was composed that afternoon. Many found their relatives after several hours, but most people could only grieve.

Two babies were orphaned and left with their nanny, as was a two-year-old French girl and two Czech children who cried continually. Through interpreters' knowledge of languages, they managed to learn their Czech nationality the following day.

A Swedish woman was saved along with two of her daughters, one of whom had contracted pneumonia on *Titanic* and became terminally ill; she lost three of her four children with her husband.

Mrs. Baxter, who was from Montreal, had an operation in Paris, a feminine matter, boarded the ship two days afterwards with her daughter and her 23-year old son. They were saved but her son was lost; he had gone to Captain Smith, who reassured him to return to his cabin and go back to sleep.

For that matter, most of the survivors thought that they were getting in the lifeboats temporarily, and as soon as *Titanic*'s damage had been fixed, they would return.

Many people have asked me to talk about some of the rumors such as were any of the survivors men who wore women's clothes? I remember a young man who had a skirt on; naturally, I didn't think that he did this deliberately; there was nothing else available that he could put on quickly.

The story of the two Chinamen who hid under the seat of the lifeboat and were thus saved is true; one of them had a small parcel.

There were numerous so-called eye-witness stories, only a fraction of which were true.

Mrs. Astor, who was said to be very beautiful, assumed almost legendary qualities; she was said to be giving money away open-handedly although she had nothing except the clothes she was wearing and kept to herself all the way to New York.

Among others, I have an excerpt from a newspaper where a woman on *Carpathia* with a vivid imagination told this story: 'the *Carpathia*'s gallant doctor, Dr. Lengyel, got in a boat and hurried to the aid of those floundering in the water. The lifeboat was equipped with a long metal rod with a hook, which the seamen used to pull the floating bodies. It was a sorry sight when Dr. Lengyel threw a human body back into the water, saying "Frozen!"' She was the only one of *Carpathia*'s passengers who saw *Titanic* while it was still sinking!

There are countless made-up stories which the New York reporters bought for a good price. A clever waiter from *Carpathia* drew the sinking *Titanic*. His minute by minute account from his imagination and this picture was published in major illustrated papers around the world; the *New York Herald* bought it for 500 dollars.

Paintings and photographs of icebergs were made by a painter on board *Carpathia* who was paid handsomely for his work.

Later, about 10 o'clock, we met two ships looking for survivors. They came very close to us so that they could inform our commander by signal that they had found none of the ill-fated passengers. One of the ships was the French *Kalifornia* [sic], the other the Russian *Burma* [sic] in the middle of the ocean.

The meals were adequate, even abundant. The survivors received theirs first, then our passengers and finally our crew. There was enough food on board for everyone for several months; our larder was full. Upon our arrival in New York, after the survivors were gone the ship was resupplied mainly with coal, medicine, dressing material and clean laundry.

On the afternoon of the 18th we were impatient to land. In spite of the bad weather almost everybody was on deck, happy that we reached the *Ambrose* lightship, twenty-six miles off the coast of New York, where the pilot, the doctor who inspected the ship and mail were hoisted aboard.

By now the rain cleared away the fog.

About seven o'clock a flotilla of small craft rented by newspaper reporters were waiting for us. There were large sign boards on each stating the names of their newspaper. They greeted us by tooting their whistles and asked to be let aboard, which the captain declined. However, one man from one of the Hearst papers got on the moving ship under the pretense that he was delivering mail, but he didn't have a chance to bother the passengers because the captain summoned him first.

As it was getting dark, flashes from cameras fired one after another, and their boats kept following us until we reached the dock. It was after nine o'clock when we reached the quay that was illuminated by electric lights; the huge electric letters spelling Cunard were brightly lit.

On landing in front of the dock building facing the Hudson River, there were a great many people waiting; it was noisy with shouting, but everyone was happy we arrived. The waiting room was full of newspapermen anticipating interviews from the passengers leaving the ship.

At debarkation the scenes witnessed on our ship at the time of the rescue were repeated. However, this time it was not only those arriving, but also the waiting relatives crying and looking for their family and friends. Ambulances from the New York hospitals showed up in full number at the dock, and they were busy with not only those who had been ill previously but also with new cases of sickness.

It also caused a lot of confusion and discomfort, since the names of those saved on *Carpathia* were listed on the 18th as dead; survivors read their names in the papers which had arrived with the mail picked up at the light ship.

Before our arrival, survivors from first class had formed a committee which collected several thousand dollars, partly for the benefit of the destitute survivors and partly for *Carpathia*'s hardworking crew. Those who could leave on their own accord went first while the sick were disembarked quickly, among them two children who had been diagnosed with rubella on the last day. They caught the infection in Europe, for we had not rubella on our ship before. Although we had a thorough disinfection done, on our return voyage another child came down with the same ten days after this case. Since they had not disembarked in between, he must have caught it from one of the child survivors.

It was late at night when it became quiet around our ship, and the crew could finally rest more peacefully. The time of departure was set for the following day, the 19th, at four o'clock. All the newspapers were full of praise for our ship; many prominent people came to visit *Carpathia*, which was crowded with flocks of reporters and photographers.

Because of the disaster some passengers had second thoughts and left the ship in New York. Among others, ten Hungarian families gave up their intention to visit their old home completely. On the other hand, *Carpathia* became so famous that many prominent passengers bought a ticket for her new voyage.

We departed at exactly four p.m., followed by cheering from thousands of people. Until we left the Hudson River and reached the open sea, cheers and farewells from people on board numerous coastal vessels also reached us. Every approaching vessel, naval vessels not being an exception, greeted *Carpathia* with a triple blast of their whistles.

On the first Sunday of the return leg of our voyage at the Anglican service held by Commander Rostron, he admitted publicly that the ship had been in grave danger indeed. The deeply religious man said with tears in his eyes that he felt he had to go amongst the icebergs, and that success would follow his deed; this is why he dared to risk his ship and her passengers.

There have been many discussions about causes of the disaster, but at this time it has not been possible to state anything definitive. Many blame the insufficiency of lifeboats. The fact remains that it is next to impossible to carry enough to accommodate every passenger, and even if enough were provided, it would be impossible to ready them for use in time, for the boats are arranged in several rows on the uppermost deck, the outer ones hanging on davits. Before lowering, they have to be turned outwards, which requires a lot of work in itself. It is only later that the inner boats can be fastened to the davits, and then, having been turned outwards, lowered. Even in the event of an emergency it would make no difference, for before they could be readied the ship would sink. *Titanic*'s collapsible boats could not all be made ready in time, and in those that had been assembled some passengers were too scared to get in.

Progress in shipbuilding technology has been miraculous, but regarding their lifesaving capability there is much to be done; there has been hardly any progress in the arrangement and the fitting out of lifeboats.

There were no condemning words to be heard from Captain Rostron; he only said that he had not seen any iceberg in this route in the last eight years and that such a heavy concentration of bergs and ice floes to be carried down from the north last occurred sixty years ago. He stated with confidence that *Titanic* would not have sunk if she had hit the iceberg head-on; the cause of the fatal outcome was that the collision took place sideways and as one side of the ship sprung, the fate was sealed partly by the entering water and partly by the boiler explosion caused by uneven pressure. He didn't speculate on the mistakes of the crew or the captain, shipping companies' race for speed, human vanity and greed, all of which may have been contributing factors.

I must end with mentioning Marconi, whose genius created the wireless telegraph, the only hope of travelers at sea which at a time of danger attracts help for those in need.

His spark illuminates the ocean, and by its virtue the travelers at sea can feel that they have not been completely cut off from the outside world.[37]

It was apparently in later years that Dr Lengyel wrote another account of his experiences on the *Carpathia*:

We left the dock of the Cunard Line on 11th April at exactly 12 o'clock noon. Despite the cold weather, we had an excellent voyage for three days. On the 14th – because of the cold – the passengers retired early in the evening. When I – at around half past twelve – went to rest along with my Italian colleague, everybody was already asleep. At this time the night was beautifully starlit and moonless, and the sea was smooth and calm. On this day until midnight, that is until 12 p.m., the second officer of the ship, the British Bisset, and the Hungarian Gusztav Rath were – because of the ice danger – on reinforced duty as watchmen. When I bid them goodbye before retiring, they said that they had already seen a number of icebergs in the distance, and that they had marked this down in the log. In order to increase safety the temperature of the sea was constantly being measured by the quartermasters, because its rapid cooling and the formation of patches of haze spreading over the surface water are the most reliable signs of the vicinity of icebergs.

I had hardly been sleeping for an hour when the captain of the ship alarmed the officers. I had a feeling that there had been some kind of an accident. I had almost finished dressing up when the British doctor came in and said the following excitedly: 'Doctor! A big thing! The *Titanic* is sinking!'

Together with him I went up to the designated meeting point of the officers. It was here that we found out that at 0.55 o'clock we had received a wireless in which the sinking *Titanic* was asking for urgent assistance. Her position: latitude 41.46, longitude 50.14.

At this moment our ship was 45–48 miles (approximately 92 kilometers) from the position of the *Titanic*. The captain asked us doctors – there were three of us: one Hungarian, one British and one Italian – to get ready for every possible kind of assistance, because if the situation really gets serious, many injured will probably have to be assisted medically.

Including the passengers in the steerage we had 1,100 passengers on board, who slept on blissfully, not suspecting anything. Those who were nevertheless woken up by the unusual commotion were told that the crew of the ship was having a night drill of abandoning ship. It was a regulation on Cunard ships that once or twice a week – during the day or in the night – a lifeboat or fire alarm drill had to be held for the personnel. This ensured that every necessary measure was learnt thoroughly and could be performed perfectly by the crew.

We, the ship's surgeons, divided up our duties in the following way: the British doctor got the first class dining saloon, the Italian doctor was in charge of the second class. I remained in the between deck's surgery close to the ship's side. It was here that we intended to lift the shipwrecked out of the water or of the lifeboats onboard our ship. I had to perform the first inspections, and after that I told them where to stay on the ship. At all three medical stations we had already laid ready in advance the tranquilizers, stimulants, medicines, instruments and syringes, of which we had an ample supply in our pharmacy. We also prepared the stretchers and the rails and wire cord needed for the reduction of fractures. We fetched brandy and whiskey from the pantries. In the kitchens we had many hectoliters of tea, coffee and nourishing liquid food made.

In order to relieve my nervousness, I went up on deck to take a walk of a few steps and to breathe some fresh air. I saw that at the railing reflectors had been set up in a circle. This made it possible to light the surface of the water around the ship well. The front-, side- and rear-lookouts on duty on the masts had been doubled. In canvas sacks every ten meters, lookouts had been posted on both sides of the ship at the level of the waterline. The safety nets, ropes and pulley blocks were already in position, so that those possibly escaping by swimming could hold onto something. Rostron, the captain, took over command of the ship, doing his job so conscientiously that he did not leave the bridge for almost five days. (And then, at the thanksgiving service – which he conducted himself – he collapsed from exhaustion.)

After half past two we noticed a blue flashing light on the starboard side of the ship. I found out later that only in this lifeboat was there a magnesium torch, the light of which can be seen far away and which even penetrates fog. Not much after we saw a number of tiny lights all around our ship. It was after three o'clock that we reached the first lifeboat. We stopped the engines and started the rescue.

This was the last lifeboat that had left the sinking ship. We threw down a rope to them from our ship, and with its help they pulled themselves to the side door that in the meantime had been opened. Those in the boat were crying and moaning heartrendingly. Hankinson, the first officer of the *Carpathia*, was encouraging and calming them down to climb the lowered rope ladder one by one. One of our seamen actually climbed down to help them. But the shipwrecked in the lifeboat were so frozen – partly from the cold, partly from the excitement they had experienced – that they were unable to climb the ladder unaided.

As soon as the rescued reached the between deck, we cut away their lifebelts. After that everyone came to the surgery beside the stairs – that is, to me. They took off their wet clothes and received dry, warm blankets and hot tea and coffee.

Partly as a result of the throng, partly of jumping in the water from the sinking ship, many people had been injured. For this reason our two sickbays were soon filled with people who had suffered bruises and bone fractures. In some boats the passengers had been in water up to their knees. Five people – first having climbed on top of an ice floe – escaped by swimming. There were some who had swum two or three hours in the ice-cold water. These included the second radio operator of the *Titanic* and two first class passengers. One seaman was pulled out of the water as 'dead' – I noticed only later that he was alive. By the afternoon he complained only of being tired. The last to board the ship were the four junior officers of the *Titanic*. They had been in charge of the lifeboats, and as befits a sailor, they had waited until all of their shipwrecked were safe.

The doctors of the *Titanic* met heroic death as well. The youngest of them was offered a place in a lifeboat, but he gave it up in favor of a woman and chose death instead. Of the crew of the *Titanic* some 250 were saved. Those who were healthy were immediately ordered on service duty on our ship. So for instance the radio officer mentioned before – although both of his ankles had been broken – offered to relieve our dead-tired radio officer. He was carried to the device in arms because he could not walk.

The survivors included Bruce Ismay, president of the White Star Line. Because the survivors blamed him for the disaster, he shut himself up in his cabin for the whole voyage and in New York left our ship secretly, accompanied by detectives.

The disaster had 1600 fatalities, we saved altogether 705 people, 42 were injured. From a medical point of view it is interesting that there were no cold-related illnesses at all. There were mostly bruises and fractures: leg, ankle, wrist, rib and upper arm. As we had only 32 sickbeds, we put the more lightly injured two to a bed. Cases resulting from nervous breakdown were more numerous than injuries. Fainting, fits of weeping and laugh[ter], tossing and turning, delirium, melancholy, attempted suicide, mass hysteria. Many women had premature menstruation.

After our rescue operation, at around ten o'clock, three ships appeared on the scene. Based on the distress signals they had received, they were also looking for the shipwrecked. Although they had been closer to the scene than we, they did not dare to move because of the ice danger. These ships were the British *Californian*, the German *Frankfurt* and the Russian *Birma*.

Our voyage back to New York was sorrowful and shocking. It was a stroke of luck that the Cunard Line stored five times more medicine and medical supplies onboard than required by the regulations. Because of this we did not have a shortage of anything. We reached New York and the brightly-lit Cunard Line dock at nine o'clock in the evening on 18th April. It was then that the new slogan of the 45-year-old Cunard Line was born: 'We never lost life.'[38]

While the *Carpathia* was bound for New York, Miss List wrote the following letter:

Carpathia
April 17 – 1912

Dearest Olga,

I bet you will be surprised to hear from me but maybe you know all about the dreadful disaster that has upset our voyage.

Last Sunday at midnight the *Titanic* one of the largest boats afloat went straight down and of 3000 people just 712 were saved who are now on our boat.

Just think of our state now we are in America again while we could be in Gibraltar by now of course its nice that our boat saved them but it will be about a month before we see Europe.

Believe me I think I'd rather stay in America after such a trip I think I've seen and heard so much of misery.

I am not well, the very first day I came aboard I was seasick and now to go all through it over again believe me I am so disgusted.

No wonder I was afraid of this boat and I don't like it anywhere near the *Carmania*.

Well if I get over it I think I won't cross the ocean very soon again.

Of course now that the *Titanic* went down I think any boat is liable to go down I don't trust them any more especially when we saved the people we were surrounded all around with icebergs and some were awful big too.

I never saw anything like it before and the crew said too that they are at sea for years but they have never seen the like.

I hope if we get to New York they will let us off so I could get some things because everything I had is near gone and we have a very long journey before us.

The weather is very rough too, and at the time of the wreck it was so calm that is why they could be saved, if it had been weather like it is now I think none would have been saved.

Well any way we thank our lucky stars that it is we who saved and not they saved us, though it would have been nicer if we could have saved all of them but she sank so quick that it was impossible.

I hope I could have a chance of seeing you once more but I can't tell if we land or if they just send a small boat out to take them off or what will be. I have tried hard to find out, but everyone says something different whereas one told me they don't know themselves yet and will only know when we're there.

If you find out anything about the *Carpathia* and you have a chance to write, well please write, and if you can cut out of the papers about the wreck if you don't send it to me now send it in your letter to Bpest.

If you write to me on the *Carpathia* maybe you could just address

A. List
Carpathia Steamer
Cunard Line
or to Bpest
A. List
Budapest
Hungary Europe
Poste Restante

I have no more news to write but send love to all of you and all my friends in [illegible] and [illegible].

I remain as ever
Your sincere friend and krisnotko
Anna[39]

'MARY'

While the *Carpathia* was returning to New York, Mary wrote a letter to 'C ...' describing the rescue of the *Titanic*'s passengers.

Mary apologised for her 'pencil scrawl' and explained that she was writing her letter while sitting on the open deck. She described how she had awakened on Sunday night and heard the ship's engines running at 'double speed' as they went to the *Titanic*'s assistance. At first she didn't realise the magnitude of the disaster, but, when she did, she hurriedly put on her clothes and went up on deck. Although the sky had just barely begun to brighten well before the sunrise, icebergs were visible all around, and Mary could see survivors being taken out of the *Titanic*'s lifeboats and was amazed that there wasn't another sign that the huge White Star liner had ever been there.

Mary wrote that 700 of the *Titanic*'s 3,000 passengers were saved and that the *Carpathia* was now filled to overflowing with people. She commented on the fact that many of the women had lost their husbands and that no more than twenty or thirty first-class men were saved. All of the *Carpathia*'s passengers took survivors into their cabins and provided them with spare clothing.

Mary wrote that the survivors were so dazed on the first day that they just sat and 'cried silently', but she was nevertheless impressed by their bravery. She commented on the fact that the survivors saved only the 'clothes on their backs' and mentioned that several little children had been orphaned. She also mentioned that all of the survivors kept repeating that they couldn't get the screams of the dying swimmers out of their ears. Mary thought it was wicked for any ship to put to sea carrying 3,000 passengers with lifeboats enough for only 900, and she wrote that 'of course' the problem was that the *Titanic* was trying to achieve a 'record run' and didn't slow down for icebergs.[40]

MARGARET MAURO

On 18 April Mrs Philip Mauro wrote the following letter to her sister and family:

Royal Mail Steamer *Carpathia*
'His Wonders in the DEEP'

My Beloved Ones: –
   The unparalleled experiences of the last four days have left me without words to write. – One fact stands forth with luminous clearness: CHRIST HAS BEEN GLORIFIED. God's mighty, mighty hand has bent circumstances to create opportunities for testimony to the NAME which is above every name.
   The haughtiness of man shall be bowed down – the Captain of man shall be brought low – and JEHOVAH ALONE shall be exalted in that Day. Amen. Amen.
   My heart is too full, dear ones. – I can write no more. My love in Christ – more warm, more deep, more tender than ever – to all the 'Sons' which GOD is bringing to GLORY among you. How often – how often have I thought of them upon the DEEP.
   My love with your precious household
   Margaret
   delighting in God's good, acceptable, perfect WILL.[41]

PHILIP MAURO

On 16 April Mr Mauro began writing a letter to his daughter Isabel and added instalments to the letter during the next two days. Mr Mauro was awakened by the stopping of the *Carpathia*'s engines. He went to his wife's cabin, awakened her and told her to dress and come on deck immediately. Mr Mauro then went up on deck:

The scene that greeted our eyes when we went on deck ... yesterday [Monday] morning is indescribable. We were lying a few thousand yards from a perfect continent of ice, which stretched as far as the eye could reach, with here and there huge ice peaks sticking up into the air. And all around us in the sea were detached icebergs glistening in the sun. It was a perfect, polar scene, and although it was only yesterday, and although we remained for hours skirting along the icefield looking for boats and bodies, it seems already like a dream – so unreal and strange does it appear. Surely the hand of God is most manifestly appearing in the affairs of men.

Mr Mauro wrote that, out of a passenger and crew tally of approximately 2,300, only 'about 745 persons in all, mostly women', survived the tragedy and were taken aboard the *Carpathia*. After remaining on the spot until the prospect of further rescues was extinguished, the *Carpathia* headed for New York.

You can imagine the depression and discomfort pervading this boat, with such a cargo of concentrated abjectness and misery added to the rather full passenger list that we had at the start. There are more *Titanic* passengers than *Carpathians*, and, of course, there are no accommodations for them in the ordinary sense.

I gave up my room which has four bunks and spent the night in a steamer chair. Do not expect to take any clothes off till we reach New York. The first- and second-class dining rooms and the writing room were filled with women lying on the floors, tables, and sofas. The smoking rooms were allotted to the men. I tried one but could not stand it. Possibly by tonight things will be better arranged.

Margaret has given away most of her things (underwear, etc.). There has been [no great demand] for masculine apparel – but I quickly parted with some stockings, pajamas, and handkerchiefs, besides the nice, felt slippers my dear Charlie gave me. The dozen toothbrushes I had were most acceptable. Of course the people had absolutely nothing but what was on their persons – not even hand togs. They were told up to the last few moments that there was no danger of the ship's going down.

Wednesday. The opportunities are opening out. A splendid one was offered this morning before breakfast. A young man, Albert A. Dick, was saved with his wife (married less than a year ago). The Lord put him in my way. He has made money (three quarters of a million, he told me) and is about quitting business, meaning to devote the rest of his life to 'doing good'. Said he was not a Christian, but had been reading the Bible trying to find out if there were a God. Was quite ready to listen, and I gave him the truth for some hours. He was in a state similar to that of the Ethiopian treasurer. I am sure the Lord sent him to me and that He gave me the word for him. He lives way off in Calgary, Alberta. Pray that the Lord may bring him clearly into the light and supply the ministry he needs. Also that his wife may also be saved. She seems disinclined to hear or to allow him to hear. When she appeared, he said 'My dear, this gentleman is telling me how he came to be a Christian, and I mean to be one too'.

Margaret has been very busy, ministering in the second cabin and steerage. And all that she has been doing is being discussed, and so is turning into a testimony. The whole shipload (with few exceptions) will have received the testimony of a living Christ.

Among the rescued passengers is a child of God, a young man named Collett, author of *Scripture Truth*. Has considerable light.

Thursday. We are expecting to reach New York this evening. The opportunities that have opened for ministry have been simply wonderful. Most of them care to Margaret. Such a day as she had yesterday! Hope she may be able to write you some of the marvelous doings of the Lord. Now I want you to send a copy of the *World and its God* to A.L. Salomon, 345 Broadway, New York ... He is a Jew, but his heart is quite tender just now. It might be good to send him 'The Shepherd of Israel'. It's only 7 a.m. now; but I have already spent more than an hour with another Jew – a wealthy London merchant.

Thursday night. Another busy day. We are quite fatigued but rejoicing that the Lord is working in His own irresistible way. We are about landing and are told we shall leave again early tomorrow.

Charlie's letter was much appreciated. Dearest love to my precious ones and comforting greetings to all the saints.

Father[42]

Mr Mauro wrote the following letter excerpt to his daughter Isabel after the *Carpathia* reached New York:

[The *Carpathia*] docked about nine o'clock ... Thursday evening. A dense crowd, filling the streets leading to the dock and estimated at 25,000 persons, awaited the arrival of the vessel in the hope of merely catching a glimpse of some of the survivors.

Note that the Mauros' daughter, Isabel French, and her husband Charles, were waiting at the wharf when the *Carpathia* came in. They saw two of the *Titanic*'s lifeboats being rowed away to a separate location and saw and heard J. Bruce Ismay, president of the White Star Line, booed and hissed as he came off the *Carpathia*, because he had allowed himself to be rescued.[43]

FRANK M. McGAULEY

After the *Carpathia* arrived in New York, Dr McGauley sent the following telegram to his mother, Mrs Thomas McGauley:

Dear Mother: – In New York again. Dr. Minahan lost; Mrs. and Daisy saved. Awful sight. We leave at 4 o'clock. Telegraph immediately, care of *Carpathia*, if all is well.
Frank McGauley[44]

Dr McGauley also sent a telegram to his friend B.J. Kremer of Fond du Lac, Wisconsin:

Dr. Minahan lost; Mrs. And Daisy safe. We leave at 4 o'clock again. Telegraph me immediately care of *Carpathia*, Cunard Line, if all is well. Notify papers.
Dr. Frank M. McGauley[45]

Before the *Carpathia* sailed again from New York, Dr McGauley sent the following telegram to his hometown newspaper:

New York
April 20

We arrived here Thursday night on the steamer *Carpathia* with 705 passengers of the ill-fated *Titanic* aboard.

From reports secured from all sources it is evident that the *Titanic's* life saving apparatus was insufficient. There were only twenty-two lifeboats to care for 2,200 persons.

The saddest part of the disaster from my point of view is the death of Dr. W.E. Minahan of Fond du Lac, who died a hero.

We found Mrs. Minahan and Daisy Minahan in one of the life boats picked up by members of the *Carpathia's* crew. Like the other survivors they were half clad and suffering terribly from exposure and their terrible experiences.

All reports of the disaster are a mass of heart rending stories of heroism on all sides.

The *Carpathia* was seventy miles south of the *Titanic* when the 'C.Q.D.' wireless flash for help came. All haste was made to reach the sinking ship, the *Carpathia* plowing through the waters at top speed while the passengers lined the rails in an effort to obtain the first glimpse of the *Titanic*.

At daybreak the sight that met our gaze was awful. The sea was strewn with wreckage from the *Titanic* and we saw icebergs in all directions. There were sixteen life boats filled with 705 half dead human beings, some of them floating helplessly about on the ocean.

All the lifeboats were picked up as speedily as possible by the *Carpathia* and all possible assistance and comfort given the survivors.

When the *Titanic* was sinking women and children were given the preference by those who were lowering the life boats and their acts of heroism will go down in history. The band of the *Titanic* was playing 'Nearer My God To Thee' when the ship went down.

The *Titanic* struck the berg at 11:45 o'clock and in two and one-half hours was at the bottom of the sea. At first it was thought that the ship was not badly damaged but she began to sink rapidly and some say that there was an explosion.

On board the *Carpathia* after the rescue of the survivors the scenes were terrible. On every side there were children without parents and wives without husbands.

Everyone on board lent a helping hand and clothed and cared for the suffering human beings. The trip back to New York was one that will never be forgotten as the *Carpathia* was well termed the 'Ship of Sorrow' on her journey into the harbor with the survivors of the greatest ocean tragedy in history.[46]

On 20 April Dr McGauley sent the following letter to R.J. Kremer. McGauley wrote that, from what he could learn, he felt sure that the disaster was due to rank carelessness on the part of the *Titanic*'s officers:

> I will never forget the sight I witnessed Monday morning when I looked out of the cabin window and saw the water literally covered with debris and floating bodies. In sixteen lifeboats were huddled the survivors, many of them half crazed and frozen.[47]

MAURICE McKENNA

After arriving in New York on 18 April, Mr McKenna sent the following account to his hometown newspaper:

New York City
April 19, 1912.

We sailed from New York last Thursday, April 11, 1912 at noon, on the steamship *Carpathia* for Naples, Italy. It was the good fortune of our vessel to save the lives of 712 people consisting of some passengers and part of the crew of the *Titanic*, which was wrecked last Sunday afternoon in the Atlantic ocean about 1200 miles eastward from this port. The night was bright, and the ocean was as calm and peaceful as it could possibly be. We on board our vessel knew nothing of the catastrophe until early next morning, when the engines on our boat suddenly ceased working.

We thought that some accident must have happened to our ship, but on looking out upon the water, we saw it was covered with lifeboats from our own ship, as well as those that were cut away from the *Titanic*. She had sunk some six hours before.

We could see the icebergs in close proximity to our ship, as it went among them seeking people who might be in the water or in some of the boats of the wrecked ship. Standing on the deck of our ship I easily counted twenty icebergs, and there were more in the distance. Some of them stood more than 100 feet in height and looked like pillars or castles of bright and brilliant glass. It was no trouble at all to see them. It is almost inconceivable to understand how the *Titanic* could have run into these icebergs on a calm, bright, starlight night, without having seen these stupendous objects. They were as plainly discernible as large castles or gigantic buildings standing in the horizon but a short distance away.

It was the good fortune of our vessel to save the lives of all these people. Had we not arrived at the time we did, there would probably not be a single survivor of the wreck to tell what had become of the palatial vessel on her maiden trip across the ocean. The scenes on board of our ship of the survivors, most of whom had lost some members of their family, or near and dear friends were very pathetic. Many of them came hardly without clothing, and having lost everything on earth.

We vacated one berth for Mrs. West, a refined lady of Southampton, England, and her two children, which was occupied by them during the four days we spent coming back to New York City from the scene of the wreck. Her husband, who was thirty-six years of age, was not allowed to enter the life boat with the family and lost his life.

There were many pathetic scenes on board, each survivor having his or her own experience, having been out on the ocean in the life boats for several hours after the *Titanic* disappeared beneath the sea. The elder of the two children of the lady, to whom I have just referred, was a bright little girl about four years of age. Her mother being indisposed, we took her up on deck with us to give her the benefit of the air. Soon after we were there, the little child asked me for a lead pencil and paper, on which to write. I asked her whom she wished to write to. She said she wanted to write to 'my daddy'. I let her take my pencil and gave her paper, and I asked her what she wanted to say. She addressed the letter 'Daddy' and started to write: 'We don't know what is keeping you. We are on this boat. We arrived before you and want you to come here'.

Pretty soon her little hand got tired of making the zig-zag marks upon the paper on which she was writing and she asked me to take her hand and steady it. I did so and asked her how she was going to send the letter. She pointed up to the mast of our vessel, on which were the lines of Marconi wire, and said that they would carry that letter to her father. Finally when she got tired of writing, she asked me to look for her father and try to find him. I didn't ask her for any description of him, but she told me herself to look for a man that had 'a white coat, a white waistcoat, white trousers and a gray hat, and that would be her father'. She said that he always wore that kind of clothes except on days when he was on particular business, and on such days of business, she always made him wear a black coat.

The scene was extremely pathetic and affective, and we all knew that her father at the time was deep in the Atlantic Ocean, but no one dared to tell the child the truth. This was but one of hundreds of heart-touching stories.[48]

MRS MAURICE MCKENNA

On 18 April, while the *Carpathia* was bound for New York, Mrs McKenna wrote the following letter to her brother, J.K. Fagan:

Atlantic Ocean
April 18, 1912

Dear Bro. J.K. and Family,

I did not think you would hear from us again until we were on the other side of the earth.

We are on a return trip to N.Y. with 850 passengers saved from the *Titanic*. Sunday night at 11:30 the *Titanic* struck a huge ice berg. Our ship, sixty miles south, was called to the rescue by the wireless. Mrs. Minahan is on board, also Colonel Astor's widow (Madeline Force). Of course all are anxious to reach N.Y. in hopes of finding their loved ones found. It was a terrible scene presented to us Monday morning. The ship was all in confusion, wailing and crying, children for parents, wives for husbands. It is wonderful 'a touch of sorrow makes the world akin'. Children were clad by passengers and everything done to console them.

I cannot write details now, but we've heard many a harrowing tale of woe. We expect to reach N.Y. tomorrow and to sail again in a few days.

I cannot write well owing to the motion of the boat. Maurice and Estella have made many friends among the children. We are well. I hope Minnie's baby and you are all well. With love,

Nellie[49]

C.T. PHELPS

While the *Carpathia* was returning to New York, Judge Phelps wrote the following letter to his daughter, Miss Christine Phelps:

Early Monday morning we were awakened by some unusual noise and confusion on deck. The sailors were trampling hurriedly about and were hauling up ropes to the deck, and on withdrawing the curtain from our porthole, the first thing we saw was several huge icebergs in the distance. Going upon the deck we found all confusion and excitement and crowded with strangers, some with scarcely any clothes at all, and some in full evening dress, others in their night clothes with wraps about them, in a half frozen condition. Upon emerging we found that the *Titanic*, the largest steamship built in the world, just making its first trip from England to this country with about 2,800 passengers on board, had just been sunken at the very place where our boat was then standing at anchor.

The *Titanic* ran into a great iceberg at about 11:45 p.m. Sunday night, and at about 2 o'clock Monday morning she sank. After the collision the *Titanic* sent out a wireless message of distress, and we happened to be about 50 miles away and received it, and started at once for the scene under full speed, reaching there about 4 o'clock in the morning and succeeded in rescuing all who were then surviving, numbering about 710 in all. These were found in the lifeboats and rafts and many perished from cold after leaving the ship. Thirty people were on the raft, and 14 died from cold and exposure before they were picked up by our boat. The people in the 16 lifeboats and on two rafts were rescued, and it is estimated that about 2,000 people, including the crew were drowned.

The passengers rescued say that the concussion with the iceberg was scarcely perceptible at the time, and they did not realize that anything serious had occurred. They were assured by the officers that they were perfectly safe, and those engaged at card playing continued at their game undisturbed for an hour after the collision, but finally the ladies were all quietly summoned on deck, and the passengers were told to put on life preservers and were persuaded to take the boats. They, however, supposing it to be an unnecessary precaution and believing they would soon return to the ship, the men were kept aboard until the women wishing to go were provided for.

There were only boats enough to take about one-fourth of the people on board and all the rest, of course, had to go down with the ship. At first all was quietly arranged without confusion or panic, but later, however, as the great ship began to list heavily to one side, the remaining passengers came to realize for the first time that they were in real danger. Then terrible panic and confusion prevailed. Mothers went mad and threw their babies overboard, and men were kept from the boats by the officers with revolvers, to let the women go first. It is reported by the passengers that the captain and first mate both shot themselves and went down with their boat. However, no one seems to be sure about this.

Many most pathetic and heart-rending stories are told by the survivors. Husbands, wives, parents and children were separated by the hundreds. A number of infant children were rescued whose parents were both [lost?] and [our ship is?] completely filled with widows whose husbands went down with the wreck. Several of them were brides on their wedding trip.

The lifeboats, after leaving the ship, rode and drifted about in the dark, keeping in touch with the others as best they could, by burning torches made of their handkerchiefs or other articles that could be spared, and by shouting until the arrival of our ship. Most of the boats were in full view of the great ship when it began to settle, and finally broke in two and disappeared with a great hissing noise and the explosion of the boilers. By the captain's orders the band continued the music until the very moment when the lights were finally extinguished by the sinking of the ship.

Before we left the scene of the disaster, all rescued passengers of the *Titanic* were called to the dining saloon and brief funeral services were held for the lost ones, as near as possible, on the very spot where the ship went down. Our ship was surrounded by floating debris and wreckage from the sunken ship, and on every side loomed huge icebergs, some of them rising to a height estimated at about 100 feet above the water and extending to unknown depths below. There were at least 25 of these great floating icebergs within sight from the place where we were anchored, and a short distance to north of us extending along the horizon for several miles, was an ice pack or floe forming a solid bank of ice several feet deep and covering probably 25 square miles in area, formed of fragments of floating ice driven together and freezing into a solid field.

After the funeral services were held and all boats were taken on or cast adrift after being unloaded, we proceeded to cruise for an hour or two in the vicinity of the wreck, and then a freight steamer, the *Californian*, came up and anchored, when we left and sailed away, headed back to New York to land the rescued, before starting again on our trip.[50]

ROD

The following letter was apparently written by a *Carpathia* crewman:

Royal Mail Steamship *Carpathia*

Dearest Earnestino,

No doubt the terrible news has already reached you about the tragedy of the *Titanic*, a most harrowing event which I shall in all my lifetime never forget.

It was just a few hours after mass that our radio operator had notified the captain about the distress signals received from the *Titanic* and after much confusion and excitement with much doubt in my mind whether a ship like the *Titanic* could possibly be sinking, orders were given for full steam ahead.

After about an hour or so we could see some rocket signals which were rather faint, but in due time we heard cries from people in the life boats who saw or heard us approaching.

Most of the crew were working throughout the night distributing as much clothes as was available attending to those who were too sick to take care of themselves. All of the bunks were occupied by the rescued and most of the crew had to take cat naps in shifts wherever there was a place to lay their tired torsos down.

Expect to visit John this spring and will let you know when so we will be together.

Rod[51]

ARTHUR ROSTRON

On 18 April, while the *Carpathia* was still at sea, Captain Rostron wrote the following report to the Cunard general manager in Liverpool:

RMS *Carpathia*
April 18, 1912
To General Manager,
Cunard Steamship Company, Ltd.
Liverpool

Sir: The following may be of interest to you. Monday, 15th inst., informed of urgent distress message from *Titanic*. Had struck ice. Required immediate assistance. Position of *Titanic* 41.16 north [sic], 50.14 west.

I immediately ordered ship turned and set course, we then being south 52 E. (true), fifty eight (58) miles from *Titanic*. Sent for chief engineer and ordered out another watch of stokers, and to make all possible speed. Gave orders to get all lifeboats prepared: spare gear taken out and boats swung out ready for lowering. Then sent for English doctor, purser and chief steward, and gave following instructions:

English Doctor – With assistants to remain in first class dining room.

Italian Doctor – With assistants to remain in second class dining room.

Hungarian Doctor – With assistants to remain in third class dining room.

Each doctor to have supplies of restoratives, stimulants and everything to hand for immediate need of probable wounded or sick.

Purser – With assistant purser and chief steward to receive passengers &c at different gangways, controlling our own stewards and assisting passengers to dining rooms &c. Also to get Christian names and surnames of all survivors as soon as possible to send by wireless. Inspector, stewards and master-at-arms to control our own steerage passengers and keep them out of third class dining hall, and also to keep them out of the way and off the deck, to prevent confusion.

Chief Stewards – That all hands would be called, and to have coffee &c ready to serve out to all our crew. Have coffee, tea, soup &c in each saloon, blankets in the saloons, at the gangways, and some in the boats. To see all rescued cared for and immediate wants attended to.

My cabin and all officials cabins to be given up. Smoke rooms, library, dining rooms would be utilized to accommodate the survivors. All spare berths in steerage to be utilised for *Titanic*'s passengers. All our own steerage passengers grouped together.

Stewards should be placed in each alleyway to reassure our own passengers should they inquire about noise in getting our own boats out &c of the working of the engines.

To all I strictly enjoined the necessity for order, discipline and quietness and to avoid all confusion.

Chief and First Officers – All the hands to be called. Get coffee &c. Prepare and swing out all boats. All gangway doors to be opened, electric sprays in each gangway and over each side. A block with line rove in each gangway. A chair slung at each gangway for getting up sick and wounded. Bo'sun's chairs, pilot ladders and canvas ashbags for children. Cargo falls with both ends clear, bowlines in the ends and bites secured along ship's side for boat ropes or to help the people up. Heaving lines distributed along the ship's side and gaskets handy near gangways for lashing people in chairs &c. Forward derricks topped and rigged and steam on winches; also told off officers for different stations and for certain eventualities.

Ordered company's rockets to be fired at 2:45 A.M. and every quarter-hour thereafter to reassure *Titanic*.

I may state that canvas ash bags were of great assistance in getting the infants and children aboard.

I am proud and happy to state that the utmost loyalty, obedience and attention was shown to me by all the officials and the men working under them also, all working with perfect willingness and without the slightest confusion or unnecessary noise.

As each official saw everything in readiness he reported to me personally on the bridge that all my orders were carried out, enumerating the same, and that everything was in readiness.

The details I left to the several officers, and must say they were most efficiently carried out. I think you will hear from other sources that we made every preparation possible.

A. H. Rostron, Captain, *Carpathia*[52]

On 19 April 1912, the day after the *Carpathia* arrived in New York, Captain Rostron gave the press a copy of a business letter he had just written to Cunard's general manager in Liverpool. Three days later, after the *Carpathia* left New York and resumed her interrupted voyage to Gibraltar, Rostron wrote the following letter to the Senate *Titanic* inquiry:

RMS *Carpathia*
At Sea
April 22nd, 1912
To the Chairman and Gentlemen of Committee
Senatorial Inquiry on *Titanic* Disaster

Gentlemen.

I beg to forward you a copy of my business letter which I sent to our General Manager, Cunard S.S. Co. Ltd. Liverpool.

This is the identical copy I gave to the Press. I gave no other account – neither oral nor written – as I was too busy, and I thought under the circumstances it only right you should know the exact source of their information. I simply told them it was my letter to our General Manager – making no other comments, except cutting out reference to letter No. 3, of which I gave a copy to your Committee in New York. You would notice from that letter it was also addressed to our General Manager.

As I later found I had omitted to include two rather important instructions, perhaps you would be good enough to attach the enclosed slip, as instructions to Chief and First Officers.

With my sincere best wishes that your Committee may be able to formulate the best and safest means to reassure, not only the travelling public, but we who go to sea, making it our profession and our calling.

And with heart-felt sympathy for all those who in any way suffered from the terrible disaster and all honour to those brave noble men who gave their lives for the 'women and children first'.

I am, Gentlemen,

Your obedient Servant

A.H. Rostron

Commander, R.N.R.

Commanding RMS *Carpathia*

Addenda for instructions given (and carried out) 15.4.12.

Lamptrimmer and one hand to have cans of oil and pour oil down ford W.C.s, either side.

All discharges over side to be stopped so far as possible.[53]

The following is the copy of the business letter that Captain Rostron wrote to Cunard's general manager in Liverpool:

I beg to report that at 12:35 a.m. Monday, 15th inst., I was informed of urgent message from *Titanic*, with her position.

I immediately ordered ship turned round, and put her on course for that position, we being then fifty-eight miles S 52 E (T) from her. Had heads of all Departments called, and issued what I considered the necessary orders, to be in preparation for any emergency.

(Please see Letter No. 3 for instructions given.)

At 2:40 a.m. saw flare half a point on port bow, taking this for granted to be ship, Shortly after we sighted our first iceberg. (I previously had look-outs doubled, knowing that *Titanic* had struck ice, and so took every care and precaution.) We soon found ourselves in a field of bergs, large and small, and had to alter course several times to clear bergs. Weather fine and clear, light airs, calm sea, beautifully clear night, though dark.

We stopped at 4 a.m., thus doing distance in three hours and a half, picking up the first boat at 4:10 a.m. Boat was in charge of Officer, and he reported to me that *Titanic* had foundered.

At 8:30 a.m. last boat was picked up; all survivors aboard and all boats accounted for, viz: 15 Lifeboats alongside; one Lifeboat abandoned; 2 Berthon Boats alongside; (saw one bottom upwards amongst wreckage); and, according to 2nd Officer (Senior Officer saved), one Berthon Boat had not been launched, it having got jammed, making 16 Lifeboats and 4 Berthon Boats accounted for.

By the time we had cleared first boat it was breaking day, and we could distinguish the other boats all within an area of about four miles. We also saw we were surrounded by icebergs, large and small, and 3 miles to N.W. of us a huge a huge field of drift ice, with large and small bergs in it, the ice field trending from N.W. round by W.&S. as far as we could see either way.

At 8 a.m. the Leyland S.S. *Californian* came up. I gave him principal news and asked him to search and I would proceed to New York. At 8:50 proceeded full speed.

While searching over vicinity of disaster, and whilst we were getting the people aboard, I gave orders to get spare hands along and swing in all our boats, disconnect the falls, and hoist up as many *Titanic* boats as possible in our davits; also, get some on fo'castle heads by derricks. We got 13 lifeboats; 6 on forward deck, and 7 in davits.

After getting all survivors aboard, and whilst searching, I got a Clergyman to offer a short prayer of thankfulness for those saved, and also a short burial service for their lost, in Saloon.

Before deciding definitely where to make for, I conferred with Mr. Ismay, and though he told me to do what I considered best, I informed him – taking everything into consideration – that I considered New York best. I knew we should require more provisions, clean linen, blankets, etc. even if we went to the Azores.

As most of the passengers saved were women and children, and they very hysterical, and not knowing what medical attention they might require, thought it best to go to New York; also thought it would be better for Mr. Ismay to get to New York or England as soon as possible, and knowing I should be out of 'Wireless' communication with anything very soon if I proceeded to Azores, it left Halifax, Boston, and New York, so chose the latter, as we would require coal, clean linen, blankets, stores etc. Again passengers were all hysterical about ice, and pointed out to Mr. Ismay the possibility of seeing ice if I went to Halifax. Then I knew from the gravity of the disaster that it would be desirable to keep in touch with land stations all we could.

I am pleased to say that all survivors have been very plucky. The majority of the women, first, second, and third [class] lost their husbands, and, considering all, have been wonderfully well. Tuesday our doctor reported all survivors physically well.

Our First Class passengers have behaved splendidly, giving up their cabins voluntarily, and supplying the ladies with clothes, etc. We all turned out of our cabins and gave them up to survivors; Saloons, Smoke Rooms, Library, etc. also being used for sleeping accommodations. Our crew also turned out to let the crew of the *Titanic* take their quarters.

I am pleased to state that, owing to preparations made for the comfort of survivors, none was the worse for exposure, etc.

I beg to specially mention how willingly and cheerfully the whole of the Ship's company have behaved throughout, receiving the highest possible praise from everybody, and I can assure you I am very proud to have such a ship's company under my command.

We have experienced very great difficulty in transmitting news, also names of survivors. Our 'Wireless' is very poor, and again we had so many interruptions from other ships, and also messages from shore (principally press which we ignored.) I gave instructions to send first all Official messages; then names of passengers; then survivors' private messages, and the last press messages, as I considered the first three items most important and necessary.

We had haze early Tuesday morning for several hours; again more or less all Wednesday from 5:30 a.m. to 5 p.m. Strong S.S.Wly winds and clear weather Thursday with moderate rough sea.

I am
Sir
Yours obediently
A.H. Rostron
Master[54]

On 24 April, after the *Carpathia* resumed her interrupted voyage to Gibraltar, Captain Rostron wrote a letter to President William Howard Taft regarding allegations that Rostron had ignored the President's earlier query about the fate of his military aide:

Royal Mail Steamship *Carpathia*
At Sea, April 24th – 12
His Excellency
The President of the United States
White House
Washington, D.C.
United States America

Sir,

I have the honour to express to you, Sir, my sincere regret that you or the Government & people who you represent should have the slightest cause to imagine that any act of mine – or those under my command – could possibly be construed to intentionally or otherwise ignore or disregard any message with which your Excellency might honour me.

I am given to understand that the USS *Chester* sent wireless from you asking if Major Butt was aboard this ship or to that effect.

I beg to state I have absolutely no knowledge of any such message.

I made enquiries from our Purser if any such message had been received. He replies, 'We got one from *Olympic* asking if Major Butt was aboard. I replied "Major Butt not on board"'.

Fortunately, this morning I came across the two first messages from the *Chester* which I enclose, also scrap copy of one of mine in reply.

The only other message I received from *Chester* was 'Yes Yes' in reply to mine asking if he could send names of 3rd class.

I hope, Sir, this explanation will be quite satisfactory to you & your Excellency may rest assured nothing could be further from my mind or any under my command to ever dream of disregarding any message or request you might make.

As I had not a spare minute & my time taken up by business etc. the short time we were in New York, I take this, the first opportunity of informing your Excellency of the actual state of affairs.

With my humble respects
I am
Sir
Your obedient servant
A.H. Rostron
Commander RNR
Commanding RMS *Carpathia*[55]

In 1913, Captain Rostron wrote the following account of his rescue of the *Titanic*'s survivors:

The *Carpathia* left New York, April 11, 1912, in fine, clear weather, bound for Gibraltar and other Mediterranean ports. Saturday and Sunday (13th and 14th) it was very fine but cold weather, and we remarked that there must be a lot of ice to the north'rd, as we had then a light northerly breeze.

I turned in about midnight on Sunday, and was just dropping off to sleep when I heard the chartroom door open (this door leads directly into my cabin, near the head of my bunk), and I thought to myself, 'Who the dickens is this cheeky beggar coming into my cabin without knocking?' However, I very soon knew the reason. I looked up and saw the first officer and the Marconi operator; the first officer at once informed me, 'We have just received an urgent distress message from the *Titanic* that she had struck ice and required immediate assistance'.

You can imagine I was very soon wide awake, and, to say the least, somewhat astonished. I gave orders to turn the ship round, and jumped up getting hold of the Marconi operator by the sleeve, and asked, 'Are you sure it is the *Titanic* and requires immediate assistance?'

He replied, 'Yes, sir.'

Again I asked, 'Are you absolutely certain?'

He again replied, 'Yes.'

'All right,' I said, 'tell him we are coming along as fast as we can.'

I then went into the chart-room and asked if he had given *Titanic*'s position, and then the operator gave me the position on a slip of paper, 'Lat. 41.46 N., Long. 50.14W'.

When in the chart-room working out the position and course, I saw the bo's'n's mate pass with the watch as they were going to wash down the decks. I called him and told him to knock off all work, and get all our boats ready for lowering, and not to make any noise; also that the men need not get excited, as we were going to another vessel in distress.

I had already sent for the chief engineer, and on coming up told him to turn out another watch of stokers and make all speed possible and not to spare anything, as we were going up to the *Titanic*, she being in trouble, having struck ice.

The chief engineer hurried away at once, and I then sent for the English doctor, purser and chief steward.

These officers were soon in my cabin, and I related the circumstances and gave the following instructions:

English doctor, with assistants, to remain in first-class dining room; Italian doctor in second, and Hungarian doctor in third-class dining room, and to have supply of stimulants, restoratives, and everything necessary.

Purser, with assistant purser and chief steward to receive the people at the different gangways, controlling our own stewards in assisting the *Titanic*'s people to the dining rooms etc. Also to get Christian and surnames of survivors as soon as possible to send by wireless.

Inspector, steerage stewards, and master-at-arms to control our own steerage passengers and keep them out of third class dining hall, also to keep them out of the way, and off the deck, to prevent confusion.

Chief Steward, that all hands would be called, and to have coffee etc. ready to serve out to our men. Have coffee, tea, soup etc., in each dining room for rescued. Have blankets near gangways, in saloons and public rooms, and also some handy for our own boats.

To see all rescued cared for and immediate wants attended to, that my cabin and all officials' cabins would be given up for accommodation of rescued; smoke-rooms, libraries and dining-rooms, if necessary, to be utilised as accommodation. All spare berths in steerage to be used for *Titanic*'s third class, and to get all our own steerage passengers grouped together.

To all I strictly enjoined silence, order and strict discipline; also to station a steward in each alleyway to reassure our own passengers should they inquire about any noise they might hear.

After receiving their instructions these officers hurried away to make their preparations.

I then went on to the bridge, and soon after the Marconi operator came up and reported he had picked up a message from *Titanic* to *Olympic*, asking the latter to have all his boats ready. (But previous to this the operator had received a message from *Titanic*, asking when we would be up there. I told him to reply, 'About four hours'. We did it in less than three-and-a-half hours.) I told the operator to inform *Titanic* all our boats would be in readiness, and also all preparations necessary.

After the operator left I gave the following instructions to the first officer:

All hands to be called and get coffee, etc.

Prepare and swing out all boats; all gangway doors to be opened.

Electric clusters at each gangway and over the side.

A block – with line rove – hooked in each gangway.

A chair – slung – at each gangway for getting sick or wounded up.

Pilot ladders and side ladders at gangways and over the side.

Cargo falls, with both ends clear and bight secured, along ship's side on deck, for boat ropes or to help people go up.

Heaving lines and gaskets distributed about the decks and gangways, to be handy for lashings, etc.

Forward derricks rigged and topped, and steam on winches – to get mails on board or as required.

Pour oil down forward lavatories, both sides, to quiet the sea.

Canvas ash-bags near the gangways to haul the children up in.

Ordered company's rockets to be fired from three a.m., and every quarter of an hour, to reassure *Titanic*.

Also arranged as to how the officers would work, should the situation require the service of our boats.

About two thirty-five the doctor came on the bridge and reported all my instructions carried out, and everything in readiness.

I was talking to the doctor as to what we might expect, and keeping at the same time a sharp lookout, when quite suddenly – and only for a couple of seconds – I saw a green flare about a point on port bow. I remarked, 'There's his light, he must be afloat still', as at one-thirty or so the operator had reported to me that he had received a message saying, 'Engine-room filling'. So, of course, I knew, on hearing that, of the gravity of the situation.

All our men were quietly but busily making preparations. It was a beautiful, fine, clear night, very cold, and every star in the heavens shining bright, the sea quite calm and no wind. We were racing along splendidly

– attaining a maximum speed of about seventeen knots – our usual speed being fourteen.

The chief engineer had been up to me about one-thirty and reported all hands were working below and doing all they possibly could. It appears some of the stokers on being called – and knowing the reason – had turned straight out of their bunks and rushed below, not even taking time to dress.

Soon after seeing the green light the second officer reported an iceberg about two points on the port bow. This berg we saw with the reflected light of a star – a starbeam – on it.

From now on we were passing bergs on either side, and had to alter course several times to keep well clear of them. You may depend on it, we were keyed up pretty tight, and keeping a bright lookout. I was also fully aware of our danger, knowing what had already occurred to the *Titanic*. So it can be imagined I was pretty anxious, thinking of my own passengers and crew and ship, as well as those on the *Titanic*. We had three-and-a-half rushing, anxious hours, and plenty to think of and plenty to do in the meantime in order to be ready.

We started sending up rockets at intervals of about a quarter of an hour, and when nearer fired the company's Roman candles (night signals), to let them know it was *Carpathia*. We saw the green light at intervals, and what with keeping a lookout for icebergs, vessels' lights, and the green light, we had to keep our eyes skinned and no mistakes to be made.

About three-thirty a.m. the purser and chief steward came up to the bridge and reported all in readiness, enumerating all the orders I had given.

Three-thirty-five or so I put the engines on the 'stand-by', so that I should know the engineers would be at the engines for instant action, if required.

About four a.m. I stopped the engines, knowing we must be somewhere near the position.

A few minutes after I saw an iceberg right ahead, and immediately the second officer reported the same. We had seen the green flare light low down not long before, and so we knew it must be a boat. I had intended taking the boat on the port side, which was the lee side if anything, but with the iceberg to consider, I swung the ship round and made to pick up the boat on the starboard side.

Another few minutes and the boat was alongside; a hail came, 'We have only one seaman in the boat and cannot work very well.'

'All right,' I replied 'I'll bring the ship alongside the boat.' We got her alongside and found her to contain about twenty-five people, and in charge of an officer.

Now comes the heart-rending part when we knew for a certainty the *Titanic* had gone down; I sent word to the gangway to ask the officer to come up to me on the bridge when he came aboard. On coming up to the bridge I shook hands and asked, 'The *Titanic* has gone down, I suppose?'

'Yes,' he replied – but what a sad-hearted 'Yes' it was – 'she went down about two-thirty.' Daylight was just setting in, and soon, in the early dawn, could be seen dozens and dozens of icebergs, large and small, all around us; here and there dotted about the calm sea we could distinguish the other boats, the boats being within a radius of about four to five miles, I should think.

We also saw the iceberg we picked up right ahead; this was about one-third of a mile off our starboard beam. Looking aft we saw a growler – a broken-off lump of ice – about ten to fifteen feet high and twenty-five feet long, a couple of hundred yards off our port quarter.

Giving instructions to the junior officer on the bridge to count the number of bergs about two hundred feet high – and pointing out several as a guide – he counted twenty-five estimated at from two hundred to two hundred and fifty, and dozens of bergs from fifty to one hundred and fifty, feet high.

From now on we were getting the remainder of the boats alongside, and one's imagination fancied these people shivering for hours during that cold night in their confined space. We manoeuvred about to reach the boats, and by eight o'clock had all the boats along-side, and we were also in the immediate vicinity of the disaster. I had arranged to hold a short service whilst we were close to the spot – a short prayer of thankfulness for those saved and a short service for those lost.

This service was held in the first-class dining-room whilst slowly cruising about. From the deck we could see little to indicate the terrible catastrophe of a few hours previous. We saw little but bits of small wreckage – some deck chairs, a few life belts and large quantities of cork; for all the world just as one sees on the seashore, merely a tide drift.

At eight o'clock we also saw a steamer coming toward us out of the ice-field. This ice-field stretched as far as the eye could see from northwest to southeast, and we soon found her to be the *Californian*. We signalled her and told news of trouble, and asked her to search round, as we were returning to New York. It was now blowing a moderate breeze and the sea rising as we were getting survivors on board.

About eight-twenty or so all the people were aboard, and by eight-forty-five all the boats we could take, and then we proceeded to New York.

I had decided to return to New York as I considered New York the only port possible under the circumstances.

We soon found our passage blocked by a tremendous ice-field. Of course we had seen this ice-field before, but did not know how compact it was, nor the extent of it. In the field were many bergs from one hundred to one hundred and fifty feet high, and the general mass of the ice perhaps six to twelve feet high. We sailed round this ice-pack for nearly four hours – quite fifty-six miles – before we could set our course for New York. We also passed several large bergs clear of the pack.

About noon we passed the Russian steamer *Birma*, bound east. We saw him attempt to cut through the ice-pack, but he had to turn out again. And I don't blame him, either.

We had been in wireless communication with several steamers that were coming up to assist, but I sent word we had accounted for all the boats, and it was useless, as we had left the *Californian* searching. They also were all a long distance.

Our own passengers began to arrive on deck soon after the first boat was alongside. It was quite remarkable the manner in which everyone behaved. There was absolutely no excitement. Our own passengers did not seem to realise what was happening or the catastrophe that had occurred.

The *Carpathia* was stopped in mid-Atlantic. The sun was just rising over the horizon, chasing away the last shades of night from a cloudless sky; beneath us a calm sea with scarcely a ripple on its gently heaving swell; everything perfectly still – a perfect sunrise and a picture before us almost impossible to imagine either as regards the colour or the subject.

All around us were dozens and dozens of icebergs, some comparatively close, others far away on the horizon, towering up like cathedral spires or assuming in one's fancy the forms of ships under full sail. The sun shining on these ice pinnacles seemed to enhance their splendour and belie the hidden truth. Dotted here and there on the quiet sea were to be seen the boats, some in groups of two or three, others singly, pulling in toward a common centre – the *Carpathia*.

Along-side were more boats more or less filled with people, more people climbing up the ship's side, others being pulled up, all having white life-belts on – no noise, no hurry.

The whole might have been an early morning improvised spectacular arrangement for the benefit of our passengers, but withal there was an atmosphere of inability to grasp that which was before them; as if it had been given to them too suddenly, and just as if they were looking on at something most unusual, and yet with an indefinable tragedy behind it all; something too great to realise. In reality, our passengers had a few minutes before been asleep in their beds, and this sudden experience of such a scene and its relative meaning was almost beyond one's comprehension. Can one wonder, with the immensity of it all thrust on their hardly awakened senses in such an unheard-of and undreamt-of dramatic manner?

However, something of the true nature soon seemed to strike our people. They seemed to understand that they had a part to play, and that this was something which was not meant for them to be merely as an audience, but in which they could and ought to act.

Our passengers mixed with the new arrivals and tried to comfort and help them, persuading them to take some nourishment or stimulant, arguing with and pressing them on the necessity for such a course. Our doctors must have been relieved to see our own passengers using their persuasion and common sense so successfully.

Then they saw the survivors required dry and warm clothing, so off they took them to their cabins to fit them out with everything they could do for them.

It was a most busy and stirring scene, our people never overdoing it and showing such excellent tact and sympathy, always ready to help and ready at any moment to do the right thing.

Our men gave up their cabins and the ladies turned out of theirs – in many instances to double up with other ladies, so leaving their cabins for the use of the survivors. The ladies were very soon self-appointed nursing sisters, getting some to lie abed, others to rest on deck, and listening to the heart-breaking tales, and doing all women can do to console and try to brighten them up.

As many of the second and third class people who came aboard were but poorly clothed, blankets and sheets were requisitioned, and many of the ladies started in to make clothes, work seeming a relief to their overwrought nerves. Some ladies – both survivors and our own – went amongst the third class and nursed, bathed, and clothed and fed the children.

The cream of human kindness was surely given with a free hand those three-days-and-a-half, and through it all an almost unnatural quietness and lack of all excitement seemed to pervade the whole ship.

Our own doctors did all doctors could do: rest and sleep seemed to be the most desirable thing for those we had taken aboard, and so everything possible was done to induce sleep.

I was astonished and more than thankful and pleased when Doctor McGhee, on Tuesday morning, reported to me all the survivors physically well. The doctor had hardly had a minute to himself – day or night – since we commenced embarking the people. It seemed almost incredible that those hundreds of people who had undergone such trying experiences should not have developed some physical trouble. I knew it meant untiring attention on the part of not only the medical staff but everyone, both our own officers and men, and our passengers also, in attending to the people immediately they arrived, and also the preparations made for them on board.

I hardly think it good taste to attempt to picture the sad, heart-rending appearance of those sorely tried people as it impressed us, but I can say how bravely they bore up under their agonising trouble, and how we one and all felt that we must get them to New York safe and sound and do all we possibly could to keep them from further trouble or anxiety.

About four-thirty Monday afternoon I received a wireless message from the *Olympic* asking for information. I gave the bare facts and also sent the official messages to the Cunard Company etc. The names of the survivors were then sent, and we continued in until about one o'clock Tuesday morning, when we got out of range.

This was the first opportunity we had had of sending any news of any kind through to shore, as the other steamers we had been in communication with earlier in the day were all too far to the eastward. It was also the last until Wednesday afternoon – and we afterward learned what an awful suspense the world was in during those three days, as we had only been able to send the formal official messages of disaster, with approximate number saved, and the names of the first and second class passengers and crew.

Our wireless instrument was only a short-distance one, limited to one hundred and thirty miles – to about two hundred and twenty under most favourable circumstances; also we only had one operator.

It was most difficult to get the names even, and the continuous strain at the instrument, the conditions under which the operator was working, and the constant interruptions made it anything but a simple matter. I must again refer to the quiet, subdued manner of everyone on board during our return to New York.

We had several hours' fog on Tuesday morning early, and again it set in thick Wednesday morning and continued foggy, more or less, all the way to New York.

The dismal nerve-racking noise of the whistle blowing every half-minute must have been very distressing to the survivors especially, and one can quite understand their suspense and agony of mind in having gone through such a terrible experience on that fateful night, and then the other terror of the sea-fog coming to augment their mental suffering. We had taken three bodies from the boats, and one man died during the fore-noon of Monday, all four being buried at four in the afternoon, Protestant and Roman Catholic services being held over them according to their religion.

At half-past eight Monday night, in company with the purser and chief steward, I went all round the ship to inspect the arrangements made for everyone, and found all that was possible to be done was either done or being done. All the public rooms were converted into sleeping accommodations. Fortunately, we had an ample supply of blankets and all spare mattresses and pillows were served out, every one having every attention given them that was at our command.

Many of our own stewards were self-appointed watchmen during the night, remaining at their posts in readiness to attend to any one requiring assistance, and to give moral support – to the ladies especially, who always found someone ready to help or to cheer them.

In speaking of the loyalty and cheerful willingness of every member of the crew, officers and men, from the moment I gave the first order to our arrival in New York (and I know for a certainty that the doctor, purser and stewards – even the little bell-boys – had very little rest until the Friday night, that is, the day we left New York again), I must also mention the assistance given by the stewards of the *Titanic* who were saved; they all turned to and assisted in every way they could.

We heard of many great and noble deeds of self-sacrifice performed by those on the *Titanic* that night: tales of heroism and bravery of men and women, of men who had everything in this world to live for, men who were sending away in the boats those who were dearest on earth to them, those in the boats leaving on the ship those most dear to them in the whole world. Men who had so much of this world's honours and riches yet at the great test they showed the world they had still greater gifts – the gift of great and noble self-sacrifice and self-command.

Standing out equal to each or any, and superbly noble, was that of a young girl.

A boat full of women and ready for lowering was found to be too full and the order was given for someone to get out, as it was considered unsafe. A young lady – a girl, really – got up to leave the boat; then some of the others tried to persuade her to remain. 'No,' she said, 'you are married and have families; I'm not, it doesn't matter about me!'

This girl-woman, in the highest and noblest sense, got out of the boat and returned to the deck of the ship. Those in the boat were saved, the girl on deck went down with the ship. From being in a position to be saved she deliberately returned to the uncertainty, and so gave her life willingly that others might have a better chance of being saved. There were many incidents – almost too numerous to mention – and incidents one does not care to recall; but one case might be cited, perhaps.

During dinner on Sunday evening a wireless message was received by some of our passengers from relatives aboard the *Titanic*. At four-thirty Monday morning, two of the relatives were brought to the state-room of our passengers, who were then in bed asleep and knew nothing of what was taking place, such was the irony of fate! The surprise – nay, stupefaction – of our passengers so suddenly roused to hear such news can well be imagined.

Wednesday afternoon about one o'clock we were in wireless communication with the U.S.S. *Chester*, dense fog at the time, and through her sent in the remainder of the names of survivors, with corrections also.

We picked up *Fire Island* light vessel from its fog-horn about four o'clock Thursday afternoon, after which the weather cleared considerably. About six we stopped off *Ambrose Channel* lightship and picked up our pilot. It was at this time we got some idea of suspense and excitement in the world. We were met by several powerful tug-boats chartered by the press and full of press men, anxious to get news. Naturally, I did not care to have any of the passengers harassed by reporters seeking information, so I decided not to allow any one on board the *Carpathia*.

As we were going up Ambrose Channel, the weather changed completely, and a more dramatic ending to a tragic occurrence it would be hard to conceive.

It began to blow hard, rain came down in torrents, and, to complete the finale, we had continuous vivid lightning, and heavy, rolling thunder. This weather continued until our arrival off Cunard dock.

It was astonishing how quiet – apparently stolid – everyone aboard was in their loyalty. Seeing I refused to hold any communication with the press-boats, all the passengers seemed to take the same view, and to all inquiries for news or photographs, or even names, a tense silence was maintained throughout.

Whilst we were stopped off the dock, getting the *Titanic*'s boats away from the ship, a press man did manage to get on board. It was reported to me and I had him brought on the bridge. I explained my reasons for not allowing any one on board, and that I could not allow the passengers to be interviewed, and put him on his honour not to leave the bridge under certain penalties. I must say he was a gentleman.

What with the wind and rain, a pitch-dark night, lightning and thunder, and the photographers taking flashlight pictures of the ship, and the explosion of the lights, it was a scene never to be effaced from one's memory. There were dozens of tugs dodging about the ship, and the lowering away of the *Titanic*'s lifeboats (we could not get into dock until all the *Titanic*'s boats were away from the ship, as seven of them were suspended in our davits and six were on the forecastle head, and so in the way of working the mooring ropes), and these boats were leaving the ship in the blackness of the night with two of the rescued crew in each boat and some of the *Titanic*'s officers in charge of them, it brought back to one's mind the manner in which these same boats were last lowered from that great and magnificent ship never to reach New York.

It did indeed seem a fitting final scene to the most tragic and greatest marine disaster in the history of the sea. At nine-twenty we got into dock and the passengers were now free to land. And so they left us, after being aboard over three and a half days – landed to meet their dear ones and friends, and to feel once more their poignant grief surging uppermost in their minds. As they landed we all felt such a relief as only those experience who have for days been under a great strain – keyed up to the highest pitch of anxiety all the time. With such anxiety for the safety of so many people placed in my care under such heart-rending and tragic circumstances, on their landing I was thankful. With the people landed, the work of the *Carpathia* was finished, so far as the part we had taken in the catastrophe.

Of all the remarkable incidents in connection with the whole history of the short life of that magnificent creation of man, not the least was the name of that never-to-be-forgotten ship.

Looking in the dictionary one finds there the definition of that ill-fated name, '*TITANIC*: a race of people vainly striving to overcome the forces of nature'. Could anything be more unfortunate or tragic in its significance?[56]

MRS J.A. SHUTTLEWORTH

After the rescue, Mrs Shuttleworth wrote the following letter to her friend, Mrs R.B. Rankins:

We went 60 miles north and found the little lifeboats with the people almost frozen in the icy water from 12 o'clock until we reached them at 3 o'clock in the morning.

The *Carpathia* rescued 650 or 660.

I will never forget the cries and moans of the ones who bade farewell to their husbands and wives and children, who went down with the magnificent steamer ... Of course, we gave out all the clothes and everything we had to the people who saved nothing but kimonos and wraps. No stockings, no shoes, no underwear or anything. Almost naked, it is a wonder how they endured the cold, floating around in the ice mountains, waiting hopeless, for some ship to come. When they saw the *Carpathia*'s lights their prayers went up as a shout.[57]

MR SPENCER (CREWMAN)

After the *Carpathia* arrived in New York, Mr Spencer wrote a letter to his father in Belfast. Spencer began his letter by saying that at about midnight on 14 April the *Carpathia* received a Marconigram from the *Titanic* saying that she had struck an iceberg and required assistance because she was sinking fast. The letter continued:

Our captain had an extra watch of firemen on the boilers, and she steamed faster than she ever did before in the direction indicated. We were about sixty miles to the southward, and we had a long way to go.

So we got all our boats ready, the baggage ports were all open, and there were small canvas bags ready for lifting people out of the boats by pulleys &c. In fact, we were ready for any rescue emergency. About one o'clock we saw a lot of rockets being fired, and we knew it was the *Titanic*, but we were a great way off. At last we reached the latitude mentioned and found ourselves surrounded by bergs like cathedrals and churches, so we had to be very careful ourselves. This would be about four o'clock in the morning. We could see nothing of the *Titanic*, but suddenly we saw a blue light burning, and we knew it must be a boat, so we steamed slowly up to her and found she was one of the *Titanic*'s boats full of women, which we cleared in a few seconds. It was just break of day, and we saw more boats, and picked up the lot of them, sixteen all told. Two we found afterwards bottom up, and we were told how the great ship went down 35 minutes after striking the berg. Now, then, if the ship had had enough boats, the lot should have been saved, hence the dreadful loss of life. If we had been but a few hours nearer to her in the first place we ourselves might have saved the lot, and never mind about the ship, but we did our best and rescued every living soul left. We served out every comfort to the rescued. I must tell you the survivors acted grandly. There was no panic, but fine discipline. We steamed up to the empty boats, picked 13 up, and got them on board and proceeded to New York, and when we got there I shall never forget the sight. Thousands of tugs full of people came to Sandy Hook to escort us to the dock. The captain allowed no reporters on board, but some got on board one way or the other, and the papers got full of a lot of rot until the right reports were sent in.[58]

❖   ❖   ❖

ERNEST ST CLAIR

In 1980 Mr St Clair, who was a waiter on board the *Carpathia*, described his vessel's rescue of the *Titanic* survivors:

On the night of the 14th of April 1912, I, Ernest St Clair, was a 19 year old member of the crew of the Cunard liner SS *Carpathia*. We were four days out from New York with a full complement of passengers on a cruise to the sunny Mediterranean. The night was dark, the sea calm and it was very cold, there was ice about. Now this was nearing midnight, I made my way forward to retire. On the midship, on the shelter deck, I was surprised to see Captain, later 'Sir', Rostron, the chief engineer and other officers in anxious conference. I learned that our 22 year old Marconi wireless operator, Harold Cottam, by sheer chance, had donned his headphone for a few minutes before turning in for the night, when he heard the 'CQD' followed immediately by the 'SOS' distress signal emanating from Royal Mail's steamer *Titanic*. She was the flagship of the White Star Line on her maiden voyage to New York. She was the largest and fastest ship in the world and reputedly 'unsinkable'.

In mid-Atlantic, at 20 minutes to twelve midnight, she had crashed into an iceberg. She was sinking fast and calling for help. She went down, to the bottom of the Atlantic, 2 hours and 40 minutes later.

Carpathia changed course. All steam was closed down from pantries, galleys, kitchens, heating apparatus. Below, the stokers worked like demons crowding on all speed. The old ship shook, she had never travelled so fast since the far-off days of her trials, as she raced to the rescue of the *Titanic*'s survivors.

Men were called for to man the life boats. The crew, of course, volunteered to a man. A list was posted on the main companion way and I was one of those chosen. We carried hundreds of blankets from the store room up to the boat deck. There we broke out the chocks and swung out the life boats, but they were never launched. It would be about 6 o'clock in the morning and in the graying dawn, from afar, we saw the flares of the *Titanic*'s lifeboats. The light of day grew stronger and the *Titanic*'s lifeboats made toward us, guided by the rockets *Carpathia* sent out. We saw then how pitifully few the lifeboats were.

The first lifeboat alongside contained only 13 survivors; an evil omen tragically borne out.

We took 705 survivors aboard *Carpathia*. 1,503 children, women and men went down with *Titanic* when she plunged to the bottom of the Atlantic Ocean.

The survivors were cared for. The dead were buried with simple, unimpressive, ceremony.

We passed floating deck chairs and other flotsam of wreckage. We passed 'growlers', which are minor icebergs, and many ice floes. As we passed over the spot where the *Titanic* had sunk a short religious service was held. We passed the enormous black-ice iceberg which sealed the *Titanic*'s doom.

So to New York; which we reached four days later. To the tragic welcome. To the court of enquiry at the dock side. To the snarling of the yellow press at 'Brute' Ismay, as they dubbed the unfortunate Bruce Ismay, chairman of the White Star Line, owners of the *Titanic*. The American souvenir hunters besieged the *Carpathia*'s crew members when they went ashore. To the dignified and touching tribute of representatives of the survivors of the *Titanic* to their rescuers: the presentation of medals inscribed 'For gallant and heroic services to the Captain, Officers and crew of SS *Carpathia* from the survivors of SS *Titanic*'.

Such are my recollections of the *Titanic* disaster, which in my memory occurred only yesterday.[59]

LAWRENCE STOUDENMIRE

After the *Carpathia*'s rescue of the *Titanic* survivors, Mr Stoudenmire made several brief entries in his diary:

Monday Morning, April 15 – Great excitement on deck ship; had received wireless of wreck of SS *Titanic* of White Star Line. Put on full steam at 1 a.m. and rushed to scene of disaster arriving about 5 a.m. to pick up survivors. The *Titanic* had sunk three-quarters of an hour after hitting an iceberg. Two thousand people drowned, the rest picked up by *Carpathia*. A terrible sight on deck. Women who had lost their husbands and sons and men who had lost everything except a pair of trousers and a shirt they wore.

Breakfast was a scene of confusion. All the survivors seemed stunned. The flags were put half-mast. The rest of the day was taken up hearing different and various stories of the wreck as told by the survivors. Dinner and supper were as usual. Gave up my cabin to two ladies of the survivors and I turned in on deck about 11 o'clock. Heard all the bells strike until 4:30 next morning. Fine day.

Tuesday, April 16 – Turned out at 4:30 o'clock. Breakfast as usual. The only thing to do was stand around and talk. Subject of conversation the wreck of the steamship *Titanic*. The following story was told me by a survivor:

At 11:45 Sunday night I with three of my mates was in my cabin when I felt the shock of the steamer hitting the iceberg. She bounded back and brushed again at the iceberg. Before she hit the second time the engines were stopped. The bulkhead doors were then ordered closed. Going on deck dressed as I am now [he pointed to his black sweater, trousers and bedroom slippers] I saw a sight that I shall never forget. At one of the lifeboats that was full of men, an officer stood with a revolver in his hand. 'Clear out of there, you men, and let the ladies into the boat first,' said he. They cleared out. About six men were sent with each lifeboat as crew. Several men were shot. A man was running along the deck; he stopped, turned around and said to me, 'Take care of them for me, will you.' I turned and saw two ladies he indicated. I grabbed them each by the hand, and, brushing by an officer with 'I am taking care of them,' we jumped into a lifeboat which was immediately lowered. The man behind me, I remember, was grabbed by the collar and flung back into the crowd on deck.

Not long after that the bow of the *Titanic* sank sticking the stern clear of the water. Then the whole cargo shifted, making a noise like a death rattle. The ship sank out of sight. We had to pull as strong as we could to overcome the suction. Then we just drifted until we saw a rocket from your ship. With a shout of joy we pulled directly for your ship and got on board about 5:30 a.m.

The teller of the story was a young man who is going to America to study theology. Dinner as usual; loafed away afternoon on deck; supper as usual; turned in at 10 o'clock; laid my blanket in front of piano in the saloon and went to sleep; awakened about 12 o'clock by a severe thunderstorm; *Carpathia* is heading for New York; heavy wind.

Wednesday, April 17 – Turned out 6:30 o'clock; breakfast at 8; stayed on deck until dinner-time; dined as usual; on deck until supper; after supper turned in on floor of smoking-room; rainy and foggy.

Thursday, April 18 – Turned out about 6 o'clock; breakfast at 8; on deck until dinner; after dinner until supper; sighted land before supper. Before ship docked the water was full of tugboats loaded with newspaper reporters, who shouted, 'How many saved, how many on board?' etc. The parade of tugs after dark was a beautiful sight. Docked about 9 o'clock. I got pass and went to mail mother a letter. It took two hours and the lieutenant of the police to get me on board again. Millions of people lined the streets. Foggy weather. Landed in a thunderstorm.[60]

In later years Mr Stoudenmire wrote the following account of his experiences on the *Carpathia*:

Sixty years ago, while I was a second-year student at Poly in Baltimore, I was given the opportunity of touring Europe. I have some nice memories of the tour, and a number of snapshots.

But far stronger than the memory of my adventures in Europe are those of a tragedy I saw from aboard the *Carpathia*, the ship on which I embarked. The *Carpathia* was one of the ships which rushed to the rescue and picked up survivors from the wreck of the *Titanic*.

But first, how did a schoolboy, and one of modest means at that, manage a European tour in the spring of 1912?

My father, the Rev. William S. Stoudenmire, a Lutheran minister, died while I was in high school. I had to drop out for five years to help support our family. I found a job at the Mar-Del Mobile Company, an automobile dealership at Charles Street and Mount Royal Avenue. Later the manager found night work for me so I could go back to school by day.

Three wealthy Baltimore women named Fowler – I think they were sisters – had bought a 1911 Packard touring car. They wanted a young man to serve as their chauffeur in a tour through Europe. My boss recommended me. I drove the Packard to New York City, had it put aboard the *Carpathia*, and went to my second-class quarters. They traveled first class.

The ladies paid all my expenses. I don't recall now how much I got but it was a generous figure. The ladies' Baltimore attorney sent my salary to my mother.

Seasoned travelers would have called it an uneventful voyage, although I was thrilled by everything I saw on my first ocean trip. Then, late at night on April 14, our wireless operator picked up the distress call of the *Titanic*.

The westbound *Titanic* and the eastbound *Carpathia* were about midway between Liverpool, England and New York City, but the *Titanic's* course was about 70 miles north. Our ship moved at full speed to the *Titanic*. We arrived about daylight.

The *Titanic* was gone, leaving no traces except some floating debris and chunks of ice sheared off the iceberg with which the ship had collided. Fortunately some lifeboats, loaded with survivors almost to the point of swamping, were afloat and waiting.

Aboard the *Carpathia*, crewmen disconnected the ship's own hanging lifeboats, and used the davits to haul aboard the *Titanic's* lifeboats.

With the last of the survivors aboard, the *Carpathia* turned and headed for New York. In days to come, the newspapers were to refer to our vessel as 'the ship of widows'.

I talked to some of the survivors. I gave my stateroom to two of the women and slept the rest of the trip here and there on the floor. More important, all of us listened while they talked. I think it was good for them.

Statistics which I read later listed 2,208 crew and passengers who had sailed from Liverpool. Of these, only 707 were saved, leaving 1,501 missing.

The *Titanic*, on her tragic maiden voyage, was known as the biggest, most luxurious vessel afloat. It had a French restaurant, swimming pool, Turkish baths. It was reputed to have every safety device possible and was known as the ship which couldn't sink. But it did.

While the ship was sinking, a survivor told me, he saw ship's officers with pistols standing by the lifeboats to see first to the safety of women and children. A few men were allowed aboard each boat to pull the oars.

On deck, tearful husbands and fathers kissed their families goodbye, got them aboard the lifeboats, then went back to stand and wait sure death.

One woman, aboard a rapidly filling lifeboat, got out and went back to the *Titanic* deck to stand beside her husband. 'We've been together all these years,' she said, 'We'll stay together.'

The *Titanic* didn't stay afloat long. The lifeboat crews pulled at the oars in a frenzy to move clear of the suction which they knew would form a large whirlpool when the ship went down. The prow of the *Titanic* dipped lower and lower, and as it did the stern lifted clear of the water. Then the vessel tilted over to a perpendicular position and went straight down, prow first.

I have snapshots of the broken iceberg which supposedly sunk the *Titanic*, and of the heart-breaking scenes of survivors aboard the *Carpathia*. But I seldom look at them. I don't need them to jog my memory of those terrible days aboard 'the ship of widows'.[61]

ELIZABETH TARKINGTON

While the *Carpathia* was returning to New York, Mrs George Tarkington wrote the following letter to her hometown newspaper:

On the morning of the 15th, we were awakened to learn that our ship, the *Carpathia*, had, in response to wireless messages, traveled 60 miles out of her course, and that we were rescuing the passengers of the *Titanic*. Hurrying over to the ship's side, we watched the half-frozen survivors hauled upon deck. The sea was beautifully calm, icebergs looming against the clear sky; 16 boats of sick, half-frozen, more or less bereaved people were drawn on deck. We beheld the distress of people who had lost families, friends, jewels and clothing.

It was a never-to-be-forgotten scene. That calm, cloudless northern morning, with scarcely a ripple where the ship went down. The moments were tense with solemn excitement that was strangely calm. One of the lifeboats, a collapsible, was set adrift containing the dead bodies of three sailors and a babe. In the early afternoon we witnessed a burial at sea; four bodies were cast into the deep. Bereaved wives turned their eyes to heaven and wept; yet withal there was a composure that seemed born of a cold, clear sky, the calm majesty of icebergs, and the great frozen fields that appeared in view. The unfortunates in the boats crowded together like sheep. On board the *Carpathia* they have been showered with courtesy and kindness. Relief has been extended by all travelers who had it in their power to help a distressed human being ... All could have been saved had there been boats enough.[62]

On 17 April Mrs Tarkington wrote the following letter to Mr and Mrs Robert Tarkington:

My Dear Friends,

Monday morning a fellow traveler called to us, 'Get up, the *Titanic* has gone down and we are rescuing her passengers'. The girls were soon on deck. After dressing warmly I followed to find that in response to a wireless message we had gone 60 miles north of our course and were rescuing the half-frozen survivors of the great steamship *Titanic*, that had struck an iceberg at five minutes to twelve on the night of the 14th.

An interesting and sympathetic throng hung over the side of the *Carpathia* while the shipwrecked were drawn up to the lower deck. Men and women in evening dress, covered by steamer cloaks, others in whatever clothing they could snatch at short notice. Wailing babies were placed in bags and drawn up the ship's side; the women, then the men, ascended in turn until the occupants of sixteen lifeboats were drawn on deck.

The library is a hospital. Our ladies are charitably giving aid to the rescued. We gave up one of our staterooms, consequently are much crowded. Lord and Lady Hamilton are on board, also Lord Gordon. The president of the White Star Line is among the rescued, also Mrs. John Jacob Astor. Mr. Astor was lost.

I shall never forget the scene – a smooth sea, a cloudless sky, white icebergs in the distance, shivering human beings drawn up from the death that overtook families and friends. In the afternoon I beheld a burial at sea, four bodies being consigned to the deep. A babe was saved in the nurse's arms, but father, mother and sister went down. Stricken wives sit on deck and turn their tear-stained eyes to heaven and grieve for their husbands. Of 2,800 passengers 600 were rescued by the *Carpathia*.

After rescuing the passengers of the ill-fated vessel we beheld the ice fields of the North crowned by stately icebergs; for miles we floated in full view of them, gigantic white mountains rising from the ice plain, grimly fascinating, serenely beautiful. The captain of the *Carpathia* headed for New York to land the *Titanic* passengers. We will reach there Thursday afternoon. After a short rest we turn our eyes again in the direction of Italy. Among the crowd rescued from the *Titanic* my daughters found a schoolmate of the Quincy Mansion School, Boston, Mass., Miss Longley, of Hudson, N. Dak. She was rescued with two aunts. Her boat was badly manned by six sailors; she took a hand at the oars, and helped to hoist the sail. Paris gowns and jewels went to the bottom of the Atlantic, but the girls are renewing school experiences upon deck. All are filled with admiration for their captain. Yesterday they voted him a loving cup and a sum of money for the crew of the *Carpathia*.

Mrs. George Tarkington[63]

JULIET TARKINGTON

On 17 April Miss Tarkington wrote the following letter to Mr and Mrs Robert Tarkington of Danville, Kentucky:

Royal Mail Steamship *Carpathia*
April 17, 1912

My Dear Friends,

I know you have read of the awful disaster at sea, but will write you a little myself, although I am not capable of making you understand just how dreadful it was, for I am half sick and seeing double at present, as the sea is very rough and we are in a big fog.

Last Sunday night our steamer, *Carpathia*, got word over the wireless that the *Titanic*, sister ship to the *Olympic*, was sinking, so our steamer put on double speed, went over 60 miles out of our own way through icebergs and secured 800 people. The message reached our steamer about 1 o'clock, and the people were in lifeboats all this time until 8 in the morning.

Over 2,000 went down. Never in your life have you seen anything so awful. Nearly everybody rescued had lost father, husband, brother, mother or children – someone who was dear to them.

Of course, all of our passengers were on deck and watched all the lifeboats in the distance, and at last they were landed. Six brides are without husbands. You have never seen such weeping and brokenhearted people. Lots of little children are on board our ship without even mother or father. So many that were rescued died afterward from exposure. Four were buried at sea yesterday. I did not look and wouldn't have watched it for anything. Lots of women who have lost husbands are mourning for their jewelry and handsome Paris gowns. Now, what do you think of that? Not saying a word about their husbands.

Then there are all kinds of people here, from the 'biggest rich' to the poorest. More women were rescued than men. Officers pointed pistols at the men's heads, and made them get out of the lifeboats so the women and babies could be saved. There were only eighteen lifeboats on that immense ship, and there were 2,800 passengers. The White Star Line certainly should be roasted in the papers.

May, you have no idea how dreadful this was. Don't you know, I was looking at the passengers being rescued and who should I see but one of my 'Quincy Mansion School' friends being brought up nearly frozen. She had two aunts with her. We have given her some clothes and she was delighted to see us. There were only two men in her boat, and she had to help row her boat all those hours.

The women were torn from their husbands and pitched into the boats. This is the steamer you told me about, and said it couldn't sink. I tell you, I am scared to death. There was a terrific storm last night and we have been in an awful fog all day, and yesterday also. 'There is no place like home.'

Talk to me about seeing Rome. 'Linwood' is plenty good enough for me. This thing of crossing the Atlantic is no joke. We are now on our way back to New York to take the rescued passengers and I suppose will land tomorrow. We have been one whole week on the ocean: all this time is lost. We will sail again next Saturday on the same steamer – another fourteen days altogether makes 22 days we have been on the ocean.

The captain on our steamer said we staked our lives to save the passengers on the *Titanic*. We were right in an awful iceberg region. After we had taken all of them on and started back we passed a solid field of ice 50 miles long, and icebergs looked like mountains, and, remember, it is said only one-tenth is above water. I tell you, we have had a trip that will long be remembered.

I could write pages, but can't stand to stay in the writing room. It is so close. We have had rough sea, wonderfully smooth sea, a storm, burial at sea, rescued people from this disaster, seen whales, sharks, icebergs – certainly have had a variety.

With lots of love,
Juliet Tarkington[64]

ROBERT VAUGHAN

In later years, Steward Vaughan wrote the following account of his service on the *Carpathia*:

In February of the year 1912 I signed on as a steward on board the SS *Carpathia*, a liner of 13,005 tons. I had previously made a few trips to New York as bellboy on board the RMS *Mauretania*, at that time 'Queen of the Seas'. The *Carpathia* left Liverpool in February on a special cruise with an itinerary of the Mediterranean ports. She was to end her cruise at New York, then begin a regular run from New York to the Mediterranean.

During the special cruise I had the job of steward to a mess comprising the ship's baggage master, ship's inspector, wireless operator, and the three members of the ship's orchestra. At this time the mess room was the second class smoke room, but when we took on regular first and second class passengers the mess room had to be used for what it really was – a second class smoke room. The members of my mess had then to be served in the second class dining room.

On April 11th we left New York with a number of first and second class passengers, and Gibraltar was our first stop. We were four days out from New York on our way to Gibraltar, the day was Sunday, and an idea day for sea travel. Below in a cabin containing eight bunks, with only five occupied, were five members of the ship's crew. Two of the five were asleep, the remaining three (one being myself) were chatting before turning in.

This cabin was our home while we remained members of the crew, and we had endeavored to make it home-like as seafarers do. Each man had his own ideas of decorating the area around his bunk. A general form of adornment was to cut out part of the ship's menu cards and fit in photos of loved ones. Also, there were pictures of stage beauties, boxers, wrestlers and other sporty characters. To hold knickknacks etc., a box nailed to the bulkhead was usual. The larger personal belongings were in sea chests under the lower bunks. On the *Mauretania* I had to watch my property as short voyages are more conducive to pilfering than on a long voyage where men seem to trust each other, knowing they will be together a long time. In my case I had no need to lock up my property, as we trusted each other. After chatting for about an hour the three of us decided to turn in, as morning came too quickly, and another day's work.

It seemed that I had hardly fallen asleep when I was awakened by someone tugging on my bedclothes. I sat up half asleep and asked the intruder what was wrong. He told me that our ship had struck an iceberg, which later proved to be wrong. At the time, however, it certainly encouraged me to get up on deck.

But this was easier said than done! The cabin was dark, as someone had swiped the light bulb (a common occurrence) to stop someone from reading or talking half the night when others wanted to sleep. My chums and I, after coming out of our sleepy state, realized that had our ship hit an iceberg we would have been almost instantly aware, as our cabin was well forward near the bow.

When dressed, I went up on deck with the others, where we met the second steward who told us to go and help get out blankets from the lockers. After this, I helped set places in the dining saloons. Here the tables were set with as many places as could possibly be set. Every member of the crew had been allotted a task. While I was doing these various tasks, I wondered what all this preparation was for. Later, my curiosity was satisfied when along with other members of the crew I was told to go to the dining saloon. Here we found Captain Rostron, who told us that we were answering an SOS. It seemed the RMS *Titanic* had struck an iceberg and that we were going to the stricken liner's aid!

He asked us to uphold the traditions of the sea when the time came to do so. Preparations had been completed, stimulants etc., to use in case of necessity. After the talk from our captain, we were dismissed and then allotted our stations where we must go when required. Till the time I was required, I was free to go where I wished. I went to the after deck where there were many of the crew watching and waiting.

I saw many icebergs of various sizes, and no doubt our ship's navigator had his work cut out to con the ship safely, and yet maintain speed. This had, in fact, been increased almost as soon as the ship was turned to proceed on her errand of mercy. By now several sources of steam had been cut off to allow extra steam for the engines.

I was cold up on deck as were others, but a bit of horseplay helped to keep us warm. In any case it would not be long until we had steamed fifty odd miles to the area where the *Titanic* had struck.

Suddenly I saw a green light – an indication that we were near the scene of the disaster. In a short time I saw the first boat of survivors. Then, as dawn became brighter, I could see boatloads of survivors at various distances apart. Our ship was not stopped, and as each boatload of survivors came alongside they were brought aboard and given into the hands of members of the crew, who took them to the saloons where they received food and every possible attention.

After escorting several survivors to the saloon, I was in the pantry getting a drink when one of the stewards brought in a child and laid it on the warm press. I did not think any more of the child until, shortly afterwards, I heard a woman crying and acting hysterically shouting 'bambino'. She was getting out of control when I remembered the baby on the press. On bringing the child to her, it was evident that it was her baby, as she relaxed with the comfort of the child in her arms, content to be led away.

Meanwhile, our ship was the scene of conflicting hopes on the part of those whom we had taken aboard. Each of these persons had hopes that their loved ones were on our ship somewhere, but it was only after a check had been made that some hopes were realized and many, many more dashed.

As our ship left the scene of the disaster, there was a short prayer service for the lost souls. During the service I thought of my shipmates who had left the *Carpathia* when she finished the special cruise. These were the three musicians, Hartley, Bricoux and Brailey. They had told me how they would enjoy the change from the *Carpathia* to the newest super deluxe *Titanic*. Little did they realize what Fate had in store.

As our ship had a good number of her own passengers, the survivors created a problem of accommodation, but part of this problem was solved by the sympathetic attitude of our passengers, who shared their cabins and also supplied clothing to those who needed it.

We left the scene of the disaster on our way back to New York with the survivors. The beautiful sunrise over a calm sea belied the fact that such a tragedy had been enacted.

On the way to our pier after picking up the pilot, the ship was besieged by small craft shouting questions, but not getting much satisfaction, as Captain Rostron was reluctant to give any information until he saw fit.

When we finally arrived at our dock and safely tied up, I was able to relax from my duties. I could not go ashore, as it was forbidden to most of the crew. However, two of my shipmates went ashore but failed to return, and I heard they sold first-hand information to reporters who, no doubt, paid them well.

New York went all out to receive the survivors. As no full information as to the number of survivors was generally known, the people of New York expected to have to deal with a full shipload of survivors. In any event, New York showed its ability to help victims of disaster.

Before leaving New York to resume our interrupted voyage, the ship was thrown open to visitors. As a result, a few guards were posted to discourage souvenir collectors who might be tempted to take small objects.

The crew of our ship were given ten dollars from the survivors and later received a bronze medal. It was at the instigation of Mrs. Brown (The Unsinkable Mrs. Brown) that these medals were given. The members of the crew were also feted at some of the ports visited in the Mediterranean. I left the *Carpathia* on our return to New York and went back to England on the RMS *Caronia*.

Although fifty-four years have passed since that SOS was signaled, it's an experience I'll never forget![65]

During a recorded interview Mr Vaughan was asked about Harold Cottam, the Marconi operator, who was one of the crewmen he served with on board the *Carpathia*:

That afternoon, you see, I had to tidy up his cabin ... the Marconi shack, if you like to call it that. [It] was up on top of this second cabin smoke room, you see, and that afternoon, Sunday afternoon, I went to clean his room and he said, 'No, don't bother with it this afternoon, steward,' he said, 'I want to stay up late tonight and so I'll sleep now'. And that's funny, because that's the night he stayed up, and as Rostron says in his book, that he was just about to unlace his shoes and he still had the headphones on, you see, when he heard this [distress call].

... The bandsmen, you know, another funny thing about the bandsmen. There was Hartley, Brailey and Hume. Well now, they left our ship. They left our ship in New York ... because the White Star Line was anxious to get bandsmen for this new liner, *Titanic*. Well now, as I said, I was their messman and they said to me, 'Well, steward, we'll soon be on a big ship and we're getting away from this lousy food', you know, the *Carpathia*'s food, and there they were. You see how fate took a hand there? They left our ship, and they went to the *Titanic* and were lost.

Vaughan was asked about his reflections of that morning:

Well, the last scene like that impressed me was the sunrise. The absolute beauty of that sunrise, the absolute beauty of it, and then to turn your head downward into the sea and see those lifeboats and the people that spent a night of horror. It seemed to be such a terrible contrast. It made you think.[66]

Unknown Steward

A steward wrote the following account while the *Carpathia* was still at sea:

At midnight on Sunday, April 14 I was promenading the deck of the steamer *Carpathia*, bound for the Mediterranean and three days out from New York, when an urgent summons came to my room from the chief steward, E. Harry Hughes. I then learned that the White Star liner *Titanic*, the greatest ship afloat, had struck an iceberg and was in serious difficulties.

We were then already steaming at our greatest power to the scene of the disaster, Capt. Rostron having immediately given orders that every man of the crew should stand by to exert his utmost efforts.

Within a very few minutes every preparation had been made to receive two or three thousand persons. Blankets were placed ready, tables laid with hot soups and coffee, bedding &c. prepared, and hospital supplies laid out ready to attend to any injured.

The men were then mustered in the saloon and addressed by the chief steward. He told them of the disaster and appealed to them in a few words as Britishers to show the world what stuff they were made of and to add a glorious page to the history of the empire, and right well did the men respond to the appeal. Every lifeboat was manned and ready to be launched at a moment's notice. Nothing further could be done but anxiously wait and look out for the ship's distress signal.

Our Marconi operator, whose unceasing efforts for many hours deserve the greatest possible praise, was unable at this time to get any reply to the urgent inquiries he was sending out and he feared the worst.

At last a blue flare was observed, to which we replied with a rocket. Day was just dawning when we observed a boat in the distance.

Eastward on the horizon a huge iceberg, the cause of the disaster, majestically reared two noble peaks to heaven. Rope ladders were already lowered and we hove to near the lifeboat, which was now approaching us as rapidly as the nearly exhausted efforts of the men at the oars could bring her.

Under the command of our chief officer, who worked indefatigably at the noble work of rescue, the survivors in the boat were rapidly but carefully hauled aboard and given into the hands of the medical staff under the organization of Dr. McGhee.

We then learned the terrible news that the gigantic vessel, the unsinkable *Titanic*, had gone down one hour and ten minutes after striking.

From this time onward lifeboats continued to arrive at frequent intervals. Every man of the *Carpathia*'s crew was unsparing in his effort to assist to tenderly comfort each and every survivor. In all sixteen boatloads were received, containing altogether 700 persons, many in simply their night attire, others in evening dress, as if direct from an after dinner reception or concert. Most conspicuous was the coolness and self possession, particularly of the women.

Pathetic and heartrending incidents were many. There is not a man of the rescue party who was not moved almost to tears. Women arrived and frantically rushed from one gangway to another eagerly scanning the fresh arrivals in the boats for a lost husband or brother.

One boat arrived with the unconscious body of an English colonel. He had been taking out his mother on a visit to three other of her sons. He had succeeded in getting her away in one of the boats and he himself had found a place in another. When but a few yards from the ill fated ship the boat containing his mother capsized before his own eyes.

Immediately he dived into the water and commenced a frantic search for her, but in vain. Boat after boat endeavored to take him aboard, but he refused to give up, continuing to swim for nearly three hours until even his great strength of body and mind gave out and he was hauled unconscious into a passing boat and brought aboard the *Carpathia*. The doctor gives little hope of his recovery. He has spoken to nobody.

There were, I understand, twelve newly-married couples aboard the big ship. The twelve brides have been saved, but of the husbands all but one have perished. That one would not have been here, but that he was appealed to to assist to man a lifeboat. Think of the self-sacrifice of these eleven heroes, who stood on the doomed vessel and parted from their brides forever, knowing full well that a few brief minutes would end all things for themselves.

Many similar pathetic incidents could be related. Sad-eyed women roam aimlessly about the ship still looking vainly for husband, brother or father. To comfort, them is impossible. All human efforts are being exerted on their behalf. Their material needs are satisfied in every way. But who can cure a broken heart?

One of the earlier boats to arrive was seen to contain a woman tenderly clasping a pet Pomeranian. When assisted to the rope ladder and while the rope was being fastened around her she emphatically refused to give up for a second the dog which was evidently so much to her. He is now receiving as careful and tender attention as his mistress.

A survivor informs me that there was on the ship a lady who was taking out a huge Great Dane dog. When the boats were rapidly filling she appeared on deck with her canine companion and sadly entreated that he should be taken off with her. It was impossible. Human lives, those of women and children, were the first consideration. She was urged to seize the opportunity to save her own life and leave the dog. She refused to desert him and has, I understand, sacrificed her life with him.

One elderly lady was bewailing to a steward that she had lost 'everything'. He indignantly replied that she should thank God her life was spared, never mind her replaceable property. The reply was pathetic. 'I have lost everything – my husband,' and she broke into uncontrollable grief.

One incident that impressed me perhaps more than any other was the burial on Tuesday afternoon of four of the poor fellows who succeeded in safely getting away from the doomed vessel only to perish later from exhaustion and exposure as a result of their gallant efforts to bring to safety the passengers placed in their charge in the lifeboats. They were:

W.H. Hoyt, Esq. first class passenger.

Abraham Harmer [David Livshin], third class passenger.

S.C. Siebert, Steward.

P. Lyons [William Lyons], sailor.

The sailor and steward were unfortunately dead when taken aboard. The passengers lived but a few minutes after. They were treated with the greatest attention. The funeral service was conducted amid profound silence and attended by a large number of survivors and rescuers. The bodies, remains covered by the national flag, were reverently consigned to the mighty deep from which they had been, alas, vainly, saved.

Most gratifying to the officers and men of the *Carpathia* is the constantly expressive appreciation of the survivors.

On Tuesday afternoon a meeting was held in the saloon attended by all the survivors of the *Titanic*'s saloon passengers. Mr. Goldenberg, who took the chair, expressed in a vote of thanks to the captain of the *Carpathia*, A.H. Rostron, R.N.R., their heart-full thanks to God for their deliverance and the unanimous opinion of the company that no words could express their gratitude to the captain, officers and crew for their self-sacrifice and unsparing efforts in the noble work of rescue.

It was unanimously resolved to immediately open a fund with the objects of presenting a loving cup to Capt. Rostron and the officers of the *Carpathia*, presenting a purse to the crew and a purse to the surviving officers and men of the *Titanic*, also to render immediate assistance to such of the survivors as had lost everything and were penniless.

I.G. Frauenthal of New York offered to act as treasurer and Mrs. J.J. Brown undertook the management of inquiring and rendering the necessary immediate assistance required. There was also read a unanimous resolution from the women survivors expressing heartfelt gratification and unrepayable indebtedness to the *Carpathia*'s officers and men, enlarging upon their tender kindness, chivalry and gallantry and their self-sacrificing devotion to the rescued.

The response to the appeal was immediate. Subscriptions ranging from $250 downward rapidly filled the list.[67]

The Cunard liner *Carpathia* – the only vessel to pick up survivors of the *Titanic*. (Author's collection)

Captain Arthur Rostron. 'Then came to our ears moans, occasional cries, intermittent shouts of men, and above it all the frequent concise orders of Captain Rostron, directing the work of rescue.' – C.A. Bernard, *Carpathia* passenger. (Library of Congress)

John Jacob Astor. 'Colonel Astor, holding his young wife's arm, stood decorously aside as the officers spoke to him, and Mrs. Astor and her maid were ushered to seats in the lifeboat.' – Carlos Hurd, *Carpathia* passenger. (New York Public Library)

Archibald Butt. '... I learned that Major Butt, when the *Titanic* struck, took his position with the officers and from the moment that the order to man the lifeboats was given until the last one was dropped into the sea, he aided in the maintenance of discipline and the placing of the women and children in the boats.' – Captain Charles Crain, *Carpathia* passenger. (Author's collection)

Harold Cottam. 'Harold Cottam, the main Marconi operator of the *Carpathia*, did not go to bed at his usual time Sunday night and as a result caught the first message of the *Titanic*'s plight.' – Carlos Hurd, Carpathia passenger. (*Washington Times*)

May Futrelle. 'Mrs Jacques Futrelle, wife of the novelist, herself a writer of note, sat dry-eyed in the *Carpathia's* saloon, telling her friends that she had given up hope for her husband ... "I feel better," Mrs Futrelle said hours afterward, "for I can cry now."' – Carlos Hurd, *Carpathia* passenger. (*National Magazine*)

Henry and Irene Harris. 'Mrs Henry B. Harris, wife of a New York theatrical manager, checked her tears long enough to beg that some message of hope about her husband be sent to her father-in-law.' – Carlos Hurd, *Carpathia* passenger. (*New York Herald*)

Joseph Bruce Ismay. 'The survivors included Bruce Ismay, president of the White Star Line. Because the survivors blamed him for the disaster, he shut himself up in his cabin for the whole voyage and in New York left our ship secretly, accompanied by detectives.' – Dr Arpad Lengyel, Carpathia passenger. (Author's collection)

Charles Lightoller. 'The *Titanic*'s second officer, Lightoller by name, had the most wonderful escape of which I have yet heard. He actually went down with the ship and was blown out by an explosion which occurred after the ship had sunk with tremendous force.' – May Birkhead, *Carpathia* passenger. (Author's collection)

William Murdoch. 'Mr Murdoch, first officer of the *Titanic*, sacrificed his life in seeing all the lifeboats away from the ship, and his display of coolness is indescribable.' – Fred Beachler, *Carpathia* passenger. (Author's collection)

Michel and Edmond Navratil. 'In my stateroom a little boy, just sick enough to keep very quiet, was placed. He was one of the two French children who had been put into lifeboats by other passengers while their father, who did not succeed in getting into the boat, was drowned.' – Carlos Hurd, *Carpathia* passenger. (Library of Congress)

Captain Edward J. Smith. 'I notice that there have been various stories afloat that Captain Smith shot himself just before the *Titanic* went down, but this does not appear to be the opinion of a great many of the survivors with whom I talked on the *Carpathia*. The majority of them say that he jumped at the last moment.' – Eleanor Danforth, *Carpathia* passenger. (*Literary Digest*)

Isidor and Ida Straus. 'Isidor Straus, supporting his wife on her way to a lifeboat, was held back by an inexorable guard. Another officer strove to help her to a seat of safety, but she brushed away his arm and clung to her husband, crying, "I will not go without you."' – Carlos Hurd, *Carpathia* passenger. (Straus Historical Society)

May Birkhead. 'The sea was dotted with tiny lifeboats from the *Titanic*, and much to my amazement there was one at our side and our sailors were pulling the passengers up onto the deck with ropes.' – May Birkhead, *Carpathia* passenger. (Unknown 1918 newspaper)

Second Officer James Bisset. 'We arrived at the scene about 4 a.m. We first saw a green light and imagined it was one of the *Titanic*'s sidelights. A little later we knew the worst. The light was a rocket fired from one of the boats. The *Titanic* was gone.' – James Bisset, *Carpathia* officer. (Author's collection)

WOVEN IN SILK.

R.M.S. CARPATHIA.

A woven-silk postcard sold as a souvenir on board the rescue ship, *Carpathia*. (Author's collection)

CARPATHIA PASSENGER
AND CREW INTERVIEWS

ROGER B.T. ANDERSON

The Reverend Anderson was asked to conduct a burial service for three bodies that were buried at sea from the *Carpathia* at 4 p.m.:

There were no others who died on the way over. While a number of them were suffering from injuries received in getting into the lifeboats or from exposure, none others succumbed. Those whom we buried died in the lifeboats. They were probably frozen to death.

The tortures which those poor victims of the wreck had to undergo while they were in the lifeboats were terrible. The water's temperature was 31 degrees. One can imagine having to stay in that for an hour even, until one could be pulled into a lifeboat, or to have to remain in a cramped lifeboat for many hours waiting for a ship of rescue to come.

They might just as well have been in the middle of the Arctic zone. I talked with a number of them and they all told me the same thing when they came aboard. The cold was killing each one of them. Had they had to wait much longer, few would have survived. Our boat fortunately came just in time.

It was midnight when we received the SOS signal from the *Titanic*. I was asleep in my stateroom, but the fearful shuffling of feet on the deck above me made me think that something was wrong. Finally at 3 o'clock I could no longer remain in my room and I dressed and came out. When I got on deck I saw our crew getting the lifeboats ready for action. The captain did not know what to expect and wanted to be prepared.

I guess it was about half-past 3 that the first light of dawn began to appear, and by straining our eyes we could see several hundred yards ahead. We stood in the bow, several of us, watching. The time seemed very long. Then I heard a man in the mast above us shout, 'Lifeboat on the starboard bow!' That changed everything. We never thought that the *Titanic* would have sunk. We believed we would get there in time to save her. But as the dawn increased and lifted the veil of darkness clear to the horizon we saw in the midst of the ice floes little boats bobbing up and down on the water, some filled with women, children and men, some half empty.

There was no *Titanic*. Our captain could not understand where the big vessel could be. I saw the officers straining their eyes to catch sight of the ship itself. Just then the quartermaster turned the wheel and we made for the first lifeboat.

It was a sight which clutched one's heart to see those people when they saw the ship. We could see the women rowing in many of the boats, and as they turned and saw us behind them they took up their oars again and seemed to have a new and strange strength as they pulled for our boat. They were taken into the hatches in the third class passengers' department for the most part, but others had to be lifted in slings right from the boats up to the top deck.

Many, when they saw the ship, began to scream in hysterics and as they came up the side they fell trembling to the deck, crying out their prayers of thanksgiving for deliverance. Others seemed remarkably composed and walked briskly down to the cabin, where coffee and food had been prepared for them.

But there were none who walked below who had left someone they loved behind on the *Titanic*. No sooner had they gained the deck than they pressed close to the side and watched with straining eyes each passenger lifted to the deck. At times a wife would recognize a husband and then a hysterical shriek of joy would sound over the whole ship.[68]

❖   ❖   ❖

J.W. Barker

Steward Barker gave the following interview to reporters on 19 April:

At eight bells, midnight, I had gone below and turned in. Twenty minutes later I heard the hiss and crackle of the wireless, but paid no attention to it until the chief officer knocked at my cabin and told me to get ready to receive 3,000 passengers from the White Star liner, which was in distress and from which an SOS call had been picked up.

All of the stewards were assembled, the storeroom was ransacked, blankets, brandy, medicines and bandages were gotten out and the dining room tables were laid to provide a large and extra fine meal for the rescued. The crew was assembled on deck and mustered to the boats, which were swung loose, ready to be lowered at a moment's notice.

In the meantime, we had changed our course and were proceeding under full speed for the spot in which the *Titanic* lay. It was three o'clock before the first sign of her had been detected. Then we noticed on the horizon a blue flare, which is a distress signal. It came from one of the lifeboats, but we could not tell that at the time. The *Titanic*, as we afterward learned, had sunk long before this signal had been sighted.

It was 4:30 and dawn was just beginning to break when we caught sight of the first lifeboat and knew that the *Titanic* had been abandoned. At the same time we got our first hazy glimpse of the giant iceberg which had destroyed the big steamship. It lay against the horizon in front of us like a green-gray monster in the early light.

As soon as the first lifeboat had been sighted, we hove to and began to send up rockets to attract the attention of any other boats which might be at hand. Soon afterward the first boat lay alongside of us, and the passengers were hoisted over the side, with Capt. Rostron of the *Carpathia* standing at the rail to receive them. In the first boat were two men, both sailors, fourteen women and two children.

The passengers had been barely picked up and the first lifeboat hoisted on deck when the second boat hove in sight. From then on, at brief intervals, boat after boat began to come alongside until we had picked up sixteen in all. Fourteen of the boats were large-sized lifeboats and these were hoisted on board and saved, the other two, as it happened, were collapsible and of slight value, and these we discarded for lack of room after the people on them were saved.

We lay in the same position until it was broad daylight, burning rockets and searching the sea with glasses on every side. At 6 a.m. we sighted the *Californian* of the Leyland Line and got into wireless communication with her at once. She informed us that she had been cruising around the spot where the *Titanic* went down and had not been able to sight a single lifeboat or any indication of any survivors. We asked her to continue the search and put about for New York with the rescued we had on board.

I was amazed at the wonderful demeanor of most of the women passengers rescued from the *Titanic*. Most of them came up over the side perfectly calm and collected. Only a few shrieked, and I did not see any of them weeping until several hours afterward. All of the rescued were immediately wrapped in warm blankets and were given drinks of brandy and coffee.

When Bruce Ismay was taken on board the first thing he did was to demand something to eat and went into the dining room for some breakfast. One of the stewards gave it to him, and he offered the man $2 as a tip. At first it was refused, but he insisted, saying that he was going to see to it that all of the 'boys' on the *Carpathia* would be rewarded generously. It was then that the steward learned that the hungry passenger was Mr. Ismay.

After the first meal Mr. Ismay kept to the stateroom which he was sharing with another passenger, and ate all of his meals there. I did not see him again in the restaurant. I did hear some talk among some of the women from the *Titanic* about his having been saved, but nothing that I can remember.

A remarkable thing was that in one of the lifeboats which was picked up were two sailors at the oars were both dead, having collapsed from exhaustion as the result of their long fight with the waves to get away from the sinking ship and avoid being within the area of suction.

The officers of the *Carpathia* and the male passengers gave up their cabins very gladly to accommodate the passengers from the *Titanic*. We slept in the steerage or anywhere we could in order to make room for the strangers. The strangers were always fed first. Most of them were without any clothing whatever and our own passengers and officers gave up their own clothing to help them out. In that fashion they all got clothing of some description.

There were five or six little children. They seemed to recover from their first fright very quickly and were soon romping about and playing. One of the children had a case of pneumonia, as it was first thought, but it turned out to be a case of measles. All the women passengers on the *Carpathia* got busy at once, knitting and sewing babies' clothing.

I have asked some of the passengers how it happened. They tell me that about 12 o'clock they heard a great noise. According to their stories when they came on deck and asked what had happened, the captain told them there was nothing to be alarmed about and that she had only poked her nose into an iceberg. It was not until sometime later that they got ready for the lifeboats.

While the sailors were busy getting the lifeboats ready, there was an explosion and it was only then that the captain ordered that every person should put on a lifebelt and that the women and children should be put into the lifeboats.[69]

Steward Barker granted the following interview on 6 May:

At midnight on Sunday, April 14, I was promenading the deck of the *Carpathia* when, hearing eight bells strike, I went below to retire for the night. I had just turned in when an urgent summons came from the chief steward, and I learned that an urgent distress message had been received from the *Titanic*.

We were then about 58 miles to the south-east of her, and Captain A.H. Rostron had already given orders for the *Carpathia* to be turned around and proceed at utmost speed in her direction. The heads of all departments were aroused and every precaution was quietly and quickly made to receive 2,000 passengers.

Blankets were placed in readiness, tables laid up, hot soups and consommés, coffee and tea prepared, and the surgeries stocked and staffed. Men were mustered at the boats and given instruction to be in immediate readiness to launch and row to the *Titanic* and bring off all passengers and crew.

Within an hour every possible preparation had been made by the stewards' department, and, to their great credit be it recorded, not a single passenger of the 1,000 we were carrying had been aroused. It was now only possible to wait and look for any signals from the distressed vessel. Their wireless had failed some time. We were then forging ahead at the utmost speed that could be got out of our engines, making us about 18 knots per hour as against our usual 13 to 14. No words of praise can be too great for the unsparing efforts of the engineering department and the firemen.

At about a quarter to three we got the first signal, a blue flare on our port bow. Shortly after we sighted our first iceberg, undoubtedly the cause of the disaster, a huge ghostly mass of white looming up through the darkness a few miles distant. A little later we found ourselves in a field of icebergs, large and small, and it became frequently necessary to alter our course.

It was a little before 4 o'clock when we came near enough to discern the first lifeboat, which came alongside at 4:10 a.m. She was not much more than half-filled with women and children, and was in the charge of an officer, who reported that the 'unsinkable' *Titanic* had foundered a little more than an hour after striking the iceberg. The survivors were taken aboard and handed over to the care of the medical staff and the stewards, under the perfect control of Chief Steward Hughes.

Day was breaking, and over an area of four miles we were able to see the other boats. We were surrounded by icebergs of all sizes, and three miles to the north was a big field of drift ice dotted with icebergs. During the next two or three hours we endured the most heartrending experiences we have ever known. Some of the incidents were almost too pathetic for description.

One woman was heartbroken and uncontrollable. She cried hysterically for her husband, and it was only with the greatest difficulty that she could be restrained from jumping into the sea to look for him. It was necessary to resort to the subterfuge of a lie, and tell her that her husband was safe before she could be calmed.

A Colonel was brought aboard unconscious. He had been swimming in the icy water for over two hours. His mother was placed in a collapsible boat which was launched only to capsize on reaching the water. Immediately he dived from the ship to his mother's rescue.

He was unable in the darkness to find her, and commenced a frantic search among the bodies and wreckage. One after another the lifeboats endeavored to take him aboard, but he resisted until the coldness of the water overcame him. He was hauled into a boat just as he was about to sink and join his mother in death. It is doubtful if he will recover. He has spoken to no one. His mother was about to pay a visit to three other of her sons.

Another young woman went down with the *Titanic* rather than desert her dog – a huge St. Bernard, and a great favorite on board. When the lifeboats were being launched a seat was prepared for her, but she demanded that the dog be taken also.

This was impossible, human lives being the first consideration, and she was urged to sacrifice the dog and save herself. She refused, and was last seen on the deck of the vessel, clasping her pet to her bosom. Her dead body was afterwards found floating by the side of her dog.

An old lady was bewailing to a steward that she had lost 'everything'. Indignantly he told her she should thank God that her life was spared, and not at such a time regret the loss of her property. Her reply was pathetic – steward, I have lost everything – my dear husband – and she burst into tears.

About 8 o'clock we had picked up the last boat and got the survivors aboard. Two were so exhausted from exposure that they died whilst being brought aboard. These, together with a sailor and steward who perished at the oars, were buried at 4 o'clock.

The *Carpathia*'s passengers behaved splendidly, giving up their cabins voluntarily, and supplying the distressed women with clothes. The captain, officers and crew also gave up their quarters and did their utmost to alleviate the sufferings of the survivors. The saloons, library and smoke-rooms were also utilized for sleeping quarters.[70]

FRED BEACHLER

Mr Beachler granted the following interview to reporters after the *Carpathia* reached New York:

The *Carpathia* left New York at noon on Thursday, April 11, for her regular Mediterranean cruise, taking the northerly course and almost immediately ran into cold weather, which continued, but with a smooth sea, until the evening of Sunday.

It was about midnight by the ship's clock when we got the *Titanic* operator's message stating that the great steamship had struck an iceberg and was in danger.

Captain Rostron of the *Carpathia* at once gave orders for full steam and set out for the distressed *Titanic*, the *Carpathia* at that time being about eighty miles distant. Before reaching the scene we got the word that the *Titanic* was badly ripped along the starboard side and soon afterward learned that the great ship was going down.

It was about three o'clock when we reached the place where the wreck occurred, and we could plainly see the huge dark iceberg which she had struck. Just as dawn was breaking the first boat from the *Titanic* came alongside the *Carpathia* and our officers and crew brought the passengers on board, removed the life preservers, wrapped the rescued in blankets, gave them stimulants and did everything possible for their comfort. The weather then was clear but very cold, and the sea smooth.

It may as well be said here that the officers and men of the *Carpathia* deserve the highest praise for their splendid work throughout the trying night, and also for their continuous work day and night until our return to New York. They worked not only unceasingly, but were cool and courteous at all times and gave the same attention and care to the poorest steerage passenger that was given to those in the first and second cabins.

It seemed nearly an hour from the time of arrival of the first lifeboat until another came up, but from then on they came more frequently and by eight o'clock the sixteenth and last to be picked up by us arrived, with a total of about 720 survivors.

The first boats to put off the *Titanic* contained mostly women and children, and many of the women helped at the oars. At first rope was dipped in pitch and burned in some of the boats to give their location, while men burned paper in other boats. Some of the boats were well filled, while others were but half full.

Bruce Ismay, president of the White Star Line, was the last to leave the boat in which he reached the *Carpathia*.

All the rescued seemed remarkably calm, some women laughing while being put on board, but, once safe, many of them went into hysterics but were quieted and looked after by our stewardess. Many of the arrivals were fully dressed, while others had very little clothing.

Since daylight we could see countless icebergs all about us, some of them of mountainous size and fantastic shape, and an endless field of ice stretched away to one side as far as we could see. A conservative estimate would be fully one hundred miles of floes. It was at once a most awe inspiring and grand spectacle, and the oldest mariners and greatest Atlantic travelers on board the *Carpathia* unite in saying they never beheld its like before nor expect to see its equal again.

It was not unlike the beautiful harbor of Rio Janeiro, with its famed fantastic shaped peaks, except that this was on a grander scale.

The large black iceberg which caused the disaster stood out like the Rock of Gibraltar, but close by also were Old Sugarloaf and Hunchback, the beautiful peaks of the Brazilian harbor, but now presented to us in huge ice mountains.

The *Californian* of the Leyland Line, having come alongside us about eight o'clock, we exchanged signals and soon after steamed for New York, a distance of more than one thousand miles, while the *Californian* remained.

The *Carpathia* had been in a dangerous position during the whole night, both from icebergs and high pressure on boilers because of the forced run we were making, but none of the passengers knew this at the time. As a matter of fact few of them left their staterooms until after daylight, and some did not learn of the *Titanic* disaster until all the lifeboats were in.

Two of the rescued from the *Titanic* died from shock and exposure before they reached the *Carpathia*, and another died a few minutes after being taken on board. The dead were W.H. Hoyt, first cabin; Abraham Harmer [David Livshin], third class and S.C. Siebert, steward, and they were buried at sea the morning of April 15, latitude [illegible] deg. 14 min. north, longitude [illegible] min. west. P. Lyon, able seaman, died and was buried at sea the following day.

It was not until noon of Monday that we cleared the last of the ice and Monday night a dense fog came up and continued until the following morning, then a strong wind, a heavy sea, a thunderstorm and a dense fog Tuesday night caused some uneasiness among the more unnerved, the fog continuing all of Tuesday.

The second cabin dining room had been turned into a hospital to care for the injured, and the first, second and third class dining rooms were used for sleeping rooms at night for women, while the smoking rooms were set aside for men. All available space was used, some sleeping in chairs and some on the floor, while a few found rest in the bathrooms.

One of the most seriously injured was a woman who had lost both her children. Her limbs had been severely torn, but she was very patient.

In talks with surviving officers and passengers of the *Titanic* the time given from the striking of the iceberg until the ship sank varies, but I learn from a reliable source, my informant being an officer of the *Titanic*, that she struck twenty minutes of twelve by the ship's clock (twenty minutes to one Navy Yard time); that the forward starboard side was ripped open about half the length of the vessel, and that great pieces of ice fell over her bow. It was nineteen minutes past two when the vessel disappeared with a report of two explosions.

I also learn on the same reliable authority, verified by others, that Captain Smith of the *Titanic* was in the water with a child in his arms, which he succeeded in placing in one of the boats. He was begged to come on board himself, but refused and turned back as though to aid others, and was not seen again.

There was little excitement, according to my informant, when the passengers were told to get up and dress and go to the upper decks, as none of the crew or passengers thought the great boat would sink, and those who had put off in the small boats felt reassured when they saw the lights from the *Carpathia*. But many failed to get overboard before the ship sank, and their screams could be heard by those who had left the vessel as the great mass went to the bottom.

One of the most remarkable escapes was that of an American barber from Philadelphia, the only American employed aboard. He was blown off as the boilers exploded and was injured, but was rescued after being in the icy waters three hours. He has made 750 ocean trips, but says he is through now.

About the first news we got told of Col. Astor's death.

Mr. and Mrs. William Carter, Miss and Master Carter, of New York, had spent last year in England and were returning. They were made comfortable by Chief Steward Hughes of the *Carpathia*. The Carter valet and a chauffeur were lost.

A boy of the ship's crew jumped for an overturned boat on which a number of men were clinging, but fell into the water. He swam for the boat but was struck on the head with an oar by one of the men. He caught hold of the man's leg and threatened to pull him into the water if he repeated the blow, and was permitted to get aboard.

Among the rescued was a Japanese and four Chinese. Two small dogs, one being a handsome chow chow, were also saved and taken care of.

On Tuesday afternoon a meeting was called of the uninjured survivors in the main saloon for the purpose of devising means of assisting the more unfortunates, many of whom had lost relatives and all their personal belongings and thanking Divine Providence for their deliverance.

A committee was then appointed to raise funds on board the *Carpathia* to relieve the immediate wants of the destitute and assist them in reaching their destinations and also to present a loving cup to the officers of the *Carpathia* and also a loving cup to the surviving officers of the *Titanic*.

Mr. I.G. Frauenthal of New York was made chairman of the Committee of Subscriptions.

A committee consisting of Mrs. J.J. Brown, Mrs. William Bucknell and Mrs. George Stone was appointed to look after the destitute.

Mr. Murdoch, first officer of the *Titanic*, sacrificed his life in seeing all the lifeboats away from the ship, and his display of coolness is indescribable.

The spectacle on board the *Carpathia* on the return trip to New York at times was heartrending, while at other times those on board were quite cheerful.[71]

C.A. BERNARD

Dr Bernard's newspaper interview was published on 19 April:

Strangely enough, I did not retire early that night. I was somewhat fond of watching the flashing and snapping of the wireless and had climbed up to the wireless cage to stand about and watch.

I went down about midnight. Hardly had I reached the smoking room when a steward, white-faced and excited, rushed by me. I saw him whisper to the second officer. Together they rushed to Captain Rostron's cabin. Then the captain in his shirt and bathrobe flashed by us. I followed. A few minutes later I learned the *Titanic* had sounded the dreaded SOS.

The ship put about quietly. It was such a night as I shall never forget. The stars were out, and at midnight the cakes of ice, heaving in the calm sea, glittered in the freakish night light. Hour after hour we went on, the *Carpathia* hewing a veritable path through the ice-strewn region in her mad haste to reach the *Titanic*.

All at once the officers began to stir. Then came orders to man the boats. Then, off to the northeast, like black logs in the sea, I saw what was left of the *Titanic*. It seemed hours before we reached the first boat. It was manned entirely by women – some twenty-seven of them, I believe, were in it. Two women were lustily working at oars and I saw a man in a heap leaning over the gunwale.

I am a strong man. I have faced death and my friends tell me I have courage, but I cried, and I'm proud to admit it. These women, heroines, clinging to each other, the stronger soothing the weaker, were huddled in their seats, half clad, bonnet-less, with eyes which seemed to blaze their horror and mute appeal in the growing dawn. Then came to our ears moans, occasional cries, intermittent shouts of men, and above it all the frequent, concise orders of Capt. Rostron, directing the work of rescue.

It was a masterly effort. God forgive us if we cheered while some poor soul was passing away, but emotions coming thick and fast, and so contradictory could not be balked longer, and we did cheer when boatload after boatload was drawn to the deck.

Probably all of the *Carpathia*'s passengers were up by this time. Along the rail they stood, men and women, with arms full of clothing, blankets, shawls, cloaks – everything, in which they wrapped the shivering, terrified figures.

Day by this time had broken strongly. Officers with glasses searched the horizon for other boats or rafts or castaways on the ice. There was none, but off to the east loomed terrifying and awful the iceberg that had sent the *Titanic* to the bottom. The hideous blue spectacle, looking amazingly like the skyline of your New York here, stretched menacingly about eighty miles, I should say. But there was no sign of the *Titanic*.

Then came the stories. And what stories! Probably the true story of all that took place that fateful night may never be told, for the reason none of the survivors seemed to be calm enough to have retained accurate impressions of the event. Those who were calm enough to see to it that the women and children got off first are beyond questioning. The versions of the disaster differ, as they always will.

I am sure that Captain Smith was in his cabin smoking a cigar with two friends when he was shunted out of his seat. The ship seemed to rise out of the water, grind on something, like a row boat striking a rock, tremble for a moment, and then slide back again into the water with an enormous splash. He must have known then that the terror of the seas had crossed his path. With his other two experiences of ill fortune, he likely did what other captains have done – found solace in a pistol shot.

I have been told by maybe twenty of the survivors that they remember distinctly the captain moving his arms calmly and shouting, 'No danger' and ordering the passengers back to their staterooms. Then came strains of music which soothed the alarm, but instantly it broke out afresh and a panic of indescribable fury broke out. It was then, when he saw his people out of his control, that he flashed his pistol and ended his life. It was then that heroic men of the Butt type retained control and saved a frightful carnage.

There were seven dead in the boats we picked up, and in the two days following there were some thirteen burials at sea. I do not credit a report that there are many dead on the *Carpathia*.[72]

After submitting her own account of the *Carpathia's* rescue mission to the newspapers, Miss Birkhead was interviewed and described the circumstances under which that account had been written:

I was so much interrupted that I thought I should never get anything done and that, when I had done it, it would be such a jumble that it wouldn't be of any use to anybody. I never even had a chance to read it over. While I had been lying in my berth during the nights after we picked up the passengers, I had been writing the story in my mind, but I never thought that the call to produce it would come when it did. I had, however, made some notes of the things I did not want to forget so I should be able to tell them to mother when I got back. You know, we are going to be far away for at least six months and it is so easy to forget things in such a long time.

The captain had given orders that private messages of survivors to their friends were to take precedence of press messages, and, though I inquired repeatedly, I found that it was impossible to get anything through. So I just had to write the things down as they came to me and trust that it would come out all right in the end.

First one person would come to me to have something done, and then another. A little 13-year-old English girl was trying to mend a tear in a coat for one of the physicians, and she came to me because she could not get it right. I showed her how, but I had done nearly half of the work before I gave it up.

Then a woman came in to borrow some ink. I hadn't any ink, but my aunt had a fountain pen. We lent her that, and soon she was back again in the cabin in worse trouble than before. The pen, poor thing, leaked, and the woman's fingers were all stained. She was nearly ready to go on shore, and at such a time as that something had to be done about the fingers. So I took some manicure powder and cleaned the fingers and began to write on my story just where I had left off.

Then when we got nearer to port I had another anxiety. Tug after tug loomed up, and I expected at any time to hear my name called out on a megaphone and have to throw overboard what I had, to somebody from the *Herald* and the *Times*. I carried what I had already written in an envelope in my shirt waist, and had a block ready to tie it to to weight it. When anything hove in sight I would go to the side and listen and then go back to write some more to add to the story already in my envelope.

We had got nearer and nearer to New York, and several tugs had been unable to approach us, and so it seemed that I would have to depend on my own efforts to get to the *Herald* office as best I could. Everybody said that we wouldn't be able to get a taxicab and that we never would get there in time.

A little German woman, who couldn't speak any English, had promised to come with me to the *Herald* office. She had taken some photographs, too, but she had separated from us in the hurry when the passengers began to go off. I had to go along without her, but everything came out right in the end. The *Herald* and the *Times* men were waiting for me at the pier. There was a taxicab waiting there, too. When it was all over, naturally I was tired, but there was nobody prouder than I to find I had every paper beaten to death.[73]

JAMES BISSET

In later years Second Officer Bisset granted the following interview regarding his experiences on the *Carpathia*:

It was Sunday night. The sky was clear and starry. We had been warned that there were icebergs about. I was on the 8–12 watch. About 12:30 a.m., after I had been in bed about half an hour, I was awakened by the sound of the captain talking on the bridge. He had retired to bed about two hours before me. I thought this strange. I listened and thought I heard him say the *Titanic* was in trouble. I jumped out of bed and went to the chart room. There was an SOS from the *Titanic*, and a message saying that her engine-room was filling. The chart showed that the ships were 57 miles apart.

We turned and went to her relief as fast as possible, although we had to watch out, for icebergs ourselves. The entire crew was awakened, and told to prepare for 2,430 passengers from the *Titanic*. We expected, of course, to find the *Titanic* afloat and no lives lost. The hurrying stewards preparing bedding and meals awoke most of our own passengers. Everyone was out of bed.

We arrived on the scene about 4 a.m. We first saw a green light and imagined it was one of the *Titanic*'s side lights. A little later we knew the worst. The light was a rocket fired from one of the boats. The *Titanic* was gone.

For the next few hours we cruised around over a distance of about 10 miles picking up survivors in boats. They were all very cold and dazed. On the spot where the *Titanic* had sunk there was an island of wreckage – bunks, deck chairs, everything.[74]

ERNEST G.F. BROWN

In 1913, Chief Purser Brown granted the following interview to a Wisconsin newspaper:

> I can add nothing to what has already been told about the tragedy. We got the CQD flash at 12:20 while we were forty-eight miles away. We got the flash by accident. We were late getting the wireless news and the operator was just about to go to bed when he decided to take one more chance on picking up something. He adjusted the headgear just in time to get the call.
>
> The *Titanic* went down at 2:25 and we did not reach the scene of the wreck till 3:45. Sixteen heavy loaded boats were floating about. There was no wreckage with the exception of a few deck chairs. Because of the large number of icebergs in the vicinity it took us till 4 o'clock to get any of the boats aboard.
>
> We did not realize the extent of the tragedy till later. The *Titanic* survivors were so numbed by the magnitude of the disaster they themselves did not realize they were figuring in the most monster marine tragedy in the world.
>
> We had 1,200 passengers of our own on board the *Carpathia*, and we had to find room for the 705 survivors. The *Carpathia* passengers were very good about sharing their rooms with the survivors.
>
> Only two passengers on the *Carpathia* knew that the rescue work was in progress. The first the rest of them knew of it was when they arose in the morning.[75]

THOMAS BROWN

Steward Brown granted the following interview after the *Carpathia* reached New York:

> The iceberg that sank the *Titanic* looked to be as big as the Rock of Gibraltar.
>
> There were 2,341 persons aboard the *Titanic*, counting officers and crew. Seven hundred and ten persons were saved; so the list of those who drowned numbers 1,631 persons.
>
> I had turned in for the night when Main [Cottam], our wireless operator, caught the SOS signal of distress. He told me it was the clearest signal of any sort he ever received. The minute he got the message he hastened to Captain Rostron and said, 'Captain, the *Titanic* is sinking; she struck

an iceberg.' Captain Rostron did not believe it. 'Here it comes again, Captain,' said the operator.

That was all the captain needed to get our crew into action; he sounded the bell for the watchman, and sent him to order all hands on deck.

I doubt if any passengers on the *Carpathia* knew of the tragedy until Jones, the first mate, sounded the emergency gong after the watchman had summoned the crew.

A few minutes after we got the signal for help we were ready for action. The SOS reached us shortly after midnight. We were then 56 miles away from the *Titanic*. Our engineer turned about and put on full speed, and we reached the *Titanic* about 3.30 o'clock Monday morning.

While the *Carpathia* was speeding toward the doomed ship, Captain Rostron summoned the higher officers together, and said he would hold every man responsible for the work assigned to him.

He told Main [Cottam] to answer the *Titanic* and tell Captain Smith that we were making for his ship, full steam ahead.

Phillips, the operator of the *Titanic*, evidently did not get our reply, or, if he did receive it, he could not answer us in any way. Captain Rostron told Mrs. Smith, the stewardess, to prepare for any emergency.

He told me to get coffee, sandwiches and other food ready for the survivors.

On our way to the *Titanic* the captain went below and told the engineer that he must get to the *Titanic* before she sank. I doubt if Captain Rostron ever got as much speed out of the *Carpathia* as he did on the way to the *Titanic*.

Long before the *Carpathia* got near the scene of the wreck our boats were ready to be lowered into the water.

Two men were stationed at each boat, and I and Thomas McKenna, seaman, were in charge of boat No. 1. We have sixteen boats on the ship, and they were hanging suspended from the davits within fifteen minutes after we received the SOS call for help.

I must not forget the women who were on the *Carpathia*. They were the most self-sacrificing women I ever saw. Their fortitude under the distressing circumstances was so remarkable that each one ought to be rewarded for the work she did after the survivors were lifted aboard the *Carpathia*.

As we got near the scene of the wreck the barometer dropped considerably. It became cold – bitter cold. We did not see the icebergs then, but Captain Rostron said that we were nearing them. Suddenly, as the iceberg loomed up ahead of our ship, Captain Rostron ran to the pilot house and took charge of the helm.

The night was clear and starlight, but we did not see an iceberg until the *Carpathia* was within a half mile of it. Of course, we had ample time to steer clear of the floes.

At 3.30 o'clock our vessel plunged into a sea of open ice. I believe there must have been thirty or forty icebergs in the water around the *Carpathia*. Captain Rostron took his ship safely through the floe and suddenly we heard a shriek. It was faint at first and then it became louder.

'The women and children, get them first,' Captain Rostron shouted to the crew on the boat deck who were awaiting the signal to cut loose life-boats. Our searchlight was trained on the sea ahead and the boats filled with the shipwrecked passengers stood out in bold relief.

I shall never forget the sight. There were many boats from the *Titanic* loaded with women and children wedged among the ice. Even before we got up to the first boat from the *Titanic* we could see the iceberg which sank her. It looked to be as big as the Rock of Gibraltar. It towered high in the air and it moved very slowly.

I believe it was over 500 feet high, and we can judge by its size by recall-ing that seven-eighths of an iceberg is submerged. Within fifty yards of the boats in the water Captain Rostron gave the signal to reverse the engines so our ship would not crash into the shipwrecked passengers.

'Ready men – go,' shouted the captain to me, and McKenna loosened the rope and our boat dropped into the water. We tugged away at the oars with all our strength. We shoved our boat alongside of boat No. 13 from the *Titanic*. It was filled with passengers. I believe there were about fifteen children in it.

Poor little things! Some were benumbed with cold; others were appar-ently lifeless, and several moaned piteously. The women in the boat were scantily clad. Their clothing was grotesque. They had on wraps, night robes, silk shawls ever their heads and men's coats around them. Many had no shoes, and all of them suffered from the cold.

McKenna and I tied a hawser to the boat and then rowed back to the *Carpathia*. Harris, the bos'n's mate, and another member of the crew helped us to lift the unfortunate ones from the boat. Some had to be car-ried up the ladder to the boat deck of the *Carpathia*.

A few could walk, but the majority were so benumbed that they could neither speak nor walk.

As fast as others of our crew could get the *Titanic*'s boats they were dragged toward the side of the *Carpathia*. We rescued twenty boatloads of passengers – 710 in all. Our ship resembled a hospital on our way back to New York, for a number of the women and children were ill.

The three physicians on the *Carpathia* told me as we were going up the bay that there were sixteen patients for the hospital as soon as the *Carpathia* docked.[76]

❖   ❖   ❖

HENRY BURKE

After reaching New York, Fr Burke and Fr Daniel McCarthy spoke with Fr J.W. Malone, who relayed their account to the newspapers. At 1 a.m. a steward knocked at their door and whispered that the *Carpathia* was trying to rescue some people on a sinking ship but that the two priests should keep the news to themselves. They dressed and went on deck, where fourteen other passengers were also gathered. The sky was star-lit and the weather bracingly delightful:

It was impossible when we got to the deck to contemplate that anything serious had happened within range of our vessel, as the elements were at peace.

We first began to realize something was not right when the orders of the captain and of the other officers rang through the *Carpathia*. They were in forms which the landsman does not understand, but the tone of voice they were uttered in spoke volumes, and we could feel the ship moving ahead as if every power within it was exerted to its limit.

Presently we came within sight of the ice floes, which the *Carpathia* cut through at top speed. We stayed on deck all the time, and as we were getting closer to the grave of the *Titanic* the lowering temperature warned us of the icebergs.

When the morning began to dawn we could see through haze and fog something that resembled a white mountain. While the ship ran fast through the ice floe, which was nothing more than smaller cakes of ice that offered no resistance, as they were swept aside with ease by her prow and sides, the captain changed course several times, and we were informed that he did so because of the danger of meeting a berg which would damage the ship.

However, there was little slackening of speed from the time that we got aboard until she slowed down when her bearings indicated that she was close to the disaster site.

As she was nearing the rescue she sent up rockets and blew the siren whistles to call the lifeboats to her. It was breaking day when we saw the first lifeboat, and in a few moments others loomed in view. They were all making toward the *Carpathia*, which had almost stopped.

The captain assigned two of the crew to take the names of the persons as they came aboard, and it was not till the first boatload was brought on that the extent of the disaster was fully comprehended on the *Carpathia*.

From daylight till between 8 and 9 o'clock Monday morning the *Carpathia* was moving in one direction after another, scouting for more survivors. After the first few lifeboat loads were taken aboard, the captain knew the *Titanic* had sunk, because one of the lifeboats was within five hundred feet of her when she went down, and if there had been the suction usually said to accompany a sinking vessel four or five other life-boat loads would have been drowned.

When the sun's rays shot through the fog and mist of the morning the most inspiring sight we ever beheld was disclosed. Three miles off, the captain said, the figure of a giant iceberg loomed a hundred and fifty feet or more above the water. It may have been the one the *Titanic* struck.

When the *Carpathia* got to the place indicated where the *Titanic* went down, there was nothing visible. Some of the lifeboats were two or three miles distant from others.

One of the survivors who had taken the last lifeboat lowered from the *Titanic* said that the crew of that ship had been making merry early Sunday night and some of them were drunk.

The reception J. Bruce Ismay, president of the company that owned the *Titanic*, got in the four days' run from the icefield into New York harbor was one that he will not forget till death, if he lives to be as old as the oldest man. The feeling against Mr. Ismay was intense. We did not bother to inquire whether he jumped into the first lifeboat or the last, but it was enough to drive him out of his head if he knew the feeling against him.

He had to have a stateroom all to himself and have every attention, while some poor women were without the ordinary comforts. That he might not be disturbed a sign was placed outside his room that he should not be disturbed. On it was written 'Don't Knock'. A big Irish stoker was passing it one of the days and kicked it with all his might. The feeling was so strong that it wouldn't take much to stir up a mob spirit to throw him overboard and put a millstone around his neck.

The description we gathered from the survivors, especially those in the nearest lifeboat when the *Titanic* sank, was that she sank gently as a big creature lying down to sleep.

The shock of striking the iceberg, they told us, was not a severe one. It was a lurch more than a sudden impact, as if the *Titanic* had run up on the side of a sloping ledge of ice and her starboard side was torn away for more than half its length. Then it seemed to settle back again in the water.

A call was sent through the entire vessel, they said, to get to the upper decks at once, but that was met by the assurance from the officers that the vessel would not sink, and could not, no matter what happened.

This served to quiet a lot of the confusion at first, but as the ship began sinking steadily into the water there was a general feeling of panic. One survivor told us he saw two of the crew shoot three Chinese cooks who were struggling to press ahead of some women. They were carried from where they fell and the bodies thrown overboard.

There was an explosion, and after that the vessel buckled, her middle going up like a hump and her stern dipping into the water.

Strange as it may seem, after the boilers exploded, or whatever it was in the hold that caused the explosion, the electric lights were lit till the last and the wireless apparatus was working, as the operator stuck to his post.

When it was realized by all on board the *Titanic* that she could not stay above water much longer, the band, which during the excitement had been playing lively and patriotic music, suddenly stopped. The first thing the band struck up when the rush was made aloft was 'The Star Spangled Banner'. It had a most soothing effect on all.

The band never stopped playing for any length of time. The players rested on their turns, and someone seemed to be working all the time.

As the strains of 'Nearer, My God, To Thee' broke over the waters the *Titanic*, as if echoing to the sentiment, plunged her nose into the water, and the stern stuck up straight into the air, and she went down gently head first.

The lights stayed lit until within a few minutes of her fatal plunge. The survivors in the adjacent lifeboats could see that all the people on deck were kneeling with their faces lifted to heaven in prayer.

When the last boatload had been put aboard our ship, and she scurried around looking for other stray boats that might have drifted off, the survivors and the *Carpathia*'s own passengers were lined up in a mass and prayers were said for those who had not been saved, as well as a prayer of thanksgiving offered to God for those who were.

All the stories that the survivors aboard the *Carpathia* were filled with hope that some other vessel had saved the rest of the people, are as far from the truth as it is possible to get. There was no less than three lifeboat loads of survivors who were within sight of the *Titanic* as she took her grave, and they saw the people go down.

Fr Burke and Fr McCarthy moved their belongings from their stateroom, gave it to a survivor and slept in the smoking room on cots. Every day the survivors gathered together and prayed for the dead. The priests said that two sisters named Murphy, who boarded the *Titanic* at Queenstown, were separated by death. The surviving sister was overcome with hysterics after landing from the lifeboat, but when she saw the priests she knelt down and asked their blessing. They told her that her sister had plenty of time to invoke the mercy of God and was probably looking down on her from heaven with all the others who had died.[77]

JOHN CARGILL

In later years, crewman Cargill granted the following newspaper interview:

Our wireless operator was just about to turn in when the message came through. We couldn't believe it. The *Titanic* in trouble. It seemed impossible.

It didn't take our captain long to react. We were the nearest ship except for the *Californian*. We told *Titanic* we were on our way, then went like a bat out of hell. But we still never thought the *Titanic* could sink.

In case we had to help we made restaurants ready and got blankets. I just stayed at the wheel looking for icebergs – and the *Titanic* ...

In describing the rescue, Cargill said:

It was pathetic. People were dressed in everything from fur coats to pajamas.

We saw a man in the water clutching two children – a boy and a girl. They had frozen to death.

We lowered sacks for the children and the babies and started looking for other boats. I'm sure to this day that one of the survivors I helped lift on board was Nan Harper.

We were all quite numb. We looked across and saw the *Californian*. If only she had come sooner.

There are two things I'll always remember. There was a huge iceberg right at the spot. It had red on it and looked like the one which sank the *Titanic*.

The other thing was the anger we all felt [later] towards the *Californian*. Everyone might have been saved if she had answered the rockets.[78]

HOWARD CHAPIN

In later years Mr Chapin granted the following interview:

We remember keenly the hours of the evening before on the *Carpathia*. One day out from New York, we were steaming along the Gulf Stream. The evening was hot, the air sultry. It was so mild that men on deck discarded their coats – even sitting in their shirt-sleeves.

At a reasonable hour – perhaps 10 o'clock, we went to our stateroom and to bed. As we went in I recalled that on the roof of the deckhouse, directly over our stateroom, was a lifeboat. Its painter was fastened to a cleat on the roof. I noticed that it was the only lifeboat that hung outward in the davits – the rest were stowed aboard.

Sometime after 11 o'clock, or just before midnight, I was awakened – by the sound of feet overhead. I heard the footsteps on top of the deckhouse and stop directly over me. There could be no reason but that a sailor was uncleating the painter of that lifeboat.

I threw on some clothing and hurried on deck. I found that the weather had changed – drastically changed. It was bitter cold. I asked the sailor what he was doing and he told me the *Titanic* had struck an iceberg. We were hastening to her rescue.

I returned to the cabin, aroused my wife, and together we dressed in our warmest clothing. We returned to the deck. We could see that we were steaming through black water, but water that was flecked with masses of ice. We were in the midst of the icefields; that was what accounted for the change in the atmosphere.

After some time we saw in the distance a light. At first we thought it was the light of a ship, but soon we saw it was too low – too near the water. We found it was a light in a lifeboat. The boat was filled with survivors of the *Titanic*. We steamed up as near as it was safe for the ship to approach the small boat. The lifeboat was rowed alongside, and the passengers came aboard.

A pitiful appearance they made. Some of the women were clothed only in their night clothing. Some of the men were in evening dress, having come directly from the halls where they were enjoying themselves. The *Carpathia* passengers aided them in every way they could, giving them extra clothing, and taking them to their staterooms.

Soon it began to be dawn, the early daylight over the water, and we saw other lifeboats. One by one they came up to us and their occupants – and most of the boats themselves – were taken on board. We learned of the striking of the berg by the magnificent steamship, and of the appalling fact that while we were speeding to her aid, the *Titanic* had gone down an hour before we arrived. Her death list was officially placed at 1,635. Capt. E.J. Smith, 40 years a mariner, went down with his ship.

The crew of the *Carpathia*, other passengers – doctors, nurses, everyone – aided the passengers as they came on board. Some needed medical assistance – some stimulants. Later, as *Carpathia* passengers who had previously been aroused came on deck, they were astonished to see the increase in the ship's load. We already had some 700 persons aboard, and here were several hundreds more.

But all took it in the best of humor. The passengers were willing to sleep on couches – bunks, on the tables, and even on the floor, until we got back to New York.

And imagine our surprise to see Miss Ostby, a lifelong friend of both myself and my wife, among those brought on board. The Ostbys had been among the guests invited to our wedding, although being abroad, they were unable to attend. They had, however, sent a present, which is still a treasured memento. Miss Ostby is now living in Brussels, Belgium, where we met her a few years ago.[79]

MRS COLIN COOPER

After arriving in New York, Mrs Cooper granted the following interview. Mrs Cooper told how Mrs Harris refused to leave her husband on the *Titanic* and stayed with Mrs Thorne until their husbands forced them to enter a collapsible boat:

> The men told Mrs. Harris and Mrs. Thorne that they wanted them to go; that the *Titanic*, they believed, would have a better chance if all who could leave her would do so.
>
> Mrs. Harris told me that all the men were brave beyond anything. When her collapsible boat had gone about 100 yards from the *Titanic*, not more, the *Titanic* sank. She saw a crowd of men, and knew her husband was one of them, rush toward the stern in an effort to save themselves when the bow began to sink. The band was playing. There were waves, but no suction.
>
> All the men stood back. The men were ordered to go below, women to the upper deck. The men went below without a word.
>
> The theory grew that, although the *Titanic* was badly injured, she would float indefinitely. Some men and women even went back to bed. Other men smoked on the deck. Among many men and women there was a strong preference displayed to stay on the *Titanic*. Many women did not go into the lifeboats until they were ordered, and even then, they told me, they expected to be called back to the *Titanic* after a little while.
>
> The whole talk of the women after they got on board the *Carpathia*, was that too many men had sacrificed themselves.
>
> 'My life is finished,' said one survivor to me, 'and these useful men stayed without a murmur'.
>
> Two hundred stokers with black faces and almost without clothes, came up from below and saw a lifeboat. Two men jumped in and started to lower it. The captain cried, 'Go back in your place, every one of you'. And every one of those men turned back and went below without a word. They said they thought all the women had been put off.
>
> The men saved were not cowards. The women repeatedly said they felt that more men should have been given a chance.
>
> One of the stewards, the last to leave the *Titanic*, told us that at the last, when the passengers realized the *Titanic* was really sinking and that there was no escape, there was painful excitement but that there were no scenes to make mankind feel anything else than proud of the courage shown.[80]

CHARLES E. CRAIN

After reaching New York, Captain Crain granted the following interview to reporters. Crain was ill in his cabin and didn't witness the rescue itself:

It had been a gay trip out, the rescued passengers told me, with dinner parties, dancing and concerts. It seemed more like a picnic party than an ordinary voyage of a transatlantic steamship.

None of the passengers with whom I talked told me anything about any great crash. So far as I could learn all they had felt was a comparatively slight shock.

Mr. Harper, of No. 31 Gramercy Park, was one of my informants. Mr. Harper was put in one of the boats with his wife because he was an invalid. According to his story, and to that of others with whom I talked, there was absolutely no confusion on board the doomed ship up to the time they left her.

Another of the survivors with whom I talked was a boy about fourteen years of age. He told me a remarkable story of his rescue through the intervention of Colonel John Jacob Astor. He said he had tried to get into one of the lifeboats with his mother, but that the sailors had pushed him back, and said: 'You're not a girl. You can't get in there. Stand back.'

Colonel Astor, who was assisting women into the boat, picked up from the deck a girl's hat, and jamming it on the boy's head, said: 'There, my boy, you're a girl now. Go ahead'.

The only thing of which any of the survivors with whom I talked complained in connection with the work of rescue was the difficulty experienced in getting the boats away from the sinking ship after they had been lowered.

This was due to a new arrangement in connection with the ropes with which the boats were lowered. The sailors did not understand it. It was a new contrivance placed on board the *Titanic* for the first time. The result was that as the boats touched the water the crew could not detach the lines and eventually had to cut them.

The intention of the officers of the *Titanic* was to place four sailors in each boat, but this could not be carried out in every case, with the result that in several of the boats passengers themselves had to take oars. In some instances, women were forced to row.

Mr. Harper told me he was in his cabin at the time the ship struck. He felt the shock, but it was not severe enough for him to be alarmed. However, he dressed and went to one of the upper decks where he remained for about ten minutes.

Then he noticed the passengers coming down from another deck who told him as they passed that they had been ordered to put on life preservers.

Mr. Harper went back to his cabin, aroused his wife, and after both had put on lifebelts they went to the upper deck. There they found the women and children being put into the boats, and Mrs. Harper was sent with them, and her husband, being an invalid, was permitted to accompany her.

The boat in which the Harpers were experienced no trouble beyond that mentioned in disconnecting the tackle. It was rowed away from the *Titanic* and the occupants watched the great ship sink.

It was twenty minutes past three a.m. on Monday when she plunged head first out of sight. Her lights had been burning almost until the last. She had sunk gradually until the water reached high enough to extinguish the fires and stop the lights. Soon after that she took the fatal plunge.

The last boat that left the wreck had only seven passengers in it, but it was one of the smallest boats. However, it could have held more and Mr. Harper is convinced that many women must have been left on board.

As a matter of fact there was no great rush to get into the boats, he said, because very few of the passengers realized the gravity of the accident. They had a natural disinclination and fear to entrust themselves to the little craft. As a matter of fact, many of them felt safer aboard the big ship. None believed she would sink.

The shock was so mild one of the women survivors told me that after she had dressed and had gone on deck she thought so little of it that she went back to her cabin and remained there until her husband went for her. Another played several games of bridge after the crash.

Of course there was a good deal of excitement at the time of the shock. Everyone rushed back and forth asking, 'What was that? What has happened?' The officers, however, seemed calm, and the word was passed that it was merely a lump of ice, so everyone seemed satisfied. The lights were not extinguished, and there was nothing to alarm them until the orders were issued to put on life preservers.

It was a beautiful night. None could believe that anything like a collision could occur in such weather. It was not an iceberg into which the *Titanic* ran, but an icefield. It was one great solid mass, more than fifty-two miles long, rising at times to a height of what seemed seventy feet or more out of the water.

We on board the *Carpathia* could form some idea of its extent because we ran past more than fifty-two miles of it on our way back from the spot where we picked up the survivors.

Four of those we took on board from the boats were dead. They had perished from fright and exposure. We buried them on Tuesday. Their bodies were committed to the sea from the side portholes after the burial service had been read.[81]

❖   ❖   ❖

In another newspaper interview, Captain Crain told of his efforts to obtain information about his friend, victim Major Archibald Butt:

> Naturally, I was deeply concerned in the fate of Major Butt, for he was not only a fellow-officer of the army, but also a personal friend of many years' standing. I questioned those of the survivors who were in a condition to talk, and from them I learned that Butt, when the *Titanic* struck, took his position with the officers and from the moment that the order to man the lifeboats was given until the last one was dropped into the sea, he aided in the maintenance of discipline and the placing of the women and children in the boats.
>
> Butt, I was told was as cool as the iceberg that had doomed the ship, and not once did he lose control of himself. In the presence of death he was the same gallant, courteous officer that the American people had learned to know so well as a result of his constant attendance upon President Taft. There was never any chance of Butt getting into any of those lifeboats.
>
> He knew his time was at hand, and he was ready to meet it as a man should, and I and all of the others who cherish his memory are glad that he faced the situation that way, which was the only possible way a man of his caliber could face it.[82]

MRS CHARLES F. CRAIN

After arriving in New York, Anna Crain granted the following newspaper interview. News of the disaster became known on the *Carpathia*, and many people lined the rails watching for the *Titanic*:

> With the aid of powerful glasses we sighted the lifeboats. The first to come into view was rowed by women. The passengers and women on the *Carpathia* were stunned. 'She has sunk,' said an officer of the ship who stood near me. And then I realized for the first time that many lives had been lost.
>
> As the *Carpathia* slowed up, the women at the oars of the first boat did not seem to be the least bit excited. They were taken on board, and their calmness was remarkable. No one of the women was crying and not one of them showed any nervousness.
>
> It was a remarkable thing – the calmness of these women. Some were thinly clad, while others were dressed in evening gowns. Other boats came into view. It seemed as though they were coming from behind icebergs. And the women in the boats were too dazed to realize their situation.

Some of the boats were only half filled and the men who had been rowing were completely exhausted.

When all of the boats had been picked up and there were no others in sight, the first outburst of grief was heard.[83]

Mrs Crain granted a second interview to another New York paper:

I never saw anything so remarkable in my life. Late Sunday we received a wireless message from the *Titanic* asking for aid. The next morning we reached a spot where the *Titanic* had called from and asked for help. There was nothing in sight and there was no wreckage. The sailors on the *Carpathia* seemed to be dumbfounded at not finding the *Titanic*. We were steaming along slowly, apparently aimlessly, when from in back of a small iceberg came a white boat. It looked very small. The captain ordered the boat stopped, and gradually the little boat drew up to us. We saw women rowing it. As they drew alongside the calmness of these women was unexplainable. They needed no assistance in climbing onto the *Carpathia*. They acted as if it were not at all unusual.

There was no crying among them, and as they came on board they yielded willingly to the many hands stretched out to them. They were taken into the dining saloon. None of them was properly clad. Those that were fully dressed were in evening gowns. The others had little or no clothing. In the dining saloon they were given clothing, and then, as if they had all been through similar experiences before, they went out on the deck and looked steadily ahead out over the ice-strewn ocean. We followed their example wonderingly and then realized the objects their eyes sought. More little white boats came into view. The same scene was repeated as they came alongside. There was no sobbing or weeping. The little band along the rail, gradually increasing in size as the boats came alongside, eagerly scanned each face as it came over the side of the boat. Then the stare ahead was resumed. The number in many of the little boats was pitifully small.

Finally the time came when all the little boats had drawn alongside. As the last one in the last boat came over the side there was a moan of anguish from one woman. It was repeated throughout the group around the railing. The hope that their relatives were in other boats had been proved wrong, and the long anxiety made the grief that followed more agonizing and heartrending.

Mrs. Astor and her maid were in the first boats that arrived, and she was immediately placed in the captain's cabin. While the bereaved among the survivors gave way to their grief, food was prepared for them and many were taken to staterooms and put to bed. Others told us of the wreck. All declared that a great many who could have come in the small boats had been so confident that the *Titanic* could not sink that they had regarded the taking to lifeboats as foolish. Many women who had not this confidence in the wrecked vessel refused to go into the small boats because it meant separation from their men folks.[84]

❖ ❖ ❖

ELEANOR DANFORTH

After the *Carpathia* landed, Miss Danforth granted an interview to a New York newspaper:

Many stories were told by the survivors, some of them almost unbelievable. One man, J.B. Thayer Jr. of Philadelphia, stuck to the ship until the last. He leaped overboard just before the ship sank. He was not far enough away to get out of the fearful suction and was drawn down twice, he said. He finally came up, however, and was rescued by one of the boats in an almost unconscious condition. Another man, whose name will never be known, I was told, had stuck to his post loading women and children into the lifeboats until the last boat was off. When there were no more women to look out for, he jumped overboard. Just after he jumped the boat sank. He was sucked down.[85]

❖ ❖ ❖

Miss Danforth granted a second interview to a Boston newspaper:

Even for anyone aboard the *Carpathia*, which merely visited the spot where the *Titanic* went down and rescued the survivors, this is the most horrifying thing imaginable. What it must mean to the people who had an actual share in it is beyond imagination. I woke soon after midnight on Monday when the rush of feet on the deck overhead indicated, as I found later, that the *Carpathia*'s wireless had picked up the *Titanic*'s call for help.

The rush of feet back and forth continued, and I remember thinking vaguely that something must be wrong. Then I decided to go to sleep again and was just drowsing when suddenly I felt our engines give a great throb which meant quickened speed.

I dressed and went to the deck, for I knew it must be something unusual. The woman in the stateroom next to mine had already rung to ask the steward what had happened, but he gave her some evasive response.

When I reached the deck someone told me of the *Titanic*'s distress. You cannot imagine the anxiety, the alternating hope and fear that beset those of us who had gone on deck when we counted the minutes in that quick terrible flight to the region from which the *Titanic* had called. It was about four in the morning when we reached it.

Our hearts grew cold with horror when we searched the sea for a sign of the vessel. All around were icebergs, large and small. About twenty miles away there drifted an icefield, dead white and ghostly. We had been obliged to skirt bergs on the way, but we did not slow up – and this meant danger to the *Carpathia* but none of us stopped to think of that.

Soon after the sun began to rise. It was a night I shall never forget. The east was drenched with rose color, and as the light caught each of the bergs it turned their peaks to crimson and suffused them with delicate shades of pink and carmine.

The glowing east colored even the distant ice floe and made spots like blood in the hollows between the waves. Someone pointed out a glistening, pink-veined mountain of ice as the berg into which the *Titanic* had run. I think it may really have been the same berg, for I learned later from *Titanic* survivors that the berg was a tall one – so tall that they saw it slide past their stateroom windows and found the deck covered with ice splinters knocked from it by the crash.

There was almost no wreckage – a chair, perhaps, or a wooden rack, but nothing to give a hint as to the size or magnificence of the vessel lying two miles beneath our keel. Of course, being night, everything had been closed up and so went down with the vessel.

At a little distance we noticed small bobbing specks on the water, and as we approached we saw with a thrill tingling to our fingertips that they were lifeboats containing the handful of survivors. I was at the rail when we picked up the first boat. The sight of those crouching women with their strained white faces and their haunted eyes is one that I shall remember always.

In one boat I saw a woman dressed in a satin evening gown. Several of the men wore evening clothes. I saw at least one woman and one man whom I know to have been insane. Most of the people as they came over the side were incredibly calm – in fact they seemed stunned. A very few were hysterical.

But on all the faces there was frozen an indescribable look as if they could not believe the thing that had happened before their eyes and as if they still heard the awful cry that went up as the *Titanic* gave her final lurch beneath the sea. Many of the [several illegible words] ... men and women when the *Titanic* finally sank was something to ring in the ears forever.

Mrs. Astor I did not see. She went at once to a stateroom and did not come out at all. Nor did I see Mr. Ismay. Nobody did. Nobody wanted to. He was busy arranging a committee meeting or something.

All we passengers on the *Carpathia* shared our staterooms with the rescued folk. A friend of mine had in her cabin six widows, none of whom was over thirty years old. The *Titanic* had carried many bridal couples among its passengers.

A man whom I knew had seven other men, all from the *Titanic*, in his stateroom, sleeping on the floor and on extra cots built over the couch and bunk.

I took charge of two little French children. I think their mother had not come with them. Their father had gone down on the *Titanic*. They were too small and frightened to tell their names. I got clothes for them from a woman who had a little girl aboard, for they were scarcely dressed at all. I heard today that one of them had died.

Not long after we picked up the survivors we had a burial service for those who died from exposure. It was a solemn and heartrending thing consigning them to the sea from which we had rescued them. All the *Carpathia* was in mourning. People have spoken of the silence as we slid into dock. Nobody wanted to talk. The wild cries that rose as the survivors went on the pier is scarcely a hint of the agonizing strain under which all of us labored.

Why, the wreck is so vast and so awful that everywhere you go you meet people whose relatives went down on the *Titanic*. Everywhere you hear people talking of the ship's band, playing knee-deep in the icy water; of the sea dotted with swimming men; of the cry that rose from the drowning victims and the answering shriek from the lifeboats.

For those of us who hung over the *Carpathia*'s rail as the white-faced women and men were swung from the rocking lifeboats, all rosy in the sunrise – for us that sunrise over the ice peaks those days those days of horror aboard the hospital ship and that tragic landing at the dock are memories that will follow us to the grave.[86]

A third interview with Miss Danforth was published a few days later:

None of us got a great deal of sleep after the survivors were taken on board. There was so much commotion and the topic of the disaster so uppermost in the minds of everyone that few could really rest.

Though I was not directly in the wreck, I lived in the atmosphere of it through the stories told by the survivors. There was no sign of any steamer and not a vestige of any wreck except the lifeboats when we arrived on the scene. It hardly seemed possible that such a gigantic craft could have completely disappeared.

Early Monday morning I awoke and went on deck as usual. The steward said, 'We are going to the help of the *Titanic*.'

It was still dark and we could see the gleam of ice. When the day fully dawned the sight was magnificent, but terrifying. Our ship was surrounded by icebergs, one icefield being 20 miles long, so the steward told me. Stationed all about the deck were sailors watching eagerly for a glimpse of the *Titanic*.

Finally the first lifeboat was sighted. We came upon it quickly. It was about half-full of people, some wearing only their nightclothes. One man wore his dress suit. Some of the women were bareheaded and in their evening clothes.

The people in the lifeboat were calm, but their faces were drawn and all were shivering with the cold. There was not the slightest panic connected with their transfer to the *Carpathia*. I stood by the side of the ship and watched the sailors as one by one they lifted the women and men by means of ropes on board the ship.

All the passengers on the *Carpathia* lent a hand and were ready to sacrifice any of their comforts for the survivors. Many gave up their staterooms, and others shared their apartments with the newcomers. Many devoted long hours to tending the survivors and planning and sewing for them.

The lifeboats reached us in quick succession, and for a while the survivors seemed dazed. They could not realize the awful truth. There were not beds enough for all of the survivors in addition to the passengers on the *Carpathia*, so the men rolled themselves in blankets and crept under the dining room tables. Others slept on the tables. Chairs were at a premium. But no one complained, whatever his lot. The people from the *Titanic* were given the best of everything.

I talked with many of the *Titanic* survivors, and it is my belief that few on board the ill-fated ship believed that she would sink. They hesitated to get into the lifeboats, feeling safer on the deck. This, I think, must account for the fact that some of the boats were only half full of passengers.

I notice that there have been various stories afloat that Captain Smith shot himself just before the *Titanic* went down, but this does not appear to be the opinion of a great many of the survivors with whom I talked on the *Carpathia*. The majority of them say that he jumped at the last moment.

Incidentally, I think the captain of the *Carpathia* showed courage when he steamed out to the scene of the disaster at such speed in the midst of the ice fields. I confess I was a little alarmed myself over the perilousness of the trip, and this feeling was shared by many of the other passengers.

We all found the captain of the *Carpathia* genial and accommodating, but stern and strict when conditions required. He was never for a moment confused or nonplussed.[87]

❖ ❖ ❖

WILLIAM DAVID

Assistant Saloon Steward David, whose name is missing from the official crew list, granted the following interview after the *Carpathia* reached New York:

Colonel Astor was walking the deck at the time the *Titanic* struck the iceberg. He was approached by a frantic waiter, I was told, and urged to put on a lifebelt. The waiter had several lifebelts in his hand. Colonel Astor waved the waiter away.

'Pooh,' he said, 'this is nothing. There is no need of lifebelts.' And that was the last seen of Colonel Astor.

J. Bruce Ismay was pulled on board the *Carpathia* from a lifeboat. He was clad only in pajamas. He collapsed completely upon reaching the deck.

At midnight on Sunday the men on the *Carpathia* received the word that the *Titanic* was sinking. They laughed at the idea, and it was not until fifteen minutes after twelve that the real situation occurred to them. Instantly torches, electric apparatus and other signal devices were prepared on the decks, masts and bridge of the *Carpathia* and provisions placed in all boats. Blankets and robes were placed in alleyways and gangways. All available men were put on the lookout and all equipped with powerful glasses.

The first light – a blue light – was sighted, and it was found to be the torch on one of the *Titanic*'s lifeboats, the only one having a light. It was for a time thought that the illumination was from the head mast light of the sinking *Titanic*. Everyone on board believed that they were seeing the *Titanic* gradually going to her grave.

But this lifeboat was positively recognized soon before three o'clock Monday morning. It was picked up and found to contain only fifteen persons, while it could easily have accommodated forty. It had on board one entire family, one sailor and five firemen.

We found the *Titanic*'s lifeboats within three or four miles of one another. All passengers rescued were lifted to the deck of the *Carpathia* by means of the jacket ropes. All were too exhausted to climb the rope ladders which were lowered. Mrs. Astor was lifted to the deck in this manner. The *Carpathia* picked up twenty-two boats. There were from thirty to forty persons in each.

Mrs. Rothschild carried a little Pomeranian when taken on board.

Surviving passengers told me that when two firemen attempted to board a lifeboat when the *Titanic* was sinking, the officer of the boat shouted to them that they would swamp it because it was already overcrowded. The firemen are quoted as saying, 'All right, Jerry.' After which they went out of sight in the icy water. I was told that the *Titanic*'s officers directed the filling of the lifeboats with drawn revolvers and that only two shots were fired and those by the second officer, who meant to intimidate several of the crew fighting to escape from the sinking ship.

The *Titanic* went down slowly. When the bridge was on the level with the water, Captain Smith, who had remained on the bridge, was picked up by two sailors, I was told, and dragged on board a floating raft. He had no sooner been taken on board than he leaped into the sea. It was not until the boilers of the *Titanic* burst that she sank fast. She went down bow first.[88]

❖   ❖   ❖

META FOWLER

Mrs Fowler, who was traveling with Amelia and Alice Fowler and Kate Steele, granted the following interview after the *Carpathia* returned to New York:

We were all asleep on the *Carpathia*, my two sisters, Miss Steele and myself, when at 4 o'clock on Monday morning we heard a great shuffling of feet overhead and the sounds of many voices. I got up and looked out the cabin window. To my surprise I found that we were in a great field of broken ice and off a short distance I saw several icebergs standing out white and glittering in the gray of dawn. It was an indescribably beautiful scene. Then I wondered why we had stopped. I thought there must be a man overboard, for I saw ropes swinging from davits and preparations as if for taking something on board or swinging a boat. As my field of vision cleared I saw a boat and in the next instant saw that it was filled with people, mostly women. I called my companions' attention and we all dressed hurriedly and went out on deck.

I shall never forget that sight. When we reached the deck we saw boat after boat, and in the water bits of broken wood and other materials evidently gathered where the *Titanic* went down. At first I could not realize that all these people seeming to come from every direction were shipwrecked human beings. At sight they appeared to be thousands who were only a pitifully few hundreds.

Captain Rostron had everything in readiness to take them aboard. Chairs were swung over the side and rope ladders and bags for the children and blankets to put over them. A hatchway leading into the third passenger section was open, ready to receive them.

And then they came aboard one by one as rapidly as they could be handled with comfort and safety. The weak and ill were carried to staterooms willingly vacated by the occupants and to the dining saloon, where improvised couches were stretched on the floor. Women on board hurriedly shared their clothing with the rescued of their sex, who were dressed lightly, some of them hardly dressed at all, some showing ball slippers under nightgowns, some only stockings under ball gowns. It was as if they had come from a dance and had been interrupted in disrobing. They were in a terrible condition from cold and exposure.

I have heard that fully 75 per cent of the women who were saved were made widows by their husbands staying on board the *Titanic* that they might have places in the boats. There were three widows occupying my room, Mrs. Meyer, Mrs. Cavendish and a Spanish woman whose name I did not learn. In Miss Fowler's room and the rooms of the others were more of widows. Many of them were ignorant of their widowhood, fondly hoping and firmly believing that their husbands would be saved.

Mrs Fowler was asked if she heard of, or saw, any disorder:

Not a particle at any time. The survivors of the awful wreck came on our boat as calmly as you could imagine and remained comparatively calm all the way in. I think the bigness of the tragedy had an influence for calm.

She was asked if any survivors were ill:

Yes, a few, but not seriously. I saw Mrs. Astor and helped take care of her when she came on board. The steward had everything ready in the way of warm food and accommodations, and we women all went downstairs and helped wait on them all impartially whether they were from the first cabin or the steerage.[89]

❖   ❖   ❖

WILLIAM HISS

After the *Carpathia* returned to New York, Mr Hiss and his wife informed friends that they would be continuing their interrupted voyage to Gibraltar on the *Carpathia*.[90]

❖   ❖   ❖

PM ALBERT HOGUE

After arriving in New York, Father Hogue granted the following newspaper interview. Father Hogue gave religious consolation to the Catholic survivors on board the *Carpathia* and read the service for the dead over the Catholics who were buried at sea:

Every lifeboat that left the *Titanic* could have carried more passengers. Members of the crew did not know what to do.

The boats were shoved off before they were filled and many a man and woman sank into the deep because that crew had not been drilled. The first boat, with room for fifteen more passengers, was sent away, an officer standing with drawn revolver to forbid others entering. These things I learned as I passed among the sufferers on our way into New York.

I was up before dawn the day we picked up the surviving remnant of the two thousand who were aboard the *Titanic*.

I knew of nothing amiss, except that sailors were running to and fro. No other passenger was about at that hour, I think.

Suddenly the *Carpathia* reversed her engines, and stopped. There came the sound of oars to starboard. I peered out in the grey dawn, and saw a little boat coming toward us.

Thirty-eight had started on that boat, only fourteen were aboard her when she reached safety – and one of the fourteen was dead. The others had died on the way, and had been cast overboard, while a woman, I know not who she was, recited prayers for the dying.

The sun was rising. To right, left, before us and behind, were other boats, some far distant. Women were rowing some of them.

In one a man lay dead, his head hanging over the side, the tiller rope in his stiffening hand, he held in death, the course of the boat true.

The sun rose. Directly in its path, far off – almost at the horizon, there was a little boat in the crimson path that lay across the waters. The figures in the boat showed black against the brilliant background, and we could see them bending to their oars. At last they came aboard and one by one, almost everyone fainted. A woman, one of the bravest I have ever seen, was acting as stroke and urging the rowers on. I never learned her name.

A few bodies were floating, and we took them aboard. They were buried at sea.

One boat was picked up and had two foot of water in it, and those aboard had abandoned rowing for an hour or more, for they were chilled to the point of death.

One died. He was, I understand, W.F. Hoyt, bound for Cleveland.

All passengers agreed in their story that 200 at least might have lived if the crew of the *Titanic* had known what they were doing. The men were brave enough, God knows – but a week of drilling would have saved ten score.[91]

❖ ❖ ❖

Father Hogue granted another interview to a New York paper:

From the habit of a lifetime I am an early riser. Even had not the noise of the *Carpathia*'s big whistle and the clatter of the ship's crew as they dashed up and down the stairways, through the halls and along the decks from a little after midnight aroused most of the sleeping passengers, I would have turned out not later than 3:30 o'clock anyhow.

And so I saw and heard and felt everything that went on aboard the *Carpathia* during those dreadful hours when we were being carried at top speed to the rescue. The crew worked like a veritable machine. Every part responded instantly to Captain Rostron's touch. Eagerness, intense, desperate, profound, shone from every countenance.

We knew only that a frantic cry had been sent by the *Titanic*. The last word received by our wireless operator indicated that the *Titanic* was sinking. And we were fifty-eight miles away when the message, horsed upon the sightless couriers of the air, had carried the heartbreaking news around the world.

As soon as I came on deck I saw the gaunt form of Captain Rostron pacing the bridge. Sailors were dashing back and forth from deck to deck obeying his commands. The sea was smooth. The whole world seemed wrapped in a perfect calm, save the low mutterings of officers and seamen in repeating the captain's orders. The sky was clear. The stars glittered gloriously. The phosphorescent lane in the wake of our swiftly moving ship shimmered brilliantly.

I held my watch almost constantly before my eyes. On, on we were going, I knew not how fast. The minutes seemed like hours. I had not the heart to interrupt the work of the ship's crew by asking how fast we were going, how far we still were from the *Titanic*'s position, or at what time we should arrive there.

I was literally transfixed by the horror and awe of it all. I do not think I moved once from the spot I took at the rail of the top deck after I learned what was going on. A little past three o'clock the darkness began to show a slight tinge of light. Then my straining eyes could see a little further ahead of the ship. But there was nothing in sight above the water.

By half past three the air was showing more plainly the pink of coming dawn. But still I could discern nothing but the rippling waters. The huge bulk of the *Carpathia* was throwing broad sprays ahead of her course.

It was just about 4 o'clock that we saw a lifeboat. The sun had not then risen, but it was almost as light as day. Before we could come alongside the first lifeboat the red sun came up over the majestic curve of the ocean.

The *Carpathia*'s whistle greeted the boat with a mighty blast. The sound crashed into the ears of the people in the lifeboat, and for the first time since we had sighted them they gave recognition of our presence by the waving of such articles as they dared detach from their shivering bodies.

I counted twenty-five persons in the boat. Twenty-three of them were women and children. The other two were seamen. It seems to me now that quicker than I can tell you we had every soul on board.

The seamen pulled desperately on their oars, bringing their boat alongside. Rope ladders were suspended from our top deck. A rope for everybody on the boat was thrown down. There were loops in these ropes.

Every woman and child, as if by instinct, put the loops around their bodies and drew them taut. Some of the women climbed the ladders. To others chairs were lowered and in those they were lifted aboard. Not a word was spoken by any one of the rescued or the rescuers. Everybody was too benumbed by horror to speak. It was a time for action and not words.

There was a solemn hush over the ocean. The sea was glassy and absolutely quiet. The awful solemnity was gnawing at every heart, burning every brain. Then as if by magic lifeboats began to bob into our vision from every direction. We were moving slowly around a narrow circle. On came the lifeboats toward us – one, two, three, four, five.

Either they came so fast or my brain was in such a torpor I could not count them readily. The air was crisp, but not biting cold. We were fairly in the midst of a great ice field that seemed to stretch into the Arctic. Tall bergs reared their white and menacing bulks ahead of us. Silently, stealthily they were bearing down upon us. A deep, low crunching sound, like death's defiant groan, came up from the placid sea.

But terror had done its worst. Not a soul seemed frightened by the ominous icebergs. There was but one thought in all the company. That was to get safely aboard the *Carpathia* every human being in the lifeboats that seemed such pigmies. We accomplished the work with marvelous celerity.

Not a tear dimmed the eyes of one of the hundreds we got on deck. The women were less excited than the men. Apparently they had all drained their tear ducts dry, for every eye was red and swollen.

Without a word of greeting or of questioning by any of us, the rescued were conducted by tender hands to comfortable places in the saloons and staterooms. Then the ship's three doctors, assisted by Dr. Blackmarr, of Chicago, a fellow voyager, set to work.[92]

Father Hogue granted a third interview to a Boston newspaper:

Captain Rostron was a very angry man when I saw him early Thursday morning. He called a dozen or more of us on deck and said, 'Gentlemen, the White Star Line officials have sent a Marconigram accusing me of having given advance information of the terrible disaster to the newspapers of New York.

'Since the collision, I have sent only one telegram and that was to the Cunard Line officials. Now, in view of what we have done for the survivors of the *Titanic* wreck – the *Titanic* having been a White Star Line steamer – I think I am a victim of a rank injustice. How do you gentlemen feel about it?'

We assured him that no person could have done more for a person in distress. Also, we told him that when he was accused in any way by the White Star officials, he was being accused unjustly. Then every man of us took off our hats and cheered him until we were hoarse.[93]

❖ ❖ ❖

LUCIUS HOYT

After the *Carpathia*'s arrival, Mr Hoyt granted an interview to an Albany, New York, newspaper:

About dawn on Monday my wife woke me and said that the whistle had given a sharp blast and the ship had stopped. I put my head out and asked the steward what was the matter. He said that the *Titanic* was in distress. We all dressed and went on deck. The lifeboats were beginning to arrive and continued to do so at intervals.

It was not unlike the rescue of a shipwrecked party in the polar regions. The ice floe extended for miles and miles both ways, with icebergs of enormous size all around. In the bitter cold of early dawn, the background of ice and the lifeboats coming toward us will not soon be forgotten. We reached the position of the *Titanic* about 3:30, but nothing was to be seen but ice and it was supposed at first that all had been lost. Often a cake of ice would be mistaken for a boat, but at last a boat appeared out of the darkness, attracted by the rockets fired from our ship. The first boat was only about two-thirds filled, and there was one Albanian aboard, Mr. Tucker.

One of the rescued men told me that there was no suction as he and his father jumped overboard, and when the ship took her final plunge they were directly under. He said they could look up and see the big screws. The water threw them away from the vessel and they caught a life raft, but the father did not have the strength and, bidding his son goodbye, sank.

Wednesday night the purser, who was occupying one of our berths, gave it up to a young man who raved all night. He was so weak that it was necessary to carry him in. A millionaire on board had to borrow money to get a shave. In some of the boats were the bodies of people who had died from exposure, and we had five burials from our ship. Very few bodies came to the surface up to the time we left the spot. I saw at least four.

A rescued passenger, a civil engineer, told me that tons and tons of ice fell on the deck of the *Titanic* and that a height of 180 feet of ice was visible when the berg struck the ship.

Mr Hoyt said that he and his party gave every piece of their spare clothing to the survivors. He and his wife surrendered their cabin to survivors and shared a cabin with Mr and Mrs Reynolds:

> One of the occupants of our cabin jumped from the *Titanic* as she was sinking and got on an upturned lifeboat. The other occupant had a similar terrible experience.[94]

Mr Hoyt was interviewed again at the St Denis Hotel with fellow *Carpathia* passengers, Charles Reynolds and Reuben Weidman. Mr Hoyt declared they were undaunted by the disaster and that they intended sailing on the *Carpathia* at 4 p.m:

> There are so many tales to tell of the wreck of the *Titanic* as we heard them from survivors that one hardly knows where to begin. I can recall now just the experience we had when we got the first intimation of the *Titanic*'s peril. The *Carpathia* made tracks for the scene of the accident immediately, and I can see now the dotted spots of white bobbing up here and there. As we came closer we saw that they were lifeboats full of people, mostly women.
>
> It seemed that everybody aboard the *Carpathia* wanted to rush at once to the rescue of those poor unfortunates. The *Carpathia*'s officers got them boatload after boatload aboard, and the survivors were quickly escorted to the dining room and given coffee and brandy. Nobody lost his head. The best kind of discipline was maintained. Yes, we gave up our cabins, we gave up everything we had to these poor [illegible] ... Why, Mrs. Hoyt and I haven't a thing to wear, having [illegible] us. I have on [illegible] underwear, and he told me that he intended to have it laundered and returned to me but that he had given it to another man.

Mr Hoyt described the German baron who tried to monopolise the *Carpathia*'s blankets, as was told to him by survivor Gilbert Tucker:

> I was standing right beside the young woman who demanded those blankets. And I heard her say to the ungrateful fellow, 'To think of it: the like of you saved and women left to drown; shame on you.' I could scarcely restrain myself from getting that fellow by the collar and ousting him

from his cozy corner into the sea. But these cases were rare indeed. On the contrary the best kind of generosity prevailed and $10,000 in cash was contributed on board the *Carpathia* for the survivors while $20,000 was subscribed.

The discussion turned to Mr Weidman's statement about the dog that Gilbert Tucker purchased in Naples and saved in his lifeboat:

Yes, and the last I saw of Tucker he was going down the gangplank with the dog under one arm and a baby under the other.[95]

MRS CARLOS HURD

After the *Carpathia*'s arrival in New York, Mrs Hurd granted the following news-paper interview:

Monday morning, about 7 o'clock, I awoke suddenly to find that the *Carpathia* had stopped. Suddenly my husband, who had gone on deck, came in at the stateroom door.

'The *Titanic* has gone down and we are taking on her passengers!' he exclaimed, and was gone again.

I ran to my stateroom porthole and looked out upon an icefield that seemed to extend for miles in the distance. Here and there in this mam-moth, sun-glittering field of ice huge icebergs rose to enormous height. The sudden glare almost blinded me for a moment. Then I gazed down below me and saw two overturned lifeboats. That was my first realization of the great tragedy.

I dressed hurriedly and rushed out of my stateroom to go on deck. As I ran along one of the gangways a passenger came out of his stateroom and asked, 'What's happened?'

'They say the *Titanic* has gone down,' I answered.

Just then a man in a blue uniform with a white star on his cap, who was standing at my elbow, stepped forward and said, 'It's true, Madame. I'm of the *Titanic*.'

I stood still and gazed at him for several moments, hardly comprehend-ing. Then the wails of the survivors who were being taken aboard our ship reached my ears. As I proceeded toward the dining room to make my way to the deck a steward stopped me, saying, 'Don't go in there, madam, please. It's a poor Italian woman who has just lost her baby.'

Then from the door of the dining room came the distracted mother, half clothed and with her hair hanging about her face, shrieking hysterically.

I could not bear to look upon the poor, distracted mother's face, and her shrieks ran through me like knife-thrusts.

I made my way to the deck just in time to see the last two lifeboats bearing *Titanic* survivors being pulled alongside by a rope. The two lifeboats were mostly filled with women and children, and one of the boats had a dead man. As the boats were being drawn in many of the women recognized friends on the deck of the *Carpathia*, who had preceded them in other lifeboats, and several lost control of themselves, cried hysterically and fell half-fainting into the arms of their companions.

The rope ladders and swings, just like the kind that children delight in, were lowered down and the people in the two boats were drawn up to the deck. The women seemed to lose absolute control of themselves at this point, and screamed and fought against ascending the rope ladders or taking seats in the swings. The men in the boats had to force them into the swings, where they clung screaming as they were drawn aboard ship.

That was the last of the rescued. Sixteen lifeboats and two collapsible boats had left the *Titanic*. One of the collapsible boats overturned and was used as a raft, and in this way several persons were brought to safety. The rescued had scattered all over the *Carpathia*. Here and there little groups gathered about, telling of their experiences.

I looked over the icefield, thinking I would see something of the *Titanic*. I thought I would see a mast sticking out of the water, but all that I saw was the two overturned lifeboats and some pieces of broken wood floating about.

In the women's cabin I saw a woman lying on a couch wrapped in a blanket. On the floor nearby was a pile of wet clothing – her clothing that had been cut from her by the stewards. She told of her ordeal aboard the sinking ship. She said she was on the deck of the *Titanic* awaiting her turn to get into a lifeboat. As the lifeboat was being lowered the *Titanic* suddenly went down. The rush of water flooded the decks and washed her off her feet.

As she was floundering about in the icy water she saw a collapsible lifeboat that had overturned and was being used as a raft. Several men were on this improvised raft, and she cried to them as she felt the *Titanic*'s deck disappear beneath her, to help her. The men paid no attention to her cries, and with desperation she threw herself aboard without any assistance. They had no oars, and the men balanced the frail craft by leaning from side to side. They drifted about in this way for two or three hours before they were picked up by one of the *Titanic*'s boats, already overcrowded with survivors. The woman who told me this story was Mrs. Rosa Abbott of Providence, R.I.

Another survivor, a man, told me of the suddenness of the *Titanic*'s sinking. He said he had been sitting in the men's smoking room playing cards. The crash as the ship struck the iceberg threw him and his companions out of their chairs. Some of the players, after getting on their feet, went on deck to see what was the matter. The iceberg was on the opposite side of the ship from where they were, and they saw nothing to alarm them.

My informant then went to his stateroom, thinking nothing amiss, and began to undress. His companions returned to their card game. Then the messengers came to each of the staterooms, to the smoking rooms and to other places and quietly ordered the passengers to put on their life preservers and come on deck. This was the first real intimation of danger.

Survivors by the dozen told me of the events that followed the warning to don life preservers and come on deck. Many women in evening dress came on deck wearing life preservers, laughing gaily, thinking the warning a joke. Some even refused to leave their staterooms. Among those who refused to leave their staterooms, thinking the warning a joke, was a family of four, accompanied by a nurse. The nurse obeyed the warning and carried the baby on deck and later to safety.

Laughing groups stood about the decks and in the saloons in evening clothes, wearing life preservers and laughing at the 'joke' being perpetrated on them by the *Titanic*'s crew. Some of them, thinking they would be back in their staterooms in half an hour, did not try to take any of their valuables with them.

One or two who took the warning half way serious seized their valuables as they left to answer the warning. No one thought for a minute that the boat would sink.

From what I could learn, the steerage passengers were more keen to realize the real danger than those in the first and second cabins. Some of the laughing passengers saw the iceberg as it loomed up alongside in the dark, but they laughed at the idea of the mighty *Titanic* being injured seriously by an iceberg. From what I could learn from the survivors the majority did not see the iceberg.

Then the crew of the *Titanic* began to lower the boats and to order the women and children aboard. Still there were many who doubted the sincerity of it all and laughed at the idea of serious danger. Many women held back, even when ordered to enter the boats. One woman with whom I talked said that she was actually kicked into a boat by an officer of the ship, who had repeatedly ordered her to get aboard.

Then as the boats were lowered and filled with passengers and pulled away into the darkness, the first real realization that the ship was in peril began to dawn upon them. Then the word went from mouth to mouth that the ship was in danger of sinking, and the rush to the decks began.

There was plenty of light aboard the *Titanic*. The electric bulbs threw their brilliancy over the crowds on the decks. It was a clear, starlight night, and the passengers could see for miles across the icefield. There were no lights in the lifeboats, however, and the suddenness of the call did not allow of time to provision them or put water aboard.

There was not much disorder as the boats were lowered away. The passengers were not panicky; in fact they did not seem to realize the gravity of the situation. The majority of the men gallantly observed the rule of women and children first. The boats were rapidly filled and lowered away.

Many women refused to leave their husbands and steadfastly refused to obey the commands of the *Titanic*'s officers to get into the boats. Many husbands had to force their wives to get into the boats. Other wives refused to be forced and remained by the side of their husbands until the last.

Lifeboat after lifeboat to the number of sixteen had been lowered away with their passengers. Suddenly there was a rush of water, then darkness. The once diamond-like ship had become a cinder. There were loud shouted orders, hoarse cries from the throats of the men, shrieks from women and then came the explosion. The water that had reached the engine room and stopped the dynamos, throwing the ship into darkness, had reached the boilers, too, and the explosion followed. Then the *Titanic* sank.

The first day aboard the *Carpathia*, when all was excitement because of the rescue, the real awfulness of the tragedy was not realized. Everyone who had been separated from a relative or friends believed that other boats had come to the rescue.

The second day, Tuesday, the real truth began to be broken upon the survivors. The women bore themselves bravely even though realizing that their loved ones had gone to their death. But still there was always a hope, and many landed in New York still hoping that other ships would rescue those from whom they parted aboard the *Titanic*.

It was a ship of tragedy that put back to New York, and those of the *Carpathia* who had witnessed it all will never forget to their dying days the sense of grief. Here was a babe that had been rescued and whose father and mother had gone down with the *Titanic*. Here were two little French boys who had suddenly been made orphans. Here was a bride of two months who had been forced from her husband's side to the lifeboats, and there was an aged woman who had been torn from the side of her companion of years.

Words cannot express the horror, the tragedy of it all. I want to forget it. I wish that the last week could be blotted from my memory, but it haunts me, sleeping or waking, like a terrible nightmare.[96]

JOHN R. JOYCE

Mr Joyce granted the following interview after the *Carpathia* reached New York:

In response to the wireless call, when we got up to the scene of the wreck we saw eighteen boats and one raft floating around. The *Carpathia* picked them all up. Four of the people on the raft were dead. They were buried at sea from the *Carpathia* on her way to New York.

On the raft were about thirty-five people, and they said that about thirty-five others had tried to get on. They were lost either off the raft or while trying to get on it. It was all fixed for the women to go first. Some of the women refused to go, and the men had to insist, and actually pushed them into the boats. To the best of my knowledge the *Titanic* stayed afloat two hours.

Some of the men were in their dinner jackets and evening clothes. As far as I know we saved about 600 passengers and 110 of the crew. A survivor I talked with said that when he was stepping into the last boat that left the *Titanic* he saw Isidor Straus. Mr. Straus was urging his wife toward the boat. She was insisting on remaining with him.

I saw Mrs. Astor come on board the *Carpathia*, and one of the survivors told me that just before he left he saw Mr. Astor drown.

Some of the people jumped from the *Titanic* and were immediately drowned. They leaped for the boats, but did not hit a lifeboat at all. I heard nothing of Major Butt. A rumor ran through the *Carpathia* after the rescue that there was a wild rush for the boats by the steerage passengers, and that three Italians were shot by the *Titanic* officers.

A survivor said that the *Titanic* was going at full speed, or at least 20 knots an hour. The iceberg struck her side on and the impact didn't even throw people off their feet. As far as I can understand it scraped along the bilge keel and dragged her plates out.

Mr Joyce was asked how Bruce Ismay escaped from the *Titanic*:

Well he got into a lifeboat. On the *Carpathia* he went to a stateroom and never said a word. There was some criticism regarding Mr. Ismay on board the boat, but he was not criticized severely. The White Star Line was criticized to some extent. People said that everybody could have been saved if there had been enough lifeboats. Among those who criticized the steamship line was the Second Officer of the *Carpathia*.

Among the wreckage that was seen at the scene of the disaster were all kinds of furniture. When she went down, there was very little suction indeed. The order was given absolutely that women should go first. Many of them hesitated, and while they did so, some of the men slipped into the boats. The majority of the survivors were in good condition.[97]

Mr Joyce made the following statement to another reporter:

> When the *Carpathia* reached the scene of the wreck, we saw eighteen boats
> and one raft on the water. The *Carpathia* picked them all up. Four persons
> on the raft were dead. They were buried at sea on our way back to New
> York. A survivor told me that some of the *Titanic*'s passengers jumped for
> the lifeboats, missed them and were immediately drowned. I heard nothing
> of Major Butt.[98]

Mr Joyce made a third statement to another reporter. Joyce repeated the experiences of a survivor who was one of thirty-five who scrambled on a raft just before the ship went down and who had a desperate time keeping his place on the raft after the sea roughed up:

> Nineteen of the thirty-five on the raft were lost before the rest were picked
> up by the *Carpathia*. They died there on the raft in the four hours of exposure. Some had only their underclothes on, and although their comrades
> did their best to look after them and to share what they had, there was little
> that could be done. There were two bodies on the raft when the *Carpathia*
> hoisted the others over the side. Most of those on the raft were men.[99]

J.F. KEMP

Dr Kemp spoke with reporters after the *Carpathia* reached New York:

> A boy and one of the last of the children to be taken from the *Titanic* told
> me that he saw Capt. Smith put a pistol to his head and then fall down. Of
> course, I cannot tell whether the boy told me the truth, but it seems to me
> hard to believe that the little fellow would invent such a tale. I was talking
> with him on the deck of the *Carpathia* when he voluntarily told me.
>
> A number of passengers spoke of the use of pistols and the firing of
> shots, but we were all too busy with the rescued and those who suffered
> from exposure to follow up any investigation of that sort.

Dr Kemp was asked if he had any reason to believe that weapons were used to keep men away from the lifeboats:

> I have not. I have heard reports on the pier to that effect, but none
> from the passengers of the *Titanic* who were taken out of the sea by the

Carpathia. I was told by a number of passengers that Col. Astor was seen to embrace and kiss his wife farewell at the rail as she went down to a lifeboat.

Mrs. Astor did not leave her stateroom on the *Carpathia* during the voyage to New York.

Kemp was asked how the *Carpathia*'s passengers first became aware of the disaster:

It is odd, but it seems to be a rule that the wireless operator on this ship quits the job about 10:30 p.m. Our operator was just getting ready to turn in and gave a last moment to his instrument, when the call came from the *Titanic.* We all knew of it in a little time, and the ship began to make its way with all possible speed for the point given in the call for help.

The anxiety aboard the *Carpathia* was frightful when the calls from the great new ship kept up and then stopped. Those of us who realized what might be happening, or could imagine the possibilities of what might happen, remained awake.

The first we saw over the rail to give us a sense of realization that the great vessel was lost were the tiny lights close to the sea miles away. They were the lanterns swung on the mastheads of the lifeboats.

The dawn began as we approached the boats. They were scattered. We could find here and there bits of wreckage, but no living human being clinging to any of it. I remember seeing the tops of tables floating on the water before we reached the boats.

We immediately began taking the boatloads of women aboard, and we found that nearly all of them were certain that their men folk were safe. Many of them still believe it now that they are in New York.

As far as I was able to learn there was only one first class woman passenger who lost her life. It seems that she preferred to stay aboard.

Kemp was asked if this woman was Mrs Isidor Straus:

I do not feel that I should answer that question.

The women aboard the *Titanic* did not seem to realize their danger when the collision with the iceberg came. Some of them told me that after the first shock they so relied on the bulkhead construction of the ship that they went to their staterooms and retired. Quite a number did this, and some of them said that when they were ordered to the boats they said that if the captain so ordered they would go off in them for an hour or so and then return to the ship. They gave me the impression that they did not for a moment believe the great vessel could sink.

Kemp was asked if any of the lifeboats were filled entirely with men:

> There was one. The men were begrimed. I think they were the stokers of the *Titanic*. I understand that they were.

Dr Kemp was asked if there was any feeling on board the *Carpathia* against Bruce Ismay, the managing director of the White Star Line:

> None at all. I only saw him once on the trip back to New York.
> The flotilla of lifeboats did not hang close together. We picked them up as fast as we could, and all the time hunted for those who might have clung to wreckage or rafts and survived the exposure. We did not get, so far as I know, a human being from the *Titanic* who was aboard her after the last boat left. Four of the men we picked up from the boats died and we buried them on Monday.[100]

Dr Kemp spoke with a second newspaper reporter:

> Our wireless operator was about to retire Sunday night when he said jokingly, 'I guess I'll wait just ten minutes, then turn in'. It was in the next ten minutes that the *Titanic*'s call for help came. Had the wireless man not waited there would have been no survivors.

Kemp described the iceberg that sank the *Titanic* as at least 400 feet long and 90 feet high, and he declared that one of the boats that the *Carpathia* picked up was filled with stokers. It had just two women aboard. Kemp also declared that the *Carpathia* cruised twice through the ice field near the spot where the *Titanic* sank and picked up bodies of three men and one baby:

> On Monday at 8:30 in the evening we held a funeral service on board the *Carpathia*. At this service there were thirty widows, twenty of whom were under twenty-three years of age, and most of them brides for a few weeks or months. They did not know their husbands were among the dead of the disaster. The *Californian* and the *Birma*, the last named a Russian steamer, cruised about the scene of the wreck for some time in a futile search for the bodies of the victims.
> Mrs. John Jacob Astor had to be carried aboard. She had to be taken into a cabin and given medical attention. She was more completely attired, however, than many of the women who were rescued.[101]

Dr Kemp spoke with an additional reporter in New York. Kemp said he saw the body of a child floating around with a lifebelt buckled around its waist and that it had been dead for at least a couple of hours:

Another sad scene was when two little children, one three and the other five years old, were taken out of the lifeboat and brought on deck. Both parents had been drowned.

There were many of the sad scenes, but perhaps the culminating point was reached in the funeral services on shipboard last Monday when four of the passengers rescued from the *Titanic*, and who had died on the *Carpathia*, were buried with all the honors of a sea funeral.

Dr. Anderson, who is connected with the Holy Cross Episcopal Monastery, officiated at the services, and after the burial services the bodies, having previously been sewn up in canvas sacks, with the feet well shotted, were placed on a plank and slid into the water, where they instantly disappeared from sight.

I saw at least twelve lifeboats hoisted from the water and at least three collapsible boats which were also taken aboard ship. I heard that there were sixteen boats in all which left the *Titanic* and learned that some were lost.

When we sighted the boats it was just a gray dawn and we could only see two small lights from the lifeboat mastheads. As the daylight grew brighter and we drew nearer the number of lights increased to ten, and when we reached the scene the light wreckage and the bodies had mostly disappeared from view.

The manner in which some of these women worked in the boats would excite the admiration of anybody. There were two college women, whose names I did not get, who rowed five hours continuously, and you can fancy how they must have felt after being rescued.

When these women got on shipboard and into the warm air they in many instances collapsed and were in a very nervous, hysterical state bordering on total collapse.

Survivors told Kemp that the *Titanic* sank gradually and that it finally lunged slightly, after which the bow sank and the stern rose high in the air. Kemp also said that a rescued boy told him that Captain Smith shot himself through the head just as the ship was sinking. The boy jumped overboard and was later picked up:

I was told by the passengers of the *Titanic* that there were many in the cabins who never came to the decks and went down with the ship. I heard of a lot of husky stokers forcing their way into a boat, and another instance of a Jap and an Armenian who got in a ship's boat in some unknown manner and were hidden in the bottom for a long time.

From all I could learn, the men in nearly every instance behaved well. It was very lucky for the passengers on the *Titanic* that our wireless operator had not retired for the night as he was about to, otherwise there would have been a different story to tell.

He was making his last call and inside of ten minutes more would have closed up for the night and the distress call of the *Titanic* would not be heard by us. We all considered that a very close call an congratulated ourselves on being able to contribute something for humanity ... [102]

Dr Kemp granted at least one additional interview to reporters, who paraphrased it as follows:

Dr. Kemp said that he was in his room on the *Carpathia* at 11:35 o'clock Sunday night when he noticed that the engines had stopped. He went out to find the trouble and was informed that a message of distress had been received from the *Titanic* and that the *Carpathia* was turning to go to her assistance. The wireless operator was about to go to sleep when the message was received, Dr. Kemp said, and five minutes later the signal might have found no response.

The *Carpathia* reached the scene of the disaster at about 5 o'clock in the morning. The boats of the *Titanic* were in a field of ice that stretched out for a mile. By 8:30 all the survivors were safe on board the *Carpathia*. Some were in very good condition and perfectly clad. There were a few who did not have much clothing, but most were attired sufficiently to have withstood the chill of the icy air. One of the boats of the *Titanic* was filled with stokers.

Mrs. John Jacob Astor appeared to be in good condition and was able to walk to her room without assistance. She did not appear on board later, but there was nothing said by any of the ship's doctors to indicate she had to be taken care of by the physicians. There were not many persons ill among the survivors. A few steerage passengers of the *Titanic* had pneumonia and others suffered from frostbite.

The *Carpathia* cruised around the scene of the disaster, and four bodies were picked up and later buried. During the return voyage four persons died on board the *Carpathia*. It was understood that they were sailors.

A male survivor told Dr. Kemp that the night was very clear. There had been no indication of icebergs and the one that proved fatal must have loomed up very suddenly. The passengers took the matter very quietly. They were persuaded to take the boats, thinking there was no danger that the ship would sink and that they might be able to return to it in the morning.

The survivor told Dr. Kemp that Captain Smith was on the *Titanic*'s bridge. A wave washed him into the icy water, and one of the lifeboats tried to rescue him. He fought, but finally was pulled into the boat. He then jumped overboard and swam back to the *Titanic*, where he was again seen on the bridge and must have died at his post.

Dr. Kemp said that, of the thirty widows on the *Carpathia*, nearly all thought their husbands had been saved in some other manner, and they were confidently expecting to get some news from them on reaching New York.[103]

JOHN KUHL

Mr Kuhl granted the following interview after the *Carpathia* reached New York. Kuhl said that many of the women in the lifeboats were scantily clad and all were suffering from the cold. Four died on the *Carpathia* as a result of the exposure:

In spite of the suffering and the crowded condition of the boats, the utmost heroism was displayed by all of the unfortunates. When they were lifted to the deck of the *Carpathia* many of the women broke down completely and there were many touching scenes. Many of the women were incoherent, and several were almost insane.[104]

Mr Kuhl granted a second interview to reporters:

Mrs. Astor was sent away in the tenth boat. Just as she was about to be placed within the boat, Colonel Astor embraced her. Astor then freed himself from his wife's embrace and, after helping to force her into the boat, turned away and stood upon the deck.[105]

H.H. LEE

Mr Lee, who was the *Carpathia*'s printer, granted an interview to reporters, who paraphrased its content:

Lee stated that he had taken in four members of the *Titanic*'s crew in his bunk, and among them was a quartermaster who saw Captain Smith calmly walk to the chart room, draw a revolver from his pocket and fire a shot through the right side of his head. This was done, Lee said, after the lifeboats had all left the doomed vessel and Smith was satisfied that he had performed his duty. The ship's printer further stated that he had been told by the *Titanic* survivors that twice previous to killing himself, the captain had been found about in the act of taking his life. On the bridge of the *Titanic*, according to Lee, Chief Officer Wilde snatched the revolver from Smith's hand and blew his own brains out.[106]

❖   ❖   ❖

ARPAD LENGYEL

Dr Lengyel spoke with reporters after the *Carpathia* reached New York:

For three days we had been having splendid weather. We hoped to make Gibraltar one day earlier than usual. Suddenly at 12:10 a.m. on the 15th we received a Marconigram with the terrible message that the *Titanic* was in a sinking condition. We instantly replied that we would give assistance. We had not heard what had happened to her, but we knew that where she was then there was ice.

It was a beautiful starlight night, but the weather was very cold. The night before it had been very dark and foggy, but the night of the catastrophe it was clear and beautiful. I came on deck in response to a call to quarters issued by the captain, A.H. Rostron, who immediately ordered all hands on deck as soon as he received news of the disaster.

The *Carpathia* was in darkness at the time the message was received, and all of her passengers were asleep. As soon as the captain's order was issued, calling the crew to the deck, the lights were all turned on and the ship became a brilliant mass of light. Preparations were made to meet every possible emergency. I was put in charge of the steerage, which was the receiving ward. The Italian doctor was put in charge of the second cabin. The captain ordered coffee prepared for 1,000 persons. Full surgical dressings and appliances of every description were taken from our well-equipped drug store.

These arrangements were made for the first, second and third class passengers. We, at this time, changed our course and started in the direction from which the message calling for help had come. When we started steaming, we saw ice, but no boats. The *Carpathia*, which makes 13 knots under normal conditions, made 18 knots during the entire time until we picked up the first boat from the *Titanic*. At 12:30 a.m. they commenced sending up rockets, which we continued to do. We went forty miles to the north. At about 2 a.m. we saw the first Coston light. This light was from a lifeboat and was not from the *Titanic*.

It was 3:30 when we picked up the first boat. This boat was filled with steerage passengers. The *Carpathia* had then stopped her engines. Suddenly we saw the sea dotted with little saltering [*sic*], appearing in and off among the ice peaks. The people we picked up in this boat were so overcome with the cold that they were brought to the deck in a helpless condition by means of a bosun's chair.

There were twenty-two people in this boat, most of whom were women. All of them had worn lifebelts. These belts were cut from them. To some we gave coffee and to others brandy. To all of them we administered massage. Some of them were crying and could not be comforted. Though I am a surgeon and used to terrible sights and scenes, I will say to you that it is beyond human belief that any man's eyes could see what mine have seen. It was terrible, even to me.

A little ahead of us just at this time we noticed a very peculiar thing. A short distance away the sea appeared as brown as if it had been painted. This marked the spot where the *Titanic* went down. The color of the sea was due to the mass of wreckage from the great ship. It consisted of small debris, settling of chairs and stools and included twelve boats upside down. Several persons whom we picked up were in their night clothes. Some of them were in evening dress.

Many of them were wounded, perhaps from jumping. When we sighted the flotilla of lifeboats, we stopped our engines and let them come to us, because it was easier for them to maneuver. Because we had no infectious diseases on our ship and because of the great number of wounded and weakened people we picked up, we used our isolation ward as well as our hospital.

Clinging to the side of the first boat we picked up were four men who had been swimming from two to three hours in the cold water. Two of them were sailors, one of them was a passenger, and the other was the second Marconi man. Although these men were swimming, automatically keeping their heads above the surface, they were mentally unconscious of the fact that they had been rescued. When we got them to the deck they appeared to me to be four dead men. I cut their clothing from them and laid them in a warm stateroom, where they recovered in about twelve hours.

Mr. Daniel, who is a banker from Philadelphia, was clothed only in a woolen sleeping garment. He was delirious. I gave him my own short [suit?]. There were a number of children taken from the lifeboats who did not have parents. There were four cases in which infants and mothers were separated, being in different boats, and being united after we had gotten the entire number of survivors aboard.

In one case there was a nursing infant separated from its mother, who was saved in a different boat. We took from the boats four dead bodies.

Mrs. Astor was not recognized because of the condition of her hair, which obscured her face. When her identity was learned she was put in the private stateroom from which she came out for the first time tonight.

Those who were dead were either frozen to death or killed by shock. They were unwounded. They were all male. These four bodies were buried at sea at 6 o'clock Monday afternoon. We picked up in all sixteen lifeboats. We have brought in thirteen of those boats. We did not have room for the other three and left them adrift. It was 10 o'clock in the morning when we had picked up the last boatload.

Then we started steaming. In one hour and a half we had reached an icefield. It took us one and a half hours to pass through this field. It was eighteen miles in width.

Lengyel spoke with a survivor who said that the survivors in his lifeboat recalled that Captain Smith shot two men who tried to climb into a lifeboat, and that he had also shot the man who had been on lookout in the crow's nest. He said that Mrs. Astor kept to her stateroom on the *Carpathia* and was not seen on the *Carpathia*'s deck until the night of the 18th, when he saw her on deck for a few minutes.[107]

Dr Lengyel also related information he had picked up while interviewing the *Titanic*'s steerage survivors:

There was a great fright in the steerage from the moment the ship struck the ice, all of the passengers told me. Some who had been on deck said that just before the crash they heard the lookout on the forward mast, just above them, shout out a warning.

Piling up to their deck, shouting and crying, dragging their bundles, the steerage men and women were at first beyond control. Sailors went among them telling them the ship had struck the ice but was not in danger, and they grew calmer. Just as the boats began to come down from the upper deck the steamship listed heavily to starboard, and the steerage passengers were piled up against the rail. This renewed their terror and they fought to extricate themselves.

Despair took possession of them, because the first and second boats lowered past them were not stopped at that deck and neither was half filled. They believed they were being deserted.

When the first boat was stopped at the steerage deck everyone surged forward to get into it, the men forcing themselves to the front and none of them, so far as they told me, thinking of anything but his own safety and his precious bundles. One woman rescued could talk of nothing but the 'beautiful goose liver and cheese' they had torn from her.

The first boat stopped was filled with men before the sailors could interfere. They had a battle to drag out the men and let the women take their places. Many of the women had enormous bundles on their heads or in their arms and they fought like demons to keep them.

The great panic seems to have begun when the stokers rushed up from below and tried to beat a path through the steerage men and women and through the sailors and officers to get into the boats. They had their iron bars and shovels and they struck down all who stood in their way.

First to come up from the depths of the ship was an engine oiler. From what he is reported to have said, I think perhaps the steam fittings were broken and many men were scalded to death when the *Titanic* listed. He said he had to dash through a narrow place beside a broken pipe and his back was frightfully scalded.

Right at his heels came the stokers. The officers had pistols, but they could not use them at first for fear of killing the women and children. The sailors fought with their fists, and many of them took the stoke bars and shovels from the stokers and used them to beat back the others. Then it seems, from what the survivors told me, the officers thought of firing in the air.

One of the stokers, a Chinaman, managed to slip into a boat. An officer saw him just as the boat was lowered and shot at him. Those in that boat with whom I talked said the bullet did not hit the stoker, and the officer seemed afraid to shoot again, for fear of hitting others.

Many of the coal passers and stokers, who had been driven back from the boats, went to the rail, and whenever a boat was filled and lowered, several of them jumped overboard and swam to it, trying to climb aboard. Several of the patients said that men who swam to the sides of their boats were pulled in or climbed in.

Dozens of the cabin passengers were witnesses of some of the most frightful scenes on the steerage deck. The steerage survivors told me that often the women from the upper decks were the only cool persons in the lifeboats, and they tried to quiet the steerage women, who were nearly all half crazy.[108]

MARY LOWELL

Miss Lowell granted the following interview after arriving in New York:

I was awakened by a strange thumping and pounding from the interior of the steamer, and I didn't know what to make of it. I lit the light and looked at my watch and saw that the hands pointed to 3:30. Then I heard some people talking outside and saying something about a sinking steamer and icebergs, so I got up and dressed.

At 4 o'clock I came on deck. Dawn had not begun to break, and the air was terribly cold. The steamer was tearing through the water at a great rate. Up in the bow there was a little crowd of people, and just as I started toward them, two or three of them shouted and pointed straight ahead. When I joined them I saw a little flickering light in the distance. It was that at which they were pointing.

As soon as this light was sighted the *Carpathia* slowed down. Her regular speed is 13 knots an hour, but when our wireless operator learned that the *Titanic* was sinking, her speed was increased by more than one third so that she was making 17 knots an hour. The speed at which she was running was responsible for the thumping and pounding which had awakened me.

Ahead of us, and on every side of us, the water was filled with ice cakes and icebergs. It was so dark at first that I could not see how far away this ice extended. The ship's surgeon who came down and stood beside me just after the light was sighted, said that he had been on the bridge for two hours with the captain and that for every minute of that time, we had been running through ice fields.

As we got nearer and nearer to the little flickering light, the sky began to grow very grey, and we were able to see a little. The sky got greyer and greyer and finally the east showed a tinge of pink and yellow. Then all of a sudden we saw two little boats among the ice cakes. We looked and looked, and then away beyond the first two we saw two more. As the sky grew brighter and brighter we kept discovering more and more boats, until we had located all of them, scattered ahead of us over two or three square miles of ocean.

The first boat seemed to creep to us and we thought it would never reach us. We didn't know what had happened or how many had been saved or anything at all about the accident; but when the little boat was close up against our side and we could look down into her we knew that the accident had been a terrible one.

The men and women who were huddled into the boat's bottom were only half dressed. Until I saw their faces I never knew what the word 'haggard' meant. They had been exposed to the biting cold for so many hours that they could scarcely move. Some of them were so frozen that they couldn't even look up or move from the bottom of the boat when it came their turn to come aboard the *Carpathia*.

Our captain had made the sailors get chairs on the ends of ropes and big bags on the ends of ropes and fix them around the rails so that they could be used in unloading the boats. It was lucky that he did, for the poor women were so frozen that when they were helped up from the positions that they had been cramped in for so many hours, they could do nothing except fall back into the bottom of the boat. So the chairs were used to get the women up on deck, and the bags were used for the children.

It was really terrible to see the poor women stagger out of their chairs and fall into the arms of the people who were so anxious to help them. The experience they had been through was such a horrible one that they were completely dazed by it. I was helping one girl when she was hoisted out of a boat, and she turned her face towards me with a smile and said in a perfectly unemotional, conversational tone, 'My husband's drowned, isn't it awful?' There was as much expression in her face and voice as if she had said, 'I've forgotten my handkerchief. Isn't it terrible?'

The children could not appreciate what they had been through, of course. When the first sack was hoisted on deck we all crowded around it while it was first being opened. When the mouth was finally undone, a little four-year-old boy was blinking at me. We pushed the bag down around his feet, and then we saw that he had a wooden soldier in his hand. He put the head of the wooden soldier in his mouth and sucked it, and didn't make a sound. Poor little boy. He'd lost his father and mother.

Nobody could watch those poor people come aboard without crying. Everyone was crying. I cried fearfully. In fact, I simply howled. Men were crying, too, and they weren't ashamed of it. I saw one sailor carrying deck chairs away from one part of the deck and stacking them up in another. He had seen the women coming aboard and heard them asking for their husbands and fathers, and as he carried the chairs down the deck the great big tears rolled out of his eyes and dropped down on his jersey.

For four hours those little boats were creeping up to our side, and survivors were coming aboard. In one of the boats there was only one man, and he was afraid. He steered the boat and the women rowed. While they rowed the man kept telling them that they would never get away alive. He was a steward. When these women got aboard, their hands were blistered fearfully from swinging the heavy oars for so many hours.

All of us aboard the *Carpathia* either gave our staterooms to the survivors or took them into our cabins. I took in Miss Dorothy Gibson of New York.

I asked her what had happened. In common with almost every survivor she said the shock of hitting the iceberg was so light as to be almost imperceptible. She had just gone down from the deck to her cabin to get an overcoat when it occurred so she went right back on deck again.

Not only Miss Gibson, but many other survivors, told me that many more persons could have been put into the boats. I saw every one of them come up to the side of the *Carpathia*, and there were only one or two of them that were really crowded.[109]

M.E. Luce

Mr Luce granted the following interview to newspaper reporters. Luce said that many of the lifeboats were only half filled:

> Several of the survivors told me that the reason the boats were so poorly filled was that the persons on the *Titanic* could not believe they were going to be compelled to abandon her. They had heard so much about her unsinkable character they could not believe her big, broad deck was not the safest place under the circumstances.
>
> On board the *Titanic* the lights were blazing and the band was playing. A voyage on the cold sea in small boats did not appeal to the imagination of many, and to that fact some of those who lost their lives certainly owe their death.

Luce said that one lifeboat was launched before the sea plug was put into position, and the occupants of the boat had to bail all night. One person died in a boat, three died immediately after being brought aboard the *Carpathia*, and two died later.[110]

Jose Mardones

Mr Mardones granted the following interview after the *Carpathia* reached New York:

> I talked with a number of people who were rescued. The passengers of the *Titanic* were confident that she could not founder. Otherwise no one would have been saved. There was no panic whatever. In fact, I was told by several of the survivors that they had jested about going into the lifeboats.
>
> One of the *Titanic*'s stewards who was rescued died coming up the side of the *Carpathia*. One of the survivors told me that Mrs. Isidor Straus said to her husband, 'If you don't come, I won't.'

Mardones said an English passenger told him that Captain Smith was washed from the bridge and then saved a woman and then a child by putting them into lifeboats, but Smith refused to be saved himself. In one of the boats picked up by the *Carpathia* were only two men; they were up to their necks in water and nearly drowned.[111]

MRS JOSEPHINE MARSHALL

Mrs Marshall spoke with reporters, who paraphrased her story as follows:

Mrs. Marshall of California gave up the stateroom that she had booked for her maid and made Mrs. Astor comfortable there. Other women gave Mrs. Astor underclothing and did the same for Mrs. Widener and other rescued women. Mrs. Astor had her meals in the steerage dining room but did not complain and gratefully acknowledged any small service done her.[112]

DANIEL MCCARTHY

Fr McCarthy spoke with newspaper reporters in New York:

Father McCarthy and Father Henry Burke helped to aid the injured survivors on the *Carpathia* and gave spiritual consolation to many. Five people they attended died of exposure, others died of injuries. They were told that there was little or no panic on the *Titanic*.[113]

LOUIS MANSFIELD OGDEN

In 1915 Mr Ogden testified at the limitation of liability hearings regarding the *Titanic* disaster, and reporters paraphrased his testimony as follows:

Mr. Ogden said that at 4:10 a.m. the *Carpathia* picked up the first *Titanic* lifeboat, and at that time, although it was dark, they sighted a large iceberg about a third of a mile away. After daybreak many large icebergs were seen. There were fourteen lifeboats of the *Titanic* not nearly filled. One had only twelve and another only sixteen persons aboard, although the capacity was sixty-eight in each case. He offered photographs in substantiation of his statement, and they were admitted as evidence. Ogden estimated that about one hundred icebergs were visible at dawn, and about thirty of these were more than two hundred feet in height.[114]

MRS LOUIS MANSFIELD OGDEN

Upon arriving in New York, Mrs Ogden spoke with reporters:

Mrs. Ogden described how she felt when she heard the *Carpathia*'s whistle sounding early in the morning. She asked her husband if there was a fog, but Mr. Ogden had left the stateroom and did not explain until he returned some ten minutes later. The ship had then slowed down perceptibly and Mrs. Ogden was pretty nervous. Then her husband returned and told her that there had been a great accident and that the *Carpathia* was going to help.

'The passengers are asked to keep to their rooms,' he said. 'There isn't any need of being frightened. There's been no fire on our boat, but there has been an accident to the *Titanic*.'

Mrs. Ogden thought that an accident to the *Titanic* was quite too ridiculous to think of, and in that she shared the impression, which, so she learned afterward, was current upon the *Titanic* after the latter had struck. Mrs. Ogden dressed hastily and went out on deck.

'I saw there on the bosom of the ocean a boatful of women and children. I suppose there must have been sailors there, too, but I did not see them. There were only one or two women in evening dress, but most of them were clad in fur coats over their kimonos or nightgowns. They had on their evening slippers and silk stockings. Some of them wore hats.

'Far in the distance were two or three other black specks which we made out also to be boats. As daylight grew we made out more and more boats, three on one side of our ship and five on the other. Still later we picked up more.

'Here and there on the ocean's surface among the field of ice were bits of wreckage from the broken *Titanic*, and there were in sight many bergs eighty and ninety feet high. The passengers of the *Titanic* were taken aboard the *Carpathia* boatload by boatload up sea ladders.

'The women, most of them, were hoisted to the decks of the *Carpathia* in swings but a few were hardy enough to climb aboard by the sea ladders. The ocean all this time was calm as a lake and it was not a difficult task to take the excess passengers aboard.

'Some of the women helped out in the rowing in the lifeboats themselves.'

Mrs. Ogden said that she saw the hands of Mrs. Astor, Mrs. John B. Thayer and Mrs. George D. Widener red from the oars. Most of the women were wet to the knees from the icy water that had slopped into the *Titanic*'s lifeboats.[115]

Mrs Ogden interviewed a surviving passenger on board the *Carpathia* and later relayed the substance of that interview to newspaper reporters, who paraphrased the interview as follows:

Mr. Ismay, according to Mrs. Ogden, had great trouble in inducing some of the women to take their chances in small boats. They could not be convinced that the shock to the *Titanic* would sink her. Most of them wanted to stay aboard. Mrs. Ogden says that Mr. Ismay left the *Titanic* in the last boat, which contained mostly men. The earlier boats had been filled with both men and women because then the danger did not seem to be imminent. The later boats took entirely women and children until the last boat, in which Mr. Ismay himself went, according to Mrs. Ogden's authority. Just before Mr. Ismay started to climb into the boat he turned to William Carter and said, 'Come on, Mr. Carter, with me.'

The first officer was standing by with his pistol. 'If you do get into that boat,' said the officer to Carter, 'I'll shoot you.'

'But,' protested Mr. Ismay, 'they need men in this boat. Let him come.'

Mr. Carter climbed into the boat thereupon and was saved.[116]

BERNICE PALMER

In later years Miss Palmer recalled her experiences on the *Carpathia*:

Miss Palmer was awakened by the cold and looked out of the porthole of her first class stateroom. It was after dawn, and she saw icebergs and people being hauled up from lifeboats.

'Something terrible has happened,' she called to her mother, and she dressed, hurried on deck and asked a crewman what had happened. 'Oh, the *Titanic* struck an iceberg last night and sank, and we are rescuing the survivors.'

The survivors stood quietly on deck, and Miss Palmer remembered that many of the 'frozen and terrified' survivors were comfortably dressed, some wearing hats. 'A well-dressed woman always wore a hat when she went out,' Miss Palmer explained.

She hurried below and got her Brownie box camera to 'get a picture of the iceberg that sank the *Titanic*'. When she returned to the deck, she recognized survivor Arthur Peuchen, the father of one of her sorority sisters, and rushed up to him. He began to apologize for the fact that he was among the living when so many others had died, and he explained that he had been ordered to take charge of a lifeboat filled with women. He offered this same explanation again and again to anyone who would listen.[117]

MRS F. PALMER

After arriving in New York, Mrs Palmer spoke with newspaper reporters about how the *Carpathia* had picked up the *Titanic*'s lifeboats:

> To reach them we sailed through a sea of icebergs. Sometimes they were so close we could almost touch them. It was bitterly cold. Many who had been in the water a long time before being picked up died from exposure before we reached them. Four seamen succumbed later and were buried at sea.
>
> It was the weirdest, most pathetic sight imaginable. We always picture mourners in black. Many of these women were gaily clad in evening dresses. Some again had only coats slipped over nightdresses. Pretty little Mrs. Dick of Calgary was one of the latter. These and the daintiest of pale blue satin slippers didn't afford much warmth.
>
> She was the last cabin passenger to leave the ship. She was in her cabin, but had not retired when the boat struck. Hurrying out to the corridor in alarm she was met by an officer who said, 'You foolish little woman, there's no danger. Go back to bed.'
>
> So to bed she went, only to be aroused later and told to put on a life preserver. Finding only women were being taken off in the boats, she refused to leave her husband. When the last boat was almost filled, the officers tried again to urge her. Failing, the officer put his hand beneath Mr. Dick's elbow and, pushing him forward, said 'Take her.' The fair little bride's fidelity saved her husband's life.[118]

MISS PETERSON

While the *Carpathia* was approaching the port of New York, tugboats carrying newspapermen steamed alongside and attempted to obtain news of the *Titanic* disaster:

> Miss Peterson stuck her head out of a porthole in answer to a megaphoned hail from the tug *Reynolds*. 'What's the trouble now?' she asked.
>
> 'Tell us about the wreck of the *Titanic*. Who are you?'
>
> 'Miss Peterson of Passaic, New Jersey.'

Miss Peterson gave the following information:

> It's almost too horrible to speak about. It seems like a dream. I was asleep in my berth. I had walked along the promenade deck until about 10 o'clock

and had gone to my room and fallen asleep. Suddenly I heard a deep blast from the horns. I awoke startled. Then came another blast. The lights were turned on all over the ship. I heard the officers and crew running up and down the decks. I dressed hurriedly, thinking something was wrong on the *Carpathia*. I hastened to the deck. It was about 2 o'clock in the morning and the stars were shining brightly overhead.

I met Captain Rostron and asked what was the trouble. 'The *Titanic* has struck an iceberg and is sinking. Great God, men,' he shouted, turning to his officers, 'get ready to save those poor souls. There must be 2,500 on board.'

Before the captain had told us of the wreck, the *Carpathia* was being turned around toward the *Titanic*. I went on the boat deck and met many of our passengers. I heard the wireless buzz, and I knew the operator was trying to talk to the *Titanic*. I tried to get below to see the wireless instrument and operator, but I was told to go on deck again. The operator was clad only in his trousers and undershirt.

Captain Rostron said, 'Can't you get her?'

'No,' replied the operator, 'she doesn't answer.'

'She's going down,' said Captain Rostron, and he ordered the engineer to put on full speed.

I don't know how fast we went, but the speed of the *Carpathia* at that time was greater by far than the way we had been traveling on our way across the ocean. You can imagine the excitement aboard the *Carpathia*. Everyone was dressed and on deck before we got to the *Titanic*, or rather what was left of her.

I guess it was about 3:30 o'clock when we got near the boats of the *Titanic*. The *Carpathia* had all her boats hanging on the davits and Captain Rostron was ready. I heard women scream as the *Carpathia* approached the *Titanic*'s boats. I shrieked with them because everyone was saying, 'Oh, oh, it's awful, awful.' I saw the first boat of the *Titanic* taken from the water.

I saw the icebergs all around the boats. I wonder now how it kept afloat. Before the *Carpathia* had slackened speed much, a lifeboat from our ship was in the water and the men were pushing toward the other boats. They tied a rope to the *Titanic*'s boats and then moved back to the *Carpathia* and the first boatload of survivors were taken from the water only a few minutes after we saw it.

There were about fifty women and children in it; some had fainted and lay motionless. Others were screaming and were hysterical. There were no men in the boat, and none of the survivors were dressed properly. They had on night robes, furs, evening gowns, anything they could find. Some were almost frozen. A little girl, they called her Emily, was shrieking, 'Oh, mama, mama, I'm sick. Oh, mama, mama.'

Her mother could not comfort her because she collapsed as soon as she was lifted to the deck of the *Carpathia*. All the women on our boat got their heavy clothing and threw it among the survivors. Captain Rostron told us to [several lines illegible] ... hour or more had passed; by that time the crew of the *Carpathia* had taken nearly all the boats from the water. I saw three loads of passengers taken from the boats and the mate of the *Carpathia* said there were about eight hundred saved. Captain Rostron had tears in his eyes while he was directing the work of rescue.

We were here, there, everywhere it seemed all at once. We got a few men aboard, but they were not taken from the lifeboats. It was women and children first.

Our ship was a hospital ship on April 15. All the women on our boat offered to give up their staterooms, and the captain ordered many of the survivors placed in our berths.

The doctors had more than they could do to care for the sick. Women fainted one after the other. Mrs. Astor was unconscious at times. She called for her husband time and again and so we dared not tell her that Colonel Astor was not aboard.[119]

BARBARA AND FLORIN POSAN

Upon arriving in New York, the two ladies spoke with reporters, who paraphrased the interview as follows:

The women declared that they saw two boats filled with women on Monday near where the *Titanic* sank. There were about sixty women in the two boats, and none of them was able to steer the lifeboat. Soon they saw both boats capsize and all were drowned.[120]

MR AND MRS CHARLES REYNOLDS

Mr and Mrs Reynolds were interviewed at New York City's St Denis Hotel:

The couple declared that they were undaunted by the disaster and intended sailing on the *Carpathia* at 4 p.m.[121]

MARY ROBBINS

Reporters paraphrased their interview with Mrs Robbins as follows:

> Mrs. Robbins said that nearly all of the women rescued from the *Titanic* wore only their nightdresses when they entered the lifeboats and most of them wore no stockings. She, as well as the other women passengers of the *Carpathia*, gave away practically all their clothing to the women survivors. When the rescue ship reached the lifeboats, women were found rowing while the men, who had formerly been at the oars, were hysterical and unconscious and lying in the bottom of the boats. She said that six boats swamped when the *Titanic* went down.[122]

JOHN RONTELS

Mr Rontels was interviewed after the *Carpathia* reached New York:

> So far as I know, none of the passengers saved anything.

He was asked about the condition of the survivors when they were picked up:

> Horrible, horrible. Every one of the persons rescued was on the open sea for hours. They had not a bite to eat, the wind coming over the sea of ice and the great bergs chilled us to the marrow of our bones. One or two of the persons in the boats were frozen to death, I believe.[123]

ARTHUR H. ROSTRON

After reaching New York, Captain Rostron made the following statement to reporters:

> I cannot yet make a connected statement. I have gone through so much since I received aboard my ship the first distress call of the *Titanic* that a complete narrative is impossible. I was between fifty and sixty miles away from the *Titanic* when the wireless sang into the ears of my operator the first call for help. The operator said that we received only one call.
>
> The silence after the first frantic appeal for relief was ominous to me. Our Marconi sent out rays that scraped the sky in vain, but there was no response whatever to any of our inquiries. I swung the *Carpathia* around

straight to the position the poor *Titanic*'s first aerogram said she occupied. Our engines were put at top speed.

The silence of the air so far as the *Titanic* was concerned made me shudder as we sped on our way to the rescue. I realized what it meant. On and on we sped. Our stokers never worked harder. When the first faint daylight came and I knew we were still miles from the spot of the tragedy, I felt we should arrive too late to be of any service.

When, however, after full daylight, we sighted the first lifeboat filled with women and children and eight or ten strong-armed and brave-hearted men of the *Titanic*'s crew, I realized that we could at least save a few human lives. I was too busy for the next hour or so to recall now just what occurred. My mind was wholly set upon saving the lives of the people who crowded the boats.

The sea was calm. There was scarcely a ripple upon its face. Great ice floes were crunching down from the north. In the distance several icebergs shimmered like mirrors. Why the lifeboats were not crushed by the swiftly moving ice floes I could not understand. The sixteen boats seemed at first to be occupied solely by women.

I remember that it occurred to me that the good God had stretched out His mighty hand and had checked further murder by His elements.

We got aboard the *Carpathia* every human being in the sixteen lifeboats of the *Titanic*. Every officer and member of our crew stood by like the brave and loyal lads they are and did his full duty.

My mind is in no condition now to tell you much more of what I heard and felt during the two hours' work of the rescue.

We took aboard 705 women and children who were alive, but some of them were unconscious. We also dragged to the decks of the *Carpathia*, four members of the *Titanic*'s crew who had been told off to man the lifeboats and were stark dead. They had been frozen to death. Their strong, horny fingers still clutched the oars that they had been desperately pulling. We buried these men in sailors' graves only yesterday from the deck of the *Carpathia*.

I am told that it was reported to President Taft by Capt. Chandler, of the scout cruiser *Salem*, that the *Carpathia* had received Monday night wireless messages from the commander of the *Salem*, asking, in the name of the President, if Maj. Butt, John Jacob Astor, Frank Millet, Clarence Moore, and Isidor Straus were aboard his vessel.

Upon my word as a man, upon my honor as a sailor, I cannot remember receiving any such message from Capt. Chandler or anyone else in the name of the President, or any other person. Had such a message been received by me I immediately would have ordered that all other business of the wireless be sidetracked until the answer could have been sent to the President that none of his friends, of whom he had inquired, was aboard the *Carpathia*.

It is possible the *Carpathia*'s wireless operator acknowledged but refused to answer messages even from the President of the United States received after Wednesday night, as he had been at his post more than seventy-two hours without rest. But he never reported such a message to me, and I don't blame him.

After I reached the Cunard pier I was asked as to the truth of reports that some passengers, and particularly some men passengers, on the *Titanic*, were kept back from the lifeboats at the point of the pistol and that two well known men were shot. Of course, I was not there. I did not see the ship go down. But from the survivors who came aboard my ship I heard no such story.

I do not give the least credence to that report. If I had to write about it I would denounce it as an abominable lie. The *Carpathia* was amply provisioned for the accommodation of the 705 passengers rescued, and, likewise, comfortable sleeping room for the unexpected increase of her passenger list by bringing into requisition the big lounges in the salons.

I thank the people who have congratulated me, but I am not entitled to any more credit than would have been due any other man of the sea, had the opportunity for the service my ship rendered been afforded to others. I thank God Almighty that I was within wireless hailing distance, and that I got there in time to pick up every one of the 705 survivors of the *Titanic* wreck.[124]

SUE EVA RULE

After reaching New York, Miss Rule granted the following interview to reporters:

Unknown to the sleeping passengers, the ship turned abruptly to the north. No one knew of the sudden change of course, and the first intimation anybody got of the fact that anything unusual was about to take place was the order given the steward to prepare breakfast for 3,000.

The tidings ran through the ship like wildfire, and long before the Cunarder had come within the scene of the tragedy we were all on deck.

Just as day broke a tiny craft was sighted rowing towards us, and as it came closer we saw women huddled together, the stronger ones manning the oars. The first to come aboard was a nurse maid who had wrapped in a coat an eleven-months-old baby, the only one of a family of five persons to be rescued. The men and women both seemed dazed. Most of them had almost perished with the cold, and some of them who had been literally thrown into the lifeboats perished from exposure.

One of the most harrowing scenes I ever saw was the service of thanksgiving, followed by the prayers for the dead, which took place in the dining saloon of the *Carpathia*. The moans of the women and the cries of the little children as their loss was brought home to them were heartrending. The hope that by some means their beloved ones would be saved never left the survivors.

How those who were saved survived the exposure is a miracle. One woman came aboard devoid of underwear, a Turkish towel wrapped about her waist served as a corset, while an evening wrap was her only protection. Women in evening frocks and white satin slippers and children wrapped in steamer rugs became common sights. Soon the passengers were almost in as bad a plight as the rescued. Trunks were unpacked and clothing distributed right and left. Finally the steamer rugs were ripped apart and sewn into impromptu garments.

My view of the first boat sighted led me to think we were picking up the crew of a dirigible. Back of the boat loomed in the shadowy dawn the huge iceberg which had sent the *Titanic* to the bottom. The lifeboat looked like the usual boat which swings from a balloon.

After an hour or so of rest, the only relief the women who had been literally torn from their husbands seemed to have was in discussing the last scenes. Shooting was heard in many of the lifeboats just before the ship took its final plunge, and the opinion of many was that, rather than drown, the men shot themselves.

Mrs. Astor was one of the first to come aboard. She was taken at once to the captain's room. Others were distributed among the cabins, the *Carpathia*'s passengers sleeping on the floors of the saloons, in the bathrooms, and on the tables throughout the ship in order to let the survivors have as much comfort as the ship afforded. One woman came aboard with a six-month-old baby she had never seen until the moment it was thrust into her arms as she swung into the lifeboat. Nothing could equal the generosity and helpfulness of the *Carpathia*'s passengers.[125]

Simon Senecal

Mr Senecal granted the following interview to New York newspapermen:

After rescuing the boatloads of women, we sighted a life raft on which were about 24 persons. One half of these were dead. One of the *Carpathia* boats went to the raft and took the live men off, leaving the dead.

The water was thick with corpses. The crew of the *Carpathia*, in their rescue work, had trouble in avoiding the bodies as they floated about in the water.

I know of seven bodies which were buried by the crew of the *Carpathia* after the rescue. If there were any other bodies buried I do not know.[126]

JAMES A. SHUTTLEWORTH

Newspaper reporters paraphrased Mr Shuttleworth's interview as follows:

> Shuttleworth befriended Mrs. Lucian Smith, whose husband went down with the *Titanic*. Mrs. Smith's father was Congressman Hughes of Kentucky. The Smiths were on their wedding trip. Shuttleworth asked Mrs. Smith if there wasn't something he could do for her. She said that all the money she had she had lost on the *Titanic*, so Mr. Shuttleworth gave her $50.[127]

LOUIS P. SKIDMORE

Mr Skidmore photographed the iceberg that officers and passengers said was the one that the *Titanic* had struck, and he described the berg to reporters:

> It looked like an immense dirigible balloon about to rise from the water.[128]

KATE STEELE

Miss Steele was interviewed by reporters along with Amelia, Meta and Alice Fowler:

> We are glad, we four, to express our absolute faith in our fine captain by sailing with him again for our original destination. We are glad to show how safe we feel in his hands.

She was asked if this was true even though Captain Rostron had doubled the stokers and steamed full speed through ice fields and past icebergs to get to the *Titanic*:

> As much because of that fact as in spite of it. We'll go as fast as the captain wants us to go when he is on such a mission as that.

Miss Steele was asked if there had been a panic on board the *Titanic*:

Absolutely none, so far as I could learn.[129]

MRS REGINA STEINER

After arriving in New York, Mrs Steiner spoke with newspaper reporters:

I saw sixteen of the *Titanic* boats picked up. It was about 5:30 o'clock on Monday morning. The poor women were in a frightful state from exposure and anxiety and all of them were holding to the hope that their male relatives whom they had left behind had been rescued by some miracle after the small boats drew clear of the sinking *Titanic*.

In one of the *Titanic* boats a sailor, one of the *Titanic* crew that was manning one of the boats, was dead of exposure before we picked them up. Later seven of those rescued died aboard the *Carpathia*.

Oh, it was terrible! Four of them, I was told, were sailors, overcome by the exposure of that terrible night, and three were passengers. They were all buried at sea. There was no ceremony for any of them that I saw, and we knew of their burial only because we saw the unmistakable canvas sacks dropped into the sea.[130]

A second newspaper interview was attributed to Mrs Steiner:

There are more than fifty women dead on the boat now. Of this I am positive. I was on the *Carpathia*'s deck when the *Titanic*'s passengers were picked up.

It was a sight that can never be described. There were sixteen boats of shipwrecked persons drawn out of the water. Many of the women were hysterical. I might say that every woman on the boats, except four who had died from exposure and fright and fifty or one hundred others who were unconscious, was shrieking.

Some of the women were mad. They could not be controlled, and I doubt if one of them escaped frozen feet and hands. Few of them were dressed. Some of them were only covered with nightgowns. Others wore raincoats or men's coats they had seized off the sinking *Titanic*.

The first boat that drew alongside the *Carpathia* contained the body of a woman who had apparently frozen to death. Then other boats came. The unconscious and dead were much less trouble to get on the *Carpathia* than the living, shrieking and frantic women.[131]

A third interview was attributed to Mrs Steiner:

> She said that sixteen lifeboats were found floating in a sea of ice and that
> the passengers were taken aboard and were aided by the *Carpathia*'s pas-
> sengers and crew.
>
> 'The survivors were lying in the bottom of the boats, all alive, but the
> majority of them unconscious. Many were suffering terribly from the
> exposure, and many were already frozen. That afternoon about twenty of
> the survivors died, and four were given burial at sea immediately.'[132]

ELIZABETH TARKINGTON

After the *Carpathia*'s arrival in New York, Mrs Tarkington granted an interview
to reporters:

> It was the most appalling thing I ever saw. I went out on deck early in the
> morning and saw the first boatload brought over the side. Most of them
> were so dazed that they could tell us nothing.
>
> They were illy clad, many wearing only their nightclothes with wraps
> over them; others were in evening dress, with lace scarves and such ill
> suited protection.
>
> When they had been somewhat revived, most of them became hysteri-
> cal, weeping and laughing, and some crying out against the officers who
> had induced them to leave the ship without knowledge of the peril of their
> husbands.
>
> It was like rescuing people on a polar sea. There was ice on every side,
> and one great berg in the distance as big as the Capitol at Washington. It
> was bitterly cold on deck, even for those of us who were well wrapped up.
> The poor people seemed half frozen. Of course, we have been frightfully
> crowded since, but we have all been busy helping those who were saved.
>
> There were thirty pet dogs on the *Titanic*, and three of those were saved.
> The women just clung to them like babies. I think it would have been better
> if they had found babies to cling to.

Mrs Tarkington said there was little panic on the *Titanic* because she understood
the officers persuaded the people they were leaving the ship only temporarily.
Therefore many were reluctant to get in the boats.[133]

George Travis

Steward Travis, whose name does not appear on the *Carpathia*'s official crew list, offered the following interview to reporters:

Travis said that when Bruce Ismay was picked up from the second boat that the *Carpathia* rescued, the only thing he said was: 'I didn't believe she could sink. I didn't know she could possibly sink. I merely got in the boat for safety.'

As I understand it, Mr. Ismay had the right to claim a place in the life-boat because of his position as an officer of the line.

I heard that he had presented to the officers of the *Titanic* a request that as an experienced and able seaman, he be allowed to take charge of a boat. He was in charge of one of the boats, and, so far as I know, conducted it capably.

There was an average of about three men to a boat among the fifteen boats that we picked up.

We picked up three dead men, two sailors and an officer. They had perished from the cold. In the boats that they were manning all of the women and children were alive. Perhaps they had given their clothes to shelter the weaker ones. We believe so.

Two died on the *Carpathia* on the way in. The five dead were buried at sea.

Those we rescued said that probably never in the lives of any living man or woman had such a scene as the scene of the sinking of the *Titanic* been witnessed by human eyes.

'And the cries!' they said. 'We saw the great vessel as we moved away in the small boats – we saw her all agleam with the blaze of her electric lights, which held full and strong to the very last. The night was clear and utterly calm.'

There was not a sound from the hundreds who were left aboard until suddenly the vessel parted amidships and broke with a dull crashing roar, broke in two and both parts settled quickly into the sea.

As they sank, there arose from the ship a sound that could not be called a scream – for it was the mingling of a thousand cries. It was harrowing. It came clearly over the water.

We knew nothing about any wreck until about 1:45 o'clock Monday morning, when we got the order, 'Proceed to the lifeboat stations immediately.' We manned the boats. In our half-asleep (wakened so suddenly) we thought at first that our own ship was going down.

I ran on deck to the lifeboat that is my station. I could see three large icebergs to the starboard, one of them being of extraordinary size.

We all stayed at the boat stations for an hour, when we were ordered away to prepare hot blankets and brandy and coffee. Still we had no idea what had happened. Next we knew we were ordered back to the boats.

The *Carpathia* began to send up rockets. About 3:45 o'clock in the morning we sighted a small boat carrying a green light, hailed her and soon reached her. We picked her up without lowering a boat. In fact, we didn't lower a boat during the whole work of rescue.

The first lifeboat was filled with women and children, except for one junior officer and one seaman. Those on board were half frozen. The men could not use the oars because of the paralyzing cold.

The junior officer said several hundred of the crew of the *Titanic* had been drowned and the ship sunk. We simply didn't believe him.

Dawn broke, and we sighted lifeboats filled with women and children on either side of us. The second boat we picked up carried Ismay and Lady Duff Gordon. The latter had been pulling an oar during the night.

Three more boats were quickly picked up. In each was a dead man and many who seemed to be at the point of death from exposure.

The women were calm because of their physical exhaustion and suffering. It was not until later on our voyage into New York that the horror of their grief was realized.

We stood by all day, probably right over the spot where the *Titanic* went down. But we found no more survivors.

Slowly we began to draw the story of the wreck from the rescued. So far as we know, Captain Smith of the *Titanic* leaped into the sea in deliberate suicide after the vessel struck the berg.

We seamen understand his action. It was a beautiful clear night – no fog, no sea. His ship – the greatest in the world – had been run to its ruin without apparent excuse. Someone said he saw the captain go over the rail after the second lifeboat was lowered. He made no attempt to reach a boat.

We understand the *Titanic* struck at 11:40 p.m. The last boat left her at 2:10 a.m. – just ten minutes before she split in two and went to the bottom.

We heard that there were not enough lifeboats on her to carry even one-third of the people on board. Two lifeboats filled with men – the last two boats lowered – capsized and all were lost.

Not a few women went down with the vessel. They were those who refused to leave their husbands.

Two Chinese were shot to death by the officers of the ship. The Chinese had tried to rush into the boats while the women and children were being put aboard.

One American millionaire offered any price to be allowed to enter a boat, but he was held back under the grim and chivalric rules of the service. He drowned.

We were informed that six ships besides the *Carpathia* received the *Titanic*'s first 'CQD' message, but that all of them refused to believe it was meant. Some of them flashed in almost facetious terms their refusal to give aid.

If we had been able to reach the scene two hours earlier than we did, we could have saved the whole ship's company together with the mails.

The survivors said that there were tons of ice on the *Titanic*'s forward decks after the crash. As I see it, she struck the submerged part of a giant berg and ground her way along it until every compartment was torn open. We heard that she was going at 21½ knots an hour when she struck.

One of the most peculiar things we noted was that none of the lifeboats had been provisioned. There is an absolute rule of the seas that food supplies shall be kept always in the lifeboats. There was nothing to eat on any of the craft that we picked up.[134]

REUBEN WEIDMAN

After arriving in New York, Mr Weidman was interviewed at the St Denis Hotel:

I have had all I want and now have one desire – to get back to Albany and try to forget some of those heart-rending scenes witnessed among the unfortunate who lost their loved ones on the *Titanic*.

No, it is not because of any fear that I am giving up the trip, but I think I am getting too old to try it again. As a matter of fact I did not intend to go abroad. I went down to the station with Mr. and Mrs. Hoyt when they were leaving Albany, and they urged me to join them again as I had done on two previous occasions. I made up my mind to go in fifteen minutes.

He described how the *Carpathia*'s passengers helped the *Titanic* survivors:

All I had to give was money, and I gave all of that I had away. But it was a little compared to just what we wanted to do.

There were millionaires aboard the *Carpathia* without enough money when they reached New York last night to buy a cup of coffee, while I don't believe there was a man on the ship with a bit of clothes that were not on his back. And oddly enough one poor Englishman lying upon my bed nearly dead from three or four hours' exposure in the lifeboats insisted that I should take his card. I never saw such discipline or such courtesy under circumstances that were trying men's very souls.

Weidman laughed and recalled the spirit of Gilbert Tucker, an Albany survivor:

He was full of life and helped to make things as agreeable and lively as possible. And when he was not looking after the comfort of his fellow survivors, he was taking care of his little dog, which he got in Naples and which he proudly held on to throughout the ordeal.[135]

H. WYKE

Mr Wyke, whose name does not appear on the *Carpathia*'s crew list, spoke with reporters:

Wyke, who was in charge of the hospital on board the *Carpathia*, said that five men were buried at sea, four the day before yesterday and one yesterday.[136]

GIUSEPE ZUPACIC

In later years crewman Zupacic recalled the *Carpathia*'s rescue of the *Titanic* survivors:

The captain ordered all of the crew to assemble and he told us about the *Titanic*. He told us that we were going to her rescue, even if it meant risking our own lives by going between the icebergs. He said, 'We have got to keep up our courage and try to get as many people as possible from the water.'

The captain doubled the shift in the engine room, trying to get as much speed as he could from her. We were fifty-eight miles from the *Titanic*, and at our normal 14 knots it would have taken four hours to get to her. That was too long.

The *Carpathia* approached the lifeboats:

We had no trouble seeing them. There was one boat that had at least sixty people in it. You could hardly have squeezed a bird in there, that's how crowded it was.

There was this one little Italian fellow, maybe he was 34 or 36, and he tried to get in one of the lifeboats but the others in the boat kept hitting his hands to make him let go of the boat. They were afraid he would tip the boat over. Anyway, he made it, even though his hands were beaten raw. He got in the boat and crawled under the other passengers' legs.

Most of the survivors were in a state of shock. A lot of them kept saying, 'Captain Smith told us, this boat is unsinkable! This boat is unsinkable!'

We circled over the *Titanic* three times and one boat we picked up had only three men in it. They were two sailors and a third officer.

Zupacic was surprised that many passengers survived in the boats:

A lot of them were wearing nightclothes.

As the *Carpathia* arrived in New York:

The band [on shore] was playing full blast. There were people crying, whether from sadness at losing the *Titanic* or happiness at seeing the *Carpathia*, I don't know which. It was an awful experience to go through.

Lady Astor ... gave everyone on the *Carpathia* a gold medal and told them that if ever they needed help to call her. She helped one of my buddies, who lost a leg in a coal mining accident in Shamokin. He sued the coal company for $60,000 but lost the case. He wrote Lady Astor and she hired two more attorneys and they fought the case for him and he won $40,000.

Zupacic was surprised that the *Titanic*'s grave wasn't marked by more wreckage:

There was hardly anything there, some bits of cork, a few bodies.[137]

❖   ❖   ❖

Unknown Crewman (Assistant Baggage Master)

We first got word from the *Titanic* at midnight. The wireless operator came down to the captain and gave him the news. The captain immediately called the crew to quarters and gave them instructions how to proceed. He ordered the engineers to go ahead at full speed. At three o'clock we caught sight of the passengers in the lifeboat and we kept moving slowly toward the field of lifeboats, working our way carefully, so that we would not run them down. We finished picking them up at 7:30. About 8 o'clock we first saw the *Californian* of the Leyland Line.[138]

❖   ❖   ❖

Unknown Crewman (Bandsman)

He said that he had spoken with an authoritative survivor who said that the *Titanic* was going twenty-two knots an hour when she struck the iceberg:

The iceberg, I have learned from a source one cannot doubt, was very much higher than the bridge of the *Titanic*. Because of some atmospheric conditions, however, the mountain of ice could not be seen until the *Titanic* was close to it. It was not thought at first that the big liner had been dealt a dangerous blow. Everybody took things comparatively easy at first. Some of the men were in the gymnasium taking exercise before turning in.

My authority tells me that those men continued with their exercises for some minutes after the *Titanic* struck, not knowing what was passing above. Not long after this, however, came the first big explosion. Then came, a moment later, the second explosion. This second explosion was the one that did most of the damage. It blew away the funnels and tore a big hole in the liner's side. The ship rocked from the explosion as if she were an eggshell. The *Titanic* careened to one side and passengers making for the boats were spilled into the water.

At one place on the deck A, so I was told, the people were piled up by this great lurch of the ship until the topmost of the pile reached to the deck roof. The order for the boats to be lowered was given after this rocking which had thrown the passengers about. There was hesitancy in a great measure, I am told, on the part of many, even the women, to be the first to leave the ship. On this account only thirteen were in the first boat that put off.[139]

UNKNOWN CREWMAN (OFFICER #1)

After we got the *Titanic*'s passengers on board our ship, it was a question as to where we should take them. Some said the *Olympic* would come out and meet us and take them on to New York, but others said they would die if they had to be lowered again into small boats to be taken up by another, so we finally turned toward New York, delaying the *Carpathia*'s passengers eight days in reaching Gibraltar.[140]

UNKNOWN CREWMAN (OFFICER #2)

Mr. Ismay reached the *Carpathia* in about the tenth lifeboat. I didn't know who he was, but afterward heard the others of the crew discussing his desire to get something to eat the minute he put his foot on deck. The steward who waited on him, McGuire, from London, says Mr. Ismay came dashing into the dining room, and throwing himself in a chair, said:

'Hurry, for God's sake, and get me something to eat; I'm starved. I don't care what it costs or what it is; bring it to me.'

McGuire brought Mr. Ismay a load of stuff and when he had finished it, he handed McGuire a two dollar bill. 'Your money is no good on this ship,' McGuire told him.

'Take it,' insisted Mr. Ismay, shoving the bill in McGuire's hand. 'I am well able to afford it. I will see to it that the boys of the *Carpathia* are well rewarded for this night's work.' This promise started McGuire making inquiries as to the identity of the man he had waited on. Then we learned that he was Mr. Ismay. I did not see Mr. Ismay after the first few hours. He must have kept to his cabin.

The *Carpathia* received her first appeal from the *Titanic* about midnight. According to an officer of the *Titanic*, that vessel struck the iceberg at twenty minutes to twelve o'clock and went down for keeps at nineteen minutes after 2 o'clock. I turned in on Sunday night a few minutes after 12 o'clock. I hadn't closed my eyes before a friend of the chief steward told me that Captain Rostron had ordered the chief steward to get out 2,000 blankets and to make preparations to care for that many extra persons. I jumped into my clothes and was informed of the *Titanic*. By that time the *Carpathia* was going at full speed in the direction of the *Titanic*.

The entire crew of the *Carpathia* was assembled on deck and were told of what had happened. The chief steward, Harry Hughes, told them what was expected of them. 'Every man to his post and let him do his full duty like a true Englishman,' he said. 'If the situation calls for it, let us add another glorious page to British history.'

After that every man saluted and went to his post. There was no confusion. Everything was in readiness for the reception of the survivors before 2 o'clock. Only one or two of the passengers were on deck, one of them, Mr. Beachler, having been awakened by a friend, and the other because of inability to sleep. Many of the *Carpathia*'s passengers slept all through the morning up to 10 o'clock and had no idea of what was going on.

We reached the scene of the collision about 4 o'clock. All was black and still, but the mountain of ice just ahead told the story. A flare from one of the lifeboats some distance away was the first sign of life. We answered with a rocket, and then there was nothing to do but wait for daylight.

The first lifeboat reached the *Carpathia* about half-past 5 o'clock in the morning, and the last of the sixteen boats was unloaded before 9 o'clock. Some of the lifeboats were only half filled, the first one having but two men and eleven women, when it had accommodation for at least forty. There were few men in the boats. The women were the gamest lot I have ever seen. Some of the men and women were in evening dress, and others among those saved had nothing on but night clothes and raincoats.

As soon as they were landed on the *Carpathia* many of the women became hysterical, but on the whole they behaved splendid. Men and women appeared to be stunned all day Monday, the full force of the disaster not reaching them until Tuesday night. After being wrapped up in blankets and given brandy and hot coffee, their first thoughts were for their husbands and those at home. Most of them imagined that their husbands had been picked up by other vessels and then began flooding the wireless rooms with messages. We knew that those who were not on board the *Carpathia* had gone down to death, and this belief was confirmed Monday afternoon when we received a wire from Mr. Marconi himself asking why no news had been sent.

We knew that if any other vessel could by any chance have picked them up it would have communicated with land. After a while, when the survivors failed to get any answer to their queries, they grew so restless that Captain Rostron posted a notice that all private messages had been sent and that the wireless had not been used to give information to the press, as had been charged. Little by little it began to dawn on the women on board, and most of them guessed the worst before they reached here. I saw Mrs. John Jacob Astor when she was taken from the lifeboat. She was calm and collected. She kept to her stateroom all the time, leaving it only to attend a meeting of the survivors on Tuesday afternoon.[141]

UNKNOWN CREWMAN (STEWARD #1)

It was between quarter after and half after 10 o'clock, ship's time, Monday morning when all the stewards were mustered and Chief Steward Hughes told us that a wireless had just come in that the *Titanic* had hit an iceberg, and probably would need help. He urged us to turn right in and get things ready for a ship's load of people. The *Carpathia* turned in the direction the wireless had called from.

We did not suppose it was so bad as it turned out, but we got hot coffee ready and laid out blankets and made sandwiches and everything like that. It seemed as if every male passenger on the boat knew about the trouble and turned out, and no wonder, for the ship was shivering like it had a fit. Capt. Rostron – and let me say there is a grand man, a soldier as well as a sailor – had shut off the hot water all over the ship and turned every ounce of heat into steam and the old boat was as excited as any of us.

After we got things ready we went out on deck. It was a glorious morning, no swell in the sea, but bitter cold. The ship's lights were on full blaze and we were there in the middle of a sea of ice – the finest sight I ever saw.

About 4:30 we passed a great black iceberg, bigger than the ship many times it seemed to me, and from what we heard after, it was the one that sunk the *Titanic*.

About 6:30, while it was yet dark, we saw way off the port bow a green light and we knew that we had the emergency ladder in sight. About twenty minutes later we came upon a boat. There were eighteen men in it and it was in charge of an officer – I don't know what one – but there were three officers saved altogether.

There were no women in the first boat and it was not more than one-third filled. All of the men were able to come up the Jacob's ladder on the *Carpathia* which we threw over the port side, and every one of them was given a hooker of brandy or as much hot black coffee as he wanted. After they were all on board we pulled up their boat.

It was bright morning by now and all around the *Carpathia* here and there about a quarter mile apart, were more boats. These were fuller than the first and there were women in all of them. The women were hoisted up in bo'suns chairs and the men, who could, climbed up the Jacob ladder, but some of the men we had to haul up, especially the firemen.

There was a whole watch of firemen saved. They were nearly naked. They had jumped overboard – just their undergarments, and one or two had on their shoes. They jumped overboard and swam after the boats, it turned out, and they were almost frozen stiff. One of them was that stiff that they had to wrap him in blankets for almost half an hour.

The women were dressed, and the funny thing about it is only five of them had to be taken to the hospital, while both the men's hospitals were filled – twenty-four beds in all. We got twelve boat loads, I think, inside of a little more than an hour, and then it was more than half an hour before we got up with any more. Then between 8:15 and 8:30 we got the last two boats, crowded to the guards, and almost all women.

After the last refugee was taken out of the last boat, we hoisted up two dead bodies. I found out later that two other dead bodies were taken out of one of the earlier boats, but I did not see them. All the dead were men – two passengers, a fireman and a waiter. The bodies were laid to one side until after the excitement was over, and at 4 in the afternoon they were buried at sea – regular service and everything.

After we got the last boat load aboard, the *Californian* came alongside and the captains arranged that we should make straight for New York and the *Californian* would look around for more boats. We circled around and around, though, and we saw all kinds of wreckage floating by, but there was not a soul on a stick of it, and we did not get sight of another soul.

While we were pulling in the boatloads, the women we saved were quiet enough and not making any trouble at all until it seemed sure that we would not find any more, and then bedlam came. I hope I never go through it again, but the way those women took on over the dear ones they had lost was awful, and we could not do anything to quiet them until they cried themselves out.

Here's the funniest thing in the whole business and the mystery of it. There were five Chinamen in the boats, and not a soul knew where they came from. No one saw them get into the boats, but they were – wherever they came from.

Of course, the most of what I know I got from the men on the *Titanic*. There were ninety-two of them saved – thirty firemen, forty-two waiters, three officers and the rest I don't know what. These fellows told us that lots more of them could have got away, only no one would believe that their ship could sink. Why, one waiter who was saved, told me he was in a card game with five more and someone put his head in the door and shouted that the ship was sinking, but the boys said, 'Don't make me laugh,' and they kept on playing, except the one mate who was telling it to me. The rest are out there yet.

And they said, also, that more women could have been saved only they would not go without their husbands or the men who were with them. The officers pulled them apart – the women from the men – and shoved the women into the boats, telling them that they wanted all the women together and all the men together, and they couldn't get the half of them to go.

They said – a woman told me this – that one beautiful old lady that everyone liked was standing near the lifeboats and they were shoving her toward the side, but she hung her arms around her husband's neck, who was with her. They couldn't get her arms loose, although the old man himself was trying to get her away from him. And neither one of them was saved.

And I don't know but what the waiters who were talking to me were right about the boat not being likely to sink, because after she bumped she did not settle for more than an hour, they said, until two explosions came right sharp together, and then she sank in a few minutes.

The steward was asked if he saw Bruce Ismay:

Oh, he was sick all the way back. All the boys said – I believe every one of them will tell you the same – Mr. Ismay did everything he could – helping the ladies first and all that. I couldn't tell you a thing about him – I didn't see him at all, you know – but all the boys said that Mr. Ismay did everything he could.[142]

Unknown Crewman (Steward #2)

When we came up within sight of the lifeboats the passengers were burning rope ends in order to indicate their position, but this was not necessary on account of the light reflected from the iceberg. The passengers were only 300 yards from the spot where the *Titanic* went down. Practically all of them saw her when she sank, for the night was clear and starlit, with no fog. When we arrived the iceberg was clearly visible.

I have followed the sea for twelve years and have never seen a bigger berg. We saw sixteen lifeboats, of which two were collapsible. Two of these boats were abandoned and two others containing the purser, the doctor and another officer capsized. We brought in twelve boats.

The explosion which demolished No. 6 bulkhead was the direct cause of the *Titanic* sinking. That bulkhead is on the port side. Bulkheads 2 and 4, also on the port side, must have been torn open when the ship struck. Bulkhead No. 6, which is about midline, broke later under the increased pressure.

The *Titanic*'s lights did not go out until shortly before she went down. If we had arrived one hour sooner with our sixteen lifeboats we might have saved the whole passenger list.

There were absolutely no provisions in the lifeboats when we picked them up and the passengers had been without food.

When the water began to rise over the bow of the *Titanic* and reached the forward bridge of the vessel the second officer of the *Titanic* struck out into the water and swam desperately away. He was picked up by a lifeboat and saved.

The Marconi operator on the *Titanic* showed the greatest fortitude. When he was brought aboard the *Carpathia* it was found that both of his legs were broken at the ankles, but nevertheless he went to work and helped the operator on the *Carpathia*.

The steward said that Bruce Ismay went to his cabin immediately after boarding the *Carpathia* and stayed there until the ship made port.[143]

Unknown Crewman (Steward #3)

One of the earlier boats to arrive was seen to contain a woman tenderly clasping a pet Pomeranian. When assisted to the rope ladder and while the rope was being fastened around her she emphatically refused to give up for a second the dog which was evidently so much to her.

The steward also said a survivor told him that one woman declined to leave the *Titanic* because they wouldn't take her pet dog into the boat.[144]

UNKNOWN FEMALE PASSENGER

The passenger said it was no wonder that none of the wireless telegrams addressed to Bruce Ismay were answered until the one that he sent yesterday afternoon to the White Star Line:

Mr. Ismay was beside himself, and on most of the voyage after we had picked him up he was being quieted with opiates on orders of the ship's doctor.

Five women saved their pet dogs, carrying them in their arms. Another woman saved a little pig, which she said was her mascot. Though her husband is an Englishman and she lives in England she is an American and was on her way to visit her folks here. How she cared for the pig aboard ship I do not know, but she carried it up the side of the ship in a big bag. I did not mind the dogs so much, but it seemed to me to be too much when a pig was saved and human beings went to death.

It was not until noon on Monday that we cleared the last of the ice, and Monday night a dense fog came up and continued until the following morning, then a strong wind, a heavy sea, a thunderstorm and a dense fog Tuesday night, caused some uneasiness among the more unnerved, the fog continuing all of Tuesday.

A number of whales were sighted as the *Carpathia* was clearing the last of the ice, one large one being close by, and all were spouting like geysers.

On Tuesday afternoon a meeting of the uninjured survivors was called in the main saloon for the purpose of devising means of assisting the more unfortunate, many of whom had lost relatives and all their personal belongings, and thanking Divine Providence for their deliverance. The meeting was called to order and Mr. Samuel Goldenberg was elected chairman. Resolutions were then passed thanking the officers, surgeons, passengers and crew of the *Carpathia* for their splendid services in aiding the rescued and like resolutions for the admirable work done by the officers, surgeons and crew of the *Titanic*.

A committee was then appointed to raise funds on board the *Carpathia* to relieve the immediate wants of the destitute and assist them in reaching their destinations and also to present a loving cup to the officers of the *Carpathia* and also a loving cup to the surviving officers of the *Titanic*.[145]

UNKNOWN MALE PASSENGER #1

A passenger on the *Carpathia* who wouldn't give his name said that he had talked with Mrs. Churchill Candee, one of those on the *Titanic*. Mrs. Candee told him that the ship was trying to make 540 knots on Sunday. When they struck the iceberg no one thought it was anything serious, because the damage was done all below the water line. She said that Major Archibald Butt had perished.[146]

UNKNOWN MALE PASSENGER #2

I was awakened at about half past twelve at night by a commotion on the decks which seemed unusual, but there was no excitement. As the boat was moving I paid little attention to it, and went to sleep again.

About three o'clock I again awakened. I noticed that the boat had stopped. I went to the deck. The *Carpathia* had changed its course.

Lifeboats were sighted and began to arrive – and soon, one by one, they drew up to our side. There were sixteen in all, and the transferring of the passengers was most pitiable. The adults were assisted in climbing the rope ladder by ropes adjusted to their waists. Little children and babies were hoisted to the deck in bags.

Some of the boats were crowded, a few were not half full. This I could not understand. Some people were in full evening dress. Others were in their night clothes and were wrapped in blankets. These, with immigrants in all sorts of shapes, were hurried into the saloon indiscriminately for a hot breakfast. They had been in the open boats four and five hours in the most biting air I ever experienced.

There were husbands without wives, wives without husbands, parents without children and children without parents. But there was no demonstration. No sobs – scarcely a word spoken. They seemed to be stunned. Immediately after breakfast, divine service was held in the saloon.

One woman died in the lifeboat; three others died soon after reaching our deck. Their bodies were buried in the sea at five o'clock that afternoon. None of the rescued had any clothing except what they had on, and a relief committee was formed and our passengers contributed enough for their immediate needs.

When her lifeboats pushed away from the *Titanic*, the steamer was brilliantly lighted, the band was playing and the captain was standing on the bridge giving directions. The bow was well submerged and the keel rose high above the water. Suddenly the boat seemed to break in two. The next moment everything disappeared. The survivors were so close to the sinking steamer that they feared the lifeboats would be drawn into the vortex.

There were preparations for a brilliant party to be given on board the next evening.

On our way back to New York we steamed along the edge of a field of ice which seemed limitless. As far as the eye could see to the north there was no blue water. At one time I counted thirteen icebergs.[147]

UNKNOWN *CARPATHIA* PASSENGERS

One tale of base cowardice, reinforced by a revolver wielded by a man passenger of the *Titanic*, was told by passengers of the *Carpathia*. The *Carpathia*'s passengers and Mr. Brown, the purser, learned from the *Titanic* survivors that this man, a dapperly dressed young fellow, forced his way into a boat containing women. He aimed a revolver at them to make them stand aside for him while he stepped into the smaller boat.

Once in the boat he lay down so as to become concealed by the women who were in it or entering it. To every rebuke he answered with a sinister pointing of his revolver. When ordered to take an oar and row, he refused and his revolver kept him immune from punishment.

As soon as the boat was picked up by the *Carpathia* this coward rushed into the first class saloon, seized blankets and made himself comfortable, lighting a cigarette. Men passengers of the *Carpathia*, hearing the accusations, advanced on the craven, who waved his revolver at them. They then informed Mr. Brown, the purser, who walked up to the man and wrenched the revolver from his grasp.

One man tried to force a fight on the coward, ordering him to pull down a curtain. The disarmed man meekly obeyed, removing any pretext to strike him. His name was given by all who related the affair.[148]

DOCUMENTS FROM
OTHER VESSELS

Captain Wood
Captain Wood sent the following wireless message to the *Olympic* about six hours after the *Titanic* foundered:

> *Asian* heard the MGY signaling on and off from [8 p.m. to 10 p.m.?] local time Sunday. Finished calling SOS at midnight. Position given as latitude 41.46 longitude 50.14. No further information. *Asian* then three hundred miles west of *Titanic* and towing oil tanks to Halifax.
> Regards, Wood[149]

Captain Couloucoundis

The lookout of the Greek liner sighted a berg two hours before the ship came abreast of it. It was half a mile long and 150 feet in height:

> This particular berg was the shape of the Rock of Gibraltar. I am sure that that is the one the *Titanic* struck, for at noon on Sunday, as my log shows, our position was latitude 41.46 and longitude 49.41.
>
> You will observe that our latitude was exactly the same as that of the *Titanic* when she sent out her cry of distress, and our longitude was almost exactly the same, the *Titanic*'s being 50.14. So that it would be very easy for the iceberg to travel the few fateful miles before midnight to bring it to latitude 41.46 and longitude 50.14 – the *Titanic*'s grave.
>
> When I sighted the iceberg I saw some ten or so smaller ones. I realized that if any ship should crash into the big one, it would be the end of the unfortunate one. We must have been the first to sight them, for we had received no warning of ice ahead, and so I ordered my Belgian wireless operator to send out warnings of the ice, giving our position and that of the iceberg, and he received acknowledgments from at least ten vessels.
>
> We were about 170 miles or so from the *Titanic* when she struck the berg, but it was not until Tuesday night that we learned of her fate. We received the sad news from the wireless station at Cape Cod.[150]

❖ ❖ ❖

Unnamed Chief Officer

After his vessel arrived in Portland, Maine on 22 April, the *Ausonia*'s chief officer spoke to a newspaper reporter:

> We entered Southampton harbor as the *Titanic* started on her maiden and last voyage. We left Southampton for Portland one day after the *Titanic* started on her voyage to New York, and while we were over 1,400 miles east of the giant liner when she went down after striking an iceberg, we learned of the disaster within 24 hours and later changed our course and came fully 60 miles south of the place where the *Titanic* struck the iceberg.
>
> By changing our course far south we avoided the ice belt entirely and did not even sight an iceberg or icefield during the entire passage. While the commander of our ship knew of the disaster many days ago he did not

notify others on board our ship, and the passengers were not aware of the disaster until we arrived in this port.[151]

❖ ❖ ❖

RMS BALTIC

Captain Ranson

On the night of 18 April Captain Ranson sent the following Marconigram to the White Star Line company at Liverpool in order to quash the belief that the *Baltic* had rescued some of the *Titanic*'s survivors:

> 11:08 New York time. On Sunday received wireless S.O.S. from *Titanic* when 253 miles east of her position. Immediately turned back. Steamed 134 miles in her direction. When hearing from the steamship *Carpathia* that assistance was no longer required continued our course to Liverpool.[152]

❖ ❖ ❖

SS BIRMA

Charles Walters

Mr Walters was a passenger on the *Birma* and wrote the following account of his vessel's connection with the *Titanic* disaster:

SS *Birma* (off Dover)
Monday, April 22.

We left New York in the *Birma*, of the Russian East Asiatic Company, on Thursday afternoon, the 11th inst., bound for Rotterdam and Libau (Russia), in splendid weather. The *Carpathia*, of the Cunard Line, sailed three hours earlier on the same day, heading for Gibraltar, and the *Baltic* departed about the same time for Liverpool, but both steamers having a somewhat greater speed than the *Birma*, and traveling the more northerly course, were soon out of touch with our ship. We received, as usual, the regular reports by wireless, our boat being fitted, not with the Marconi service, but with the De Forest system. The installation is owned by the steamship company and operated by two English wireless operators under contract with the Russian steamship concern.

The regular Press reports were received nightly from Cape Cod, Massachusetts, the American coast station, and were published on board our ship for the benefit of the first and second class passengers, and although the Marconi Company, for obvious reasons, holds no intercourse by wireless with ships not installed with their instruments, we were, nevertheless, in touch with the usual number of steamers along the coast up to the banks of Newfoundland, a voyage occupying about three days – i.e. from Thursday noon until Sunday evening.

On Sunday evening, the 14th inst., at 11.45 p.m., while the wireless operators were receiving news items of the day, the service was suddenly interrupted by a distress signal reading in the wireless code, 'C.Q.D.' and sent out a call designated as 'M.G.Y.' The latter stands for the letters of the *Titanic*, and our news service was at once stopped so that we could get into touch with the *Titanic*. We were, I believe, the first vessel spoken to by the *Titanic*, and our response was immediate. Mr. J. Cannon, of Palmerton Road, Bowes Park, N., our telegraphist, and his colleague, Mr. Thomas George Ward, of Bussett, Southampton, telegraphed to the *Titanic* immediately after reporting to Captain Stulping, who at once altered our ship's course to the north. At that time we were some 100 miles away from the scene of the tragedy.

The full message from the *Titanic* read to the effect that the ship had struck an iceberg; that she was sinking fast, and that the position of the ship was in lat. 41.44 N., long. 50.14 W. Our messages to the *Titanic*, to the effect that we were rushing there at full speed, met with the response that we must hurry and that they were grateful to us. Fifteen extra stokers were rushed to the fires, and at fullest speed possible (14½ knots) we hastened northward to the position given us. Our officers and crew are Russians, but the freemasonry of the sea knows no nationality, and it is impossible to describe the big-hearted energy which at once possessed the hearts and souls of these brave mariners.

The head steward, believing that in six to eight hours' time he would be called upon to feed, warm and comfort, as we hoped and fervently prayed, hundreds and hundreds of survivors after exposure to icy cold in open boats, rushed every man in his department to prepare food, the ovens were kept steaming with bread baked in enormous quantities, food of every sort was prepared, stewards and stewardesses got ready rooms, couches, even blankets, in the saloons, for the reception of travelers in distress. Everywhere was activity, coupled with the intensest anxiety which I have ever witnessed.

Meanwhile the captain and all officers were grouped on the bridge, with grave, set faces, counting the minutes. The cry of distress heard through the wireless had stirred the hearts of all, so that perhaps never were prayers uttered more earnestly than that God should grant us speed to help, to save, to minimize the horror which we knew but too well would be appalling. Hardly a word was spoken on the bridge as we sped through the darkness. The operators in the wireless room hailed first Cape Race, giving them briefly the facts as then known, and then getting in touch with, first, the *Baltic* (which ship, however, was so far to the east that its signals were not distinguishable); then the *Megantic*, known to be in the locality; then the *Frankfurt*, a German steamer back of us; and from time to time giving words of comfort to the operator of the *Titanic*.

For this, the time was very brief, for great care had to be exercised that the message would not 'jam' the instrument of the *Titanic*. With all the ships speaking at once, there was a danger of none being received accurately. The *Frankfurt*, being a slower boat, was about 100 miles to the rear of us, and although we knew they were loyally rushing to the *Titanic*'s aid, we were fast outdistancing them.

We ascertained from the *Frankfurt* that the ship's position, as given by the *Titanic*, had been confirmed by them. Nevertheless, the position was given wrongly, and the only explanation pending official facts would seem to be the one that the *Titanic*, having struck an iceberg, must have been shrouded in fog or hazy weather, and, this being so, may have had such uncertain atmosphere preceding the disaster that the position was ascertained by dead reckoning, i.e. that the officers of the *Titanic* thought they were in lat. 41.44 N. and long. 50.14W. while in reality the true position was a different one, as our continued recital will show. The *Carpathia*, which in the morning picked up the survivors, was at that time not heard of by us.

After a delay of perhaps twenty minutes after the first signal of distress had been heard by us (and it may be remarked here that the distress signal being C.Q.D. in American usage, and S.O.S. in European code, it was given in both descriptions by the *Titanic*'s operators at the first and subsequent instances), we again spoke the *Titanic*, repeating our position and distance, and she answered clearly as follows: 'O.K. – O.M.' This in wireless talk stands for the cordial and fraternal saying, 'All right, old man.' She then called C.Q. (which means 'anybody'), saying she could not last much longer and that the passengers were being put into the boats. At 1.30 the *Titanic* sent a report that the women and children were then in the boats and that the ship was sinking fast, with all the rest aboard.

Immediately following this call the end must have come, for all further signals we sent were unanswered; not even the usual 'A.R.', which is the finish sign, or the good-bye, so that we fear the end came quicker even than it was possible for the operators to send a word as their last. During the night we were called by several boats installed with the Marconi system of wireless i.e. M.W.L., which is the SS *Californian*; M.G.N., which is the *Virginian*; and M.G.T., another Marconi-fitted boat, &c., all asking us for reports, which were willingly given.

After daylight we reached the position given us, and found at once that it must be wrong, for although we passed enormous icebergs of a size seldom seen at this season of the year so far south, yet it was obvious that none of those could have damaged the *Titanic*, for to the north-east of us lay enormous ice floes, extending for miles. The *Titanic*, coming westward, would have been warned by these floes that large bergs were about. We soon heard by wireless that the *Carpathia* was picking the boats up north of the ice-floe, and this is the first intimation we or the boats we had spoken to had of the presence of the *Carpathia*. We soon sighted the *Carpathia*, and then got in touch with her boat, and seeing that they were then taking in the survivors, we steamed round the ice-floe. Captain Stulping ordered our operators to offer our help to the *Carpathia*, and the reply came asking us to 'stand by'. We came closer, and then we offered provisions or stores, if needed, as we had heard that twenty boatloads of women and children had been taken up. The reply to this query was again 'Stand by', and nothing further, and when we asked if we should send provisions, the reply came 'Shut up'. This is vouched for by the two operators. Mr. Ward is an experienced telegraphist, who would make no mistake, and the same signal came to us many times in the subsequent attempts to gain or give information.

It is a known fact that the Marconi Company will give no information to any ship not Marconi-fitted, nor answer its calls unless the ship is in distress. This may be a commercially fair system, but, at the same time, while our ship was not in distress, we were trying to help. When it was found that our help was not needed, there came no word of thanks, no reply to our questions as to whether more boats might be adrift, but only a salute from the flag at the stern of the *Carpathia* as she steamed on her way to the west. All day, and days following, we were refused any information. Every ship we spoke to replied, 'Are you a Marconi ship? If not we have orders to give you no information.' This after the energy of our officers and crew, and the thirty hours vigil day and night to help!

I attach herewith a statement, signed by the officers and operators, to show that the facts are as stated. There is no rancor or envy in this report. No one questions the usefulness of the Marconi system nor their commercial right to protect their interest in a commercial sense, and we gladly and with grateful joy welcome the fact that the *Carpathia* reached the scene in time to save life. What our officers have done has been done for humanity, in the broad spirit of Christianity, which is never so feelingly shown as on the deep, 'for those in peril on the sea'. There was and is no question of precedence in this matter. The *Carpathia* got there in time and saved the survivors, whether by chance in striking the position or warned in time by being on a different course; but the fact remains that we did all in our power and met with a refusal to tell us even the most vital facts. The writer holds no brief for the De Forest or any other system, the officers or the operators, but he is an Englishman by blood, if not by naturalization, and is solicitous that England should give credit where credit is due.

What followed? On this Russian ship a handful of Englishmen gathered to hold a memorial service for their dead last Sunday. No English flag being available, one was made on board. The captain and officers were present at the service and joined with full-hearted love in the English hymns and prayers.

We firmly believe, and have convinced the officers of this ship, that the error lies not with the management of the Marconi Company, but with the employees on the ships. These men are in a more or less subordinate position, and tied by hard and fast rules, and it is even to an extent excusable that an operator, in the midst of the hustle and excitement – perhaps with the memory of the famed Jack Binns, of the *Republic* disaster, in mind – exceeded his authority or good judgment in forcing the rule of keeping other ships 'incommunicado' at a time when a man of riper judgment would have set rules aside in the common eagerness to help save life. The near future, when I intend to have the matter brought before Parliament, will show to what extent this suggestion is correct. No harm has been done in any event, for no ship could have reached the sinking vessel in time. The night, while dreadfully cold, was favored by a perfectly calm sea, so that with care even in a panic those boats which got away would be picked up without difficulty. As stated before, the only feeling aboard of this vessel is one of rejoicing that the saving of even twenty boats was possible, irrespective of the nationality of the actual salvage-craft, though it is a matter of pleasure to realize that the English vessel was in a position to render help.

We herewith enclose a rude chart, drawn for the purpose of illustrating the course of the steamship *Birma* on the memorable morning of the 15th inst., and the approximate location of the disaster. The ice-floe was approached by us from the south-west until we reached the point marked X, when it was obvious that the location given must be wrong. We then saw the *Carpathia* on the north-easterly side of the floe, and, being asked merely to stand by, and seeing the vessel engaged in picking up the boats with the survivors, we circled around the floe, first to the south, in order to avoid being crushed by the ice; then, after turning the lower corner, we turned north-eastward, up to the point marked XX, which is the spot on which the *Carpathia* 'stood' while picking up the boats.

When we reached the *Carpathia* men of her crew were still in the rigging, keeping a vigorous outlook for further boats, and she steamed in a circle while we were within hailing distance, then she turned to the west at full speed, and as our question, whether some boats were still missing, was not met with a reply, and the constant order by the Marconi operator 'Shut up' could only convey the one thought that the ship was trying to talk with the Cape Race station, and our 'cutting' in would 'jam' her instruments, we steamed back to our course.

The night having been dark and the sea calm, it is presumed that the twenty lifeboats circled around the spot until daylight, and that the *Carpathia* then appearing, of course, was enabled to render immediate help. Since then we have had practically no facts beyond those to which we were witnesses, excepting an erroneous report which went the rounds of all Marconi boats to the effect that we, the *Birma*, had picked up five boats with their survivors. This is entirely wrong, as we kept a look-out for the entire Monday but saw no sign of life.

The icebergs such as we passed on the south-westerly side of the floe were photographed, but, owing to the distance, the picture is not clear. The largest bergs were on the south and north-easterly side, but, while a magnificent sight, they could have little bearing on the tragedy, as the ice-floe lay between them and the course of the *Titanic*. Hence it is obvious that one of the bergs we photographed on the easterly side must have caused the disaster. The ice-floe was larger than has ever been seen so early in the year in this part of the Atlantic, and the bergs extended as far south as 41 deg. In fact, our last effort after the tragedy was to wire all Marconi boats and all west-bound vessels to be on the look-out for the enormous bergs, so as to prevent further loss of life.

The sight of the *Carpathia* steaming to the West, her ensign hanging at half-mast, was one to leave intense sorrow in the hearts of all. The terrible masses of ice surrounding us told their story but too well. More than likely the reason why no wreckage of any kind was seen is due to the fact that the ice-floe was dragged by suction towards the grave of the big ship, and then, like a pall, spread itself over the spot. The approximate depth in that location is about 2,000 fathoms, or 12,000 ft., more than two miles in extent, and the spot is comparatively near the scene of the *Republic* disaster. The Cuion liner *Alaska* struck a berg near this scene in the early eighties, but it is unusual that a ship meets with icebergs so far south during the early part of the year, as is the case now.

Captain Stulping, First Officer Nielson, the wireless operators, the head steward, in fact, all those in command of any department of the *Birma* are entitled to the credit and gratitude of English men and women for what they tried to do in the darkest hour of British marine service. They worked like heroes and set regulations aside to be of service, and the writer feels this point is of vital interest.

OFFICERS' CERTIFICATE

To the Editor of the *Daily Telegraph*.

Dear Sir – We, the undersigned, commander, first officer, wireless operator and wireless operator's associate, of the SS *Birma*, herewith beg to state that the facts in the foregoing report, handed you by Mr. Charles Edward Walters, journalist, of San Francisco, California, are correct, to our knowledge and belief.

The chart attached thereto has been prepared by Captain Stulping, of the SS *Birma*. The photograph has been taken from the bridge of the *Birma* on the morning of the rescue of the survivors by Mr. Nielson, first officer of this ship. The facts stated re: the wireless reports are correctly given, as entered upon the log of the wireless station on SS *Birma*, and Mr. Walters has carefully stated all the facts as we know them correctly, in substance and detail. They are given herewith for the first time to the Press, after careful and painstaking preparation, with the object of furnishing a true and correct report, free from bias or animosity against other ships, officers or operators, but with the desire to record facts and minute details of a disaster the like of which has never befallen any other nation.

[Signed]
Ludwig Stulping, Captain
Alfr. Nielsen, First Officer
C. Hesselberg, Purser
Joseph L. Cannon, Wireless Operator
Thomas George Ward, Wireless Operator

Witness to all the above signatures:
Charles Edward Walters [153]

❖   ❖   ❖

SS *CALIFORNIAN*

Ernest Gill

On 24 April Second Donkeyman Gill swore out an affidavit regarding his vessel's activities on the night of 14 April. He made his statement in the presence of four fellow crewmembers, who assented to his statements but refused to make any statements of their own for fear of losing their jobs:

The night of April 14 I was on duty from 8 p.m. until midnight in the engine room. At 11:56 I came on deck. The stars were shining brightly. It was very clear, and I could see for a long distance.

I looked over the rail on the starboard side and saw the lights of a very large steamer about ten miles away. I could see her broadside lights.

I turned in but could not sleep. In half an hour I turned out, thinking to smoke a cigarette. Because of the cargo I could not smoke between decks, so went on deck again.

I had been on my deck about ten minutes when I saw a white rocket about ten miles away on the starboard side. I thought it must be a shooting star. In seven or eight minutes I saw distinctly a second rocket in the same place and I said to myself, 'That must be a vessel in distress.'

[When I went back on duty on my next shift] I went down into the engine room on watch and heard the second and fourth engineer in conversation. J.C. Evans is the second and Mr. Wooten is the fourth. The second was telling the fourth that the third officer had reported rockets going up on his watch. I knew then that it must have been the *Titanic* I had seen.

The second engineer added that the captain had been notified by the apprentice officer, whose name I think is Gibson, of the rockets. The skipper had told him to Morse with a light to a vessel in distress. Mr. Stone, the second navigating officer, was on the bridge at the time, said Mr. Evans.

I overheard Mr. Evans say that Morse lights had been shown and more rockets went up. Then, according to Mr. Evans, Mr. Gibson went to the captain again and reported more rockets. The skipper told him to continue to Morse until he got a reply, but no reply was received.

I am quite sure the *Californian* was less than twenty miles from the *Titanic*, which the officers report to have been our position. I could not have seen her if she had been more than ten miles distant, and I saw her very plainly.

I have no ill-will toward the captain or any officer of the ship, and I am losing a profitable berth by making this statement. I am actuated by the desire that no captain who refuses or neglects to give aid to a vessel in distress should be able to hush up the matter.
[signed] Ernest Gill[154]

Charles Groves

In later years Third Officer Groves wrote an account describing his vessel's proximity to the sinking *Titanic*:

The *Californian*, owned by the Leyland Line, was a four-masted steamship with a gross tonnage of 6,223 and a maximum speed of about 14 knots.

She had accommodation for 50 passengers and carried a crew of 55 all told. Leaving London on Good Friday, April 5th, 1912, bound for Boston, USA, with a full cargo but no passengers, she was commanded by Captain Stanley Lord, a tall, lean man who had spent some 20 years at sea, much of which time had been in the North Atlantic trade. He was an austere type, utterly devoid of humor and even more reserved than is usual with those who occupy similar positions. Owing to a certain concatenation of circumstances he had obtained command somewhat earlier than was usual.

The Chief Officer was G.F. Stewart, a competent and experienced seaman nearing middle age who was well versed in the ways of the Western Ocean and was a certificated Master.

H. Stone, the Second Officer, had been some eight years at sea, the whole of which period had been spent in the North Atlantic and West Indian trades. He was a stolid, unimaginative type and possessed little self confidence. He held a certificate as First Mate.

The Third Officer was C.V. Groves who had followed the sea as a career for six years and was in possession of a Second Mate's certificate. For three years his voyages had taken him mainly to South America and the Mediterranean. Latterly he had been engaged as a junior officer in the Indian and Colonial trades. Signaling was a strong point with him, for which he held the Board of Trade's special certificate, and he had made some progress as an amateur in wireless telegraphy.

The *Californian* carried one Apprentice and this was J. Gibson who had completed three years of his indentures with the Leyland Line, the whole of which time had been spent on the North Atlantic and West Indian runs. He was a bright lad, keen on his profession and one who showed every sign that he would make headway in it.

The voyage proceeded normally until the afternoon of Sunday April 14th, when, at a few minutes before 6.00 p.m., Mr. Groves went on to the bridge to relieve the Chief Officer for dinner. The sky was cloudless, the sea smooth and there was a light westerly breeze. Away to the southward and some five miles distant were three large flat-topped icebergs. Nothing else was in sight and the ship was making 11 knots through the water. Captain Lord was on the bridge talking to the Chief Officer as they scanned the horizon. A few minutes later they both went below for their meal, after which Mr. Stewart returned and relieved the Third Officer.

Mr. Groves went on watch again at eight o'clock to take over until midnight and was told by the Chief Officer that wireless messages had been received giving warning of ice ahead. Shortly afterwards, the Chief Officer went below. Almost immediately Captain Lord came up with similar information, telling him to keep a sharp lookout for this ice. The night was dark and brilliantly clear with not a breath of wind, and the sea showed no sign of movement, with the horizon only discernible by the fact that the stars could be seen disappearing below it. The lookout was doubled, there being a sailor on the forecastle head and another in the crow's nest. The Captain remained on the bridge with the ship proceeding at full speed, when suddenly the Third Officer perceived several white patches in the water ahead which he took to be a school of porpoises crossing the bows. Captain Lord evidently saw this at the same moment and as he was standing alongside the engine room telegraph he at once rang the engines full speed astern. In a very short space of time and before the ship had run her way off she was surrounded by light field ice. This was about 10.30 p.m. Despite the clarity of the atmosphere this ice was not sighted at a distance of more than 400 yards, nor was it seen by the lookouts before it was seen from the bridge.

Captain Lord went below shortly after the ship had lost her way through the water, leaving instructions that he had to be called if anything was sighted. Absolute peace and quietness now prevailed save for brief snatches of 'Annie Laurie' from an Irish voice which floated up through a stokehold ventilator. At 11.15 a light was observed three points abaft the starboard beam of which the Captain was immediately advised, and his reply to the information that it was a passenger ship was, 'That will be the *Titanic* on her maiden voyage.' This light was some 10 miles distance but he did not go up to look at it. Mr. Groves kept the ship under close observation and at 11.40 he saw her stop and then her deck lights were extinguished, or so it appeared to him. The time of the stopping of the ship is accurately fixed by the fact that at that moment the *Californian's* bell was struck once in order to call the men who were to take over the middle watch. The dowsing of the lights caused no surprise to the Third Officer because for the preceding years he had sailed in large ships where it was customary to put the lights out at midnight to discourage the passengers from staying on deck too late.

Captain Lord was told of the ship having stopped and at a few minutes before the close of the watch he went up on the bridge and after looking at the distant ship observed, 'That's not a passenger ship', to which the Third Officer replied 'It is, Sir, – when she stopped she put all her lights out.' The Captain then left the bridge saying that he must be told if that ship made a move, or if anything else hove into sight. The ship remained stationary. The drama had commenced.

At midnight Mr. Groves was relieved by Mr. Stone, to whom the Captain's orders were passed. The two young officers chatted for a while until the newcomer's eyes had got accustomed to the darkness. Mr. Groves then bade him 'Good night' and walked along the boat deck in order, as was his wont, to have a yarn with the sole Marconi Operator, Mr. Evans, before turning in. The Operator lay asleep in his bunk with a magazine in his hands. His visitor woke him up with the query 'What ships have you got, Sparks?' Dreamily he replied 'Only the *Titanic*.' He was then told she was in sight on the starboard beam. Almost mechanically the Third Officer picked up the wireless 'phones which lay on the operating table and placed them on his head to listen to what the ether might convey. He heard no sound, for he had failed to notice that the clockwork of the magnetic detector had run down, thus no signals could be received until it had been wound up. He could read wireless signals when sent slowly. Mr. Evans had dropped off to sleep again and the 'phones were replaced on the table. The Third Officer closed the door and went to his room to turn in. The time was then 12.25 a.m. and that was ten minutes after the *Titanic* had commenced to send her messages of distress. The *Californian's* operator slept peacefully on. The *Titanic* realized she was doomed and was lowering her lifeboats, and twelve hundred souls had seen their last sunrise.

About 6.45 that Monday morning the Third Officer was awakened by hearing ropes being thrown on to the boat deck above his head, and he realized that the boats were being prepared for swinging out.

Almost immediately Mr. Stewart came into his room to tell him to turn out as 'The *Titanic* has sunk and her passengers are in her boats ahead of us.' Jumping from his bunk Mr. Groves went across the alleyway to the Second Officer's room and asked if the news was true, and received the reply 'Yes, I saw her firing rockets in my watch.'

Amazed at hearing this, he went up on the bridge and found it to be a brilliantly fine morning with a light breeze and slight sea. There were more than 50 icebergs, large and small, in sight, and the ship was making slow way through the water. Some five miles distant a four-masted steamship with one funnel was observed, and she proved to be the Cunarder *Carpathia*. She lay motionless with her house flag flying at half mast. The *Californian* arrived alongside her at about 7.30 and semaphore signals were exchanged from which it was learned that the *Titanic* had struck an iceberg at 11.40 the previous night and sunk two and a half hours later. Some 720 of her passengers had been rescued and the *Carpathia* was returning to New York forthwith. Would the *Californian* search the vicinity for further possible survivors? The *Carpathia* then got under way by which time it was nine o'clock, and less than 20 minutes later disappeared from view, hidden by the icebergs.

The sea was covered by a large number of deck chairs, planks and light wreckage. The *Californian* steamed close alongside all the lifeboats which the *Carpathia* had left floating, and it was particularly noted that they were empty. Scanning the sea with his binoculars, the Third Officer noticed a large ice floe a mile or so distant on which he saw figures moving, and drawing Captain Lord's attention to it, remarked that they might be human beings. He was told that they were seals. The *Californian* now made one complete turn to starboard followed by one to port and then resumed her passage to Boston passing the Canadian Pacific steamship *Mount Temple*, and another steamship of unknown nationality.

Before noon the *Californian* had cleared all the ice, and among many wireless messages she intercepted was one addressed to Mr. W.T. Stead, a passenger who was with those lost in the *Titanic*, offering him a dollar a word for his story of the casualty. It was sent by a well known New York newspaper.

The New England coast was approached in a dense fog out of which loomed a tugboat containing a number of American newspaper men expecting to obtain a story. Their journey was a vain one.

What was the complete story of events aboard the *Californian* during the middle watch of that fateful morning of April 15th? The passage of time has not dulled the recollections of all who were in any way concerned. Mr. Stone and the Apprentice Gibson saw the ship which Mr. Groves had reported as being a passenger ship fire eight rockets, the first of which was seen at 1.10 a.m. This is the number which the *Titanic* is believed to have sent up between 1.00 and 2.00 a.m. and at 2.20 a.m. Mr. Stone reported to Captain Lord that the distant ship had 'disappeared'. It is known that the *Titanic* foundered at that time.

Officers of the *Titanic* and many others aboard her reported having seen the lights of a ship which was stopped a few miles away from her, and the passengers on the ill-fated vessel were reassured on being told by the officers that this ship would soon come to their assistance.

All that middle watch the *Californian* remained stationary for news of the rockets being seen did not stir her Captain into action, Mr. Stone lacked the necessary initiative to insist upon his coming to the bridge to investigate things for himself, and it did not occur to him to call the Chief Officer when he realized the apathy of the Captain, who apparently slept peacefully whilst this drama was being enacted about them. Mr. Stewart relieved the bridge at 4.00 a.m., when the events of the watch were related to him. Half an hour later he roused Captain Lord and when told about the rockets which had been fired, he replied to the effect that he knew all about them. Shortly before 6.00 a.m. Mr. Stewart was instructed to call the wireless operator to see if any information could be obtained regarding the distress signals, when advice was received from several ships of the sinking of the *Titanic*. Slowly at first but eventually at full speed, the *Californian* got under way until she arrived at the scene of the disaster.

Many questions will forever remain unanswered concerning the failure of the *Californian* to render assistance to the stricken ship. Mr. Stone knew without a shadow of a doubt that there was trouble aboard the vessel from which the distress signals had been fired, but he failed to convince his Captain. But did Captain Lord need any convincing? Was Mr. Stone afraid that if he was too insistent he would arouse the wrath of his superior?

Why did Captain Lord take no efficient steps to render assistance before 6 o'clock? Did he consider problematical damage to his ship was of more importance than the saving of lives?

Many times the question of Captain Lord's sobriety on that occasion has been raised, but it cannot be too strongly asserted that he was a most temperate man and that alcohol played no part in the matter.

Does an experienced shipmaster lay down fully-clothed and in such circumstances sleep so heavily as he said he did on that night? Surely, surely, that is open to the very gravest of doubts.

Probably it would not be far from the mark if it is stated that the fate of those twelve hundred lost souls hinged on the fact that Mr. Groves failed to notice that the magnetic detector was not functioning when he placed the 'phones on his head in the wireless office at which time the ether was being rent by calls of distress which he would not have failed to recognize. And what of those figures on the ice floe? Were they only seals, as the Captain asserted? It has already been stated that all the *Titanic*'s lifeboats which were left afloat were closely examined and found to contain no occupants. A month later in almost the same spot the White Star liner the *Majestic* picked up one of these boats, and in it were found the bodies of passengers who had evidently died of starvation, for the ship's doctor who examined them reported the men's mouths contained fragments of cork from the lifebelts. Had these passengers escaped from the sea on to the icefloe and then eventually got into the boat as it drifted past?

What is the probable explanation of the *Titanic*'s deck lights appearing to go out when it is beyond dispute that they burned right up to the moment when she sank? She was approaching the *Californian* obliquely, and when she stopped she put her helm hard over and thus foreshortened her perspective thereby giving the appearance of the extinction of her lights.

The whole unfortunate occurrence was a combination of circumstances the like of which may never again be seen, and a middle watch which will not soon be forgotten.[155]

❖ ❖ ❖

RMS *Caronia*

George Gregory
On 17 April Mr Gregory, a passenger on the *Caronia*, wrote a letter to O.W. Brown of Lynn, Massachusetts, and described how his vessel had narrowly missed colliding with an iceberg:

The *Caronia* passed the iceberg sometime on Sunday previous to the disaster, and the wireless operator on the *Caronia* spoke to all westbound steamers advising them, including the *Titanic*, and when the accident occurred the *Caronia* reports the *Titanic* was going 22 knots an hour through a heavy fog.

Mr Gregory wrote that he and his friend Mr Beals were trying to get the *Caronia*'s wireless operator to obtain the American League baseball scores when the *Titanic*'s CQD arrived:

The operator told us to keep quiet and forget about baseball and said he had something more important off the wire than the score of the Boston Red Sox. He told us that a ship was calling for help and dropped enough hints to us to let us know that something big had happened. Later, just before Mr. Beals and myself retired to our cabins, the operator told us that the *Titanic* had hit an iceberg and tore half of her bottom away, sinking in less than two hours after the collision.[156]

❖ ❖ ❖

RMS *CELTIC*

Mr W.J. Napier

After the *Carpathia* arrived in New York, Mr Napier – a crewmember on the *Celtic* – wrote the following letter:

The all absorbing topic at present is the disaster to the *Titanic*. It is certainly very appalling to us on the *Celtic*, who knew a great many of the *Titanic* crew. We were a little more than a day's steaming behind the ill fated ship and received the news by wireless on Monday. It was kept very quiet and only a few were in the secret. The captain was afraid of a panic amongst our passengers. We were also in the ice region. We made all possible speed to the scene of the disaster. Hoping to pick up any boats that had not already been taken, but there was no sign of anything, not even wreckage, though we passed right over where the *Titanic* had sunk. We too had a very anxious time, as we encountered a lot of ice and fog. The captain hardly left the bridge, night or day, till we were out of the danger zone.

On Tuesday we passed a field of ice, supposed to be one hundred miles long, but I think this is greatly exaggerated. Quite a number of men left the ship to sail with the *Titanic* on her maiden voyage, but only two of them were saved. One of these lives near me in Birkenhead and I was more than glad to see him in New York when we arrived on Saturday. The other man was telling us that when the ship started to sink, he and a friend dived into the sea and were swimming about in the icy water for two hours. At last his friend said he was getting tired and sank before his eyes. Almost immediately afterwards the other man got hold of a deck chair and kept afloat, until he was picked up and dragged quite unconscious into a boat. The strange thing about it was that before he left the ship, he had helped a lady to put on her lifebelt and showed her the way to the boat. She thanked him and shook hands, saying what she thought was a last good-bye. He was pulled into the same boat as her, quite unconscious.[157]

❖ ❖ ❖

SS *CINCINNATI*

Kurt Schoenherr

After arriving in London, Marconi operator Schoenherr described his vessel's response to the *Titanic*'s distress message:

The *Cincinnati* was the first to answer the CQD call of the *Titanic*. I heard it distinctly despite the fact that the *Titanic* was 450 miles away. After having ascertained the position of the disabled liner I was interrupted by the distant and loud sending of the *Olympic*, which was much nearer the scene of the catastrophe, and told not to interfere with the important work of the sister ships.

I discontinued my communication with the *Titanic* and followed the traffic of the two steamers, which was handled in a most admirable manner at that period of excitement.

The *Cincinnati* was too far away to be of any assistance. It would have taken us about twenty-seven hours to reach the position of the sinking ship.

It was a mere accident that I was able to hear the *Titanic*'s cry for help, for it came at a time when the Marconi operators on fast steamers are obliged to take the press news of the Marconi station at Cape Cod.

They adjust their receivers for a long distance wavelength of about 1,500 miles, and it happened the signs sent by the Cape Cod station containing the press news for the daily paper which is published on Marconi steamships were so faint and unintelligible that I changed for a moment to short distance in order to ascertain what was going on at the regular wavelength.

It was noteworthy that during those few minutes I received the *Titanic*'s call for help.

It is a fact the *Amerika* and *Prinz Friedrich Wilhelm*, both of which were only a few hours from the *Titanic*, were unable to receive the CQD because during those hours they had adjusted their receivers for a long distance wave for the purpose of getting press news.

If this service occupied only the ordinary time necessary for transmitting such news the calamity might have been averted, but the Cape Cod station, in order to secure exactness, compels wireless operators to receive press news four times, one after another, and this, together with private messages, takes up more than three hours, during which time we can receive no other communications. For several hours at night the Marconi service on the most important steamers is kept busy in this way, and it is impossible for the operators to hear during that long period a call coming on the regular wavelength.

It is most deplorable that for such a long period the Marconi outfits on the boats are rendered incapable of serving the main purpose of the wireless of keeping in touch with steamers, of controlling the ocean for messages sent in regular order, to avoid collisions or to hear at once the CQD in times of danger. It is exactly as if a fire department were shut down in the night time.

There is not the slightest doubt in my mind that the *Amerika* and *Prinz Friedrich Wilhelm*, which were so near the *Titanic*, instead of being compelled to receive news and private messages for three hours, would have received the *Titanic*'s cry for help and they were so nearby that they could have gone to the assistance of the sinking vessel and the passengers could probably have been saved.[158]

❖   ❖   ❖

RMS *CYMRIC*

Miss Wills

Miss Wills arrived in New York on the *Cymric* and wrote the following letter to her brother, Henry T. Wills, from her home in Portland, Maine:

We left on the same day as the *Titanic*, and our course was a very northerly one, on account probably of coal shortage. At all events, it was very dangerous. We were in a dense fog for two days with the ice all about us, and it was bitterly cold. The fog horn blew every two minutes.

The Captain and crew were most cautious. The Captain did not leave the bridge for forty-eight hours or more. He picked up a wireless message about the *Titanic*, but as she was a faster boat we could not have rendered assistance, but he was on the lookout for wreckage. The fog, however, was too thick to have made it possible to see anything. He was wise not to tell the passengers, as in our own dangerous position it would naturally have made everyone very unhappy.

We knew nothing of this terrible thing until the Custom House officers came on board, and then it was awful. There was a large cabin list, as we took on all the *Teutonic* people, as she had been taken off on account of the coal strike.[159]

❖ ❖ ❖

SS FRANCONIA

Winfield Thompson

Mr Thompson, who was on the staff of the *Boston Globe*, sent the following message from the *Franconia* on 17 April:

> *Franconia* established communication by wireless with the *Carpathia* at 6:10 this morning, New York time. The *Carpathia* was then 498 miles east of Ambrose Channel and in no need of assistance. She is steaming thirteen knots. She expects to reach New York at 8 p.m. Thursday. She has a total of 705 survivors aboard. The *Franconia* is relaying personal messages from the *Carpathia* to Sable Island.[160]

❖ ❖ ❖

SS FRANKFURT

Captain Hattorf

After the *Frankfurt* arrived in Bremen, Captain Hattorf issued the following statement regarding his vessel's activities on the night the *Titanic* went down:

> At midnight of the 14th inst. we were in latitude 39.47 north and longitude 52.23 west. At 12:10 we received a message from the *Titanic* asking us to communicate our position, which we did. In reply, the *Titanic* informed us that she was caught fast in the ice in latitude 41.54 north and longitude 50.24 west, and in urgent need of help. The *Frankfurt* was then 140 sea miles from the *Titanic*. I informed the *Titanic* that the *Frankfurt* could not reach her till eleven on the following morning. At 12:15 the signal 'C.Q.D.' came from the *Titanic*, and at 1:15 communication with the *Titanic* was broken off. I supposed she had sunk by then. We reached the scene of the disaster at 10:50 in the morning, and we sighted three great

and seventeen small icebergs, also huge icefields ten to thirty miles across. I estimated that the largest berg was 140 ft. high and 1,000 ft. long. We cruised among the bergs and searched for castaways. The British steamers *Carpathia* and *Virginian* and the Russian steamer *Birma* were also on the spot seeking for survivors ... As further search was useless and I wanted to get free of the ice labyrinth I resumed my voyage at noon.[161]

❖   ❖   ❖

SS *LAKE MANITOBA*

Second Officer Duck

The *Lake Manitoba* sighted the *Titanic* on Friday, 12 April when she was nearing Fastnet Head on her voyage from St John to Liverpool. The *Titanic* was about one day out from Fastnet Head, and Second Officer Duck later spoke about his vessel's encounter with the great liner:

> We were remarking what a beautiful thing she was. When she passed us, about a mile to the northward, we could distinctly see the passengers walking up and down her decks. Everyone was passing remarks on the beauty of the ship. She towered above the waterline like a mountain. 'Surely,' said one of us, 'that is the very last word in ship-building.'

Second Officer Duck said that his ship exchanged complimentary wireless messages with the *Titanic*:

> It is hard to believe that that beautiful vessel is now a smashed thing two miles below the surface of the water, and that many of the passengers who so gaily waved their hands to us are now corpses at the bottom of the sea. When we read in the Liverpool papers some days later that the *Titanic* had foundered, not one of us believed it. We all thought that the report was sent out by some sensational correspondent and that probably it was founded on the fact that the big vessel had met with some mishap.[163]

❖   ❖   ❖

SS *LA PROVENCE*

Captain Vesco

On 17 April the *La Provence*'s Captain Vesco wrote the following account for his company, the Compagnie Generale Transatlantique. The report was countersigned by the ship's wireless operator and the government commissioner, Monsieur Bernard:

La Provence, April 17, 1912. On the 15th of April at 3 o'clock Greenwich time, after the receipt of a press telegram by Poldhu, we heard the *Titanic* send the signal 'C.Q.D.' (distress) and the following message: 'Position 41.46 N., 50.14 W. Require assistance.' We called immediately to inform the *Titanic* that we had received her appeal, but our power would not permit us to reach the *Titanic*, which was 700 miles distant.

At 3:30 in the morning, Greenwich time, the *Titanic* said, 'C.Q.D. We require assistance. Have struck an iceberg'.

The *Caronia*, which we found within our limits, made for her and succeeded in receiving the telegram of the *Titanic*. At 3:55 in the morning we heard the *Frankfurt* working with the *Titanic* and gave her position 39.47 N., 52.10 W., which would give about 150 miles of distance separating these two vessels.

The *Titanic* continued her calls and managed to get in communication with two other ships, the *Virginian* and the *Cincinnati*. About 4:50 in the morning we heard the *Olympic*, which sent the *Titanic* the following message:

'Latitude 40.32 N., longitude 61.18 W. I am lighting up all possible boilers as fast as I can – Haddock.'

It should be remarked in passing that we received this message from a distance of nearly 1,200 miles. The *Frankfurt*, which was within a nearer range, made many calls to the *Titanic* which were not replied to. It seems that the *Titanic* wished to keep in communication only with the ships of her company.

At 5:10 a.m. we were in communication with the *Celtic* going west. We transmitted to it the telegrams from the *Titanic*, and about 5:30 we heard Cape Race, which said to the *Virginian* that the weather was quite fine and very clear and that the *Titanic* had put her boats in the sea and that the women had taken their places therein.

La Provence, the *Baltic*, Cape Race, the *Virginian*, the *Caronia*, the *Olympic* and the *Frankfurt* all called the *Titanic*, but the transmissions were somewhat entangled. The *Titanic*, however, remained in communication with the *Olympic* only, and seemed to refuse every call from the other ships.

At 6:30 Greenwich time, the *Baltic* sent out the following wireless: 'Captain Smith, *Titanic*: The *Baltic* is coming; we are 234 miles east.'

It is possible that the apparatus of transmission of the *Titanic* was out of order, although its apparatus on receipt seemed to remain excellent all the time.

At 7 o'clock in the morning the night passed away, and with it the far-off signals which gradually became more feeble and with it those signals of alarm sent out by the *Titanic*, which messages we were powerless to reply to in the matter of going to her aid.

At 11:30 we began again to receive press telegrams sent out by Poldhu, and it was with growing impatience that we waited for some fresh news which might assure us of the issue of the drama which was unfolding itself in the distance.

Soon after having put in new powers, we were able to receive a telegram from the *Celtic* saying that the *Titanic* had sunk and that 600 persons had been saved. Later still came another message which brought the information that the victims of the catastrophe would reach 1,800 and that the first boats arriving near the scene of the disaster were the *Carpathia* and the *Baltic*.

It is probable that if the *Titanic* had replied to the signals of the *Frankfurt* that vessel would have reached the sinking *Titanic* before those two ships.[162]

❖ ❖ ❖

CS *MACKAY-BENNETT*

Frederick Hamilton

Mr Hamilton, who was a cable engineer on the cable ship *Mackay-Bennett*, kept a diary describing his vessel's voyage from Halifax to recover the floating bodies of the *Titanic*'s victims:

1912. April 17th – At 6.50 p.m. Having taken in a supply of ice and a large number of coffins, cast off from the Wharf en route for the position of the *Titanic* disaster. The Reverend Canon Hind of 'All Saints' Cathedral, Halifax, is accompanying the expedition, we also have an expert Embalmer on board. Cold and clear weather.

April 19th – The fine weather which has prevailed until now, has turned to rain and fog. We spoke to the *Royal Edward* by wireless to-day, she lay east of us, and reported icebergs, and growlers (lumps of ice, some of considerable size). At 6 p.m. the fog very dense, lowered cutter and picked up an Allan Line lifebelt.

April 20th – Strong south-westerly breeze, beam swell and lumpy sea. French liner *Rochambeau* near us last night, reported icebergs, and the *Royal Edward* reported one thirty miles east of the *Titanic*'s position. The *Rhein* passed us this afternoon, and reported having seen icebergs, wreckage and bodies, at 5.50 p.m. the *Bremen* passed near us, she reported having seen, one hour and a half before, bodies etc. This means about twenty five miles to the east. 7 p.m. A large iceberg, faintly discernible to our north, we are now very near the area were lie the ruins of so many human hopes and prayers. The Embalmer becomes more and more cheerful as we approach the scene of his future professional activities, tomorrow will be a good day for him. The temperature of the sea at noon to-day was 57N, by 4 p.m. it was 32N.

April 21st – Two icebergs now clearly in sight, the nearest is over a hundred feet high at the tallest peak, and an impressive sight, a solid mass of ice, against which the sea dashes furiously, throwing up geyser like columns of foam, high over the topmost summit, smothering the great mass at times completely in a cascade of spume as it pours over the snow and breaks into feathery crests on the polished surface of the berg, causing the whole ice-mountain, which glints like a fairy building, to oscillate twenty to thirty feet from the vertical. The ocean is strewn with a litter of woodwork, chairs, and bodies, and there are several growlers about, all more or less dangerous, as they are often hidden in the swell. The cutter lowered, and work commenced and kept up continuously all day, picking up bodies. Hauling the soaked remains in saturated clothing over the side of the cutter is no light task. Fifty-one we have taken on board to-day, two children, three women, and forty-six men, and still the sea seems strewn. With the exception of ourselves, the bosun bird is the only living creature here. 5 p.m. The two bergs are now in transit, the heavy swell has been rolling all day, must be a gale somewhere. 8 p.m. The tolling of the bell summoned all hands to the forecastle where thirty bodies are ready to be committed to the deep, each carefully weighed and carefully sewn up in canvas. It is a weird scene, this gathering. The crescent moon is shedding a faint light on us, as the ship lays wallowing in the great rollers. The funeral service is conducted by the Reverend Canon Hind, for nearly an hour the words 'For as must as it hath pleased – we therefore commit his body to the deep' are repeated and at each interval comes, splash! as the weighted body plunges into the sea, there to sink to a depth of about two miles. Splash, splash, splash.

22nd April – We steamed close past the iceberg today, and endeavored to photograph it, but rain is falling and we do not think the results will be satisfactory. We are now standing eastwards amongst great quantities of wreckage. Cutter lowered to examine a lifeboat, but it is too smashed to tell anything, even the name is not visible. All round is splintered woodwork, cabin fittings, mahogany fronts of drawers, carvings, all wrenched away from their fastenings, deck chairs, and then more bodies. Some of these are fifteen miles distant from those picked up yesterday. 8 p.m. Another burial service.

April 23rd – Icebergs and growlers still in sight. Both cutters busy all day recovering bodies, rain and fog all the afternoon, fog at times very dense. 7 p.m. The 'Allen Line' boat *Sardinian* stopped near us and took dispatches from our cutter. The fog had lifted slightly, but shut down denser than ever, soon after she had signaled 'good-night' on her flash light.

April 24th – Still dense fog prevailing, rendering further operations with the boats almost impossible. We hear that the *Sardinian* is waiting some thirty miles away. Noon. Another burial service held, and seventy-seven bodies follow the other. The hoarse tone of the steam whistle reverberating through the mist, the dripping rigging, and the ghostly sea, the heaps of dead, and the hard weather-beaten faces of the crew, whose harsh voices join sympathetically in the hymn tunefully rendered by Canon Hind, all combine to make a strange task stranger. Cold, wet, miserable and comfortless, all hands balance themselves against the heavy rolling of the ship as she lurches to the Atlantic swell, and even the most hardened must reflect on the hopes and fears, the dismay and despair, of those whose nearest and dearest, support and pride, have been wrenched from them by this tragedy.

April 26th – The *Minia* joined us today in the work of recovery, and lays two miles westwards of us. Her first find, was we hear, the body of Mr. Hays, the President of the Grand Trunk. At noon we steamed up to her, and sent the cutter over for material, and soon after set our course for Halifax. The total number of bodies picked up by us is three hundred and five, one hundred and sixteen have been buried at sea. A large amount of money and jewels has been recovered, the identification of most of the bodies has been established, and details set out for publication. It has been an arduous task for those who have had to overhaul and attend to the remains, the searching, numbering, and identifying of each body, depositing the property found on each in a bag marked with a number corresponding to that attached to the corpse, the sewing up in canvas and securing of weights, entailed prolonged and patient labor. The Embalmer is the only man to whom the work is pleasant, I might add without undue exaggeration, enjoyable, for to him it is a labor of love, and the pride of doing a job well.

April 30th – 8.25 a.m. Took Pilot on board off Devils Island, and are now proceeding up Halifax Harbor. Crowds of people throng the wharves, tops of houses, and the streets. Flags on ships and buildings all half mast. Quarantine and other officials came on board near Georges Island, after which ship stood in to the Navy Yard, and hauled in alongside. Elaborate arrangements have been made for the reception of the bodies now ready for landing. 10 a.m. Transferring of remains to shore has begun. A continuous procession of hearses conveys the bodies to the Mayflower Rink. It is a curious reflection, that when on February 12th, we picked up the waterlogged schooner *Caledonia* and returned to Halifax to land her crew of six, these men walked ashore unnoticed, and two lines in the Daily Paper was sufficient to note the fact that they had been saved. While today with not one life to show, thousands come to see the landing, and the papers burst out into blazing headlines.[164]

Unknown Correspondent
Another record was kept of the *Mackay-Bennett*'s recovery of the *Titanic*'s victims:

April 20th: ... passed a berg about 200 feet high and some small ice evidently broken from large bergs. 7 p.m. passed an enormous berg; run for 45 minutes and stopped for the night. A lot of wreckage drifting about.

April 21st: 5 a.m., started steaming for position of wreck. 6:45 a.m. picked up first body, a Danish boy, and during day picked up 51 bodies, four being females and a child of two or three years, a boy. 5 p.m., hoisted boat for the night. Undertaker embalmed 30 bodies, 6 being left for morning. 8:15 p.m., burial service was held on forecastle deck, when 24 bodies were buried, these being mostly of the crew and not identified.

April 22nd: 5:30 a.m., lowered boat for a body. Enormous quantity of wreckage. Came upon a lifeboat bottom up with its side smashed in. Steamed away after trying to pick up boat. This day we picked up 27 bodies, that of Col. J.J. Astor being amongst them. Everybody had on a lifebelt and bodies floated very high in water in spite of the sodden clothes and things in pockets. Apparently the people had lots of time, and discipline must have been splendid, for some had on their pajamas, two or three shirts, two pairs of pants, two vests, two jackets and an overcoat. In some pockets a quantity of meat and biscuits were found, while in the pockets of most of the crew quite a lot of tobacco and matches besides keys to the various lockers and stateroom doors were found. On this day we buried 15 bodies some of them very badly smashed and bruised.

April 23rd: This day we came across the worst bodies. The sea was dotted with bodies as far as one could see. Started picking up bodies at 6:20 a.m. At 6:15 p.m. we had picked up 125 bodies. The decks being covered with them. At 8 p.m. we had a funeral service when 17 bodies were buried.

April 24th: Heavy sea and very foggy. Could not see a ship's length. The bodies from yesterday were being searched and tagged and stowed away, nobody being buried this day.

April 25th: Started at six a.m. and picked up 87 bodies, keeping all on board. Bodies searched and tagged in proper order. Heard that cable ship *Minia* was coming to relieve us. *Minia* arrived at midnight.

April 26th: Started again at 6:15 a.m., picked up 6 bodies. Put boat to *Minia* for embalming field. Picked up 2 more bodies, then started for Halifax, having on board 190 bodies. We buried 116 bodies.[165]

Reverend Hind

The Reverend Canon Hind wrote the following account of the *Mackay-Bennett*'s recovery of the *Titanic*'s victims:

Strange to say, there is far less to tell than people seem to imagine about the mission of the *Mackay-Bennett* in her trip to look for bodies from the wreck of the ill-fated *Titanic*. When passing steamers sent the message that they had seen wreckage and bodies floating about, the *Mackay-Bennett* was chartered to go and see what could be done in finding them.

We left Halifax shortly after noon on April 17th and had not proceeded far when fog set in, so that our journey was slow. We reached the vicinity of the wreckage on Saturday evening. Early on Sunday morning the search for bodies began, when the captain and other officers of the ship kept a lookout from the bridge. Soon the command was given 'Stand by the boat', and a little later the lifeboat was lowered, and the work began of picking up the bodies as they were pointed out in the water to the crew. Through the day some fifty were picked up, all were carefully examined, and their effects placed in separate bags – all bodies and bags being numbered.

It was deemed wise that some of them should be buried. At 8 p.m. the ship's bell was tolled to indicate all was in readiness for the service. Standing on the bow of the ship, as she rocked to and fro, one gazed at the starry heavens and across the boundless deep, and to his mind the Psalmist's words came with mighty force:

'Whither shall I go then from Thy spirit, or whither shall I go from Thy presence, if I second up to heaven Thou art there; if I make my bed in the grave Thou art there also; if I take the wings of the morning and dwell in the uttermost part of the sea, even there shall Thy hand lead me, and Thy right hand shall hold me.'

In the solemn stillness of the early night the words of that unequalled burial office rung across the waters: 'I am the resurrection and the life, with the Lord; he that believeth in me, tho' he were dead, yet shall he live, and whosoever liveth and believeth in me shall never die.'

When the time of committal came, these words were used over each body:

'For as much as it hath pleased Almighty God to take unto Himself the soul of our dear brother departed, we therefore commit his body to the deep to be turned to corruption, looking for the resurrection of the body (when the sea shall give up her dead) and the life of the world to come, through Jesus Christ, our Lord, who shall change our vile body, that it may be like unto His glorious body, according to the mighty working whereby He is able to subdue all things to himself.'

Then the prayers from the burial service were said, the hymn 'Jesus, Lover of My Soul' sung, and the blessing given.

Anyone attending a burial at sea will most surely lose the common impression of the awfulness of a grave in the mighty deep. The wild Atlantic may rage and toss, the shipwreck mariners cry for mercy, but far below in the calm untroubled depth, they rest in peace.

On Monday the work began again early in the morning, and another day was spent in searching and picking up the floating bodies, and at night a number were buried.

On Tuesday the work was still the same until the afternoon, when the fog set in and continued all day Wednesday. Wednesday was partly spent in examining bodies, and at noon a number were committed to the deep.

Thursday came in fine, and from early hours till evening the work went on.

During the day word came that the cable ship *Minia* was on her way to help and would be near us at midnight.

Early on Friday some more bodies were picked up. The captain then felt that we had covered the ground fairly well and decided to start on our homeward way at noon. After receiving some supplies from the *Minia*, we bid good-bye and proceeded on our way.

The *Mackay-Bennett* succeeded in finding in all 306 bodies, of which 116 were buried at sea, and one could not help feeling as we steamed homeward, that of those bodies we had on board, it would be well if the greater number of them were resting in the deep.

It is to be noted how earnestly and reverently all the work was done, and how nobly the crew acquitted themselves during a work of several days, which meant a hard and trying strain on mind and body.

What seems a very regrettable fact is that, in chartering the *Mackay-Bennett* for this work, the White Star Company did not send an official agent to accompany the steamer in her search for the bodies.[166]

F.H. Lardner

When the *Mackay-Bennett* returned to Halifax with the recovered bodies, Captain Lardner granted the following interview to the newspapers:

The ship was put under charter to put out to the scene of the wreck and to bring in all bodies found, but owing to the number of bodies and other conditions, such as adverse weather, this unfortunately proved impossible. We were unable to carry out the letter of our instructions, and some of the bodies were buried at sea after appropriate religious service by the chaplain here.

We left Halifax on the afternoon of Wednesday April 17. Fog and bad weather delayed us on our run and we didn't arrive on the scene until Saturday at 8 p.m.

On Saturday at noon, having asked all ships within our wireless range to report to us any evidence of the wreck, we received a communication from the German liner *Rhein* that in latitude 42.1 north, longitude 49.13 west, she had passed much wreckage and had seen several bodies.

Our course was shaped north 34 degrees east, and while we were heading this way, later in the afternoon, we spoke to the steamer *Bremen*, which told us of having passed three big bergs and several bodies in latitude 43 north, longitude 49.2 west. Roughly speaking, these two reports showed that the drift was to the north and east, and so I made up my mind to try to go over the trail that the bodies had taken.

We reached the spot where I thought the *Titanic* had sunk just after the first watch began, and we shut down and let the ship drift with whatever current chose to carry her, on the theory that where the ship would be carried there we would find the bodies.

Four hours after we began floating north by east on the rise of a gentle swell three bodies were sighted. This was in the mid-watch, and at the same time we saw quantities of lighter wreckage, steamer chairs, hatches and pieces of wood.

We kept a sharp watch on the bodies and at daylight on Sunday two boats were lowered, and though a heavy sea was running we succeeded in recovering 51 bodies. We had to work slowly and carefully, and it was well along towards six o'clock that we got the last of the bodies aboard.

They were in pretty fair shape. Now and then some would be found in mutilated condition. We judged this to be due to the seas smashing over the *Titanic* as she settled and throwing the men against the railings and fixtures, breaking their heads and otherwise hurting them. Then, again, some may have been hurt by the screws of passing ships.

The bodies that were in worse shape from these wounds or from being in the water we concluded to bury at sea, so at eight o'clock that night twenty-four of them were recommitted. Canon Hind spoke the service and we helped out as best we could. The bodies were almost all those of the crew. In some cases the undertaker didn't think it was safe to try to keep them. That night we did not bury any bodies that had been identified.

Monday, at daylight, when we resumed work, we found the bodies scarce. After a long, careful search all we got was twenty-five. We followed a line of wreckage for sixteen miles and then a batch of bodies was discovered just at dark.

The ship drifted pretty well on the course the bodies were taking during the night, and at dawn we were not far off. With the findings of the night before, we had a good start on Tuesday's work.

Finishing with one pack we ran into another. It was our best day's work. By noon we had ninety aboard.

One pack we sighted at a distance the bodies looked like seagulls swimming on the water, and the flapping in the breeze of the loose ends of the lifebelts made the resemblance to wings almost complete.

When we bore down upon them the bodies looked like swimmers asleep. They were not floating, but bolt upright, with heads up. The arms were outstretching, as if aiding to support the body. All faced one way – the way they were drifting.

We saw a big berg when we made this pack. It might have been the berg that sunk the liner. She was long and low lying, rising perhaps 125 feet, or maybe 160 at her highest point, which was well in from a bunch that sloped into the water. It was surrounded by wreckage and several bodies.

The bodies were floating, some near together, some far apart. There seemed no order among them – none hand in hand or embraced. We would come upon them within a few feet of each other in big numbers and then stretched out at great lengths from each other.

Tuesday afternoon the weather came on and so we only got twenty-nine. There was a thick fog all day Wednesday and it was blowing fresh from the south-west, so we headed to wind and sea. All day we saw nothing. At midnight the weather eased and we shaped to where we expected to find them.

At 4:30 Thursday morning one was seen from the bridge through glasses. With so little showing above the water the bodies were not easy to pick out against the water, and the job was harder when they were surrounded by bits of wreckage, which aided in concealing them.

As soon as we sighted the body we stopped and drifted. We had got back on the track, and that day we picked up thirty-seven more. This was the day we got word that the *Minia* was on the way to join us in the work. She spoke to us just after midnight by wireless and after getting our position came alongside about a quarter to one Friday morning. At daylight the two ships began the search together. She confirmed to us having the body of Charles M. Hays aboard.

The second burial we had was on Monday night when twelve bodies were sunk. We had the final service on Wednesday morning when the weather kept us from our work, so we used our time to bury 78 bodies. The task was no easy one.

At noon the *Mackay-Bennett* picked up sixteen more bodies. We then left for Halifax, having as many bodies on board as we could look after. We experienced bad weather and returned home, coming south of Sable Island.

As the bodies were hoisted up to the deck each body was searched, was numbered and all the contents of the pockets and valuables were put into a canvas bag bearing the same number as the body. Close examination of the contents of the bag led to later identification. Each bag was separately examined at night after the work of the day was finished.

Five men were sent, in each boat sent out from the ship, to pick up the bodies. In bad weather there were four or five boats, and in fine weather eight or nine. The bodies were found sixty miles northeast of the disaster in the cold water north of the Gulf Stream. The ship swept a square of thirty miles and picked up all of the bodies in that square.

There were three burial services at sea. The boats were kept within a reasonable distance of the ship. The bodies found were all standing upright in the water.

There were doors, chairs and wood from the *Titanic* spread over thirty miles. We found an empty broken lifeboat upside down with a few bodies near it. It was a flat boat of the collapsible type. We saw no sign of shooting on any of the bodies. We found several men dressed in evening clothes, but found no bodies lashed to doors. Those whom we found it necessary to bury were not men of prominence.

Regarding the body found at first and supposed to be that of Mr. Widener, it has since been established that it was Mr. Widener's valet, with some of Mr. Widener's papers on his person. He was buried at sea. The body was badly damaged. The body of Mr. Widener is not on board, and his son is satisfied that the body buried is that of his father's valet.

The *Minia* had seven bodies on board when we left.

We believe that all the bodies which were buried were members of the ship's company, and most of these were in such condition that they could not possibly have been brought ashore. In all we picked up 306 bodies and buried 116 of them. We are satisfied that we have properly identified all of the bodies of passengers which we took up. Those brought back unidentified I think were members of the crew.

As to Mr. Widener, we were never altogether satisfied as to his identity, because, though his papers were found on the body, his underclothing did not look as though it would be worn by him. It was of a poorer texture than he would be expected to wear. The name of the valet was Edwin Keeping. His head was so badly damaged that the body could not have been kept. His watch bore the initials 'E.K.' These same initials were also found on the overcoat.

We did not find the bodies of many women – eighteen, I am told, in all.

Most of the bodies look as if the people had been asleep. Over 100 bodies were embalmed. Had the bodies got on the edge of the Gulf Stream, they would have spread over many more miles. I don't think the *Minia* will get any more.

It is my opinion that the bulk of the bodies are in the ship. I think when she went down the water broke into her with great force and drove them into the hull. Mrs. Straus's body was not yet found.

I explain the reason that so many of the bodies picked up were members of the crew because they probably jumped before the ship took the fatal plunge. They were used to the ways of the sea and knew the danger of staying aboard her until the end. The passengers stayed aboard her and went down with her. They were crushed down in her as she sunk, and deep in her body they are finding their graves.

Those aboard her, the doctors think, were killed almost instantly by the terrible pressure in the vortex. Those who got away died later from freezing. I think few were drowned.

I had only one embalmer aboard and he treated something like 100 bodies. We took them in the order they came; no preference was shown. That is, the passengers were given consideration over the crew because the crew must expect such things when they put to sea, and we felt that in cases where great estates and large wills depended upon the body as proof of death it was best for us to do all in our power to have the body in shape to bring back.

I have no doubt that the families of the crew would like to have had their bodies sent to them, too. So far as we could, we did. But I thought it proper to give the preference to the men of affairs and, besides, it is fit and proper for a sailorman to be buried at sea. He lives by the sea and so he should be willing to be buried in the sea.[167]

Gerald Ross

After the *Mackay-Bennett* returned to Halifax, Electrician Ross spoke about the voyage to recover *Titanic* victims:

> I saw the recovery of Col. Astor's body. Like the others it was floating buoyed up by a lifebelt. Both arms extended upwards. The face was swollen, his jaws injured. His body was clothed in a business suit and tan shoes. His watch, a costly thing, studded with diamonds, was dangling from his pocket. It had stopped at 3:20. Practically all the other watches on bodies we recovered had stopped at 2:10. His watch chain was of platinum and so were the settings of the rings he wore.

Ross said that, by some remarkable coincidence, every male body recovered was floating face down and every female face up, and he corroborated John Snow's statement that many of the bodies buried at sea were recognisable and well preserved. He said that his vessel encountered the fatal berg, which was 'very long' but projected only fifty feet out of the water and had a jagged hole in its side in which the *Mackay-Bennett* could have berthed:

The *Titanic* gave the berg a hard bump. All kinds of wreckage was floating around the berg. We picked up a deck chair or two as souvenirs.

Captain Lardner felt as badly as anyone to be obliged to put any bodies back into the sea, but what was he to do when we were overcrowded and lacked accommodation?

We came across a diamond smuggler, a Swede traveling in the steerage. He was among the 116 consigned to an ocean grave.

I felt a peculiar hard lump in the back of his coat. I told my workmate and we ripped the lining and found a half-dozen fine diamonds sewn there. This man was not identified. The diamonds were turned over to the purser with the other valuables taken from the unidentified bodies and all placed in the custody of the White Star Line.

The property taken from the unidentified bodies was placed in little white bags bearing numbers similar to the body label. The steamship officials will undoubtedly have considerable miscellaneous property for which no heirs can ever apply. Take the diamonds, for instance. There can be no claimant for them, surely.

The hold was stacked with ice and the bodies were packed on it. The decks and every nook and cranny were stocked with them. The first few nights all hands felt creepy. I know I did, but after a while we got used to it.

When we handled the bodies aboard a few of us were selected to search the clothing for valuables and marks of identification. Some were so distorted in limbs and swollen we had to cut the garments off. If we couldn't get our hands into pockets we were ordered to slit them with our knives.

Many of the women were in evening gowns. We picked up one young married couple – Mr. and Mrs. A. Robins – the only husband and wife found. She wore a beautiful low-neck dress, and around her neck was a costly string of pearls.

When we found Colonel Astor's body, his watch was found to have stopped at 3:20. I think it was because his was better made and stood the water better. His money belt held $2,000 in gold. He had other effects, all of which, I think, were appraised at from $50,000 to $75,000.

The bodies buried were sewn into canvas shrouds and heavily weighted after a service had been held over each. We ran out of canvas and burlap and got some from an Allan liner. We were all glad to end the journey, and I for one never care for another cruise like it.[168]

John Snow, Jr

After arriving back at Halifax, funeral director Snow described the *Mackay-Bennett*'s recovery of the bodies of *Titanic* victims:

Our task was entirely indescribable. It is impossible to give you any clear idea of its character. Among the bodies we recovered is that of a two-year-old baby boy – he came floating to us with little upturned face, the only body recovered who wore no lifebelt. Nothing I saw at sea made such an impression upon me.

On last Monday we found fifty bodies all in a group, and nearby a life-boat which evidently had capsized, all within it being drowned. There was a red skirt found tied to a stick with which it is supposed that those in the boat had sought to attract attention, and failing, had gone down to their terrible death.

We secured, about forty miles from the scene of the disaster, the bodies of twelve women. The reports stated that there was an explosion and this probably explained the terribly mutilated condition of many of the bodies – arms and legs shattered, faces and bodies mangled.

We picked up many lifebelts 170 miles from the wreck.

Many of the bodies picked up were of persons in full evening dress. And it is a remarkable fact that all the watches worn by the men stopped at precisely ten minutes past two to the second. There was not the very slight-est deviation.

On Sunday, the 21st, we buried 24 bodies.

On Monday, 15 bodies, on Wednesday 77 bodies.

We recovered in all 306 bodies and buried in all 116, and we brought home 190.

There was awful evidence of the fierce struggle for life, hands clutching wildly at clothing, faces distorted with terror. But it is no use to try to describe what we saw. To do so is impossible. As I said, ours was a sickening task.

There was a special service for each body buried at sea, 'Jesus, Lover of My Soul' being sung.

We found the 'black iceberg' which caused the wreck. It was an immense iceberg but badly shattered, and was photographed.

We also picked up many lifebelts fully 170 miles from the scene of the disaster.[169]

Mr Snow later granted a second interview to another reporter:

The bodies had suffered greatly by being washed against ice cakes and wreckage. That was the only thing that made identification difficult. Some of them had broken arms, legs and skulls, caused after death by the action of the waves. It was wounds or bruises only that made identification diffi-cult or impossible in only scattered instances. The cold water and ice acted as preservatives.

Captain Lardner was distressed by the contradictory wireless orders. First he would be told to do one thing and in a short time would be commanded to do something else. Finally he did not know what to do.

I embalmed 106 bodies on the trip single handed. I would be embalming bodies at the outset, when I would receive orders to quit and then other orders would be to proceed. It is true that the bodies buried were as well preserved as those on board, but I think the captain did not understand just what he was expected to do, so many contradictory wireless messages came aboard. It is my opinion from what transpired that he supposed he was to bury all recognized until a tardy message made the situation clear and all were saved after that. Captain Lardner should not be criticized with the delay. Fog held us up.

We left this port April 17, a Wednesday, two days after the *Titanic* went down with her dead. We met bad weather and lots of ice. We did not come in sight of any bodies until a week ago Saturday night, but it was too late to lower small boats that night. There were several icebergs about us, and the floe was thick. We had to move slowly.

Bright and early Sunday morning the harvest began. One of the first bodies picked up was that of a baby not more than two years old. She had flaxen hair and a round chubby face like a doll, and she was floating right past our porthole. The boys who picked her up said that she seemed to be looking up at them with her big, appealing blue eyes, as though she was about to speak.

If her body is not claimed, the crew of the ship is going to give her a fitting burial and erect a suitable monument in her memory.

Colonel Astor's body was in an excellent state of preservation. It was clad in full evening dress. Colonel Astor's handsome gold watch was dangling from the chain out of one of his pockets as though he had looked at it just before he took the final plunge. There was $2,500 in cash in his pocket. His body is in a good state of preservation. There is no doubt about his identity judging from the effects found on him.

The body thought to be that of George B. Widener of Philadelphia is badly disfigured. The skull is crushed. Arms and legs of many were broken. Everybody we hauled in had a lifebelt.

In one group, thirty bodies, among them many women, were found. Near this group was found a lifeboat with a woman's red skirt attached to an oar. It had been used as a signal by those in the boat to attract the attention of any passing steamer. A number of bodies were floating alongside the boat. They were evidently those who had taken refuge in the boat. There was every indication that the boat had been afloat some time after the *Titanic* had gone down.

From the circumstances we read a sad, tragic story of the sea. The men and women in the boat had evidently become separated from the other boats and had perished when their craft capsized. If they had been seen by the *Carpathia*, all would have been saved.

Of the 190 bodies brought in by the *Mackay-Bennett*, nineteen are still unidentified. As fast as the bodies were embalmed they were placed in all of the coffins which we had on hand. When the coffins gave out, we bound them in tarpaulins. There are bodies of two women among the victims, and about fourteen women were buried at sea.

I found no trace of bullet wounds nor any indications of suicide. Two of the male passengers whose bodies were found had revolvers in their clothing, but the chambers were full. We kept picking them up for several days in little clusters of from four to six.

The purser took charge of all the valuables taken from the bodies. I don't know how much the combined jewelry is worth. It runs high, but I did not hear them say aboard that the cash from the bodies would aggregate $17,000.

The burial services by Canon Hind of All Saints Cathedral, the Anglican church here, were impressive. I shall never forget the scene. There were icebergs sullenly drifting all about, a lead sky and dusk just creeping on us. Canon Hind read the simple service over each body in turn, and as everyone was committed the full crew of nearly 100 all on deck with bowed and uncovered heads, the officers on the aft deck, sung loudly 'Jesus, Lover of My Soul', the flag fluttered at half peak astern and over all was a hush. In this manner we committed 24 bodies on Saturday, 15 on Monday and 77 on Wednesday of last week. It was grueling business, I tell you, but all hands acted with true sympathy and spirit. If any mistakes were made they were unintentional and due to confusing orders from headquarters. Yes, I think we might have brought all the bodies ashore, but then I don't know what the real orders were. I was merely an undertaker on board.[170]

❖ ❖ ❖

RMS *MAURETANIA*

A Passenger Delegation
On the night of 17 April the *Mauretania* sent the following wireless to New York:

The saloon passengers of the *Mauretania* desire to express their profound sympathy with the relatives of those who perished in the terrible *Titanic* disaster; also with the White Star Line. The second cabin passengers have passed similar resolutions. The collections for the seamen's charity are £175; no concerts; band silent.[171]

F.A. King

Mr King, who was a passenger on the *Mauretania*, spoke about the *Titanic* disaster:

> When we received word Monday that the *Titanic* had met with an accident, there was intense excitement on the ship and many women were on the verge of a nervous breakdown.
>
> After receiving the position of the iceberg our steamer changed its course to the south lane. Wednesday special bulletins were printed giving a vivid description of the disaster.
>
> We came within four miles of the icebergs, and the sight was a solemn reminder. There were 2,000 passengers on the *Mauretania*.[172]

A.A. Booth

Booth, the managing director of the Cunard Line, was on board the *Mauretania* and was asked about the *Titanic* disaster:

> It seems to have upset all of our convictions.

A reporter asked, 'Could the *Mauretania*'s boats, for instance, take care of all who are on board of her now?' He replied:

> Do you consider that a fair question?

Booth then squeezed himself into a restricted space between a lifeboat and a rail and brought the interview to an end.[173]

SS *Mesaba*

Stanley Adams

After his vessel arrived in New York, wireless operator Adams was interviewed about his vessel's activities on 14 April, the day of the disaster:

> From 7 o'clock in the morning through the whole of that day we were skirting the edge of an enormous area of ice. The floe was greater than Captain Clarke had ever seen in all his voyages across the Atlantic and was

filled with great bergs. We had great difficulty keeping out of the field and had to alter our course to southward in order to do so.

At 7:50 o'clock that night we were out of the floe area, but a heavy mist began to drop down on us. I heard the *Titanic* talking to Cape Race, and I thought I'd better send back warning of what we had just escaped.

So I sent out the *Titanic's* call, M.G.Y., and got an answer immediately. Then I sent the following message: 'Latitude 42 to 41.25 north, longitude 49 to 50.30 west, saw much heavy pack ice and great number icebergs. Weather clear. [signed] Clarke, Captain, *Mesaba'*. Within a few minutes I received the following acknowledgment from Phillips on the *Titanic*: 'Thanks, M.G.Y.'

At 9 o'clock I began to think again of the danger we had just escaped and wondered if I had better call the *Titanic* once more and repeat the warning, but I knew that the wireless operator aboard her had already made acknowledgment of my message and had probably reported the same to the captain, so I did not send a second message.

Adams didn't have his instrument tuned to the *Titanic's* frequency at 10:30 and didn't receive her distress call. He didn't learn about the disaster until he overheard the *Olympic* talking about it to the *Parisian*.[174]

CS *MINIA*

James Adams
On 5 May 1912, while the cable ship *Minia* was returning to Halifax with the recovered bodies of *Titanic* victims, First Officer Adams wrote the following letter:

SS *Minia* At Sea
May 5th, 1912

My Dear Earl:
    We are now on our way to Halifax after a job somewhat out of our usual rut. When the *Titanic* went down the *Mackay Bennett* was sent out from Halifax to pick up any bodies that might be floating about, and a week later we were sent out to relieve her.

    When we got out she had picked up over three hundred and pretty nearly got all that were round, so after she left we had to search round for those that had got scattered. After a week's search, during which time we covered an area about sixty miles square, we got seventeen, two of them we buried and the others we are taking in. The only well known one in our lot is President Hays of the Grand Trunk, the most of the others members of the ship's company. I have no doubt there are many more still afloat, but they are getting so widely scattered now that looking for them is like trying to find a needle in a hay-stack. The temp. of the water was 34 degrees so the bodies were well preserved but they are gradually nearing the Gulf Stream where the water is nearly 60 degrees, and when they get there they will soon decompose. It was a terrible disaster, but only what might have happened to any of the fast boats during the last twenty years, and what may happen again so long as there is a demand for passengers and mails to be rushed across the Atlantic in the shortest possible time. The immediate effect of it will be that all ships will be compelled to carry sufficient boat accommodation for everyone on board. Had the *Titanic* been so supplied, happening as it did on a fine night with smooth water, the loss of life would have been comparatively small, on the other hand, had there been a heavy sea running, very few, if any, of the boats would have got away from the ship. Just imagine [one line of the letter is unreadable]. We have a job waiting for us on the Newfoundland coast and will be getting out again as soon as we can coal. Our stay in port for the last two or three months have been very short and not much sign of a letup in sight. I don't see much hope for a day's fishing this Spring. Hoping everything is going well with you. With kindest regards,

Faithfully Yours

Jas Adams[175]

H. Ward Cunningham

After the *Minia* returned to Halifax, the Reverend Cunningham described his vessel's voyage to recover the bodies of the *Titanic*'s victims:

The *Minia* had rough weather. We experienced only two pleasant days. I myself only saw two icebergs, one of them shaped like a great tent, with two sprawling branches protruding from its base. The officers told me that they, however, sighted a number of bergs in the distance.

We reached the scene of the wreck at 9 o'clock Thursday night. About ten minutes to nine I asked Captain De Carteret about how long it would be before we arrived there. He told me, and I went below and put on my surplice, and the whole ship's company assembled, speaking only in whispers. I can give you no idea of the feeling aboard ship as we realized that we were at last on the scene of that stupendous catastrophe which the whole world is mourning.

I conducted a solemn memorial service, composing a special prayer therefor, and we then dispersed to our several duties.

On the Wednesday before we sighted a bell buoy adrift and passed quite close to it but could discover no name or letters. It was ringing away in the ocean solitude, and the sound of its pitiful tolling was weird in the extreme. One could almost imagine that it had been dispatched by command of the guardian of the souls of the mighty deep to traverse the limitless ocean whithersoever wind and current might take it, and ring a dirge for all the lost in the ocean's depths. To us on our mournful mission its sound came with a special message.

The bodies we recovered were found miles apart from each other, and such success as we attained was due to expert navigation and good luck.

The first body recovered was that of C.M. Hays and we concluded that we had come across the first class passengers, hoping to find Mr. Wright's body.

But such was not the case – our next find was that of a fireman.

We found one body with 'J. Watson' or 'Ribson' on the inside of a Norfolk overcoat, and the initials 'H. R.' on his handkerchief. It was the body of a man in full dress, and we were in hopes it was that of H. Rood of Seattle, whose gentle wife has shown so much thoughtfulness in connection with the unidentified dead recovered by the *Mackay-Bennett*. It proved, however, not to be his body. Mr. Rood was five feet nine inches in height. This is the body of a man five feet three. He wore gold cuff links inscribed 'S.G.' and in his pocket was found a bunch of keys bearing 'Café Parisienne' upon them, from which we concluded he might be one of the chief stewards.

All the bodies wore lifebelts – only one, so far as the ship's doctor could judge, died by drowning, the death of the other sixteen being due to exposure.

Cunningham was asked how long the ship's doctor thought the victims had lived in the water:

About four hours. The temperature of the water was about 34 degrees and death from exposure would, it was calculated, ensue in about that time.

Save in two cases there was no mutilation, and no evidence of struggle. In one of these the eyes had been gouged out. In the other a foot had been cut off.

I was impressed with the willingness of all on board to work, and the recovery of the bodies was extremely difficult. It was, indeed, almost impossible to descry them in the crested waves.

Not a single ship reported to us as having seen bodies floating. Not one.

Cunningham was asked about the ship's arrival at the scene of the disaster:

Now all was quiet and far below lay the remains of the noble ship, the culmination of modern skill. No icebergs were near, tho' the breeze was laden with chill.

At 5 a.m. on Friday morning Mr. Hays' body was picked up. I knew him from his photos in the papers. Letters of identification were on his person, also a gold watch presented to him by his associates in the Wabash railroad.

Our next find was an engineer, then a Norwegian, then a fireman, then an Italian warder, then a Syrian who wore his scapular and rosary, also a feather belt with apparently gold coins in it.

The fireman had no marks of identification upon him, and we buried him at sea.

Papers and belongings of the recovered bodies were given to the captain, who in turn handed them to the purser. By the latter they were enclosed in envelopes and carefully numbered, the chaplain being required to keep a tabulated record and to prepare a canvas-duck square with a corresponding number, which was fastened to the body.

On the body of a Finn were found $40 in American money and a lot of Finnish notes.

At 9.15 on Saturday, 27 April was recovered the body of a fireman. In his pocket was a printed sheet of Christmas carols of St Patrick's Church, Ballymacarrett, near Belfast. There were no marks of identification on the body, and it was buried at sea. Cunningham forwarded the carols to the rector of St Patrick's church with all particulars about the body and its burial.

Cunningham said that the presence of wreckage was a poor guide to finding bodies. The last body recovered was that of Steward C. Howell. Among the items picked up from the sea were a deck chair in good condition, a drawer from the first class pantry, a lady's boa, a lifebelt and other ship's fittings.

On Tuesday, 30 April at 1:30 the body of T.W. Kink [King] was recovered along with his keys labelled 'Assistant Purser'. He was described as a fine fellow of full height who was wearing an officer's greatcoat and kid gloves. The body was undamaged and the face wore a natural look.

At 6 a.m. on 1 May the body of J. Finney [Fynney] of Liverpool was discovered. One foot was off and the leg fractured at the ankle. He had a commutation ticket on the London and North-western Railway. He was a member of a well-known rubber firm, but from notes found on his person he was engaged in evangelistic work.[176]

William De Carteret

Upon arriving in Halifax, Captain De Carteret gave a newspaper interview describing the *Minia's* body-recovery activities:

There is no doubt that other bodies are afloat but are drifting rapidly to the gulf stream, and once within its warmer waters decomposition will rapidly take place, but there is the chance that a small, hardy vessel, equipped for a month's stay on the ground, may recover perhaps a dozen or so.

We covered a large portion of the ground from longitude 49.25, where we met the *Mackay-Bennett*, to longitude 48, where the Arctic waters meet those of the gulf stream, and saw no groups, only single bodies. We also went north from latitude 41.20 to 42.30. Thus we covered as much ground as possible, but I do not pretend that I have searched every square mile, as that is impracticable, and such an attempt alone would occupy many months.

I received willing aid from every man on the ship, even some of the watch below constituting themselves additional lookouts, engineers off duty and others all taking an active part in the search.

The ship's doctor assisted the undertaker in embalming and preparing the bodies. Rev. H.W. Cunningham assisting the purser in recording the identifications found on the dead and in other ways when required.

With only one exception, none of the bodies had water in the lungs, showing death to have been due to exposure.

One had been killed by contact with the ship's fittings when she made the final plunge, as one foot was broken off at the ankle and the other dislocated. Another man appeared to have been killed by the explosion, as his face was either burnt or scalded and one eye gouged out.

There was certainly an explosion, as pieces of coal were found with the hair in the seat of a saloon chair which was badly damaged.

We recovered a large section of the saloon staircase.[177]

In May Captain De Carteret wrote a report to the Hydrographic Department regarding the winds and currents in the area where the *Minia* recovered bodies of *Titanic* victims:

CS *Minia*
Halifax, N.S.
May 8, 1912
The Hydrographer
Hydrographic Office
Washington, D.C. U.S.A.

Dear Sir,
Yours of the 4th May to hand.

I herewith attach a blue print showing the positions of the bodies recovered. This print also shows the northern limit of the Gulf Stream as noted by me.

I met the C.S. *Mackay-Bennett* in about Latitude 41.38 N, Longitude 49.24W, she reported having cleaned up the western edge of the drift. This position was about S72E, 40 miles from the position given for the *Titanic*. After making allowance for possible wind drift, and taking the direction of the drift of wreckage on a smooth day, it appears that the actual drift was S60E true, but as I found bodies over fifty miles east true from the above position, and since my return to port have seen that bodies were passed about S25E true twenty miles also from that position, it makes the direction of the stream somewhat uncertain, but it shows that the bodies did not travel in the same direction, nor at the same rate. During the search a large berg 70 ft. high was passed close to in Lat. 41.40N, Long. 49.15W, and a few days after this berg was seen in Lat. 42.50N, Long. 49.07W. I supposed it to be the same berg as it was of a peculiar shape, not often seen; it resembled a giant lying on his back with legs wide apart, headless, with legs stretched out about 200 feet long, the toes pointing upward about 25 feet from the ankle to the knee submerged, and the seas washing up the fork. This was the view from the east; from the west it looked like a lean-to shack, with lines criss-crossing all over its west side, resembling sled or ski tracks; that portion had not been awash as it still had snow on it. If I am correct in supposing it to have been the same berg it shows that at times a current or strong wind may set icebergs to the north. I may say that 70 miles east of C Race I have seen bergs go past an anchored buoy, traveling north true at one mile an hour against a light north wind.

Although information given to a captain regarding positions of bergs may put him on his guard, it is extremely unlikely that he would find them in the same spot 24 hr. after, and any action taken by him to avoid that spot would as likely as not lead him on the berg he was trying to avoid. The berg I have described seems to have gone north at the rate of 15 miles a day, and that is not an unusual rate for a berg to travel.

In my cable work during the early months of the year between Jan. 15th and March 31st, East and N.W. of Newfoundland, I have had to force a passage through heavy Arctic field ice for over 150 miles, and on two or three occasions have actually repaired a cable in a large lake of clear water, with heavy ice all around the horizon, which closed in just as the repair was completed. It has been necessary to attach hawsers to icebergs and tow or cant them so they would not ground on a cable and crush it; and I have known them to ground on the Banks of Newfoundland in 42 fathoms and crush a cable; but I have never known them to remain in or near the same spot for even 12 hr. unless they were near the shore on rocks or shoals. Therefore it is apparent that positions of icebergs given to a captain are merely in the nature of a warning that they are around.

It may interest you to know where the northern limit of the Gulf Stream was on April 30th. I have therefore indicated its position on the blue print; but perhaps a short explanation is necessary.

I had followed wreckage from 41.30N 48.40W eastward, picking up two bodies in about 48.15W. When I saw a wall of fog to leeward in a S.E. direction, I realized it was caused by the Gulf Stream and decided to examine its border for bodies and wreckage. There was a short heavy sea which caused the ship to plunge bow-under when at half speed, and a lot of wreckage trending S60E (true) in the cold water and N65E in the warm.

As the ship's bow was about to enter the fog the sea temperature was 35 degrees, and as her stern entered it the temperature was 56 degrees. As the fog was too dense to see anything, I returned to the cold water, and repeated the tests with the same results. It was clear to the N.W. of the stream. The color of the cold water was a grayish blue, and in the stream a purple blue.

The change in direction of the wreckage was quite marked as it was caught in the waters of the stream.

I found that with a South or S.E. wind there was little or no fog, but the cold North or N.W. winds brought down the fog at once.

Temperatures taken in the vicinity of icebergs showed no difference from those taken in other parts of the same currents. I also noticed that the streams are not running in a straight line side by side, as bays of varying widths and depths are found in which the waters of one current run into those of the other; and it might so happen that a captain taking the temperature of the sea might judge that he was near field ice because it was lower than he had it a short time before; or, being higher, conclude that all danger of ice was passed; yet in both cases he is liable to be wrong, as bergs are seen in both cold and warm waters. He may run a hundred miles in cold water and not see a single berg. Running to Halifax, I passed through several bays of warm water running into the cold, a change taking place in less than half an hour; yet no icebergs were in sight, nor field ice near.

If heavy masses of field ice were to leeward of a ship it is possible a decided change in the temperature would be noted, as the passage of the mass might leave a cold wake behind it; or if a current moved faster than the rate at which the mass was moving, then to leeward of it cold water might be found. But the whole thing is so uncertain that no captain would be justified in making any alteration in his course from the changes in temperature only.

All bodies recovered in the cold water were frozen, and had to be thawed in the sun before embalming; but one found on the edge of the stream was soft, and decomposition had set in.

No field ice was seen, no soundings taken, and no buoys anchored.

On April 24th I passed a large Bell Buoy in Lat. 42.56N, Long. 57.18W, with white and black bell supports, body red and white, four swinging hammers; rivets on manhole cover appeared to form the letters G K D.

Observations were scarce, obtainable only on two days of the week I was on the ground.

My operations covered Longitudes 49.30W to 48.00W and no field ice was seen at any time, but at first a large number of icebergs were seen, from the lofty berg to the growler; then they disappeared, and only one was seen on the return trip. It is my opinion that few bergs remain in Latitudes 41.30 to 42.00N in the longitudes between 48.00 and 49.00.

The *Minia*, although fitted for only 200 mile wireless communication, was able to keep in touch with Cape Race the whole time at a distance of 350 to 370 miles, but only at night, and not always through the night. It sometimes happened that after receiving 'Go Ahead' from C. Race and the msg. being sent, on asking if C.R. had it, no reply would be forthcoming, the signals having failed; and after a few hours they would be as good as ever. This perhaps explains why so many messages went astray and were not answered at the time of the accident.

It seems to me that the time has arrived when all ocean going vessels should be compelled by law to have a wireless outfit of not less than 100 nautical miles whether they carry passengers or not. A vessel near the one requiring help might as well be a hundred miles off if she has not got wireless, for all the help she can render.

I am, dear Sir, yours faithfully,
William De Carteret[178]

Francis Dyke

Mr Dyke was serving as the *Minia*'s temporary wireless operator when he wrote the following letter to his mother on April 27th:

Anglo-American Telegraph Company
Cable Ship *Minia*
April 27th/12
2:20 a.m.

My Darling Mother,

I expect you will be surprised to receive this written on this paper, but I am on watch now in the wireless room so thought it a good opportunity to write you. This is the most remarkable trip the old *Minia* has ever been on as we are looking for bodies from the *Titanic* wreck. You know I wrote that we were up north on Cable repair when we heard she had sunk – we arrived in Halifax about three days after and it was reported that we had some of the rescued on board but we had not and the reporters that came to meet us were disappointed ...

We began the search yesterday + the first we picked up was C.M. Hays of G. Trunk Rail. It was no trouble to identify him as he had a lot of papers on him + a watch with his name on.

We picked up 10 more bodies yesterday (waiters + sailors). All those who are identified are embalmed and packed in ice + are to be sent to N. York. I can tell you none of us like this job at all but it is better to recover them and bury them properly than let them float about for weeks. The Revd. Cunningham came out with us to bury those not identified. When we passed over the spot where the *T.* sank he held a short service in the saloon, which I thought very nice of him. I expected to see the poor creatures very disfigured but they all look as calm as if they were asleep. Mack and I have had to keep 6 hours watches all this trip, so as to keep in touch with all ships + give them news – it is difficult to keep awake all night but I am getting used to it now ...

... the bodies are much scattered, ... they go very fast when in the Gulf Stream – very likely many will be washed up on the Irish Coast as they are all going East.

... The *Titanic* must have blown up when she sank, as we have picked up pieces of the grand staircase ... most of the wreckage is from below deck, it must have been an awful explosion, too, as some of the main deck planking 4 feet thick was all split and broken off short.

... I am sorry to say that we have to go out again in about two days up North the same place where we were in when we heard about the *Titanic* Etc. etc.

Your loving son,
Francis Dyke[179]

J. Durant
After his vessel's arrival in St John, NB, wireless operator Durant gave the following interview about how he received the *Titanic*'s distress call:

I was lying in bed reading with the telephone over my ear, at 12:11 New York time when I caught the first call. Immediately getting out of bed, I answered, asking the position of the ship. This was sent back with the addition, 'Come at once, have struck berg'.

As soon as I got the message I notified Captain Moore, who at once doubled the watch of firemen below, called all hands on deck and changed the ship's course toward the position of the *Titanic*. Then I went back to my instrument and sat there. I did not call the *Titanic* again because other ships, which I judged to be closer, were working and I did not wish to jam them. At 12:21 I heard the *Carpathia* answer the CQD calls of the *Titanic* and heard the operator on that ship give his position, adding, 'Have struck iceberg; come to our assistance at once.'

At 12:34 I heard the *Frankfurt* answer *Titanic*. That ship asked, 'What is the matter with you?' The answer was, 'We have struck an iceberg. Please tell captain to come.' To this the operator on the *Frankfurt* replied, 'Oh, I will tell the bridge right away.' The answer to this was, 'Yes, quick.'

All this time the CQD message was being sent out incessantly, and at 1:06 I heard the *Olympic* answer the call. To this steamer the *Titanic* said, 'Captain says get your boats ready. Going down fast by the head.' Five minutes later the *Frankfurt* struck in with, 'Our captain will go to you.'

At 1:21 the *Olympic* sent another message which the *Titanic* answered, saying, 'We are putting the women off in the boats.'

Another five minutes of anxious waiting passed when the agonized CQD again cut the air, accompanied by the words, 'Engine room flooded.'

Out of the darkness the *Olympic* again asked, 'How is the sea around you?' To which the reply was, 'The sea is calm.'

Another four minutes passed when the operator of the *Frankfurt* was heard asking the *Titanic*, 'Are there any boats around you already?' To this there was no reply, and two minutes afterwards the *Olympic* sent a message to the *Titanic* which the latter barely acknowledged by the code letters 'R.D.'

That was the last message I heard, and I presumed the flooding of the engine room had put the wireless out of commission.

It was 4:40 a.m. when we arrived at the position of the *Titanic*, having been much delayed by the ice. At that time we saw no sign of the ill-fated ship nor any wreckage. About forty minutes later we saw the *Carpathia* and *Californian* with the Russian steamer *Birma*. There was also a tramp steamer cruising about.

As soon as I saw the *Carpathia* I asked for news of the *Titanic* but got no reply. Other ships asked the same question, but she kept silent to all. It was not until 8:30 that the *Carpathia* gave out anything, and then the only information was that she had picked up twenty boats.

At the time I received the first message I would judge the *Mount Temple* to be fifty miles from the *Titanic*'s position, and when the big ship went down there was still twenty or twenty-five miles between us.[180]

❖   ❖   ❖

James H. Moore

After his vessel arrived in St John, NB, Captain Moore made the following statement:

> We received a wireless message after midnight Sunday from the *Titanic* stating that she had struck an iceberg and to come at once. We turned about at 12:30 o'clock and steamed back to the position given us, arriving there at 4:30 o'clock. We encountered so much ice, however, that we stopped until daylight. We cruised about but could not see any sign of the ship. About 6 a.m. on the other side of an immense field of ice studded thickly with bergs, we saw the *Carpathia*. We also saw the *Californian*, which was to the northward of us, steaming west, then coming to the southward, and she met us. She did not communicate anything. At 8:46 o'clock, ship's time, we received a general message that the *Carpathia* had picked up twenty boats. We asked if they wanted assistance, but got no reply. Shortly afterward we received another general message stating, 'Nothing more can be done; no need to stand by'. We then left the scene and proceeded on our way.

Captain Moore stated that, when he resumed his course, the steamers *Carpathia*, *Californian*, *Birma*, *Frankfurt* and a tramp steamer were in the vicinity. He also responded to silly allegations by some of his passengers and crewmen that his vessel had come within sight of the sinking *Titanic* but had deliberately declined to take part in the rescue:

> Furthermore, what do the people who were on board my steamer know what I was doing or where I was going? How could they tell in what direction I was sailing? It was past midnight and they were below. The statement is absurd. Leaving humanity out of the question, do you not think that I would have liked to have been the lucky one to pick up those people?[181]

F.C. Quitzrau

On 29 April 1912 Dr Quitzrau submitted the following affidavit to the Senate *Titanic* inquiry:

DOMINION OF CANADA
Province of Ontario
City of Toronto

Dr. F.C. Quitzrau; being first duly sworn, deposes and says that he was a passenger, traveling second class, on steamer *Mount Temple*, which left Antwerp

April 3, 1912; that about midnight Sunday, April 14, New York time, he was awakened by the sudden stopping of the engines; that he immediately went to the cabin, where were already gathered several of the stewards and passengers, who informed him that word had been received by wireless from the *Titanic* that the *Titanic* had struck an iceberg and was calling for help.

Orders were immediately given and the *Mount Temple* course changed, heading straight for the *Titanic*. About 3 o'clock New York time, 2 o'clock ship's time, the *Titanic* was sighted by some of the officers and crew; that as soon as the *Titanic* was seen all lights on the *Mount Temple* were put out and the engines stopped and the boat lay dead for about two hours; that as soon as day broke the engines were started and the *Mount Temple* circled the *Titanic*'s position, the officers insisting that this be done, although the captain had given orders that the boat proceed on its journey. While encircling the *Titanic*'s position we sighted the *Frankfurt* to the northwest of us, the *Birma* to the south, speaking to both of these by wireless, the latter asking if we were in distress; that about 6 o'clock we saw the *Carpathia*, from which we had previously received a message that the *Titanic* had gone down; that about 8.30 the *Carpathia* wirelessed that it had picked up 20 lifeboats and about 720 passengers all told, and that there was no need for the *Mount Temple* to stand by, as the remainder of those on board were drowned.

Dr. F.C. Quitzrau[182]

Captain Smith

On 13 May 1912 the White Star liner *Oceanic* encountered a lone lifeboat bobbing up and down on the calm, sunlit sea, and Captain Smith later sent the following wireless message ashore:

May 13, latitude 39.56 north, longitude 47.01 west, picked up collapsible boat containing three bodies. Committed same to deep. One apparently Thomson Beattie; one sailor; one fireman, both unidentified; also coat with letters in, addressed Richard N. Williams; one cane [care] Duane Williams. A ring also in boat, inscription Edward and Gerda.[183]

Marjorie Ide

Miss Ide was returning to New York from Madrid on board the *Oceanic* when her vessel encountered the drifting lifeboat, and she later wrote the following account of that encounter:

It was only when a wave from the wash of our ship went gently over the whaleboat and the people in it didn't stir that I had my first premonition. We lowered a boat and as the first officer and the ship's doctor climbed in I asked, 'Is it the *Titanic*?'

'Oh, no,' they said, 'every boat was accounted for.'

They rowed over and looked at the lifebelts while our ship's engines and passengers remained in silence. Then our captain's voice from the bridge called out, 'What line is it?' And the answer came, 'White Star, sir.'

In silence they rowed back to the liner for a prayer book and the weighted flags and canvas for a burial at sea.

Standing by my rail and looking down into the boat, I could see the occupants, whose hair had been bleached fair by the salt water and sun. One man was in evening dress with an overcoat with a fur collar. He was lying in the stern, with his legs over one seat and feet under another as if for purchase.

Beside him in the same position lay a stoker, while in the bow in navy-blue jersey and trousers was a young seaman.

Our boat returned to them, and the doctor read the burial service. Then the bodies were lifted and placed in the canvases. But as they took hold of the young seaman's arms to lift him, one long white arm pulled completely out of the blue sleeve.

When lifted aboard to be taken back to New York the lifeboat was proved to be the *Titanic*'s number fifteen. In the bottom of it were women's wedding rings, side-combs, a man's walking stick and a baby's comforter. As our engines restarted, the stewards went around the decks banging gongs, for a long-delayed lunch. But only the children aboard could swallow.[184]

Dr R.S. French

Dr French was one of the *Oceanic* crewmen men who rowed over to the *Titanic*'s derelict lifeboat, and he was later interviewed about his experience:

In the bow of the boat was the body of a fireman. It seemed to have been dragged there. I believe myself that the two survivors at the time of his death tried to throw his body overboard but could not. At the other was the body of a sailor and that of a cabin passenger, dressed for dinner with an overcoat pulled over his evening clothes. We found a tailor's tag inside his coat pocket indicating that he was Thomson Beattie of Chicago.

That there had been other people in the boat was shown by a double ring, which we found wrapped in paper, as though taken by the survivors for the purpose of identification. It was such a thing as a widow might cause to be made of her own and her husband's wedding ring; the two had been fused together. On the inside of half of the ring was the inscription 'Edward to Gerda' and some figures, apparently a [illegible] which we could not make out.

There was also a fur overcoat which seemed from the inner tag of the pocket to have been made for a man named Williams.

The thing which broke my heart, though, was the indication of starvation.

I found that [Third Officer] Withers was quite right when he said it would not be practicable to bring any of the bodies aboard this ship. To bury the poor creatures at sea was the only thing to do.[185]

❖ ❖ ❖

RMS *Olympic*

Loudon Charlton
On 16 April 1912 Mr Charlton of New York, a passenger on the *Olympic*, wrote the following dispatch to the Associated Press:

On board the steamship *Olympic*, At Sea, April 16 – The *Olympic* received news at midnight Sunday that the *Titanic* had struck icebergs. She started immediately for the scene, but resumed her course eastward at 5 o'clock in the morning upon hearing that *Titanic* had sunk at 2 A.M.

The only details known are that six hundred and seventy persons were saved, mostly women and children.

All the crew, except those manning the boats, are believed to have been lost.[186]

❖ ❖ ❖

Earl ____
The following letter was written by an unknown *Olympic* passenger on 15 April 1912:

On board RMS *Olympic*
April 15, 1912

Sweetheart,
Monday morning, and a great morning it is too. The sea has quieted down some, and the sun is shining today. A wireless this morning early

tells us that the *Titanic*, a sister ship to this is in distress off the coast of Newfoundland. We have altered our course since three o'clock this morning and we are racing to her at full speed. Are making twenty-five knots an hour, and expect to reach her about three o'clock this afternoon. This may not interest you dear, but it looks like a little excitement for us fellows here. This will give the White Star Line a black eye, as it is the *Titanic*'s first trip, and you may remember, the *Olympic* was smashed up on her first trip also. Latest wireless messages say that she struck an iceberg and was sinking, the passengers having taken to the lifeboats. You will hear all about this, before you get this, so why go into detail?

I didn't get to finish this morning dearest, but it doesn't matter now. We were too late to be of any assistance to the *Titanic*. We won't be able to get full particulars until we get ashore, but we do know that the ship has gone down and a great many lives lost. The last wireless says that only 750 people were taken off. The crew alone amounted to more than that, and they would be the last to leave. Any amount of our sailors here had fathers and brothers that they will never see again. Believe me, it is a sad thing to see big strong men break down and cry like they are doing here. I'm absolutely sick of the sea now, and when I get back again – finish.

How are you people getting on by this time? Did you get home okay Saturday night? I thought about you Saturday eve, and all day Sunday. Couldn't seem to get you off my mind all day. I couldn't possibly think of anyone better could I?

Well dearest, I will stop for tonight. Will go out on deck and walk a while and then go to bed. Do you love me?? Good night sweetheart,

Yours with love and kisses

Earl[187]

Herbert Haddock

When asked about the allegation that his vessel had sent a wireless message claiming that the *Titanic* was being towed to Halifax, Captain Haddock replied:

The story that I sent the report about the *Virginian* towing the *Titanic* is a flagrant invention. So soon as I heard of the disaster from the *Carpathia*, I dispatched the news by wireless to New York, informing the White Star officials of the number of persons saved and of the foundering of the *Titanic*. That was on Monday afternoon.

The *Olympic* steamed nearly 400 miles before discovering that she would be too late to render any aid.

The *Olympic* first heard the *Titanic*'s call for aid about twenty minutes after the mishap occurred. It came through the steamer *Celtic*, and we never heard direct from Captain Smith. Five hundred miles separated the *Olympic* and the *Titanic*, and utilizing every pound of steam the *Olympic* pressed forward at a pace never before steamed by her – between 24 and 25 knots an hour.[188]

Roy W. Howard

Mr Howard, who was general news manager of the United Press Association, sent the following Marconigram to his organisation on 17 April 1912:

On board the steamship *Olympic*, east bound, by wireless to Cape Race and land lines to New York, April 17 – The bodies of some, at least, of the victims of the lost *Titanic* will be brought, probably to Boston on the Leyland liner *Californian*. Wireless advices reaching us from the scene of the disaster say that some already have been recovered. They will be tenderly cared for, and we understand that they will be taken to port as soon as the *Californian* resumes her interrupted voyage, just when we do not know.

The *Olympic* is proceeding. She could do nothing. The realization of the tragedy, followed by the knowledge that the younger sister of the *Olympic* went to the bottom while this great vessel was rushing to her aid at top speed and hoping against hope that she would get there in time, has stopped all on board.

The captain's seat in the dining salon, his cabin, everything about the *Olympic* is a reminder of Capt. E.J. Smith, first commander of the *Olympic*, who lost his life on the bridge of the sister ship. There is little talking among the passengers. In hushed whispers, passengers and sailors alike discuss the tragedy which is brought squarely home to everyone here.

Since the word was received that the *Titanic* had struck a berg the apprehension has been very great. As soon as Capt. Haddock received the first wireless word of the disaster he turned the *Olympic*'s prow toward the scene and sent her ahead at full speed. There was hope that we might arrive in time. That hope was shattered when we got into wireless reach of the *Carpathia* and the full news of the tragedy was received.

The word of the tragedy shocked and appalled every one. The *Olympic*'s orchestra was hushed; the instruments were put into their cases, and will not be heard again on this voyage, at least.

The helplessness of all was apparent. This was best shown by the heavy contributions made to the fund for the sailors and their dependents, which immediately was raised. After remaining almost stationary most of Tuesday, relaying with melancholy exactitude the list of survivors from the *Carpathia*, Capt. Haddock was ordered to proceed on his voyage. Not until then was the use of the wireless permitted for any other purpose.[189]

When the *Olympic* reached Plymouth, England, Mr Howard wrote the following letter describing how the *Olympic* received word of the *Titanic* disaster:

It was not until the English papers were brought on board here today that the terrible horror of the *Titanic* disaster was realized by the vessel's company. No details of the death list had been furnished here and only the most meager details of the great tragedy had been published on board of the ill-fated *Titanic*'s sister ship.

As far as possible Captain Haddock and the officers of the *Olympic* minimized en route the tragedy because they feared of the effect on the ship's company. But when the British papers were brought on board here and the great black faced lists of the dead were read, the magnitude of the tragedy came home to all of us.

Some of the women passengers on the *Olympic* were on the verge of fainting when they read the names of friends and acquaintances who had gone down.

Money was freely offered for the relief funds. Mortimer L. Schiff, the New York banker, headed the list with a subscription of $500 and within a very few minutes $7,500 had been raised. Lady Ashburton, who was formerly Frances Belmont, the New York Floradora beauty, gave $500 and Madame Imone gave a similar amount.

The first news of the tragedy came to us in the form of rumors while we were at breakfast on Monday. There was no confirmation of verification until noon, when a bulletin was posted in the smoking room and in the woman's lounge. This announced that the *Titanic* had collided with an iceberg but that all of the passengers were safe. I tried to communicate this to land by wireless but the purser said this would be impossible because the wireless was being utilized to its fullest capacity to get news of the tragedy and to communicate with the *Titanic*, which we passengers later learned was even then at the bottom of the sea.

Later the purser offered to accept a bulletin to send to the United Press. He carefully edited the first message but later returned it saying he could not send it. Finally, however, he did send through one message.

Immediately after dinner on Monday night, Captain Haddock caused to be posted bulletins announcing that the *Titanic* had been totally destroyed and that all of her company had gone to the bottom with the exception of 675, who were then on the *Carpathia*.

Efforts to send word to land by the wireless from then on proved to be futile. It was stated that the wireless was in constant use for line business.

There was a rumor among the stewards that the officers of the *Olympic* knew that the *Titanic* had sunk several hours before they posted the news but withheld it in the hope that there might be an error. They were almost unable themselves, to credit the dreadful news.

The holding up of the wireless messages I believe was more due to excitement than to any desire on the part of the *Olympic*'s officers to establish a censorship.[190]

B.M. Joseph

On 15 April 1912, Mr Joseph wrote the following letter to *Titanic* passenger Washington Dodge:

> On board RMS *Olympic*
> At Sea April 15 – 12
> Dr. Washington Dodge:
>
> Dear Sir,
>   I want to congratulate you, Mrs. Dodge & your child on your escape from the awful disaster. We on the sister ship have been rushing to your aid all day, but alas to no effect. We have absolutely no news of the disaster except a partial list of survivors among whom I was so happy to see your name.
>   Hoping that your family suffers no ill effects I remain
>   Yours truly,
>   B.M. Joseph, with Raphael, Weill & Co.[191]

E.J. Moore

When asked if the *Olympic* held back news of the *Titanic*'s sinking, Mr Moore, who was the *Olympic*'s senior wireless operator, made the following statement about the time he had first received definite news that the *Titanic* had gone down:

> About 3:30 on Monday afternoon, and within a very few minutes Captain Haddock wrote messages conveying the information both to New York and Liverpool.
>   I at once cleared both messages to Cape Race, and, speaking from memory, it was certainly not after 4 p.m. when Cape Race had the news. What delay occurred in transmitting the message by the land lines to New York, if any, I cannot say.

Regarding the story that the *Titanic* had called the *Frankfurt*'s wireless operator a fool and refused to communicate with him, Moore said:

[The *Frankfurt*'s operator] probably spoke little or no English, and when Phillips picked up the *Carpathia* he did exactly what any of us would do under similar circumstances, refused to waste valuable time in arguing. Anyhow, the *Frankfurt*'s operator could and should have listened to the conversation between the *Titanic* and the *Carpathia*, which was equally applicable to him, and from the fact that the *Frankfurt* eventually reached the scene of the disaster he evidently did.[192]

Mme Simone

Mme Simone, an actress, described how a bulletin was posted on board the *Olympic* saying that the *Titanic* had met with a slight accident and that her passengers would be taken on board the *Olympic*. Miss Simone said that a festive air pervaded the *Olympic* at the news of this planned activity, and she continued:

The *Olympic* turned and went toward a point where the *Titanic* should have been. It was a joyous evening, the whole ship being lit up and all ten decks full of people. The next morning we learned by a notice posted up that our course toward Europe had been resumed and that the *Titanic* had foundered, only a few hundred persons escaping. It seemed as if one single cry went up from the whole ship. I heard shrieks and sobs all around me. A majority of the passengers had friends or relatives on the *Titanic*, and the stewardesses had husbands or sisters working there. The people met each other silently and with reddened eyes and dared not speak to each other or ask for news.[193]

Unknown Correspondent

After the *Olympic* arrived in England, an unnamed correspondent wrote the following account:

Captain Haddock of the *Olympic* has just made to me the following important statement concerning the early reports circulated on Monday that the *Titanic*'s passengers were all safe and that the vessel was being towed toward Halifax:

'On the passage from Cherbourg to Southampton I received a letter from two newspaper correspondents requesting me to explain the telegram which has appeared in the newspapers that "all the *Titanic* passengers are safe" and that "the *Titanic* is proceeding slowly toward Halifax under her own steam", which telegram caused a drop from 60 guineas to 20 guineas in the reinsurance at Lloyd's on Monday afternoon. It was suggested that the telegram emanated from the ship, because it came through Reuter's. They asked whether that message was sent from the ship, and if so how it came to be sent if it was not true. The message that came to the *Olympic* was from one of our old passengers – a lady in New York. It was this: "Are all *Titanic* passengers safe" or "saved?" The lady had friends of hers on the *Titanic*. That message was received on Monday at about 10:20 or 10:27 New York mean time, which is equal to 3:20 or 3:27 Greenwich time. At another period of the day – I think it was earlier – the *Olympic* was in communication with the ship *Asian*, from which I tried to get information about the *Titanic*. She could give me very little indeed, but among the words used were that she was towing an oil tank steamer to Halifax.

'I have sent the following letter to my owners in Liverpool:

"I, in the presence of our Marconi operators, have denied that such a message was received or sent from this ship. The only solution I can offer for the Reuter message is the enclosed Marconigram, which may have been tapped in transmission and the 'are' missed, the remaining words, '*Titanic* making slowly for Halifax' being suggested by the *Asian* message, a copy of which is already in your possession. The message is very probably from a constant White Star traveler, and I on the receipt of the message made the same mistake. I left out 'are' and telephoned the inquiry office (that is the purser's office) on the ship to put up a notice reading 'All *Titanic* passengers safe'. Nothing more was added. We have been most carefully through every message from the ship. No copy of my error, plain or in code, was sent from this ship."

H.J. Haddock, Master'

I spent this morning on board the *Olympic*, the *Titanic*'s sister ship. She has had a sad home-coming. There is hardly anyone in her crew who has not lost a friend or a relation, and today scores of firemen and engineers have gone back to bereaved homes. An *Olympic* stoker told me that he has lost a brother as well as four mates, with whom he has gone to sea scores of times, but the fact is that the crews of all liners plying from Southampton are bound together by friendship or still nearer ties. The blow is a domestic one here in a way impossible among the scattered and international community of passengers. It was not until the *Olympic* reached Plymouth on Saturday that members of the crew got the list of the saved, so that since Monday many men were in as painful a doubt as the widows in Southampton. The *Olympic* was berthed at two o'clock this morning, and most of the crew rushed home at once, eager to talk over the disaster in their homes. When I arrived a thin stream of passengers were entraining for London, and there was a group of Italian emigrants looking curiously desolate in a sort of pen waiting to be told where to go. I found the mighty ship almost deserted by officers and passengers. I learned that the *Olympic*'s share in the tragic events of the week was much as follows: At midnight on Sunday, or thereabouts, her wireless operator deciphered the frantic call for help from the *Titanic*. At once she put about and headed for the place. Her stokers heard what had happened and worked like niggers. She went ahead north-west at 23 knots an hour, and then, some time on Monday evening, she heard from the *Carpathia* that all the boats and all the possible survivors had been picked up. Realizing that no more could be done, the *Olympic* returned to her proper course, and she has arrived here 24 hours late.

'When we picked up the *Titanic*'s message,' Captain Haddock told me, 'we were about 505 miles away. We steamed toward her for fourteen hours before we picked up the *Carpathia*'s signals. When we heard from her we knew there was nothing we could do, and we resumed our course. A week before the *Titanic* sank the *Olympic* passed over the very spot, or a few miles north of it, in bright daylight. We never saw a particle of ice of any description, and from the bridge of the *Olympic* we could see about twenty miles on either side. The observations in that locality were perfect. There was no sign of ice. That is the tragedy of the thing. The field ice must have been traveling south far more rapidly than on any occasion I can remember.'

The *Olympic*'s passengers did not hear of the disaster until the Monday. A collection was made for the survivors, to which all the firemen contributed a day's pay. The first-class passengers collected £700. Altogether £1,500 was raised. The ship was a place of mourning above and below decks. There was no music on board for the rest of the trip.

As I made a tour of this huge, empty hotel I found on the top deck the men busy hauling fresh collapsible boats on board. The immediate effect of the sinking of the *Titanic* is that the *Olympic* will in future carry about forty extra collapsible boats and rafts. She made her last voyage with about the same equipment as the *Titanic* – namely sixteen lifeboats and four rafts. It is evident that no more risks are going to be run, whatever the Board of Trade ordains. The *Olympic* is a replica of the *Titanic* on a very slightly reduced scale. I gained a sharp impression of what must have happened in these huge gilded saloons and lordly corridors, where everything is done to make you forget you are not in the Metropole or the Cecil in London. It is an effort to remember you are on a ship at all. You do not see the water through the stained-glass windows, Looking over from the top deck, where the boats were lowered that dreadful night, is like peering over the edge of Dover cliffs. The coaling barges below are dwarfed to toy boats. Her neighbors in the harbor, the *Majestic* and the *Philadelphia*, ships of 15,000 tons or thereabouts, seem no bigger than the Isle of Wight paddle-steamers. From here you look down on Southampton as from a hill. The *Olympic* is the last word in luxury and size. But on this glorious morning one paced the long saloons in melancholy, not in admiration.[194]

On the following day the same unnamed correspondent wrote the following:

As I wirelessed you on board the *Olympic* in the English Channel last night, everything points to the probability that the wireless messages had been tapped in transit in mid-Atlantic by amateur, unskilled operators at some unknown port and been jumbled or wrongly read by them, [and] were responsible for the false reports of the *Titanic*'s safety which were circulated throughout the world after the *Titanic* had gone down.

Thus a question received on board the *Olympic*, 'Are *Titanic* passengers safe?' was transmitted into an affirmative statement, 'All *Titanic* passengers safe'. To this was added just a fragment from a long message of the captain of the steamship *Asian* to the *Olympic*, wherein he said: 'Towing oil tanks to Halifax'. The confusion of the words 'oil tanks' from this message and the combination of the latter would make the statement 'All *Titanic*'s passengers safe; towing to Halifax'.

I joined the *Olympic* on Saturday when she arrived outside Plymouth harbor and have been a passenger on her in her journey across the channel and back to Southampton, where early this morning the last of her ship's company, most of them in black for lost friends, are on their way to London.

The *Olympic* with her powerful Marconi apparatus was the ocean clearing house for messages relating to the *Titanic* disaster from the moment when the first midnight call for help flashed across the seas. It was not until breakfast on Monday morning that the rumor first spread among the passengers of the *Olympic* that a major disaster had befallen the *Titanic*. Although Captain Haddock had got the message asking for aid and had instantly altered the ship's course and was making at the *Olympic*'s highest speed for the ice floe where the *Titanic* was shattered and sinking, the saloon passengers taking their early promenade on the deck had seen the lifeboats being uncovered and made ready with ropes coiled, so that not an instant's time would be lost if they should sight the survivors in time. Only the officers knew that five hundred miles separated the *Olympic* from her stricken sister ship, and soon at a speed of 24 knots an hour, the *Olympic* could scarcely arrive in time if the hurt was as urgent as they had heard.

Beds had been prepared by the stewards and stewardesses and a private order went around that the fresh water should be sparingly used in order to provide for the emergency in case the *Titanic*'s passengers and crew were reached in time to be brought on board alive. At 11 o'clock on that Monday morning a notice in red chalk was on the bulletin board. It was a message similar to that which later raised such false hopes in the minds of thousands who were waiting for news in New York and London. It was the first message that the *Olympic* had, although since dawn the liner had thrilled with rumors of ominous tidings. The message as posted read: 'New York reports all *Titanic* passengers safe'.

The welcome news snapped the tension on the *Olympic*, but still the boat continued its race to the *Titanic* with every furnace going and fifty extra volunteer stokers working below.

About four hours later, without any further official message being given out, the *Olympic*'s passengers noticed that the giant steamship was making a swerve while still more than 100 miles from the scene of the disaster and was turning her head homeward on the old course. Still no further alarm was felt, for it was generally believed that the shipwrecked passengers and crew had all been picked up by other vessels and that the *Olympic* had only turned away because help was not needed.

This last surmise was true, but in its more tragic sense, for Captain Haddock had even then received this terrible news from the *Carpathia*: 'Reached *Titanic* position daybreak, but found boats and wreckage only'.

She had also reported to the *Olympic* that the *Titanic* had foundered at about 2:20 a.m. This was the message which added that all the *Titanic*'s boats were accounted for and that about 675 people had been saved from the crew and passengers, the latter nearly all women and children. This notice, the first official admission of the full extent of the wreck, was posted on the *Olympic* board at about 6 p.m.

On the instant a hush fell upon the ship with sorrow, which was all the sharper and more poignant because it had followed a period of seven hours of joy and relief among those who did not share the tragic secret. As indicated in my Marconigram yesterday, Captain Haddock was for a long time reluctant to make any statement in regard to the matter.

In conjunction with a correspondent of the *London Daily Express*, H. Leatherdal, who was the only other newspaper correspondent aboard, I wrote to Captain Haddock after various other messages had proved unavailing, a letter in which we pointed out that the 'All *Titanic* passengers safe' message had caused a drop in the *Titanic*'s reinsurance at Lloyd's from 60 guineas to twenty guineas an asking whether you (Haddock) ever received a message and, if so, if you know whence it came?

Captain Haddock gave us his assurance that no such message was ever sent or received by the *Olympic* and the Marconi operators, Messrs Bagot and Moore, corroborated this.[195]

SS *Ottawa*

Thomas Cook

On 6 June 1912 Third Officer Cook wrote the following letter to the Chief of the US Weather Bureau:

> June 6, 1912
> Chief, U.S. Weather Bureau,
> Washington, D.C. U.S.A.
>
> Sir:
> In latitude 44.16 North & Longitude 38.21 West we picked up the body of a man wearing a lifebelt. We put our boat out & picked him up, & searched his clothes & found a wallet bearing the initials W.T.K. & evidently a passenger of the *Titanic*, but not sure. It contained a love letter & a business card, 'Apartments' in Margate, Kent. The man was buried with ceremony of the Church of England. The body was much decomposed especially the hands & face. There was no name in the lifebelts, as it had been washed off.
> We have since arriving ascertained that his name is W.T. Kerley & was an assistant steward on the *Titanic*. The finding of the body was True North 74 West Distance 543 mls from *Titanic* position.
> Thomas Cook
> 3rd Officer[196]

SS *Parisian*

Captain W. Hains

On 16 April the *Parisian*'s Captain Hains sent the following message to Halifax:

> I have no survivors of the *Titanic* on board and no official information as to the fate of the ship. Expect to reach Halifax early tomorrow morning.[197]

After arriving in Halifax, Captain Hains told reporters that the *Parisian*, *Californian* and *Mesaba* had all been trying to reach the stranded oil tanker *Deutschland*:

None of us got her, though, for the prize fell to the *Asian*, coming from the west. We were all from the east. The tow is following us into the harbor and will be here in a couple of hours.

The icebergs were very thick. The *Carpathia* passed us Sunday night at 9 o'clock. We were both avoiding the bergs, which were there in hundreds. We exchanged notes on the ice and courses were slightly altered in accordance with information given and received.

It was clear where we were, but 150 miles gives opportunity for essential difference in weather conditions. It might be thick a comparatively short distance from us, though we had it clear.

The ships nearest to the *Titanic* were the *Californian* and the *Carpathia*, probably not more than fifty miles off, though I can't speak as to distances, for I have not the means of doing so exactly.

It was at 4 o'clock on Monday morning, at the same time that we heard the *Asian* had picked up the *Deutschland*, that we learned the *Titanic* had gone down.[198]

Captain Hains made another statement to reporters:

We never received a call for assistance from the *Titanic*. We never knew that anything had happened to her until after 4 o'clock Monday morning. We sent her a wireless message at 10:30 o'clock Sunday night, asking to have it relayed to Cape Race for us, as we wished to notify the Allan agents where we were.

That message was received, for our operator, D.D. Sutherland, received the notification that it would be sent along. We don't know yet whether it was sent or not from the *Titanic*.

The reason that we did not receive any call for assistance from the *Titanic* is due to the fact that our Marconi man, Mr. Sutherland, turned in just after he had sent our message to the White Star liner. That shut out all hope of help from us, apparently.

We were ahead of the *Titanic* and also to the south of her about 150 miles. Of course, she was coming along at a clip that put ours somewhat to shame, for I have no doubt that she was logging about 19 miles to our 13. It was due to the fact that she was so far north of us that we wired her to relay a message to Cape Race, as that point was too far away for our wireless.

So that possibly when she met with her mishap she was rapidly overhauling us. There could be no comparisons of weather that far apart, but it was clear for us. However, sometimes it is clear at one spot and not at another within ten miles.

The *Carpathia* and our boat swapped courses on the assumption, perhaps, that he thought the course I had followed would be safe for him and the course he had threaded would be clear for me. We began to feel the approach of the ice Sunday and so we swung off somewhat about 9 o'clock that night to the southwest to take the *Carpathia*'s course.[199]

Captain Hains made yet another statement to reporters:

There is no question that the course used at this time of the year was never so invaded by ice in the knowledge of even the most experienced seamen. It has been extraordinary. The truth is that northeasterly gales began very early last winter and were almost continuous. The result has been to drive the ice hundreds of miles further south than is usual. Moreover, in the swift drive of the great current from the north bergs shot off the turn that it takes off the Breton coast as mud might fly from a wheel, and these bergs by the score got into a course usually considered free of such dangerous impediments at this season of the year.[200]

Donald Sutherland

After arriving in Halifax, Marconi operator Sutherland spoke with reporters:

The night was so clear that the *Parisian*'s lookout several times mistook stars on the horizon for ships' lights. You have seen beautifully clear winter nights when you went skating and it seemed just like day. It was just such a night. You could have played a game of football.

On Sunday, the 14th, I was at my instrument until 10 o'clock at night. The *Mesaba* of the Atlantic Transport Line was ahead of us. The *Californian* was about fifty miles in our rear and the *Titanic* was following the *Californian* at a distance, I judge, of 75 to 100 miles. The *Mesaba* was passing me warning messages about the unusual icy condition of the course, and warned me of the presence of big bergs. I passed the information to the *Californian*. I sent this message repeatedly: 'Running into ice – very thick – and big bergs'.

I assume, although I do not know, for I did not talk directly to the *Titanic*, that the *Californian* passed to the *Titanic* the messages I had sent and which I had myself previously received from the *Mesaba*.

I left my instrument at exactly 10 o'clock. I was ordered to do so by Captain Hains because I had been up many hours in an effort to get a ship to go to the aid of the tank steamer *Deutschland*, which I had heard was in distress. The *Deutschland* had no wireless, so I could not get into direct communication with her, but our information was that she was pretty far to the south, and Captain Hains was heading in that direction as fast as he could go.

He wanted me to get on the wireless at 4 o'clock next morning and do what I could with the wireless to discover if possible what news was crossing the sea regarding the *Deutschland*. But next morning, when we were fifty miles further south of our course than the *Parisian* had ever gone before, our route being between Glasgow and Boston, with Halifax as a port of call, and we were on our way to Halifax, but of course had to dig southward to avoid the ice line, I got a wireless from the *Asian* stating that she had picked up the *Deutschland*, and so we came on to Halifax.

I received a query on the night of the disaster from Captain Haddock of the *Olympic*, the *Titanic*'s sister ship, traveling east, as to the conditions of the ice, and I sent him the same message that I had relayed from the *Mesaba* to the *Californian* and that, of course, I believe was as promptly relayed to the *Titanic*: 'Running into ice – very thick – and big bergs'.

I want to add that I have been traveling on this course for seven years, and there has never been in my experience such a condition of the ice as we found on this voyage.

The floes have come extraordinarily early and have spread way out of the usual run of what is known as the ice belt.

Certainly the *Titanic* when struck was far south of what the chart defines as the 'ice line'. She was fully 75 to 100 miles south of it.

The first news of the disaster I got about 10 o'clock on Monday morning from the *Carpathia*.

It was suggested to Sutherland that an iceberg on a clear night might create its own humidity and an accompanying haze that would endanger mariners, but he declared that this notion was absurd:

Why, on a clear night you can see a berg away off by its glitter. They glisten like an illuminated glass palace.

Operator Sutherland was a friend of Jack Phillips, the *Titanic*'s chief wireless operator:

Jack and I knew each other for years. He was born in Godalming, Surrey, England. He was only about thirty-six years old and wasn't married. It was a big post for so young a man – chief operator on the biggest ship in the world. I can't understand it – he must have got my messages, for he was the kind of a man that never failed in his job and would certainly be there at a time when the vessel was in danger – nearing ice under unusual conditions.[201]

SS PORTLAND

The steamship *Portland*, which was carrying a shipment of timber from Mobile to Grimsby, passed the *Titanic* on Sunday afternoon but did not speak to her. The *Portland* had passed a large number of icebergs early on Saturday and continued to do so until Monday. Her crewmen did not learn of the *Titanic* disaster until their arrival at Grimsby.[202]

SS PRINZESS IRENE

The North German Lloyd liner *Prinzess Irene*, from Genoa, reached her pier in Hoboken at 11 o'clock on the night of 25 April and reported that on the previous Wednesday she had intercepted a wireless message between two ships, the names of which were not learned, to the effect that one of them, in passing fifty miles from the scene of the *Titanic* disaster, had sighted an iceberg on which were the bodies of more than a dozen men.

All wore lifebelts and the bodies were huddled in groups at the base of the berg. It was the opinion of officers of the ship sighting the gruesome scene that the men had climbed on the mass of ice, perhaps within an hour of the foundering of the *Titanic*, and had frozen to death as they were swept to the southward. The fact that the bodies were huddled in groups led the captain of the ship to suppose the men gathered close to keep warm. No attempt was made to take off the bodies.

The day following the sinking of the *Titanic* the *Prinzess Irene* picked up the wireless message that the *Titanic* was being 'towed to Halifax'. It was not till the next night that the news of the tragedy was learned aboard the North German Lloyd liner. There was a terrific storm at the time, and the *Prinzess Irene* was slowed down to four knots. It was while the storm was at its height that the wireless picked up the message about the disaster from an unidentified ship.[203]

William Warner
After the *Prinzess Irene* reached Hoboken, passenger William Warner spoke with reporters:

> I have crossed the ocean thirty-eight times but cannot recall a voyage where the passengers were as nervous and uncomfortable as they were after hearing of the *Titanic* disaster. The first word we received was that the

Titanic had struck an iceberg but was not damaged badly and was proceeding under her own steam to Halifax. That was last week. We did not hear anything more until last Monday. There was consternation among the passengers when they heard the awful details and learned that so many lives were lost.

We had fearful weather Monday night and heavy seas. At least three-fourths of the passengers remained awake during the night and few undressed. The dining saloon was crowded during the whole of the night and men with pale faces gathered in the smoking room and tried to comfort one another. I did not consider the sea extremely dangerous, but it was difficult to assure the passengers that all was well. Women cried and became hysterical and men spoke to one another in broken voices. Truly it was a night of terror.[204]

❖   ❖   ❖

SS *Rappahannock*

Chief Officer Smith

Late on the night of Saturday, 13 April the Furness liner *Rappahannock*, bound from Halifax to London, came out of a heavy rain squall and found herself abeam of the *Titanic*. The big liner's lights were burning brightly, and she sounded her deep whistle, which caused the *Rappahannock* to alter her course slightly to give her more room. Chief Officer Smith admired the sight of the *Titanic*:

> She was traveling at about twenty-one knots and soon disappeared into the darkness. We had come through the icefield which the *Titanic* struck later on. It stretched some hundred miles northward. It had come this far south a month before the usual time, and we could not escape it, but ran into it, suffering considerable damage. Our rudder was twisted and our bows dented, and other injuries were inflicted on us by the ice.
>
> I saw some packs of a thousand square feet in area, and the ice was bunched together and heaped up in some cases. This is in all probability the pack which the *Titanic* struck. The ice was three or four feet above the surface of the sea and twenty-odd feet thick.
>
> It is astonishing to me that Captain Smith should have struck the pack if he sighted it in time. Of course, he may have taken it to be slob ice which is soft, and through which it would be safe to run even at twenty-one knots: but the ice we encountered was not slob ice, and when we sighted it we went dead slow. The *Titanic*, if she scraped one of those ice packs, would have had the bottom practically ripped out of her going at the speed he was.

What I cannot understand, and what most seafaring men wonder at, is why it should have been necessary for the *Titanic* on a clear night to strike an ice pack at all. I may say that we did not see any icebergs during the voyage.[205]

❖ ❖ ❖

SS *SARDINIAN*

Robert McKillop
The Allan liner *Sardinian* responded to the *Mackay-Bennett*'s request to give her canvas and burlap with which to cover the bodies of recovered *Titanic* victims. Captain McKillop later described the scene for a St John reporter:

> We saw a lot of wreckage such as cabinet furniture, including chairs, writing desks, camp stools etc. We also passed close by two bodies, but we made no attempt to get them as the *Mackay-Bennett* was close by. There was one on either side of us about thirty or forty feet away. One was apparently that of a lady wearing a short seal sack, but I could not tell what the other was, whether male or female.[206]

❖ ❖ ❖

RMS *SISMIC*

William Hopper
After sailing from England to Portland, Maine, William Hopper spoke to reporters on behalf of himself and his friend Claude Kent, both of whom had originally booked their passages on the *Titanic*:

> We decided to come on the *Sismic*. It was just a chance, as I cannot tell you why we concluded to change our passage. It was a very fortunate thing for us, I can assure you.
>
> We sailed a day ahead of the *Titanic*, but she passed us. We received word that the ship was sinking, but the captain did not tell the passengers anything about it as he was afraid it might cause a panic. Later we got a message that the vessel had gone down and we were told about the accident. Then we were warned about the icefields. On Wednesday we struck them, and old sailors told us they had never seen anything like them. We barely crawled through them. Some of the bergs were fully 200 feet high. They were all around us. Some of us were very anxious, but the officers of the *Sismic* were very careful and we got through without trouble. We saw

some of the *Titanic* wreckage, pieces of planking and the like, but we found no bodies. In all probability the ice carried them away from us.

My cousin William Allen took passage on the *Titanic*. We had our passage booked, but we decided to come a day earlier and sail on the *Sismic*. My cousin did not change his passage and was lost.[207]

❖ ❖ ❖

UNKNOWN PASSENGER VESSEL

Unknown Correspondent

During a voyage to Halifax, an unknown passenger kept a journal describing his ship's encounter with ice in the days preceding the *Titanic* disaster:

Thursday, April 11th: ... but freezing hard. Stayed on deck till midnight.

Friday, April 12th: On deck at 4:30 a.m. Wonderful sight! As far as one could see nothing but thick ice, fringed with large icebergs; and then to see the sun rising up over it all! I wouldn't have missed the sight for worlds. Four other boats were also in sight – a huge Hamburg American, the *President Lincoln*, etc. They had all laid to for the night. We turned tail and started to steam East again, and then took a southerly course for 70 miles. It took us five hours to clear the pack, so it gives one a good idea of the tremendous area of the ice. We were looking for it all yesterday afternoon, as the temperature had dropped to freezing point. We can't reach Halifax, N.S. now till Sunday. There are on board 47 first class passengers, 461 second, and 1,239 third: total, 1,747. We did only 153 miles in the last 24 hours – rather a drop from 350. Still, it is not too bad.

Sunday, April 14th: Arrived at Halifax, N.S. at 3 a.m. Anchored in mid-stream and came alongside at 8 a.m. Left Halifax in a special train at 5 p.m., and hope to reach Montreal in about 24 hours.[208]

❖ ❖ ❖

SS *VIRGINIAN*

George Clark

During the *Virginian*'s voyage to Liverpool, passenger George Clark made the following journal entry on 15 April:

All went well until one o'clock, when we received a wireless stating that a steamer, the biggest afloat, had struck an iceberg, so we wheeled to the south to rescue the party. The ship had over 2,000 on board. At about six o'clock the stewards told us to make all the room possible for the rescued, and we made the beds and prepared for them. They got the lifeboats ready, and life-ropes, and the gangways, but another wireless came to say that the ship had gone down with over 2,000 souls and that another ship, the *Carpathia*, had turned and rescued all who were in the lifeboats, so we turned east again but came across some large icebergs. Then when we got closer we discovered it was a large icefield covered with icebergs, so we had to turn around for 50 or 60 miles to get round the icefield. We then came to the south end of it, and are now taking an eastern direction again. The sailors are now taking in the gangways from the side and taking in the lifeboats also. As I look now I can see icefields from the west horizon to the east covered with large icebergs, some of which are most beautiful as the sun strikes them.

Clark also stated that the water in the vicinity of the disaster was tested and that people on board his ship estimated that a person could not live in the 32 degree water for more than an hour.[209]

J.T. Gambell

Upon arriving in Liverpool, the *Virginian*'s Captain Gambell prepared the following report on the wireless messages he received after the *Titanic* struck the iceberg:

Leaving Halifax at 3:51 p.m. on the 13th inst., I came south of Sable Island and steered a course to cross long. 50 deg. West in lat. 43.30 North. Wind light N.W. and fine weather. At 12:40 a.m. (ship's time) on the 15th inst. I received the following message by wireless from Cape Race: – '*Titanic* struck iceberg. Wants immediate assistance. Her position 41.46 North and 50.14 West'. My position then was 43.27 North, 53.37 West. The *Titanic* bore from me South 55 ½, East true – distance 178 miles. I at once altered my course to go to her assistance, and advised Cape Race and Messrs. H. and A. Allan, Montreal, to that effect.

At 1:20 a.m. I got a further message from Cape Race which read: – '*Titanic* reports ship sinking and putting women and children in boats. *Olympic* making all speed towards *Titanic*, but much further off than *Virginian*. Her position lat. 40.32 North, long. 61.13 West'. At 1:57 a.m. (ship's time) *Titanic* signals ceased abruptly as if power suddenly cut off. At 3:45 a.m. I was in touch by wireless with the Russian steamer *Birma* and gave her the *Titanic*'s position. She was then 55 miles from the *Titanic* and going to her assistance. At 5:45 a.m. I was in communication with

the *Californian*, the Leyland liner. He was 17 miles north of the *Titanic* and had not heard anything of the disaster. I Marconied her as follows:–
'*Titanic* struck iceberg. Wants assistance urgently. Ship sinking. Passengers in boats. Position lat. 41.46, long. 50.14'. Shortly after this I was in communication with the *Carpathia*, *Frankfurt* and *Baltic*, all going to the *Titanic*. At 6:10 a.m. I Marconied *Californian*: – 'Kindly let me know condition of affairs when you get to *Titanic*'. He at once replied, 'Can now see *Carpathia* taking passengers on board from small boats. *Titanic* foundered about 2 a.m.' At 10 a.m. I received the following message from the *Carpathia*: – 'Turn back. Everything O.K. We have 800 on board. Return to your northern track.'

At the same time the *Carpathia* sent the following message to the *Baltic*: – 'Am leaving here with all on board, about 800, chiefly third class and a lot of stewards. Proceed on your voyage to Liverpool. We proceeding to Halifax or New York under full steam.' I then altered my course to the eastward and proceeded on my voyage. In addition to the above message I learned from messages passing between the *Carpathia* and *Olympic* that all the *Titanic*'s boats had been accounted for, and a careful search made for survivors among the wreckage and ice floes. I later learned that the *Californian* was going to remain in the vicinity for some time, and that the *Carpathia* had left for New York with 675 survivors on board. At 11 a.m. I sighted a field of ice and bergs to the north-east. At 11:20 a.m. in latitude 42.3 and longitude 50.20 I came up with a large field of heavy, close-packed ice, with numerous bergs stretching north and south as far as could be seen. I coasted round this to the south and south-west, and rounded the southern edge in latitude 41.20, longitude 50.02, and steering east true. Finally cleared the ice in latitude 41.20, longitude 49.50, the ice from that point trending away to the north-east. At 1 p.m. I saw a steamer to the eastward, presumably the *Californian*, at the position of the wreck, but the icefield was between us and too heavy to take my ship through without incurring great risk of damage.

Gambell was asked how close he came to the place where the *Titanic* went down:

I passed it at a distance of about six or seven miles. I had to go round the icefield. There was a close-packed field of ice between me and the *Titanic*'s position. There was no boat or wreckage to be seen.[210]

NOTES

CHAPTER 1 – *CARPATHIA* PASSENGER AND CREW LETTERS

1   *St Louis Times*, 18 April 1912.
2   *Brooklyn Daily Eagle*, 19 April 1912.
3   Courtesy of the Straus Historical Society, Inc.
4   *New York Herald* and *St Louis Republic*, 19 April 1912.
5   *New York Tribune*, 18 April 1912. Note: Blackmarr's own copy of the message contains his notation about the bribe.
6   *Chicago Daily Tribune*, 20 April 1912.
7   Transcription courtesy of Jim Harper.
8   Transcription courtesy of Jim Harper.
9   *New York Herald*, 19 April 1912.
10   *Providence Evening News*, 19 April 1912.
11   Courtesy of the *Providence Evening Journal*, 18 April 1937.
12   *Brown Alumni Monthly*, April 1913.
13   *The Outlook*, 27 April 1912.
14   Courtesy of the *Titanic* Historical Society and *Titanic* Museum.
15   *Rochester Democrat & Chronicle*, 21 April 1912.
16   *New York Times*, 19 April 1912.
17   Courtesy of Craig Sopin.
18   *Chicago Record Herald*, 23 April 1912.
19   *New York Herald*, 19 April 1912.
20   Original letter is owned by Robert Dalby and was published in the April 2000 issue of *Antiques and Collecting Magazine*.
21   *Evanston (Ill) Index*, 4 May 1912.
22   *Evanston Index*, 4 May 1912.
23   *Chicago Record Herald*, 23 April 1912.
24   *Fond du Lac Daily Reporter*, 19 April 1912.
25   *Fond du Lac Daily Register*, 20 April 1912.
26   *Fond du Lac Daily Reporter*, 20 April 1912.
27   Courtesy of the *Titanic* Historical Society and *Titanic* Museum.
28   Courtesy of Robert M. Barbour, Beverly Anne Mitchell and Helen L. Ryder.
29   *New York World*, 19 April 1912.
30   *St Louis Post-Dispatch*.
31   Courtesy of the Society of Professional Journalists.
32   Courtesy of the *Titanic* Historical Society and *Titanic* Museum.
33   *Pittsburg Press*, 21 April 1912.
34   *Pittsburg Press*, 21 April 1912.

35   *New York American*, 19 April 1912.
36   *St Louis Globe Democrat*, 20 April 1912.
37   Courtesy of Kalman Tanito.
38   *Magyarorszag* (1980), translation courtesy of Kalman Tanito.
39   Courtesy of the *Titanic* Historical Society and *Titanic* Museum.
40   Original letter is owned by the Portsmouth Athenaeum.
41   Gordon Gardiner, *Champion of the Kingdom: The Story of Philip Mauro*, courtesy of Virginia Birt Baker.
42   Gordon Gardiner, *Champion of the Kingdom: The Story of Philip Mauro*, courtesy of Virginia Birt Baker.
43   Gordon Gardiner, *Champion of the Kingdom: The Story of Philip Mauro*, courtesy of Virginia Birt Baker.
44   *Fond du Lac Daily Reporter*, 19 April 1912.
45   *Fond du Lac Daily Reporter*, 19 April 1912.
46   *Fond du Lac Daily Reporter*, 20 April 1912.
47   *Fond du Lac Daily Commonwealth*, 22 April 1912.
48   *Fond Du Lac Daily Commonwealth*, 22 April 1912.
49   *Fond du Lac Daily Reporter*, 20 April 1912.
50   North Adams Transcript, 20 April 1912, courtesy of Craig Stringer.
51   Courtesy of the *Titanic* Historical Society and *Titanic* Museum.
52   *New York World*, 20 April 1912.
53   William H. Taft papers, reel 440.
54   William H. Taft papers, reel 440. A slightly altered version of the letter was published in the *New York Times*, 20 April 1912.
55   William H. Taft papers, reel 440.
56   *Scribner's Magazine*, March 1913.
57   Courtesy of the *Louisville Courier-Journal*.
58   *Belfast Newsletter*, 6 May 1912.
59   Courtesy of Les St Clair.
60   *Baltimore Sun*, 22 April 1912.
61   *Baltimore Sun*, 6 August 1972.
62   Courtesy of the *Louisville Courier-Journal*.
63   *Washington Post*, 28 April 1912.
64   *Washington Post*, 28 April 1912.
65   Courtesy of the *Titanic* Historical Society and *Titanic* Museum.
66   Courtesy of the *Titanic* Historical Society and *Titanic* Museum.
67   *New York Sun*, 19 April 1912.

CHAPTER 2 – *CARPATHIA* PASSENGER AND CREW INTERVIEWS

68   *Baltimore Sun*, 20 April 1912.
69   *New York Times*, 19 April 1912.
70   *Daily Sketch*, 6 May 1912.
71   *New York Herald*, 19 April 1912.
72   *New York Evening World*, 19 April 1912.
73   *Los Angeles Times*, 26 April 1912.
74   Courtesy of *The Argus* (Melbourne), 16 April 1949.
75   Unknown Milwaukee newspaper, 17 April 1913.
76   Jay Mowbray, *The Sinking of the* Titanic.
77   *Scranton Times*, 20 April 1912.
78   Courtesy of the *Daily Record*, 21 February 1977.

79   Courtesy of the *Providence Evening Journal*, 18 April 1937.
80   *Providence Evening Bulletin*, 19 April 1912.
81   *New York Herald*, 19 April 1912.
82   Jay Mowbray, *The Sinking of the* Titanic.
83   *Edmonton Bulletin*, 20 April 1912.
84   *Brooklyn Daily Eagle*, 19 April 1912.
85   *New York Evening World*, 19 April 1912.
86   *Boston Herald*, 20 April 1912.
87   *Portland Evening Express & Daily Advertiser*, 23 April 1912.
88   *Mt Vernon Daily Argus*, 19 April 1912.
89   *Baltimore Sun*, 20 April 1912.
90   *Buffalo Morning Express*, 21 April 1912.
91   *Niagara Falls Gazette*, 20 April 1912.
92   *New York American*, 20 April 1912.
93   *Boston Globe*, 20 April 1912.
94   *Albany Journal*, 19 April 1912.
95   *Albany Times-Union*, 19 April 1912.
96   *Boston Globe* and *New York Evening World*, 19 April 1912.
97   *New York Times*, 19 April 1912.
98   *Brooklyn Daily Eagle*, 19 April 1912.
99   *New York Call*, 20 April 1912.
100 *New York Times*, 19 April 1912.
101 *Newark Evening News*, 19 April 1912.
102 *Boston Globe*, 19 April 1912.
103 *New York Tribune*, 19 April 1912.
104 *St Louis Republic*, 19 April 1912.
105 *Pine Plains Register*, 25 April 1912.
106 *Brooklyn Daily Eagle*, 19 April 1912.
107 *New York Times*, 19 April 1912.
108 *Charlestown Gazette*, 25 April 1912, and *Washington Post*, 21 April 1912.
109 *Boston Post*, 20 April 1912.
110 *St Louis Republic*, 20 April 1912.
111 *New York Times*, 19 April 1912.
112 *St Louis Republic*, 22 April 1912.
113 *Scranton Times*, 19 April 1912.
114 *New York Times*, 2 July 1915.
115 Marshall Everett, *The Wreck of the* Titanic.
116 *New York Sun*, 19 April 1912.
117 Courtesy of the *Philadelphia Inquirer*, 18 April 1982.
118 *Vancouver Daily Province*, 20 April 1912.
119 *Philadelphia Evening Bulletin*, 19 April 1912.
120 *Baltimore Sun*, 23 April 1912.
121 *Albany Times-Union*, 19 April 1912.
122 *St Louis Times*, 19 April 1912.
123 *Toronto Star*, 19 April 1912.
124 *Washington Herald*, 19 April 1912.
125 Marshall Everett, *The Wreck of the* Titanic.
126 *Brooklyn Daily Eagle*, 19 April 1912.
127 *New York Sun*, 19 April 1912.
128 *Brooklyn Daily Eagle*, 21 April 1912.
129 *Baltimore Sun*, 20 April 1912.

130 *New York Tribune*, 19 April 1912. Note: Mrs. Steiner's name was variously reported to be 'Regina Steinhert' or 'Virginia Steiner', but the present version of the name appears to be correct.
131 *Pittsburg Daily Dispatch*, 19 April 1912.
132 *Baltimore Sun*, 19 April 1912.
133 *New York Tribune*, 19 April 1912.
134 *New York American*, 19 April 1912.
135 *Albany Times-Union*, 19 April 1912.
136 *New York American*, 18 April 1912.
137 Courtesy of the *Valley News Dispatch*, 14 April 1980.
138 *New York Sun*, 19 April 1912.
139 *New York Sun*, 19 April 1912.
140 Logan Marshall, *The Sinking of the* Titanic.
141 *Philadelphia Evening Bulletin*, 19 April 1912.
142 *Indianapolis Star* and *New York Evening Journal*, 19 April 1912.
143 *New York Sun* and *St Louis Globe Democrat*, 19 April 1912.
144 *Philadelphia Inquirer*, 20 April 1912.
145 Logan Marshall, *The Sinking of the* Titanic.
146 *New York Sun*, 19 April 1912.
147 *Portland Evening Express & Daily Commercial*, 19 April 1912. Note: the *Illinois Journal* of 19 April 1912 mistakenly attributed this interview to Samuel Goldenberg, a *Titanic* survivor.
148 *Pittsburg Post*, 20 April 1912.

CHAPTER 3 – DOCUMENTS FROM OTHER VESSELS

149 *New York Evening Journal*, 23 April 1912.
150 *New York Tribune*, 24 April 1912.
151 *Portland Evening Express & Daily Advertiser*, 23 April 1912.
152 *New York Sun*, 19 April 1912.
153 *Daily Telegraph*, 25 April 1912.
154 *Los Angeles Herald*, 25 April 1912.
155 Courtesy of Joan Webb, David Billnitzer and Bill Wormstedt.
156 *Lynn Evening News*, 29 April 1912.
157 *Birkenhead News*, 4 May 1912.
158 *Rockford Republic* and *London Free Press*, 1 May 1912
159 *New York Times*, 25 April 1912.
160 *New York Tribune*, 18 April 1912.
161 *Manchester Guardian*, 25 April 1912.
162 *New York American*, 26 April 1912.
163 *Montreal Star*, 4 May 1912.
164 Courtesy of the National Maritime Museum.
165 *Halifax Herald*, 1 May 1912.
166 *Halifax Herald*, 1 May 1912.
167 *Sioux Falls Daily Press*, 4 May 1912.
168 *Newark Star* and *New York Herald*, 2 May 1912.
169 *Halifax Herald*, 1 May 1912.
170 *Philadelphia Inquirer* and *Erie Dispatch*, 1 May 1912, and *Mahoning Dispatch*, 3 May 1912.
171 *New York Sun*, 18 April 1912.
172 *Milwaukee Journal*, 23 April 1912.
173 *New York Herald*, 20 April 1912.

174 *Richmond Times Dispatch* and *Newark Evening News*, 19 April 1912.

175 Courtesy of Steve Santini, *Titanic* Concepts.

176 *Halifax Herald*, 7 May 1912.

177 *Halifax Herald*, 7 May 1912.

178 National Archives.

179 Courtesy of the Maritime Museum of the Atlantic.

180 *New York American* and *Denver Post*, 26 April 1912.

181 *New York Times*, 25 April 1912.

182 Senate *Titanic* Inquiry.

183 *San Antonio Express*, 16 May 1912.

184 Courtesy of Anita Leslie.

185 *New York Evening World*, 16 May 1912.

186 *Richmond Times-Dispatch*, 28 April 1912.

187 Courtesy of the *Titanic* Historical Society and *Titanic* Museum.

188 *Providence Evening Bulletin*, 20 April 1912.

189 *St Louis Times*, 17 April 1912.

190 *Trenton Evening Times*, 20 April 1912.

191 Washington Dodge, *The Loss of the* Titanic.

192 *New York Times*, 23 April 1912.

193 *New York Times*, 12 May 1912.

194 *Manchester Guardian*, 22 April 1912.

195 *Edmonton Bulletin*, 23 April 1912.

196 National Archives.

197 *San Antonio Express*, 17 April 1912.

198 *Halifax Herald*, 18 April 1912.

199 *Providence Evening Bulletin*, 18 April 1912.

200 *Philadelphia Inquirer*, 19 April 1912.

201 *Philadelphia Inquirer*, 19 April 1912.

202 *London Globe & Traveller*, 27 April 1912.

203 *New York World*, 26 April 1912.

204 *New York Herald*, 26 April 1912.

205 *New York Times*, 27 April 1912.

206 *St John's Evening Telegram*, 4 May 1912.

207 *London Advertiser*, 22 April 1912.

208 Unknown Tunbridge Wells newspaper, England, around 30 April 1912.

209 *Belfast Evening Telegraph*, 27 April 1912.

210 *Manchester Guardian*, 22 April 1912.

INDEX

If you enjoyed this book, you may also be interested in …

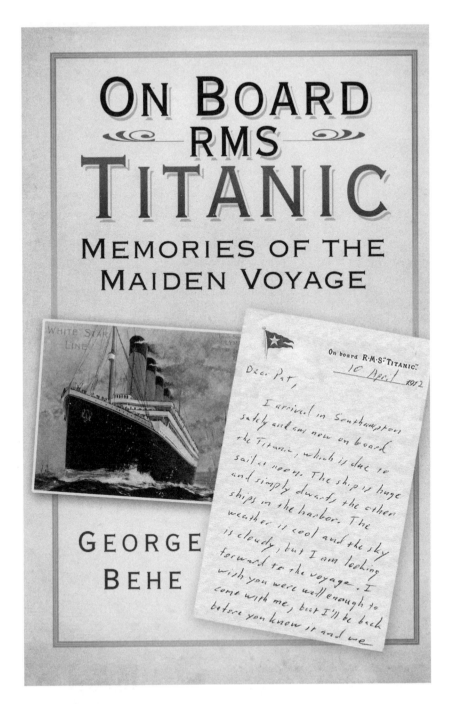

ON BOARD RMS TITANIC

MEMORIES OF THE MAIDEN VOYAGE

GEORGE BEHE

9780752483061